DINING BY RAIL

JAMES D. PORTERFIELD

Dining by Rail

THE HISTORY AND THE RECIPES
OF AMERICA'S GOLDEN AGE
OF RAILROAD CUISINE

For Martin Yan:

Antecedents to your project on behalf of United Airlines.

Best wishes

James D. Porterfield

ST. MARTIN'S GRIFFIN ☙ NEW YORK

Design by Jennifer Dossin

Library of Congress Cataloging-in-Publication Data

Porterfield, James D.
    Dining by rail : the history and recipes of America's golden age of railroad cuisine / James Porterfield.
       p.   cm.
    Includes index.
    ISBN 0-312-18711-4
    1. Cookery, American. 2. Railroads—United States—Dining-car service—History.
I. Title.
TX715.P848   1993
641.5973—dc20   92-34987
                                                           CIP

First St. Martin's Griffin: June 1998

10 9 8 7 6 5 4 3 2 1

CONTENTS

Section II: The Railroads and Their Cuisines

Section III: Appendices

ACKNOWLEDGMENTS

This work reflects the involvement of a great many people. To compile the information on the various railroads, and to collect the more than 7,500 recipes from which the 325 presented here were selected, meant corresponding with more than 300 people, from a student at Tuskegee Institute in Alabama, Kenneth Poole, to a retired officer in England, Major S. R. Elliot. As the following list of acknowledgments indicates, it is perhaps unique to railroad research that fans and collectors are often as, if not more, important than archives as a source of information. For example, the recipes of the Great Northern Railway came from a chance meeting with an officer of the Railroadiana Collectors Association Inc., from whom I learned of a collector in Chicago who in turn referred me to two other collectors in Minnesota who had both a booklet of that railroad's 1920s recipes and a pantry box containing another 300 recipes.

I am especially indebted to Peter Bordi, on the faculty in The Pennsylvania State University School of Hotel, Restaurant, and Institutional Management. Pete, who teaches food preparation, reviewed every recipe included here, plus several hundred more that were ultimately cut from the manuscript. He spotted missing ingredients (railroad chefs, like many others, often left a key but unrecognizable ingredient out of shared recipes for their specialties); suggested ways to modernize ingredient lists; and worked to reduce the often institutional portions to ones suitable for serving six or eight. Moreover, he instructed me in some of the dated techniques used, and opened his private collection of cookbooks to me, resulting in the discovery of several dozen rare recipes included here. Without Pete Bordi's help, this book would not have been possible. I am deeply grateful to him and want to thank him here.

I, however, am the one responsible for the recipes you see here. My goal, to provide historically accurate recipes and leave to you to experiment on your own, guided me in deciding which of Pete's recommended changes to incorporate, and which to leave out. All recipes not tested by dining-car departments (which often compiled handouts for their interested passengers) were tested here, to either the satisfaction or chagrin of my wife and children.

My 300-plus correspondents cannot all be acknowledged here, although each played some role in my research. I nonetheless do want to thank the following people and/or organizations for their unselfish help in providing recipes from the railroads included here:

Atcheson, Topeka and Santa Fe Railway System: Bill Burk, vice president, Public Relations.

Atlantic Coast Line Railroad: Ralph L. Progner, the assistant vice president, Passenger Traffic, with the Family Lines Rail System.

Baltimore & Ohio Railroad: Walter C. Figiel and members of the Baltimore & Ohio Railroad Historical Society, and William F. Howes, Jr., with CSX Transportation, Inc.

Boston & Maine Railroad: Richard Conrad and members of the Boston & Maine Historical Society, Inc.

Canadian National Railways: Major (Retired) S. R. Elliot.

Canadian Pacific Railway: Richard Karberg.

Chesapeake & Ohio Railway: Tod Hanger and the Chesapeake and Ohio Historical Society, Inc.

Chicago, Burlington & Quincy Railroad: Dee, Brad, and Grace Joseph and the crew of the Private Car Limited.

Chicago, Milwaukee, St. Paul & Pacific Railroad: Lorraine Hartwick and Paul Woehrmann of the Milwaukee Public Library's Milwaukee Road Collection.

Erie Railroad: Tim Stuy.

Great Northern Railway: Craig and Marty Neros (the Club Car) and the Minnesota Historical Society.

Gulf, Mobile & Ohio Railroad: David P. Wagner and members of the Gulf, Mobile & Ohio Historical Society.

Illinois Central Railroad: Carole Swanke and Robert W. O'Brien and the Illinois Central Gulf Railroad.

Kansas City Southern Railway Company: Jack B. Austerman

Louisville & Nashville Railroad: Mark D. Brainard and members of the Louisville & Nashville Railroad Historical Society.

Missouri-Kansas-Texas Lines (M-K-T or Katy): Chris Cruz and members of the Katy Railroad Historical Society.

Missouri Pacific Railroad: Dale L. Walker and members of the Missouri Pacific Historical Society.

New York, New Haven, & Hartford Railroad: Marc and Faith Frattsio and Wayne Drummond of the New Haven Historical and Technical Society.

Northern Pacific Railway: William A. McKenzie and the Minnesota Historical Society.

Pennsylvania Railroad: Theodore J. Holland and the staff of the Railroader's Memorial Museum, and members of the Pennsylvania Railroad Technical & Historical Society.

St. Louis Southwestern Railway Lines (Cotton Belt Route): Jim Bennett and members of the Cotton Belt Rail Historical Society.

Southern Pacific Lines: Fayette G. Taylor

Southern Railway System: William F. Geeslin, assistant vice president.

Union Pacific Railroad: Don Snoddy, George Cockle, and the Union Pacific Museum.

Western Pacific Railroad: Ellen Schwartz and the California State Railroad Museum and Library.

The Pullman Company: Carol Semmes and the Newberry Library.

Homer H. Noar, retired Superintendent of the Union Pacific Railroad's Dining Car and Hotel Department, and John M. Chappell, a collector, provided many of the recipes found among the miscellaneous railroads. Joyce W. Koeneman of the Association of American Railroads was invaluable for her help with illustrations and primary research.

Help with the illustrations is acknowledged in the individual picture captions.

Gratitude is owed my editor, Jim Fitzgerald of St. Martin's Press, first for sharing my belief that there is a need for this book, then for his patience in waiting for me to learn the hard way just how long it takes to compile such a work. Thanks also to my agent, Mark Frisk of the Howard Buck Agency, for doggedly pursuing potential publishers for a book idea he believed held promise. Thanks, too, to Sherry Korczynski, who typed all the recipes (learning in the process not to come to work without eating) and the many quotes found in this book. And thanks to the following people at St. Martin's Press, who played an important role in seeing to it that a quality book resulted: Alexandra Kuczynski and Eric Meyer.

Finally, know that any oversight, in thanking people for their help or in confirming the facts presented, is a reflection of my record-keeping abilities, not my intentions.

PREFACE

Edwin Kachel, for more than twenty-five years a steward in the Dining-Car Department of the Great Northern Railway, observed that "on a dining car, three elements can be considered—the equipment, the employee, the passenger." In other words, "the whole is constituted by two-thirds of human parts." [1]

What Mr. Kachel failed to mention was a fourth element of dining-car service: the food. From his perspective, the omission is understandable. At a time when hundreds of passenger trains criss-crossed America daily, outstanding food was expected, even commonplace. As the practice of feeding passengers on public transportation deteriorated into what we know today, the high quality of food served by yesterday's railroads has taken on mythic proportions. Section II of this book reveals that myth for what it is: the truth. And it serves to remind us, in an age when we are urged to excellence, that we have already demonstrated both that we are capable of achieving it, and that we are just as able to let it slip away.

But for those fortunate enough to have ridden America's great passenger trains at their peak, no part of the experience survives so vividly in memory as a meal in the dining car. This is the story behind the making of that experience, which began early in railroad history and reached a high point in 1930, when 1,732 railroad dining cars were registered with the Interstate Commerce Commission. By comparison, at this writing Amtrak operates a total of sixty-seven full diners nationwide.

Share a meal on one of those Amtrak dining cars with someone old enough to remember such pleasures and the conversation nearly always becomes a reminiscense of the meals once enjoyed on the trains. The Southern Pacific Lines recipes here came from such a random dinner companion, a tax attorney encountered on the *California Zephyr* who thought so highly of the food on the Espee *Lark* that he'd saved a cookbook from that railroad all these years. Others you meet recall riding the train just to enjoy a meal. Some of the recipe selections from the Illinois Central Railroad were suggested to me by a travel agent who recalls his family catching the New Orleans-bound *Panama Limited* for just that purpose, boarding the Chicago-to-Champaign run on Sunday afternoons and returning home later on a local. Still others marvel at the level of service encountered, at stewards and waiters whose likes today can only be found in the most exclusive restaurants or clubs. Rail fan and writer Lucius Beebe recalled an incident his father had while dining on the Seaboard Air Line's Boston-to-Palm Beach *Orange Blossom Special.* The train's steward reminded the elder Beebe that fifty years earlier, on that very night, he had been served lobster aspic in the Gold Suite of the Vendome Hotel. The server had been that steward—the occasion, the eve of Mr. Beebe's marriage.

A book celebrating this, one of the high points of civilized transportation, is appropriate if only to preserve an important aspect of genuine American fare. The recipes selected for inclusion are dishes for which the trains and railroads were noted by their patrons, foods native to America and prepared fresh just prior to serving. Many, like the Texas & Pacific's Cantaloupe Pie, or the New York Central's Scallopines of Pork Tenderloin with Riesling Wine Sauce, are unique. And, though thought has been given to the sensual pleasure to be derived from food, today's lighter eating habits also influenced selections. So you'll find recipes for the Great Northern's famous Baked Wenatchee Apple and the Southern's pineapple fritters, because they are worth remembering for the regional flavor which highlighted every major railroad's menu. But most stress today's lifestyle: good and healthy food done with style and speed. Gone is the Illinois Central's "King's Dinner," made up of a Manhattan or martini cocktail, selected appetizers, shrimp or crabmeat cocktail, imported wine, special salad, steak, potato, vegetable, dinner bread, cheese with fresh apple wedges and toasted saltines, coffee, and a liqueur. Instead, you'll find the Union Pacific's Fruit Salad with Special Sauce and the Atlantic Coast Line's Fillet of Sole with Spanish Sauce. These and other recipes would make dining-car service feel at home with today's fast pace. They had to be easy and quick to prepare, require a minimum of cookware, and use fresh ingredients that could be restocked en route.

The recipes in this account of railroad dining, then, are taken from forty-eight major intercity railroads. Over 7,500 recipes were collected and reviewed to select the 325 presented here. That is about the same number of recipes one would find in a food-service manual for any one railroad. And, while arranged by railroad in the chapters, they are divided by courses in the index, just as they were in such manuals. And, with one exception—the Fred Harvey station restaurants—recipes from the many fine station and railroad hotel restaurants, themselves a remnant of dining on the trains that lasted well into the 1950s, have not been included. Dishes from private cars, whether those of railroad executives or other wealthy travelers, are excluded because they are associated with a particular chef and not a railroad, and were not commonly available to patrons of the railroads. Many recipes attributed to chefs from the trains by secondary sources, but not verifiable by the subject railroad's food-service personnel or documents, have also been excluded.

I wrote this book to preserve a record of one of the ways we used to eat, to help prevent us from losing these details of our heritage and our national experience. The recipes selected are historically significant and deserve to be collected, saved, and shared. As presented here, the often strong regional emphasis the railroads took in creating a menu further contributes to preserving an aspect of food history now fading in a mobile America. It reminds us of the benefit of resisting a food chain dominated by giant food processors who wish we ate only one strain of tomato—a square one that bounces to ease packing and reduce spoilage. More, I wanted to produce a book that can be used, whether you are preparing a meal for visiting dignitaries, a family picnic for the Fourth of July, or a brown-bag lunch to take on your next train (or plane) trip, or just want to produce a meal with an interesting history.

But most of all, this book is written for fun. Whether you are a fan of railroads, good food, or popular culture, or some combination of all three, I hope you enjoy reading about dining in the cars and trying the great foods associated with them. If, upon completing the opening chapters of this book, you feel you have just returned from riding an extra-fare all-Pullman Limited, the dining experience fresh in your mind, and are longing to taste such food again, this book has accomplished its purpose. And I defy you to read the recipes for long before you find yourself wondering if you have enough of each ingredient to go to the kitchen and try one. I'll wager you do.

The recipes are intended for use by cooks with only a modicum of experience in the kitchen—say anyone who knows the difference between a potato and an onion. A section of basic recipes is found at the front of Section II: The Recipes, and you are referred there as necessary throughout the pages that follow. If you are more railroader than cook, and want to try your hand at recipes but can't tell your citrus zester from your basting brush, see one of the many excellent general basic cookbooks. I'm partial to Zoe Coulson's *The Good Housekeeping Illustrated Cookbook* (New York:

Hearst Books, 1980) because of the fine illustrations, which show how to skin a boiled ham or cut up a whole chicken, and the instructions which make absolutely clear how to top a pie with a woven pastry lattice or determine what to avoid when buying an eggplant. My kitchen skills, sufficient to prepare everything described here, came from this volume, but any similar cookbook will do.

Some other notes for the reader/cook:

1. Where possible, use fresh ingredients, as was the recommended practice on the trains. Food-service manuals provided to dining-car personnel often tipped off the steward to where along the route of his train fresh ingredients could be replenished by wiring ahead.

2. If fresh ingredients are not available, canned or otherwise packaged substitutions can be made, but in my opinion with slightly less positive results.

3. The recipes, where necessary, are adjusted from the often institutional portions found in research, to accommodate the number of servings noted with each recipe.

4. All recipes have been kitchen tested, either by the railroads themselves or, in the cases where portion adjustments were necessary, by the author.

Presented here, then, is the experience of eating on the train, from the earliest days when soot-covered food awaited arriving passengers trackside at the station, through the introduction of on-board snacks from a "butcher boy," to the invention of the hotel car and its evolution into the full-service dining car where these recipes originated. Where possible, first-hand accounts, anecdotes, and reminiscences drawn from the traveler's experience and point of view have been used. Thus, the reader will learn how dining cars on railroads both major and minor came to serve the unique, delicious, award-winning foods for which they are remembered.

Bon appetit!

SECTION I

From Soot to Soufflé: Eating on the Train

DINING CAR FORWARD

December 1952. You have just boarded a train, heading home from your last trip before the holidays. You busy yourself arranging your personal effects to satisfaction in the private room you've booked for the trip. Your room in order, you head for the observation lounge, take up a seat by an oversized window, and order a drink. You are brought from your reverie by the soft melodic tones a passing white-jacketed waiter plays on his chime.

"Last call to dinner. Last call to dinner. This is your last call to dinner," he announces.

A glance at your watch surprises you at the lateness of the hour, for you've been engrossed in a magazine since sights of the city began to fall behind the solarium. Outside, darkness has blotted out the cold, bleak landscape of farms and woods, but the light from the lounge windows shows up the dirty patches of snow along the railroad. What a night to be driving, you muse, as a pair of headlight beams race the train, then fall back.

In the vestibule there's a breath of icy wind. Forward in the sleeper you duck into your roomette to wash up and straighten your jacket. Then you walk through two sleepers, past the doors marked A, B, C, past the pair of porters checking space diagrams, up to the door labeled DINER.

Steward. (COURTESY OF THE ASSOCIATION OF AMERICAN RAILORADS)

The aisle leads left around the galley and along a row of windows so low that you have to lean down to see out. The smell of warm food and a flood of humid air comes out of a side kitchen exit. When you reach the end of the short passageway, a man wearing a black suit with a white vest comes up to you as you enter the dining section.

"Good evening, sir. Table for one? Right this way."

He shoves aside the aisle seat and pulls back the window chair.

"How's this?"

There really is nothing comparable to a diner—the sparkling silverware, the vase of cut flowers, the starched tablecloth and napkins, the glass pitcher of "pure spring water."

The steward places a menu before you, scribbles on a check, and places it with a pencil at your elbow. A waiter comes over and fills your glass with ice water.

On the cover of the menu is a tasteful sketch of a private school in the East and the accompanying text tells of its history and scholastic standing—and the fact that it is adjacent to the railroad's mainline. You open the menu and there is the difficult matter of selection. You're hungry, of course; and tonight any one of the main entrees would fill the bill. The Lobster à la Newburg is a specialty of this road, but you had seafood last night. Chicken pie—say, that sounds good; but just a minute. You haven't had a steak in weeks and this railroad has access to the best cuts of beef available. You write on the check and hope the waiter can decipher it; he scans it quickly, lays it face down on the table, and goes back toward the galley.

As you are squeezing a lemon over a tall glass of tomato juice, the train slows and corner street lights begin passing by. You peer out but miss the station sign in the darkness. The diner stops before the bay window of a telegraph office. Inside, a man with a green eyeshade is busy at the typewriter. It's quiet in the diner, with just the monotone of the climate control machinery—that, and the conversation, and the sound of dishes from the galley.

"Steak, sir?"

"Right here." You chew on a stalk of stuffed celery and contemplate the large plate before you. And the side dishes, the tossed salad with the railroad's specialty dressing, the platter of hot rolls,

the pot of steaming coffee. As you lift your fork, the train is moving: no jolt, no jar, just a sort of fluid motion. Automobiles are waiting bumper-to-bumper behind the crossing gate and the main street has Christmas lights hung across it—then darkness again, and the steady, muffled drumming of the wheels.

The steak is done to perfection and the coffee is hot and rich.

"For dessert, sir, we have French apple or lemon pie, cherry cobbler, ice cream, or sherbet."

"Apple pie, I think."

The pie is superb—baked green apples with a light flaky crust and crisp graham-cracker topping, with rich brown nutmeg sauce poured over and running down into the dish in little rivers. Mmm, mmm.

The waiter comes over to your table. "How's everything?

"Very good." You push the last dish away and pour half a cup of coffee. The steward comes over, quickly jots a total on your check, you pay, and he digs his fingers into vest pockets for change. He places your change on the silver tray, thanks you, and departs.

There's an icy breath in the vestibule and the observation lounge at the rear is beginning to fill up. Ah, here's a seat. As you settle in you can't help wonder about the eighty-five-foot dining car, a streamlined restaurant running through the night at seventy miles an hour. How did such a convenience come to be at your disposal? How the devil does that chef turn out a meal like you've just had, with only a handful of square feet of working space? You have enough trouble at home in a kitchen that seems bigger than the whole diner. And you don't have waiters underfoot, or a hundred people to feed, or a five-entree menu. And where does he get all that food in the first place, and how does he keep it so fresh and attractive? And that waiter. How does he balance that loaded tray over his head on just the palm of one hand? They were busy tonight, yet your meal came off without a hitch. Marvelous. You can't wait for breakfast.

A reenactment of the run of the "Best Friend of Charleston," the first scheduled passenger train. (COURTESY OF THE ASSOCIATION OF AMERICAN RAILROADS)

1

A Half-Hour to Indigestion

On Christmas day in 1830 the first locomotive built entirely in America pulled the first regularly scheduled steam-powered train in America out of Charleston, South Carolina. The Charleston and Hamburg Railroad thus launched railroad passenger service in this country. The locomotive *Best Friend of Charleston*, dragging one freight carriage and two coaches in its wake, raced along six miles of track at twenty-one miles an hour. Some 141 citizens, occupying hard wooden benches in unsprung open cars, enduring ear-splitting noise, smoke, and hot cinders, and literally facing a potentially fatal scalding, nonetheless participated as passengers.

There can have been no thought by the managers of the Charleston & Hamburg about feeding its first patrons en route. After all, "when the first passenger trains were established, the primary thought of the railroad operator was to sell transportation and little consideration was given to the comfort of the passengers."[2] This no doubt characterized the thinking of those running the Camden and Amboy Railroad who, in September 1833, advanced the concept of passenger service by offering America's first scheduled passenger-only train. They promised to make the thirty-four mile trip between Bordentown and South Amboy, New Jersey, in three hours.

But if management was not concerned with feeding passengers, the passengers themselves quickly learned to be concerned with eating. While early train trips were scheduled to be of short duration, all manner of occurrence contrived against such plans. Derailments, ambling livestock, a slow-moving train, the delayed arrival of a connecting train, and even sabotage often turned a scheduled two-hour trip into an all-day adventure. "About ten miles from Springfield [Massachusetts], we came to a dead stop and the whole train stood motionless for three hours," wrote George

Early meals for passengers were provided by trackside vendors. Wood-burning locomotives passed the food first, depositing a layer of soot over any item not protected.

Combe in 1839. The delay was "enlivened only by occasional walks in the sunshine and visits to a cakestore, the whole stock of eatables in which was in time consumed, the price of them having risen from hour to hour in proportion to the demand. . . . At half-past seven (after another one-and one-half hour delay in Worcester) we started again and arrived in Boston about ten o'clock, with pretty good appetites, as we had breakfasted at half-past seven in the morning and been allowed no meal since that hour."[3]

On occasion, the cause of delay could simultaneously serve the hunger of the stranded passengers. "The engine and tender had been thrown off the rails in a collision with a herd of cattle and two oxen had been crushed to death . . . a detention of eight hours and the loss of breakfast were the only sufferings to be borne, and some of the passengers were indisposed to forego their breakfasts without an effort to provide a substitute. There was plenty of beef alongside the line and the sage brush could be used for fuel. The sage brush was soon in a blaze but the meat could not be procured with equal rapidity. Cutting through an ox hide and carving out a steak with a pen knife was a task that baffled the passenger who made the attempt."[4]

And not everyone could count on the good fortune of F. Barham Zincke, who recounted that "on one occasion an acquaintance with whom I was traveling that day and myself both happened to have had no dinner. We mentioned this to the conductor and asked him if he could manage in any way to let us have some supper. 'Oh yes,' he readily replied, 'I will at eleven o'clock stop the train at a house in the forest where I sometimes have supper myself. I will give you twenty minutes.' I suppose the other passengers, none of whom left their seats, imagined that we stopped to repair some small damage or to take in wood or water, for on returning to the car we heard no observations made to the delay."[5]

Trackside vendors offered one early solution to the problem of eating when riding the train. They awaited the arrival of the trains at station stops and served those on board while the locomotive was being serviced and refueled.

Almost immediately, passengers were registering complaints about the practice. In 1838 a traveler noted, "At every fifteen miles of the railroads . . . the cars stop, all the doors are thrown open, and out rush all the pas-

sengers like boys out of school, and crowd around the tables to solace themselves with pies, patties, cakes, hard-cooked eggs, hams, custards, and a variety of railroad luxuries too numerous to mention. The bell rings for departure, in they all hurry with their hands and mouths full, and off they go again until the next stopping place induces them to relieve the monotony of the journey by masticating without being hungry."[6]

These early eating stops were nearly always described as terrible. The bitter black coffee may have been brewed only once a week. The ham could be dry, salty and tough. Hard-cooked eggs were stored for an indeterminate period of time in limed water to keep them from discoloring. Fried eggs may have been cooked in rancid grease and certainly were served on stale bread. Here also one found leaden biscuits—their nickname, "sinkers," giving a clue as to their quality—and something which earned the euphemism "railroad pie." The recipe was thought to be to take two crusts of cardboard and fill them with thickened glue. "The eating stations all along the route call for great improvement; some of them are moderately good but as a rule the food is ill cooked and worse served. . . . Needless to say, the ubiquitous pie is to be found in all its glory in these places. The number of victims to intemperance in pie-eating must be enormous. A light hand for pastry would be useless in making these pies: a hand that can manufacture a pie, every inch of which means a nightmare for a week, is the one most in request."[7] Menu selections such as waffles with rye whiskey offer further testimony to the hearty constitution needed if one wanted to participate in eating while riding the train.

Buying food at the station and carrying it along on the train had disadvantages beyond mob behavior and questionable quality. A reporter commented, "The bouquet from those lunches hung around the car all day and the flies wired ahead for their friends to meet them at each station." This same problem attended the alternative practice of some resourceful passengers, the timeless practice of carrying along a basket of eatables popularly called the "box lunch."

Early riders also encountered barefoot boys running alongside the train beneath the windows, shouting of the availability of fresh fruit of the season from nearby orchards. Assuming a steady aim and honesty in the seller, something delectable

This scene at Gordonsville, Virginia, of coffee and fried chicken being served to passengers on the Chesapeake and Ohio after the Civil War, demonstrates the increasing popularity of rail travel. (COURTESY OF THE ASSOCIATION OF AMERICAN RAILROADS)

Feeding the crew of the Boston train. (COURTESY OF THE BETTMANN ARCHIVE)

A patient railroad traveler encounters the news butcher in the 1850s. (COURTESY OF THE BETTMANN ARCHIVE)

The demon butcher boy. (COURTESY OF THE BETTMANN ARCHIVE)

could be had amid the bedlam. In addition, an enterprising crew might set up a small bar in the baggage car—men only, of course—to supplement their income and satisfy passengers. In an extreme case, the engineers of the Philadelphia & Columbia Railroad, running through Pennsylvania Dutch country in Lancaster County, could be counted on to stop their trains every few miles to allow hungry passengers the opportunity to toil across working farmland to a nearby stagecoach stop or farmhouse for a glass of whiskey, fresh doughnuts and coffee, apple pie with milk, chicken fricassee, waffles and fish, gingerbread, and spruce beer.[8]

But not all railroads ran by orchards, nor had the luxury of construction along a built-up stagecoach thoroughfare. The episodes recounted by Messrs. Combe and Zincke hint of the first organized efforts to satisfy the hunger of train passengers. Someone thought to carry the cakeshop on board the train, giving birth to an eventual army of young men, called "news butchers," known for their relentless and fanatical hustling of assorted goods. Meanwhile, as railroads began operating trains over more considerable distances, passengers were either provided with or could obtain meals at hotels or station restaurants at points along the route. Trains stopped at such "eating houses" for the same twenty minutes Mr. Zincke and his friend were allowed while passengers detrained for breakfast, lunch, or dinner, or simply for refreshments.

News butchers, making their appearance on New England railroads in the late 1840s, boarded a train at one station and sold food items to the passengers while the train passed on to the next station. It was a practice that proved highly unsatisfactory, and was condemned universally. "The moment the cars start," observed Alfred Bunn in 1853, "a string of filthy lads stream in offering for sale sweetmeats, apples, books, and other important wares . . . and in many trains . . . [the passengers] hand around tumblers of cold water . . ."[9] On another train, Charles Mackay encountered the versatility of the pesty butcher, one who on this occasion passed through as a book hawker "then, changing his literary business for that of a dealer in maple candy, peppermint drops, cakes, and apples, he allowed us no cessation from importunity until we arrived at the city of Rochester, where a new set of plagues of the same kind took possession of us and accompanied us the whole way to Niagara."[10]

The ceaseless presence of the news butcher, often more than one, was perhaps the most odious aspect of their work. "No want can arise in the traveler's mind that there is not someone in the train ready to administer to [it]. Every town you pass pelts you with its daily papers. If you stop for

Charles Weld, in the 1850s, wrote: "The process of watering the passengers, as it is called, is [a] feature peculiar to American railway traveling. A man or boy, often a Negro, carrying a tin can and tumblers in a frame passes frequently through the cars dispensing iced water to the numerous applicants for that indispensable refreshment during an American summer, which is provided at the expense of the railway company." (COURTESY OF THE ASSOCIATION OF AMERICAN RAILROADS)

ten minutes at a central station a quack is sure to come into the car and inform everyone that Dead Shot Worm Candy is now selling at twenty-five cents the packet, that Vestris's Bloom, the finest cosmetic in the known world, is to be had for a half-dollar the quarter pound, or that Knicker-bocker's Corn Exterminator makes life's path easy at a dime the ounce packet. Presently you fall asleep and awaken covered with a heavy snow of handbills about Harper's reprints and Peterson's unscrupulous robberies from English authors. Anon, [comes] a huge fellow with enormous ap-ples, two cents each, peaches in their season, hickory nuts, pecans, or maple sugar cakes. To them succeed sellers of ivory combs, parched corn, and packets of sweet meats."[11]

Experienced news butchers started their rounds with salted peanuts to build later sales of soft drinks and ice cream. The sandwiches they carried might be of unknown origin, or be misrepresented, as when cheap and plentiful rabbit meat was substituted for the advertised and more expen-sive chicken. And short-change experts marked their ranks. "Say that a customer gave me a fifty-cent piece for a five-cent newspaper. I'd assume it was a quarter . . . and return him twenty cents in change, meanwhile, however, retaining a quarter in the palm of my hand. If the customer no-ticed the discrepancy, why, I was quick to drop the quarter into his hand and say, 'Sorry!' Half the time, at least, the customer didn't notice, and I was twenty-five cents ahead."[12] Major William Shepherd, writing in 1885 of his *Prairie Experiences*, concluded, "This itinerant trader certainly should be suppressed; his prices are extravagant and his office unneces-sary."[13]

Opinions on the station restaurants and eating houses were not so unan-imously negative. For one thing, everyone realized some provision for feeding train passengers was necessary. "We stopped at ten different sta-tions," wrote J. S. Buckingham of his three-hour, forty-four mile trip from Worcester to Boston in 1839, "to put down and take up passengers and at each of these were comfortable and well-furnished waiting rooms for ladies and gentlemen separately, with ample refreshments for those who needed them."[14] Mark Twain observed the frequency with which well-pre-pared travelers carried a little shot bag filled with silver coin to pay for meals along the way.

And in a time when the track was not of standard width, and a frequent change of trains, baggage and all, was necessary for someone traveling any distance, layovers were an expected part of the travel experience. William Ferguson described a trip he took in 1855 from Boston to Charleston, South Carolina. It involved a total of fourteen railroads and provided these eating experiences: "The train stopped twenty minutes at Springfield [Massachusetts] for an early supper. Bodily refreshment is never lost sight of in the arrangements of American travel. . . . Before leaving [Richmond, Virginia], however, we have to amuse ourselves the best we can for more than half an hour. We fill it in by securing an early breakfast in a miserable eating house attached to the station. . . . The distance [to Weldon, Virginia] is sixty-four miles and we get there at 11:00 [A.M.] on the Petersburg Railroad. . . . This time both trains of cars are in the same station. We dine here and at 12:00 are off again for Wilmington by the Weldon and Wilmington Railroad. . . . About 11:00 [A.M. two days later] we were at a place called Fair Bluff, a clearing in the forest where the up and down trains meet, and stopped to dine. It was a forest dinner. Our host said he found great difficulty in procuring supplies [as] provisions are so scarce."[15] In such circumstances, twenty minutes for a meal here and there posed no inherent problem.

The earliest sanctioned eating houses got their start in a random and informal manner. "While I was station agent at Waukegan, Illinois, back in 1856," one such founder, Charles George, wrote, "I established what was, if not the first, among the first railroad station eating houses in the United States. My wife, who was a thrifty New England housekeeper and noted for the excellence of her cooking, began to bake a few pies, a little cake, and some doughnuts for 'the boys' who wanted refreshments. I had these articles set out on a little table for sale. One day the superintendent, W. S. Johnson, stopped at the station and noticed this lunch stand with its modest display.

"'Who's this for?' he said. 'A good idea. You can have one end of the station for a lunch counter if you want it, Charley.'

"So I fitted up a neat little refectory at one end of the dingy old station, and Mr. Johnson and the trainmen soon got into the habit of lunching there every time they stopped. The superintendent of the Chicago & Milwaukee road had the conductors and brakemen announce refreshments on their trains just before reaching Waukegan. It was not long before there was a large and regular patronage. Within a year, the place was known from Maine to Minnesota.

"My passengers on the road were constantly doing kind things to help my eating house along, making suggestions or giving presents as occasions came up. Dr. V. C. Price, the originator of the famous Price's baking powder, gave me one of the first cans of powder he made. My wife always used this preparation in her cooking, and she attributed a great part of the success of our eating house to this fact."[16]

The propensity of a railroad employee's wife to the kitchen appears to be a common element in the memorable early station eating houses. William H. Boot, in the 1880s a conductor for the Pullman Company in what was soon to become the state of Washington, recounted how "the providing of satisfactory meals and refreshments for patrons at convenient times has always been a problem. Leaving Dayton about 4:00 P.M. for Bonneville en route to Portland, it was necessary to arrange for something to eat that evening, and the railway company provided a counter and a row of high stools across one end of the Walla Walla station waiting room. The wife of Conductor James Cutting, who lived very near the depot, arranged to do the rest. She made a specialty of pot roasts and pies. These were prepared at home and with the necessary condiments and coffee taken to the station just before the arrival of the evening train."[17]

Perhaps most important, railroad management learned extra revenue could be generated by operating, or granting others a license to operate, eating houses in one corner of an existing railroad station. Thus, train conductors and brakemen played an increasingly important role in building the business of these station eating facilities, as Charles George acknowledges.

The early promotion of eating facilities by conductors on arriving trains became a formality with the advent of the telegraph. A conductor could then pass through the train before its scheduled arrival at an eating house and determine how many passengers planned to eat. Then, at the next way station, he could telegraph ahead to advise the station restaurant manager of how many portions to prepare.

Other eating houses employed handbills or announcements in train schedules to drum up business. This notice appeared in a brochure promoting the Delaware Railroad:

HO! FOR REFRESHMENTS!!

—— at ——

R. E. SMITH'S
RESTAUARANT

MIDDLETOWN STATION. DELAWARE RAILROAD.

Where the hungry traveller will find,
Good refreshments of almost every kind;
Pie and Milk, with hot coffee too;
Broiled Chickens, or an Oyster Stew.

Buckwheat Cakes and Sausages, fresh from the pan
Apples, Cakes, and good old Ham;
My house is small, but never fear,
But if you stop you'll get good cheer.

Ten Minutes allowed at this Station for REFRESHMENTS.

THE LOGAN HOUSE:
THE STATION RESTAURANT DONE RIGHT

The city of Altoona, in rural mountainous central Pennsylvania, was important early on to those building the Pennsylvania Railroad connecting Philadelphia with Pittsburgh. The railroad bought up farm land there in the early 1850s to construct locomotive and car-building and repair facilities, and to ready trains for the assent over the Allegheny mountains. Among the first problems the railroad encountered with its new site was how to retain the craftsmen it recruited and sent there from urban centers. Altoona resident Thomas McCaully may have offered an explanation when he wrote of the arrival of a train carrying fifty-six people in its one passenger car on the morning of June 14, 1851: "Rain was pouring down and mud was knee-deep everywhere. [There were] no hotels and but one reasonably-sized restaurant. How those people ever found their way through the mud or where they spent the night I can never tell you." Many such arrivals were moved to board the next train East and seek other employment.

In addition to the daily arrival of the railroad's newly hired skilled mechanics, hundreds of unemployed job-seekers poured into Altoona as well, as did numerous agents seeking to do business with the rapidly expanding railroad. They were accompanied by businessmen looking to purchase land, and by those realizing for the first time the thrill of riding a passenger train, this one through the scenic Juniata River valley. And the mainline, for the first time carrying through trains, was about to be opened. Thomas A. Scott, a daring vice-president of the railroad, saw in this situation the opportunity not only to meet the need for a hotel in Altoona, but the chance to promote his railroad as well. Scott was well aware of the public-relations value of a memorable dining experience. Patrons would anticipate the meal en route, reminisce about it among themselves during the remainder of the trip, tell friends about it on arrival, and recall the food later, perhaps when deciding which railroad to ride the next time.

Scott thus arranged construction of the Logan House, a railroad hotel and eating house named after Chief Logan, an influential vice-regent of the Delaware Indians. Built during

1854–1855 by Thomas Bricknell, a foreman of the railroad's carpenters, the hotel adjoined Altoona station at trackside. Known as the most luxurious hotel between New York and Chicago, it greeted new arrivals with heavy red velvet deep-pile carpets of a rose design which produced the "sensation of walking

The Logan House as depicted in a 1912 brochure. (COURTESY OF THE BLAIR COUNTY HISTORICAL SOCIETY)

The Logan House in full operation, fronted by the train shed erected to protect arriving passengers from the elements, with a special train hauling steel magnate Charles M. Schwab's private car in attendance. Altoona's train station can be seen to the left of the train shed.
(COURTESY OF THE BLAIR COUNTY HISTORICAL SOCIETY)

on clump grass"; four-foot-high wainscoting painted cherry, walnut, and white; black walnut and mahogany woodwork; and other appointments that brought a touch of Oriental splendor. Humorist Bill Nye remarked that "its halls are as long as the State of Rhode Island." The fact that it was one of the largest hotels in the state (and the nation) when it was built makes clear that it was intended for patrons of the railroad, not for the citizens of Altoona. These residents numbered only 2,500 in 1855, with 1,000 of them working for the Pennsylvania Railroad.[1] Logan House was operated by the Keystone Hotel Company, a creation of the railroad set up to manage it and other hotels along the Pennsylvania Railroad mainline.[2]

Early on, while the hotel was under construction, train passengers found dining tables made of boards laid across trestles, and wooden benches instead of chairs. But the completed Logan House had every modern contrivance. A signal system installed along the track approaching Altoona from either direction notified the hotel of an arriving train. Waiters set about preparing tables for the guests. The head waiter would step out onto the porch and take up a position alongside a large Chinese gong to await the train. When it came to a stop, he would beat the gong to summon passengers to eat before resuming their journey. A bench was placed outside the hotel on the verandah at the main entrance to the dining room. Here were placed a row of water basins with a towel above each. Soot-covered passengers who wished to could wash up before partaking of their meal. Trains allowed the customary twenty-minute layover at this, the only eating facility at the station.[3] "The hotel had been perfectly still all the forenoon," wrote William Ferguson in 1856, "but for ten or fifteen minutes [at] about one o'clock it became a scene of great bustle. The east and west trains meet for dinner. The long tables in the dining hall stood in all order of great preparation one moment; the next they were overrrun by the hungry passengers. In a few minutes provisions and people had alike disappeared and Altoona was once more left in quiet."[4]

Guests were greeted by a dining room that extended 104 feet, between hotel offices to the west and parlors for hotel guests to the east. Divided into three sections, the dining room, the largest room in the hotel and in all of Altoona, could seat 400 patrons comfortably. A fresco of Chief Logan decorated the main wall in the center of the dining room. The kitchen and commissary were adjacent to the dining room and "all equipment was thoroughly up-to-date. All breads and pastries were from the Logan House bakery. An exclusive recipe for ice cream"—one writer declared the Logan House vanilla ice cream to be the best in the world—

"won raves for excellent texture and flavor."[5] A second-floor parlor was set aside for use by salesmen there to display wares. Former railroad news butcher Thomas Edison, a guest on September 2, 1893, met forty-five Altoona businessmen there and reportedly kept his phonograph playing all day long.[6]

Its central location, easy accessibility by rail, and reputation for high cuisine and sumptuous rooms, put the Logan House on many people's itinerary. Men from Pittsburgh would go for a weekend to enjoy what some considered the best meals in the country. Presidents Hayes, Grant, Harrison, and Taft, Union Generals Phil Sheridan and William Tecumseh Sherman, industrialist Andrew Carnegie and Pennsylvania Governor Andrew G. Curtin were frequent guests. Some thought of it as a resort. General Sherman's family spent several summers there, as did Mary Todd Lincoln.[7] It was the site, on September 24, 1862, of the historic Loyal War Governor's Conference, called by Governor Curtin. The governors of thirteen northern states arrived hurriedly in trains from as far away as Maine and Iowa to meet in secret following a string of military and diplomatic reverses in the war with the South. They issued a "ringing pledge of loyalty and confidence in the cause of the North and in the leadership of Abraham Lincoln." It helped stave off wavering home support for the war and potential involvement by European powers.

The Logan House earned widespread praise and demonstrated from nearly the very beginning that railroad eating houses could be done right. It was described by one visitor as a "mansion in the wilderness," and by another as "unsurpassed." The latter noted, "We rarely sat down to a better table." An English visitor declared it "better than any in Europe and equal to any in America." It was a genteel place where "men in spats and straw hats escorted women in cotton, ribbon and lace dresses, high-topped shoes, and silk parasols, listening to band concerts and dining in the hotel's fine restaurant."[8] Dismantled in 1927, the Logan House was more than twenty years ahead of the famous Harvey Houses (see page 24).

Amidst the commotion created by an arriving train, passengers had to step off, find the eating house, eat, and reboard, all in less than twenty or thirty minutes. Little wonder passengers rejected the railroad's term, "meal stop," preferring instead to call it an "indigestion stop."

This scene at Hornellsville, New York, in 1876 provides evidence of the prominence of the eating house and gives a clue as to how difficult such an arrangement for feeding passengers was.

The eating house experience survived for nearly sixty years. Some eating houses were known to be quite good. At Hornellsville, New York, patrons of the Erie Railroad could look forward to chicken and waffles. At Altoona, Pennsylvania, it was the sweet vanilla ice cream of the Logan House station hotel which sent passengers back to the trains happy. Other noted stops were at Cumberland, Maryland, and Poughkeepsie, New York. The latter was run by the Johnston brothers, who also had eateries along the New York Central Lines in Albany, Rochester, Syracuse, and Buffalo. Garnett Eskew, a frequent guest at the Poughkeepsie eating house, recalled "[the] glass of milk had a big, thick layer of cream on it. And there were always crullers and pies and coffee and country-ham sandwiches on the table; and everybody made a grab for them as soon as they got within reaching distance. The earliest eating houses had no chairs. Nobody ever thought of sitting down to eat while the train waited. They simply stood around the counter, stuffing for all they were worth, afraid the train would leave. The station platform was not quite long enough to accommodate all the cars in the train. So when the trains pulled in there was a general crowding forward by everybody toward the front entrance of the front car, in order to get there first." Even so favorable a commentator could not escape noticing that "gulping rich food, and running for one's seat on the train, resulted inevitably in dyspepsia and all its attendant discomforts."[18]

Station eating houses, especially those of the western railroads, were glorified by travel journalists. Typical is this comment in the 1876 edition of *The Pacific Tourist*, a pamphlet instructing travelers on what to expect on a train ride that could by now span the continent with only a few changes of trains:

"The trains of the Union Pacific Railroad are arranged so as to stop at excellent stations, at convenient hours, for meals. The only disarrangement is at Laramie, which seems to be unfortunate to passengers from either direction. To travelers from the East it furnishes a very early supper, just after dinner at Cheyenne, and to those from the West, it gives a very late breakfast, just before dinner; but there is no other place for an eating station, except at this point. At Como, just west of Laramie, there is a little booth where the western train coming east, about 7:00 A.M., often stops ten minutes for hot coffee, sandwiches—an excellent convenience.

"Usually all the eating houses on both the Pacific railroads are very excellent indeed. The keepers have to maintain their culinary excellence under great disadvantages, especially west of Sidney, as all food but meats must be brought from a great distance.

"Travelers need to make no preparations for eating on the cars, as meals at all dining halls are excellent, and food of great variety is nicely served; buffalo meat, antelope steak, tongue of all kinds, and always the best of beefsteak. Laramie possesses the reputation of the best beefsteak on the Pacific Railroad. Sidney makes a specialty, occasionally, of antelope steak. At Evanston you will see the lively antics of the Chinese waiters, probably your first sight of them. Also, they usually have nice mountain fish. At Green River you will always get nice biscuits; at Grand Island they give all you can possibly eat; it has a good name for its bountiful supplies."

A closer look at the Evanston, Wyoming, stop at this time was provided by a reporter for *Leslie's Weekly* traveling on a special excursion train for newspapermen. Datelined November 24, 1877, his story recounted his experience at the Mountain Trout Hotel, located parallel to and near the Union Pacific Railroad's mainline station: "In the little hotel, a gem in its way for neatness and order, we find the dining room given over to the Chinamen's presiding influence and nothing can be more soothing to the traveler's nerves than such a silent, soft-stepping, light-handed attendant, gliding behind one's chair like a shadow, always smiling and deferential." Trout was a hotel specialty, with a large dish of them, fresh caught and on ice, adorning a window facing arriving passengers. Abundant servings made the long verandah fronting the hotel along the tracks welcome as a place to exercise briefly before departing. Some travelers, so taken with the place and its food, refused to depart after the meal break. The hotel was more than happy to provide a clean room for the smitten, wherein they could freshen themselves, get a good night's sleep, and depart on the next train through.'[19]

Returning to the account offered in *The Pacific Tourist*, one learns, "At Ogden you will be pleased with the neatness and cleanness of the tables and service. At Cheyenne the dinners are always excellent, and the dining room cheerful. To any who either from desire to economize, or inability to eat three railroad meals per day, we recommend to carry a little basket with Albert biscuit and a little cup. This can be easily filled at all stopping-places with hot tea or coffee, and a sociable and comfortable glass of tea indulged in inside the car. The porter will fit you up a nice little table in your section, and spread on a neat white tablecloth.

"When the tourist reaches the Central Pacific Railroad he passes beyond the domain of the Pullman Car Company; nevertheless, the new coaches of the Central Pacific Railroad are just as elegant and convenient.

"All the dining stations of the Central Pacific Railroad are bountiful in their supplies; at all of them fruit is given in summertime with great freedom. Fish is almost always to be had; no game of value. The food, cooking, and service by Chinese waiters is simply excellent. The writer has never eaten nicer meals than those served at Winnemucca, Elko, Battle Mountain, and Colfax. The Humboldt Desert is far from being a desert to the traveling public, for its eating-stations always furnish a *dessert* of good things and creature comforts.

"A little lunch basket nicely stowed with sweet and sustainable bits of food will often save you the pain of long rides before meals, when the empty stomach craves food and, failing to receive it, lays you up with the most dismal sick headaches; it also serves you splendidly whenever the train is delayed. To be well on the Pacific Railroad eat at regular hours, and never miss a meal. Most of the sickness which we have witnessed has arisen from irregular eating or injudicious attempts at economy by skipping a meal to save a dollar. We have noticed those who were regular in eating at every meal passed the journey with the greatest ease, most comfort, and best health. Those who were irregular, skipping here and there a meal, always suffered inconvenience.

"In packing your little lunch basket, *avoid tongue, by all means,* for it will not keep over a day or two, and its fumes in a sleeping car are anything but like those from 'Araby the blest.' Avoid all articles which have odor of any description.

"Lunch counters are attached to all eating stations, so that you may easily procure hot coffee, tea, biscuit, sandwiches, and fruit if you do not wish a full meal.

"The uniform price of meals at all stations overland, is one dollar greenbacks. On the Central Pacific, if you prefer, pay seventy-five cents in silver; at Lathrop pay fifty cents silver—the cheapest and best meal for the money, of your whole tour."

A detached observer, travel writer and diarist W. G. Marshall, detailed three station stops mentioned by *The Pacific Tourist*. First, "Thirty miles beyond Julesburg on the Union Pacific Railroad we came to Sidney, an eating station and therefore a place of importance. We stopped half an hour to hurry out and get breakfast. Tearing into the stationhouse past a man standing at the doorway who was vigorously proclaiming on a loud-sounding gong that the feast was ready prepared and spread within, we found ourselves in a room furnished with many neatly arrayed tables. We had plenty of time to eat and plenty of room to spare. There were given us eight little dishes apiece containing hot beefsteak, two slices of cold roast antelope, a bit of cold chicken, ham and poached eggs, a couple of boiled potatoes, two sticks of sweet corn, stewed tomatoes, and four thin buckwheat hot cakes laid one on top of the other, to be eaten with golden syrup

The tranquility surrounding the eating house at Burlington depot in Lincoln, Nebraska, in the mid-1870s belies the experience one had eating there. (COURTESY OF THE ASSOCIATION OF AMERICAN RAILROADS)

the last thing of all. We were all served alike, everyone was given the same as his neighbor. Knives and forks were lamentably scarce, as usual. One knife and fork to each to last through the whole meal is the order of the day out here. Cold tea in tumblers with a quantity of sugar added seemed to constitute the popular beverage, if it was not cold milk. There was hot tea and coffee for those who preferred. All ate as if for their very lives, and the result was that we were all through together a quarter of an hour before it was time to start."

At Ogden, "we were received by such a clanging and booming of gongs, together with such an uproarious babble of voices from a number of excited individuals directly [as] we stepped out of the train, that it looked as if we had come to a place where everyone had taken leave of his senses. What did it all mean? In a word, it meant dinner. There were four or five insignificant-looking little inns hard by the Ogden station and the runners of these hotels, each armed with a big gong, came fourth upon arrival of our train and made the most of the windfall. As we had a couple of hours to wait we began to turn a favorable ear to their vehement declarations, but so passionately did they address us and so violently did they abuse one another that I thought more than once that there was going to be a free fight. One of them promised us a clean meal for seventy-five cents, one promised us one for fifteen cents less and offered to get in addition some young ladies to wait on us. A third promised us a fifty-cent dinner, young ladies to wait, and a good bottle of wine besides. Needless to say, we closed with this last mentioned offer. . . . Dinner . . . was served half cold and what was served was half cooked." Marshall makes no mention of the role of the young ladies, but others complained of the presence of prostitutes at eating house stops.

And finally, "at 8:30 A.M. we reached Elko. Elko is an eating station and we turn out for breakfast. A gong, as usual, proclaims loudly that the feast is quite ready, and we rush out of the train ahead of everybody, for, before eating, we have our toilets to attend to after such a night as we have been obliged to put up with. The white salinous dust brushed up by the train came sweeping in at the doors of the car intermittently opened during the night and completely covered us, curled up though we were on the two seats of our section, with handkerchiefs tied around our necks and a rug thrown over us, making shift the best we could under the unpleasant circumstances. But everything had to be done in a hurry, for we had only twenty minutes allowed us before our journey would be resumed. So when we were through with our ablutions we hurriedly seek the meal room which the uproarious clatter of knives and forks renders not very difficult to find. Politely conducted to our seats by a Chinaman, we indulge in a repast that might be called sumptuous, considering our location."[20]

These writers, while generally praising, reveal several weaknesses of even the best eating-house system. Eating times, even with good intentions and on-time trains, were occasionally inconvenient. Passengers were also at the mercy of others in avoiding odors ranging from unpleasant to unbearable. And, while depot restaurants were strategically located, the strategy was often thrown aside by either chaotic schedule maintenance or devious practice. One popular fraud was perpetuated on passengers who were asked for the fifty-cent cost of the meal in advance. The food was brought out too hot to eat. At that moment, the conductor sounded the "all 'board" bell and the travelers scrambled back to the coaches without touching their food. They were right in thinking that the dishes they'd just passed up were merely saved and brought out again for the next group of victims. Whether or not the train crew was paid off for their role in this scam, the outcome for passengers was the same.

And so, if glorified by the railroads and those inclined to or dependent on them, station restaurants were just as often vilified by the independent parties, the patrons/victims. First, a mild complaint from Catherine E. Bates: "On this occasion the delay lasted only some two hours and the chief practical inconvenience lay in the fact that we were turned out next morning at 6:00 A.M. to get food as best we might at some roadside station. Anyone who has been condemned to eat three meals a day at railroad stations may be safely fed on dried-up sandwiches or fossil buns for the remainder of his life and still be thankful."[21]

Or this from Walter Thornbury: "By this time we were near Buffalo [New York] and breakfast. The train slackened and stopped and out poured the hungry swarms. Five gongs of five opposition breakfast places banged and thundered for our custom. In a minute I was seated with some thirty other hungry souls stowing away white piles of hominy, pink shavings of corned beef, and bowls of stewed oysters, while a Negro boy waved a plume brush of wild turkey feathers over my head to keep off the greedy

[TOP] *Five seconds for Refreshments! The relatively deserted environs of the rural eating house did not protect one from chaos as a main feature of the meal stop.*

[MIDDLE] *The scene inside is no better as pandemonium accompanies a station restaurant meal.*

[BELOW] *And reboarding was no less frightful.* (COURTESY OF THE ASSOCIATION OF AMERICAN RAILROADS)

flies."[22] Another traveler writes of having to run the gauntlet of fourteen hotel runners at a station, all extolling the benefits of various eating establishments. Still another debated with a companion whether it was soot or flies that was seen dotting the food.

One reporter in Texas offers this final account to bring the entire experience into focus: "As you climb upon a high stool and stick your elbows in a lump of grease on the counter, you are cheered by the sight of the glittering nickel-plated coffee urn, and a feeling of sanguine expectancy creeps over your inside as your eye ranges over the cards hanging behind the counter, which read: Turkey, 10¢; Coffee, 10¢; Lamb Chops, 15¢; Pies of all kinds, 10¢; Oysters, every style, 15¢; etc. The man who waits on you wears a dirty apron and a sad tired-of-life-and-of-dishing-out-pies-and-coffee expression of countenance. When you attract his attention and give him your order he goes off with great enthusiasm to get it, but he is stopped by the hungry mortals

all along the line of the counter, who clamor for various articles of food. He dashes a dab of butter on a little plate at the man in the linen duster, jams an empty plate under the nose of the red-faced man with the cinder in his eye, throws a plate of doughnuts to the drummer who is trying to suppress his ravenous appetite with pickles, fills the brakeman's order for a glass of cold tea and a ten-cent chunk of custard pie, and flings a ham sandwich at the sleeping-car porter, who carries it off to gnaw it at his leisure in the retirement of the sleeping-car dressing room. Then there is a clash of plates and glasses, and of knives and forks that turn around in their handles, and the sad-eyed miscreant brings you the coffee and turkey with a take-it-or-leave-it-just-as-you-please air. Before he comes back with the salt and mustard an interval elapses during which he serves seven more hungry passengers, and dives into an anteroom where, he seems to you, to rest for five or six minutes. You feel that your system demands bread. You imagine that the 'fifteen minutes for refreshments' are about up, and, in desperation, you load your internal economy with indigestible doughnuts because you are afraid to wait for the bread, [and] you scald the lining of your mouth with the hot, gritty fluid called coffee. Everything is gritty and tastes of coal dust, and you feel uncomfortable and unclean, and you wish you were dead. Then you pay the caitiff behind the counter fifty cents, and you wish you were dead some more while you rush out thinking that the train is moving off, but you find you have only been pampering your appetite in the banqueting hall for five minutes, and that you have yet ten minutes to spare, and you go back to the lunch counter and buy two cigars for a quarter. As the train pulls out and goes thundering past farmhouses, where you know are stacks of home-made pies, piles of flaky biscuits, churns full of hilarious buttermilk, and tables groaning with yellow-legged chickens and mealy Irish potatoes. . . your two-for-a-quarter cigar begins to swell up in the middle and fray at the edges."[23] Little wonder such travelers cursed the railroads they traveled for allowing the "grasping, hydra-headed, and smoke-begrimed lunchstand monopoly" to exist at all. And little wonder too that the stops were known as "the half-hour indigestion rushes."

But it was competition, not howls of protest from passengers, that brought about a change in the eating-house system. As transcontinental railroads were built or assembled from existing shorter lines, and competition for passengers increased, a more systematic approach to eating became necessary and desirable. Long-distance passengers demanded comfort almost in direct proportion with the length of trips. By 1858, a traveler could set out from New Orleans to New York with through passage on a combined river steamer and railroad route. That year, an ad for The Great Southern Route & U. S. Mail Line appeared in *The Crescent City Business Directory* offering river-packet passage from New Orleans to Memphis, and on to Washington by way of the Memphis & Charleston, the East Tennessee & Virginia, and the Orange & Alexandria railroads. There, additional routes were available to Philadelphia, New York, and Boston. Passengers could not be expected to spend days on the railroad portions of these trips without sleeping or eating. They had not been expected to do so on the riverboats. In fact, one explanation for the emergence of splendid sleeping and dining cars relatively early in railroading's history is that the traveling public had already been indoctrinated in accommodations defined as luxurious by the lavish riverboats and great metropolitan hotels and the spread they put before travelers on such trips.[24]

Eventually, as railroad technology improved, and as mechanical and power advances enabled increased train speeds and longer operating distances, pressure on the railroads mounted to find some method for providing meals on the train itself. It was no longer practical to stop a high-speed train running on a tight schedule, to match or best a competitor, merely to allow passengers to debark for a meal three times a day.

The successful evolution of dining cars gradually, and in some cases abruptly, ruined a number of famous eating houses, celebrated for their food and service among travelers who were more accustomed to rush from the train and bolt a meal. Seldom, after the turn of the twentieth century, did eating houses cater to those riding on through trains. The railway eating houses, though, were still thriving even into the 1950s in locations where they had become something of a local institution, or where the station continued to play a key role as a travel hub or urban center. Noting the closing of one of the last—a Gulf, Mobile & Ohio eating house in Artesia, Mississippi—in the early 1950s, columnist Emmet Calhoun recalled how "there had to be extra coaches put on the branch trains from Columbus and Starkville to accommodate those persons who wanted an extra-fine dinner—especially was this the case on Sunday nights. Always, too, on these Sunday-night events dozens of the cadets of the A & M College [now Mississippi State University] near Starkville came on the Starkville train."[25]

FRED HARVEY, HARVEY HOUSES, AND THE HARVEY GIRLS

In 1850, at the age of fifteen, Frederick Henry Harvey arrived in America from England and went to work as a two-dollar-a-week dishwasher in New York. With money saved from that meager salary, he moved to New Orleans and continued to work and accumulate knowledge in the restaurant business. After a bout with yellow fever in 1853, he again moved, this time to St. Louis. After six years there he realized one of his ambitions: he and a partner opened a restaurant. When the Civil War engulfed Missouri a year later, his partner followed his loyalty South, restaurant assets in hand. Suddenly broke, and now married, Harvey took a succession of jobs, first with Missouri River Packet Line, then with the St. Joseph Post Office, where he sorted Pony Express mail in the first railway post-office car, then worked for the Hannibal & St. Joseph and North Missouri railroads, finally ending up as Western Freight agent for the Chicago, Burlington & Quincy Railroad in Leavenworth, Kansas. His work for the various railroads gave him a first-hand opportunity to see what was wrong with the way railroad passengers were treated at meal stops on the western railroads of the 1870s.

Combining his experience in the restaurant business—he and a new partner even then had

The Harvey House system map. (COURTESY OF PARAGON HOUSE)

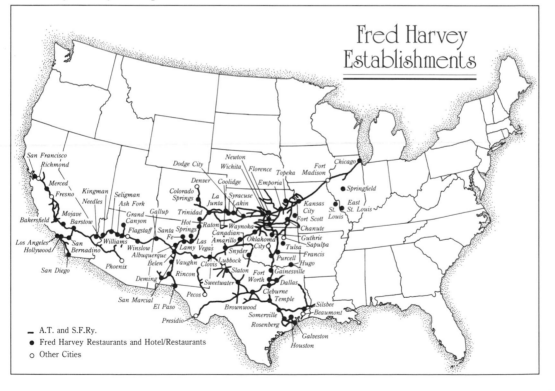

three restaurants along the Kansas Pacific Railroad—with his knowledge of railroad operations, Harvey approached his employer with a proposal to build a network of restaurants that delivered good food and superior service in attractive surroundings to the increasing numbers of travelers in the West. When the Burlington Route's management turned him down, they referred him to the Atcheson, Topeka & Santa Fe Railroad, then building and operating trains across the southwest. Santa Fe Superintendent Charles F. Morse, himself a gourmand, agreed to allow Harvey to open a restaurant on the line in Topeka, Kansas. It was immediately successful as passengers, trainmen, and townspeople quickly and regularly filled it to capacity. Within one year, Harvey, after buying out his less ambitious partner, was serving as many as 5,000 meals a day. Harvey Houses soon dotted the route of the Santa Fe, built at a distance of about 100 miles apart. Publicists for the Fred Harvey Company later asserted this was necessary "to keep western traffic from settling in one place where Fred Harvey served his incomparable meals." In addition to eating houses, at some points west of Kansas City, Harvey opened moderate-priced hotels. East of Kansas City, the Santa Fe attached dining cars to its long-distance trains.

Fred Harvey's formula for a successful eating house was to offer an above-average setting, good food prepared by an established chef, pleasant and efficient service, all at a reasonable price. To these ends, he boasted of never using canned food nor eggs that had been stored in a refrigerator, paid the Harvey chef at Florence, Kansas, twice as much as the town's next-highest-paid resident [the bank president], and coordinated menu planning in Kansas City to insure that no guest along his system encountered the same selections at different stops along the way. This strategy was augmented by the Santa Fe's willingness to provide the buildings and necessary coal, water and ice, a ready market among its passengers, and free transportation of equipment and furnishings, food and supplies, and personnel. Harvey recruited waitresses back East to staff his growing number of establishments with a newspaper advertisement that read: "WANTED: Young women 18 to 30 years of age, of good character, attractive and intelligent, as waitresses in Harvey Eating Houses in the West. Good wages with room and meals furnished."

Thus was born Fred Harvey's second contribution to Western history, the Harvey Girls. The women he recruited were paid $17.50 a month and were under the careful supervision of Mrs. Harvey, who inspected each applicant to insure standards were kept. All signed one-year "no-marry" contracts, although this clause's effectiveness is in doubt, as Fred Harvey personally went to congratulate a woman who remained single for six months. An estimated 20,000 of the roughly 100,000 girls recruited did marry their customers. Humorist Will Rogers quipped that Harvey "kept the West in food and wives." At least one railroad "boomer" agreed, saying, "The Harvey House was not only a good place to eat; it was also a Cupid of the Rails." And it's still possible for many western families to boast that mother was a Harvey girl. Other conditions of employment included a 10:00 P.M. curfew and close supervision by mature head waitresses, known as "wagon bosses." All of this may have been necessary to recruit young women for work where it was said "there are no ladies west of Dodge City and no women west of Albuquerque." Perhaps to contrast the painted ladies in frontier saloons, the Harvey girls wore plain black floor-length skirts, shirtwaists, shoes, stockings, and ties, appointed with white bib aprons. One railroad brakeman described

The Harvey Girl. (COURTESY OF THE CARSTENS PUBLISHING COMPANY)

The Harvey House lunch counter at Gallup, New Mexico, set up for arriving passengers in the early 1900s. (COURTESY OF SPECIAL COLLECTIONS, THE UNIVERSITY OF ARIZONA LIBRARY)

Harvey waitresses as "respectable as hell." A Harvey manager's wife, confronting the matrons of one city who questioned the moral standing of the newly arrived girls, pointed out that "we see that the wrong girls don't stay."

Service at a Harvey eating house was a model of efficiency. As a train sped toward a meal stop, a brakeman would pass through the cars announcing "Dinner in one hour at Florence. Fred Harvey service. Dining room, six bits, lunch counter, pay from the card." He would then count up his orders and pass them to the conductor. When the train stopped at the station before Florence, the conductor would wire ahead to notify the manager what to have prepared in both the dining room and at the lunch counter. As the train neared the eating-house stop, its whistle blew at the one-mile marker. A Harvey girl on the station platform would strike a gong alerting those inside to arrange the first course on the tables or counter. As the passengers dashed in and were seated, waitresses took orders for drinks and arranged cups and glasses in a coded position to notify the drink girl what to pour at each location. In a non-stop ritual, as one course was completed, another would be delivered hot from the kitchen. The high point of a meal was the Harvey manager bringing in a huge platter of sizzling steaks for all to see.

Laura White, who with her mother served as a Harvey girl in the early 1900s, described the dining experience from a Harvey-girl point of view: "All eight-seaters in the dining room ought to have been set, ready for the customers. It wasn't unusual for one girl to serve sixteen people a full meal in twenty-five minutes." During World War I, troop trains put an added strain on the dining services and the pace of women like Ms. White was accelerated: "A waitress with two eight-seater tables, resetting twice each meal for three meals, could feed ninety-six of Uncle Sam's boys in three meals, besides her regular train customers and town trade. I'll never forget the day I had a total of four eight-seaters for three setups at one meal! My trays were so heavy that the cooks lifted them to my shoulder and someone else had to take them off when I got to my station. During big rushes we washed our own dishes at the tray stand, reset our tables, and then held up our hands to show we were ready for more boys from the big line that stretched out through the lobby onto the station platform. When a girl began to reel, we would say, 'Buck up girl, they will be putting in lots of overtime for you before long.'" It is not surprising that "by 10:00 all of us were walking in a daze. We would climb the stairs and throw ourselves across the bed, clothes and all."

The praises earned by such service included verses such as these:

> I have seen some splendid paintings in my day,
>   And I have looked at faultless statuary;
> I have seen the orchard trees a-bloom in May,
>   And watched their colors in the shadows vary;
> I have viewed the noblest shrines in Italy,
>   And gazed upon the richest mosques of Turkey—
> But the finest of all sights, it seems to me,
>   Was the Harvey girl I saw in Albuquerque.
>
> Leiger Mitchel Hodges,
> in the *Philadelphia North American* (May 5, 1905)

One crisp December Morn—
Chilly was the day,
I sat behind my coffee
In a Harvey House Cafe.

Fred's coffee is a nectar—
A beverage supreme,
And the girl who serves it
Adds glamour to my dream.

Since Congress made amendments
And set aside the toddy,
Harvey has a substitute
To cheer us, soul and body.

The aroma most enticing,
Blending with the steam,
The face across the hazy cup—
The vision of a queen.

I like my morning coffee,
Before the busy noon,
When she has time to chatter,
While I dally with my spoon.

All dressed in spotless linen,
Her hair all in a curl,
So purely sweetly winning,
Is the happy Harvey girl.

John Moore,
Amarillo Globe (December 24, 1931)

When dining cars became standard on Santa Fe trains through to the West Coast, Fred Harvey restaurants continued to play a role in their communities. In St. Louis' Union Station, the second-floor Harvey restaurant was the most fashionable and popular in the city from 1894 until it temporarily closed during the Great Depression. In World War II it re-opened to serve meals twenty-four hours a day to thousands of GIs moving through the station. The Harvey lunch counter just off the Midway—the section separating boarding tracks from the waiting room—was, from the beginning, the undisputed heart of the station's life. Meanwhile, Harvey personnel managed the operation of the Santa Fe's dining cars, carrying on the tradition of good food associated with that railroad.

Fred Harvey's chain of Harvey House restaurants, by guaranteeing travelers the same delicious menu in predictable and clean surroundings anywhere along the Santa Fe's route, could be called the birthplace of the fast-food industry. At its peak, fifty-four Harvey lunch counters and dining rooms could feed 6,703 patrons in one sitting. The largest individual dining hall was in Kansas City's Union Station, where 525 could sit at once. The system eventually extended 3,000 miles, from Cleveland to the Pacific Coast, and included resorts, hotels, restaurants, retail shops, and news stands.

2

THE DINING CAR

In 1819, a dozen years before train travel in America became a reality, Benjamin Dearborn of Boston sought money from the United States Congress to support "a mode of propelling wheel-carriages [for] conveying mail and passengers with such celerity as has never before been accomplished [by means of] carriages propelled by steam on level railroads, furnished with accommodations for passengers to take their meals and rest during the passage . . . and that they be sufficiently high for persons to walk without stooping." Congress didn't share Dearborn's vision and buried his request, the first formal proposal to build dining cars, in the Committee of Commerce and Manufactures, where it went unanswered.[26]

But the idea of eating on the train was introduced, however haltingly, almost immediately after the first trains started running. Between 1832 and 1838, the Philadelphia, Germantown and Norristown Railroad acquired new passenger cars the length of two four-wheeled coaches. In addition to such innovations as seats divided across the width of the cars in the center to allow passage down the middle, and entrances placed at each end instead of at the sides, two of these cars, the *Victoria* and *President*, had a bar and several shelves at one end. The absence of any cooking facilities indicates the cars were catered at terminals.[27]

A reporter for the *Baltimore Chronicle* on October 21, 1838, recounted his experience aboard what may have been the first sleeping car in scheduled operation, on an overnight train between Baltimore and Philadelphia, and concluded that "nothing now seems to be wanting to make railway traveling perfect and complete in every convenience, except the introduction of dining cars, and these we are sure will soon be introduced."[28] The *American Railroad Journal*, on June 15, 1842, echoed that forecast, saying "on the whole it would be difficult to imagine any improvement [on new Davenport & Bridges coaches delivered to the Boston & Worcester Railroad] that could be desired, though we dare say, these down-Easters will rig up some new notion ere long that will furnish board and lodging as well as mere passage on the railroad."[29]

The first account of a meal served on a train appeared in the *Baltimore American* of Saturday, November 5, 1842. The article described the run of a special train on November 3 which carried the President and Directors of the Baltimore & Ohio Railroad, "and a few gentlemen invited to accompany them," over the 178-mile mainline out of Baltimore to celebrate and show off the completion of the new fifty-five-mile stretch connecting Hancock with Cumberland, Maryland. "As it was not designed to stop on the road, an elegant cold collation was prepared in one of the cars, fitted up for the purpose, under the direction of Mr. Barnum of City Hotel, whose skill in such matters is too well known to need commendation. The attention of the company was equally divided between the excellence of the fare and the novelty of thirty or forty gentlemen comfortably enjoying a collation while traveling at the rapid rate of twenty-five or thirty miles per hour."[30]

Called "refectory cars," these B & O creations and their imitators on other railroads served on similar occasions for nearly twenty years, the pace of dining innovation apparently at rest. But even this earliest account includes mention of three elements that were to characterize dining-car service for the next 125 years. The food, even in the remote and primitive "wild regions of the Allegheny hills," was termed "elegant." The creative source of the food was the menu of an already-famous hotel, a practice many in railroad management realized established instant credibility among those who frequented first-class intercity trains for their dining-car service. And a renowned chef oversaw the operation. One description was to be dropped. Dining-car meals well into the twentieth century were far from a "collation."

It wasn't until the Civil War period that food was systematically prepared and served on trains. Then, boxcars containing straw mats and hammocks were used to carry wounded troops from the battlefield to treatment facilities in the North and East. At first, food was prepared on primitive stoves in the individual boxcars. But by 1863 fully realized hospital trains were in operation and included a kitchen car containing a range, cupboards and sink, a storage compartment, and a dining area with a long table and benches. Food could be eaten there or delivered to the soldiers lying in converted boxcars and coaches on either end.[31]

The first dining cars to be called such and to be part of the established make-up of a scheduled train also appeared during the war, in 1862 on the Philadelphia, Wilmington and Baltimore Railroad. H. F. Kenney, general superintendent of the PW&B described these two cars as remodeled day coaches, each fifty feet in length and each fitted "with a partition running through the center, crosswise, one end being for smokers, and the other as an eating bar, fitted with steam box and other fixtures usually found in a first-class restaurant. Each of these cars made a round trip daily. The articles served were prepared at the terminal stations and placed in the steam box just before the train departed.[32] In October 1863, *Appleton's Railway and Steam Navigation Guide* noted that "The management [of the PW&B] has placed a new refreshment car upon the road to take the place of the one destroyed by an accident some weeks ago. The experiment of supplying passengers with comfortable meals, including all the delicacies found in first-class hotels, has proved a great success."

Newspaperman Edward P. Mitchell rode one of the dining-car-equipped PW&B trains as a boy. "The diner of 1862 was a baggage car, retired from heavy work on account of long service in the transportation of trunks, and bare as to the interior except that it was furnished in the middle with an oblong counter around the four sides of which the patrons ate while seated on high stools. . . . From the inside of the oblong viands were served by colored waiters in white jackets. If memory does not betray me, the bill of fare of the diner on the *Washington Express* consisted chiefly of oyster stew, pie, crullers, and coffee."[33]

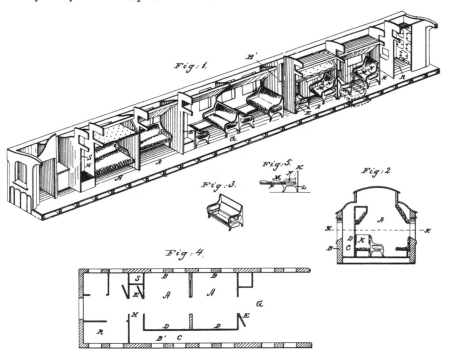

The drawings in patent No. 89538, dated April 27, 1869, for George M. Pullman's hotel car.
(COURTESY OF THE NATIONAL ARCHIVE)

A Dining Car by Definition

The rapid growth of the railroad industry following the Civil War, to serve industry in the East and to link the growing agricultural community in the Midwest and population centers on the West Coast with the rest of the nation, created confusion over equipment and the terminology used to describe such equipment. To address this problem, the Master Car-Builders' Association appointed a committee to create a dictionary of the terms used in building railroad cars. This daunting task, consuming eight years before the first *Car-Builder's Dictionary* was published in 1879, eventually demanded illustrations as well as words to identify the thousands of parts and details used to construct freight and passenger cars. The original and subsequent editions of the *Car-Builder's Dictionary* provide interesting insights into the evolution, early on, of the standard floor plan for a dining car, and to the increased importance of this car to passenger operations.

The first attempt to define eating facilities on trains did not mention dining cars, but rather offered, without floor plans, these definitions:

Hotel Car. A sleeping car with a kitchen for cooking and arrangements for serving meals. Restaurant cars have kitchens, etc., but no sleeping berths.

Restaurant Car. A car provided with a kitchen and cooking appliances and arrangements for serving meals as in a restaurant. Hotel cars also have similar arrangements for serving meals, but they also have sleeping berths.[1]

The *Revised and Enlarged Edition* of the dictionary, published nine years later, notes that the restaurant car is now more properly known as a dining car, and that "hotel cars seem to be passing out of use in favor of dining cars." True to these observations, the definition of a restaurant car was merely transferred to under dining car. Added, however, was that "the more modern cars [have] nearly all their cooking done on the car itself," with the already

Reflecting the change in vocabulary, this same illustration in the 1879 Car Builder's Dictionary *was labeled simply "Restaurant Car."* (COURTESY OF SIMMONS-BOARDMAN BOOKS, INC.)

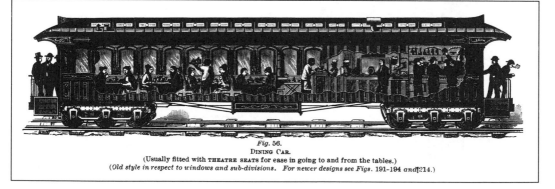

Fig. 56.
DINING CAR.
(Usually fitted with THEATRE SEATS for ease in going to and from the tables.)
(*Old style in respect to windows and sub-divisions. For newer designs see Figs.* 191-194 *and* 214.)

standard qualifier, "and alone among the more luxurious classes of cars [are] generally run by the companies themselves and at a slight pecuniary loss, with the object of attracting travel." It closed with understatement: "They are in wide and increasing use."[2]

Ten years later, entries for restaurant cars and hotel cars had disappeared. The 1898 edition of the *Car Builder's Dictionary* did, however, provide three paragraphs describing the dining car. Additions to the text noted that "the term *diner* is in bad taste, since the car has not the capacity *to dine.*" Now described as in "general use," two types were noted: "A *dining car* is a place where a full-course dinner may be cooked and served with the service usually furnished in hotels, and the whole car is given to that end. They are frequently attached to a train for a few hours only at about mealtime. A *lunch car* partakes more of the character of a lunch counter, and the food served is not cooked on the car. It is a revival of the earliest dining car. . . ."[3]

Twenty-one years later, the 1919 edition of the *Car-Builder's Dictionary and Encyclopedia* reflected the explosion in innovation occurring as dining-car departments struggled to match the eating preferences of an expanded ridership and tried, still in vain, to stop the financial drain having dining service on trains created. Distinctions are made among six different cars:

Dining Car. Regular dining car, for the use of passengers in transit, fitted with regular kitchen, tables, chairs or seats, with or without bar, carrying cooks and waiters.

Buffet Car. Car for the transportation of passengers and fitted with small broiler or buffet to serve simple meals to passengers; cooking and serving being done on removable tables by a regular porter in charge of car. With or without facilities for serving liquor.

Cafe Car. A car fitted with a kitchen, usually in center of car, one end used as [a] cafe where meals are served, also liquor and smoking allowed, the other end of car fitted with either regular dining room or smoking and card room; carrying cooks and waiters.

Grill Room Car. Very similar to cafe car.

Cafe Observation Car. Car fitted with cafe at one end, kitchen in center or extreme end, having observation compartment fitted with stationary or movable tables and observation platform at rear.

Dining and Parlor Car. A car fitted with dining compartment, kitchen and compartment for passengers, fitted with chairs, stationary or otherwise, carrying regular cooks and waiters.[4]

A final check, in the *1953 Car Builder's Cyclopedia of American Practice,* finds a short Dining Car entry. In addition to blandly noting their purpose, "for serving meals," the entry mentions one of the last major innovations, the twin- or dual-car diner, in which the dining car in such a unit has "no kitchen but is given over entirely to table service."[5] This can be explained in part by the fact that the railroads were introducing every conceivable variety of combination now to both retain ridership and, as always, reduce losses. Such configurations as a "dining-lunch counter car," a "buffet-bar-lunch room car," "dining and kitchen-lounge car," "dining-lounge car," and "kitchen-centered, double dining room car" appear.

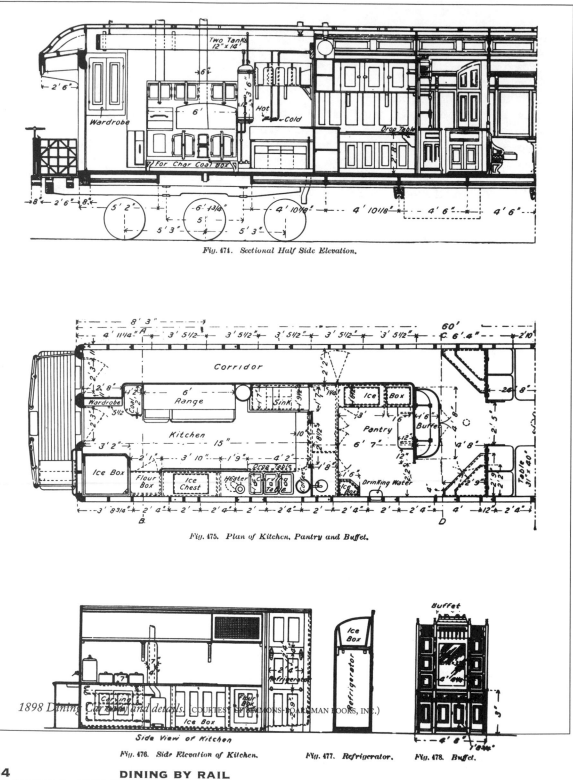

Fig. 474. Sectional Half Side Elevation.

Fig. 475. Plan of Kitchen, Pantry and Buffet.

1898 Dining Car plan and details. (COURTESY OF SIMMONS-BOARDMAN BOOKS, INC.)

Fig. 476. Side Elevation of Kitchen.   Fig. 477. Refrigerator.   Fig. 478. Buffet.

DINING BY RAIL

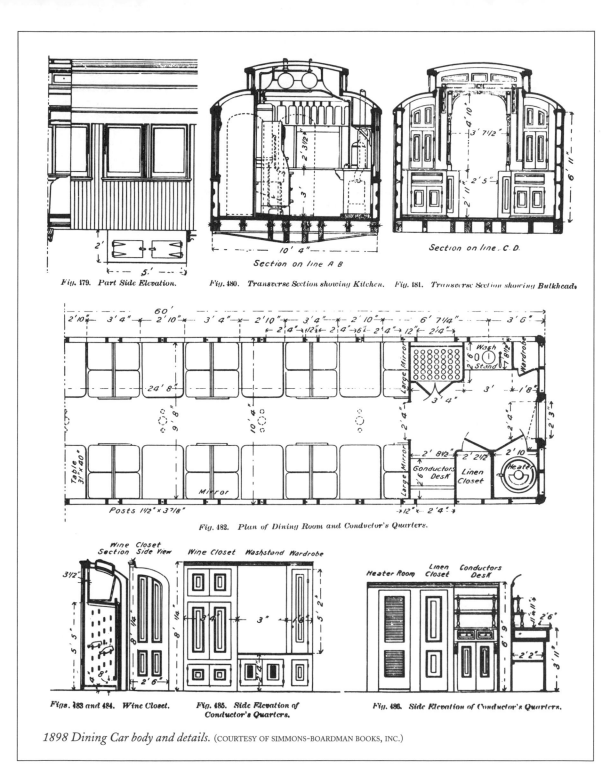

Fig. 179. Part Side Elevation.

Fig. 480. Transverse Section showing Kitchen.

Fig. 181. Transverse Section showing Bulkhead.

Section on line A B

Section on line, C. D.

Fig. 482. Plan of Dining Room and Conductor's Quarters.

Figs. 183 and 484. Wine Closet.

Fig. 485. Side Elevation of Conductor's Quarters.

Fig. 486. Side Elevation of Conductor's Quarters.

1898 Dining Car body and details. (COURTESY OF SIMMONS-BOARDMAN BOOKS, INC.)

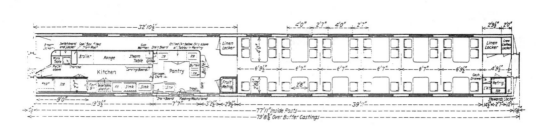

This 1931 Chicago, Milwaukee, St. Paul & Pacific dining car floor plan typifies the standard steel diner found throughout America. (COURTESY OF SIMMONS-BOARDMAN BOOKS, INC.)

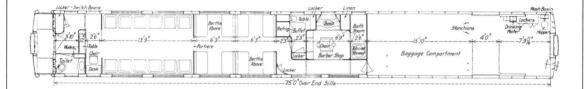

In 1916, a steel, Pullman Company Buffet Baggage Car for the Union Pacific held this floor plan. (COURTESY OF SIMMONS-BOARDMAN BOOKS, INC.)

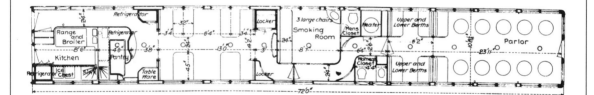

A 1906 Pullman Company Café Parlor Car built for the Chicago, Burlington & Quincy Railroad. (COURTESY OF SIMMONS-BOARDMAN BOOKS, INC.)

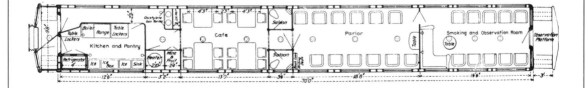

The Pullman Company's Observation Café Car for the Chicago Great Western Railroad in 1906. (COURTESY OF SIMMONS-BOARDMAN BOOKS, INC.)

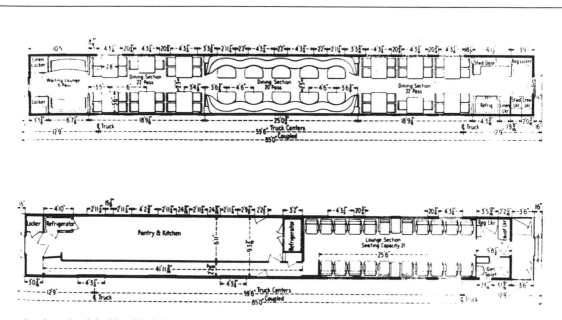

A twin unit of the New York Central System in 1953 features both a dining car and a combination kitchen-lounge car. (COURTESY OF SIMMONS-BOARDMAN BOOKS, INC.)

The first primitive dining cars continued in operation for just three years, with no public note made on the cause of their demise. But again, precedents were set by the PW&B experience. First, the cars were introduced on trains traveling what had early become a busy rail corridor, New York to Washington. Competition for passengers, perhaps already intense, may have been the motive for launching the service. Second, busy wartime travel may have helped make the dining cars profitable, something that wasn't to happen again for the railroads until World War II.

In 1867 a revolutionary turn in the way people ate while riding the train occurred. George Pullman introduced his "hotel car." Named *President*, it was the first railroad car designed and built for the purpose of preparing and serving meals on board and en route, and awakened travelers and railroadmen alike to the full potential of eating on a train.

George Mortimore Pullman, who in 1865 first introduced American train travelers to a comfortable night's sleep en route with his sleeping car *Pioneer*, was a self-taught "practical engineer." Born in 1831 in Brockton, New York, Pullman had received the minimum schooling provided by "that little red schoolhouse on the hill" when at the age of 14 he went to work for forty dollars a year in a general store in nearby Westfield. He was remembered by townspeople for his inventiveness, love of riddles, and everpresent carving knife and piece of wood. Pullman's brother offered him work in his furniture shop and so he moved to Albion, New York, to make bookcases and cabinets and repair furniture. Here, too, he began tinkering with engineering problems and doing occasional work applying his ideas and skills. One such application saw him successfully move a number of buildings back from the banks of the Erie Canal when it was being widened.

Pullman conceived his first ideas for improved rail travel during this period, when he took an overnight train from Buffalo to Westfield. A sleepless night in a crude board bunk set him to thinking about ways he would remedy the problems encountered in long-distance train travel, but it would be a number of years before he put his ideas into practice. Meanwhile, after accumulating enough money from his workworking and odd-job engineering, he moved to Chicago. There he quickly established himself as a problem-solving engineer. One of his first jobs called for him to raise several blocks of stone-and-brick buildings, including the Tremont House Hotel, to secure them from the waters of Lake Michigan.

Pullman's reputation as an engineer spread, bringing income in its wake. Enough so that, when presented with the opportunity to try his plans for providing better railroad travel facilities by the Chicago & Alton Railroad, he had both the means and the skills required. His earliest effort was to rebuild two C & A coaches into sleeping cars. They could be converted into two berths by lowering a bunk from over each set of facing benches and moving the bench seats down to bridge the gap that separated them when set up for seating passengers. Crude as they were, the berths proved a hit with travelers, who "seized upon them with avidity" when available on a train.

This episode both emboldened Pullman to attempt a whole new car of his own design, and demonstrated to him that his equipment, when placed in competition with others', came out the winner. So, to increase the market for his sleeping cars, Pullman would offer a prospective railroad's owners a challenge: "Let's leave it to the people to decide. Run both—your sleeping cars and mine—on the same trains for a while. If the traveling public thinks the beauty of finish and increased comfort are worth $2 per night, there are my $24,000 cars all ready for them. If, on the other hand, they are satisfied with less attractive surroundings for $1.50 per night, the cheaper sleeping cars are at their disposal." It is reported that, after but a few days, the only men who could be found in the older sleeping equipment—women, of course, would not enter the crude sleeping quarters and lie down in the company of men regardless of the accommodations—were those grumbling over their inability to buy space in Pullman's cars. Such rapid and widespread acceptance of improvements sought by the traveling public was to play an equally significant role in the spread of the use of dining cars on trains.

What has not been pinpointed is when Pullman conceived of his plans to create entire trains offering all the amenities of a fine hotel, and to interchange cars between not just trains but whole railroad lines. Early on, he appears to have sought to make it possible to run Pullman sleeping cars over any and all railroads, switching them from one road to another at terminals, enabling his "guests" to remain in his space for the duration of their trip. Such a plan required being able to "provide for the wants of the inner man during his journey." To do so, a way had to be found to avoid passengers having to take meals at eating houses while the train waited. So, just two years after *Pioneer* rolled out of his shops, he introduced the hotel car *President,* which combined sleeping accommodations, a lounge, and dining facilities in one car.

The hotel car gave passengers access to all the conveniences of a hotel of the day while proceeding on a protracted journey. With a kitchen measuring three by six feet, a pantry, a wine cellar built into one end, and a crew of four or five, it offered an extensive menu for its size. Here is the menu on the *Western World,* the second hotel car built, during one of its inaugural trips:[34]

THE COOK IN HIS WELL-EQUIPPED KITCHEN
ON A HOTEL CAR.

THE HOTEL CAR'S WINE CLOSET.

Oysters

Raw	50 cents
Fried and Roast	60 cents

Cold

Beef Tongue, Sugar-cured Ham, Pressed Corned Beef, Sardines	40 cents
Chicken Salad, Lobster Salad	50 cents

Broiled

Beefsteak, with Potatoes	60 cents
Mutton Chops, with Potatoes	60 cents
Ham, with Potatoes	50 cents

Eggs

Boiled, Fried, Scrambled, Omelette Plain	40 cents
Omelette with Rum	50 cents

INSPECTING THE HOTEL CAR'S LINEN CLOSET.

PREPARING THE DESSERT
FOR HOTEL CAR PASSENGERS.

Chow-Chow, Pickles

Welsh Rarebit	50 cents
French Coffee	25 cents
Tea	25 cents

The Pullman hotel car carried 133 food items, a wine chest under the floor, 1,000 napkins, and 150 table cloths, and the china, glassware, and utensils needed to serve on a trip of from four to seven days' length. When meals were to be served, tables were installed at the seating sections and the porter became a waiter. A writer for the *Detroit Commercial Advertiser* observed that "the crowning glory of Mr. Pullman's invention is evinced in his success in supplying the car with a cuisine department containing a range where every variety of meats, vegetables, and pastry may be cooked on the car, according to the best style of culinary art." Put into service on the Great Western Railroad of Canada, the popular success of the *President* prompted Pullman to build additional hotel cars.

In 1870, one traveler described his experience on a hotel car this way: "The first trip in one of these cars forms an epoch in a traveler's life. No

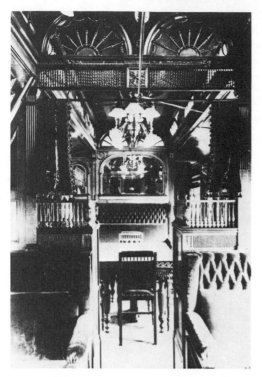

Hotel car Western World, *described by* The Chicago Times *on March 21, 1867, as* "elaborately orna-mented by pictures of good taste and appro-priateness. It is replete on the inside with all the conveniences of a modern hotel. The car is much higher and wider than any which had been constructed heretofore. It ran on sixteen wheels; was hand-upholstered in purple plush; elegantly painted; was heated by a large furnace in cold weather and cooled by a large ventilator in warm weather." (COUR-TESY OF THE ASSOCIATION OF AMERICAN RAILROADS)

royal personage can be more comfortably housed than the occupant of a Pullman car, provided the car be a hotel one. In the train by which I traveled one out of three sleeping cars was of the latter descrip-tion. The hotel car is divided into sections forming staterooms wherein parties of four can be accom-modated. Between these rooms are seats arranged in the usual way. At the rear is a kitchen, which, though small, contains every appliance necessary for cook-ing purposes. There are water tanks in which is stored a supply of water for washing and drinking sufficient to last the journey. A wine cellar contains the liquors which are likely to be in demand and an icehouse preserves the ice for the gratification of those who prefer cold beverages. At stated intervals the conductor walks around taking passengers' or-ders, who make their selections from the bill of fare. The choice is by no means small. Five different kinds of bread, four sorts of cold meat, six hot dishes, to say nothing of eggs cooked in seven different ways and all the seasonable vegetables and fruits, form a variety from which the most dainty eater might easily find something to tickle his palate and the ravenous to satis-fy his appetite. The meal is served on a table temporarily fixed to the side of the car and removed when no longer required. To breakfast, dine, and sup in this style while the train is speeding at the rate of nearly thirty miles an hour is a sensation of which the novelty is no greater than the comfort. An additional zest is given to the good things by the thought that the pas-sengers in the other cars must rush out when the refreshment station is reached and hastily swallow an ill-cooked meal."[35]

With such civilized accommodations, women joined in overnight trav-el. Lady Duffus Hardy provides this commentary on her experience on a hotel car in 1881: "It was here [Chicago to Omaha via the Chicago & North Western Railway] for the first time we enjoyed the luxury of the hotel car. We were getting hungry and curious to know what good things the gods would provide us. Presently a good-humored Negro clothed all in white brought us a bill of fare from which to select our meal. There were so many good things that we held a consultation as to what would form the most desirable meal. We decided on mulligatawny soup, broiled oys-ters, lamb cutlets, and peas. A narrow passage, every inch of which is uti-lized, separates the kitchen from the rest of the car. How is it that in so many private houses the odor or roast and broil travels from the kitchen and insinuates itself into the remotest corner of the house? Here the occupants of the car but a few feet off have no suggestion of dinner until it is placed before them. We are curious as to the working of the culinary department and animated by a noble desire to obtain knowledge, we penetrated the sacred precincts of the cook. The kitchen was a perfect gem of a place about eight feet square. A range ran along one side, its dark shining face breaking out into an eruption of knobs, handles, and hinges of polished brass or steel. Curious little doors were studded all over it. Pots, steamers, and pans were simmering on the top. Every requisite for carrying on the gastronomical operations was there in that tiny space in the neatest and most compact form. Scrupulous cleanliness reigned supreme over all. There was the pantry with its polished silver, glass, and china in shining array. The refrigerator, with a plentiful supply of ice, and the larder were side by side. The wine and beer were artfully arranged beneath the car. Thus every inch of space was realized to its utmost extent. Toward 6:00 every table was spread with dainty linen and the dinner was exquisitely served according to the previous order of each traveler. The simplest dish as well as the most elaborate was cooked to perfection and everybody fell to with a will. Early hours were kept here as in our other traveling home and the same routine was pursued. . . ."[36]

Why Pullman went on to introduce a car devoted exclusively to dining so soon after he launched hotel car service is unclear. There were, to be sure, problems with the hotel car. Traveler Benjamin Robbins Curtis complained, "Today we made our first trial of a hotel car and although the dinner is hot and the food well cooked and of good quality, the dust and cinders pretty effectually spoil the repast, for, as the kitchen occupies a large share of these hotel-cars, it is almost impossible to keep the windows closed."[37] The lingering scent of food after a meal in the sitting and sleeping accommodations of the car contributed to travel sickness among some passengers. For blue bloods, the idea of having a kitchen in one's sleeping quarters was a practice common among the lower classes, and thus neither pleasant nor acceptable. The ratio of crew to passengers, even if the car was filled, was considered high. And the investment in kitchen equipment and utensils, linens, and service pieces made the hotel car a more risky financial venture than ordinary sleeping cars.

It has been argued that "Pullman hoped to solve these defects by building a special car that did nothing but prepare and serve meals. A complete diner could provide more and better food for everyone aboard the train. It would be cheaper, since it would leave more revenue space in the sleeping cars and would surely cut labor costs."[38] Indeed, it could also be set off the train when not in use, saving the expense of the car's large crew altogether for much of a trip and of hauling unused (and thus financially un-productive) space for so many unnecessary miles.

But the introduction of dining cars is so proximate to that of hotel cars that one had to have been in development as the other was being built. Anyway, a hotel car could feed as many as forty people, only eight fewer than the earliest dining cars, and more than the thirty-six seated in most dining cars built shortly after their introduction. And at capacity, the crew of four or five was small by comparison to the ten or more required of a full diner.

That dining cars would put an end to the demand for hotel cars could not have been Pullman's plan. After all, he continued to build hotel cars for more than a dozen years. His knowledge of railroad operations of the time may have led him to believe there was room for both types of equipment. Through trains were rare in the 1860s, their destinations less numerous, their passengers well-to-do if not wealthy. In such an environment, and with nation's railways of an increasingly standardized gauge, it is conceivable that Pullman planned to have some trains under his complete control. Operating as a fine hotel on wheels, these trains could be passed from one railroad to the next onward to a completion of their journey. Other, smaller hotels (those contained in one car) could be passed from train to train en route to their destinations under the jurisdiction of one or more railroads. It was the rapid growth in the number of destinations, and its subsequent effect on the management of sleeping cars, that made sleeping car operations unique and inapplicable to dining-cars. Strings of Pullman sleepers could be broken up where routes interchanged, then picked up by various other through trains and sped to their final destination. The logistics needed to support dining cars, however, as well as the limited but certain need for their presence in long-distance trains, prevented similar flexibility in their operation. The realization of this difference, as much as the inherent money-losing aspect of dining-car operations, may have been behind the Pullman Company's eventual decision to get out of the business of staffing and operating full dining cars. This became fact by the early 1900s.

Hotel-car construction continued as late as 1879, but they remained in service into the 1880s. Their final assignments came when, as dining-car service began to appear on the eastern railroads, some were temporarily pressed into service as dining cars until either the Pullman Company or the railroad's own shops could supply and outfit new full dining cars. Other hotel cars were reconfigured as new types of cars, or phased out of service altogether.

Meanwhile, in 1868 Pullman rolled a luxurious new car out of his shops that was dedicated exclusively to preparing and serving food to passen-

gers. Named the *Delmonico* in honor of the nationally known New York restaurant of the same name, it was in operation on the Chicago & Alton Railroad between Chicago and Springfield, Illinois, within a year of the introduction of the hotel car.

Although the *Delmonico* was considered "a natural and speedy development," dining cars were very much a curiosity to the majority of traveling Americans even four years later. Charles Nordhoff, who wrote annual travel guides, alludes to this scarcity in 1872, when he describes his first experience on a dining car: "From Chicago to Omaha your train will carry a dining car, which is a great curiosity in its way. I expected to find this somewhat greasy, a little untidy, and with a smell of the kitchen. It might, we travelers thought, be a convenience, but it could not be a luxury. But in fact it is neat, as nicely fitted, as trim and cleanly, as though Delmonico had furnished it; and though the kitchen bay be in the forward end of the car, so perfect is the ventilation that there is not even the faintest odor of cooking. You sit at little tables which comfortably accommodate four persons; you order your breakfast, dinner, or supper from a bill of fare which contains a quite surprising number of dishes, and you eat from snow-white linen and neat dishes [with] admirably cooked food, and pay a moderate price.

"It is now the custom to charge a dollar per meal on these cars; and as the cooking is admirable, the service excellent, and the food various and abundant, this is not too much. You may have your choice in the wilderness, eating at the rate of twenty-two miles per hour, of buffalo, elk, antelope, beefsteak, mutton-chops, [and] grouse. . . ."[39]

An English newspaperman, writing in *The London Telegraph*, offered yet another advantage for travelers considering whether or not to seek out a train equipped with a Pullman dining car: "There will be another traveling infliction, besides Dyspepsia and Discontent, which will be speedily laid in the Red Sea. I mean the ghost of Ennui. Luncheon or dinner on board a Pullman palace car will surely banish Boredom from railway journeys."[40]

There was much to banish boredom, as this early description of a Chicago & North Western din-

Naming his first dining car Delmonico—shown here in a cutaway view—Pullman began an early tradition among the railroads of naming their dining cars after famous restaurants or maître's de cuisine in their territory. (COURTESY OF THE ASSOCIATION OF AMERICAN RAILROADS)

A Grand Trunk Railway Company dining car interior of the 1870s. (COURTESY OF THE ASSOCIATION OF AMERICAN RAILROADS)

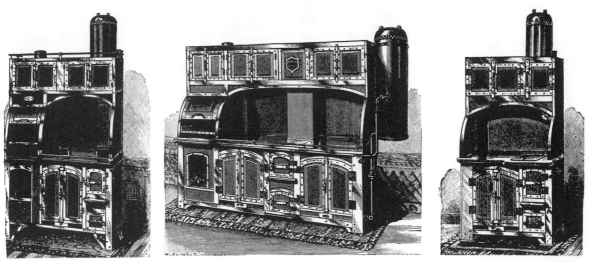

Three ranges—used in the kitchens of a hotel car, a dining car, and a private car—all from the 1880s. The Hotel Car range featured a broiler and hot water tank; the Dining Car range featured a broiler, hot water tank and fuel closet; and the Directors'-Car range merely a hot water tank. (COURTESY OF SIMMONS-BOARDMAN BOOKS, INC.)

ing car illustrates: "Each car is sixty-nine feet in length over all, the bodies being sixty-two-and-a-half-feet long by ten-feet wide. They have six-wheel trucks, thirty-three-inch Allen paper wheels, and well-adjusted springs for easy riding. The main or dining saloon is thirty-two feet in length, and is divided into five sections on a side, with a table and seats for four persons in each. Large plate-glass mirrors cover the end partitions, and also the wide window panels, the effect of which is to make the size of the room seem much larger than it is. At the end of each double seat is a large window, the panels over the seat backs are narrow and those over the tables wide, with three alcoves for tumblers, salt, spices, etc. The seats are covered with maroon leather, and the floor laid with three-inch alternate strips of walnut and maple. The seat ends and frames and the inside finish are cherry trimmed with mahogany; five Adams and Westlake two-light chandeliers with argand burners hang over the aisle—one to each pair of tables. These, and all the metal trimmings of the car are gilt. The head linings are decorated oak, paneled with mahogany moldings. Those below the clear story have paintings of game, fruit, and flowers. Hartshorn roller shades are used instead of blinds, and roll up out of sight under box moldings. The windows are all double, the outside ones of the kitchen having game and fish designs ground in the center. The kitchen is thirteen by eight feet, and built of solid walnut, with all requisite utensils and conveniences. Water is carried in a long cylindrical reservoir in the clear story overhead. Between the kitchen and the dining saloon is a pantry four-and-a-half by eight feet. In the end corner of the car is an ice closet with glass-bottomed drawers opening into the kitchen, also a closet for small stores. At the opposite end is a Baker heater, linen and wine closets, lavatory, and ice chest. Without particularizing further, it may be said that these cars are believed to embody all the improvements pertaining to their class, and are unsurpassed in their luxurious accommodations and handsome finish by any others in the country. The outside is painted a dark wine color relieved with gilt tracery and ornamental designs representing storks, passionflowers, cornucopias, etc."[41]

The only problem remaining was enabling people to get to the dining car safely. Passengers had to brave leaping the gap between car-end platforms, a task made more difficult by the up-and-down, side-to-side twist a train in motion produces where cars meet. Devices to assist passengers in these circumstances were patented for as early as 1836. In 1847 a canvas canopy, or hood, was used. Other contraptions, whose names embrace the limited advances being made, included the Garvey Buffer and Canopy Frame (1852), Atwood's Covered Passageway (1855), Childley's Covered Passageway (1865), Waller's Face Plate Buffers (1871), and Smith's Car Platform Hood (1882).

But characteristically, it fell to the Pullman Company to claim a patent on the last major innovation needed to assure the success not just of the dining car but of the concept of a land-based traveling hotel. The Sessions Vestibule, actually a series of patents awarded in 1887, permanently altered the appearance of passenger trains, making them virtually a single unit of greatly enhanced safety for passengers. Elastic diaphragms mounted on steel frames were attached to the ends of the cars. When a train was made up, the faces of the diaphragms were pressed firmly against each other by powerful springs which held the diaphragms in place and reduced the vibration characteristic of trains in motion. Passengers could safely cross the now nonexistent gap between the platform end of one car onto that of the connecting car. It was perfectly feasible to leave your seat or room and walk the length of the train to enter the dining car.

In all, the ideal vestibule served five purposes: 1. to resist the injurious effects of a collision by preventing one car from riding up over another and splitting it open; 2. to prevent oscillation between cars; 3. to lessen air resistance; 4. to insure good ventilation; and, 5. to make a covered passageway that afforded safety to passengers.[42] Only the Sessions design performed all five. No more safety bars, canvas hoods, or life-threatening leaps. It is not surprising that "vestibule trains," wherein each car was equipped with a vestibule, were quickly adopted by the railroads to gain a marketing edge. The Pennsylvania Railroad introduced the first such train in April 1887. In only a few years, every railroad using Pullman equip-

The Car-Builders Dictionary *noted that cookstoves such as this one with an oven were installed in immigrant cars: crude and inexpensive equipment used to haul immigrants from East Coast ports to towns along the mainline. Eating-car ranges were more elaborate and attached to a wall. Both types were connected to a chimney by stove-pipe through their car's roof, instead of by brick as used by home builders. (*COURTESY OF SIMMONS-BOARDMAN BOOKS, INC.*)

Early on-train food service included the possibility of a trip to the baggage car, set up by the train's crew to provide food and drink, with or without management's knowledge. A Canadian National lunch counter car of the twentieth century is evocative of this early practice.
(COURTESY OF THE BETTMANN ARCHIVE)

ment had adopted vestibule cars.[43]

Chicago gets credit for having been the inaugural point of dining-car service. *The Railroad Gazette* in 1882 summarized these developments: Regularly scheduled dining-car movements from and to Chicago began on the Michigan Central Railroad in 1876 or 1877. The Chicago, Burlington & Quincy and the Chicago & Alton followed suit. The Chicago, Rock Island & Pacific Railroad was next, followed by the Chicago & North Western, then the Wabash Railway. In 1882, the Chicago, Milwaukee, & St. Paul Railway became the last major railroad then out of Chicago to initiate dining-car service. In late 1881, the eastern railroads began offering dining-car service. "Strange as it may seem, the conservative Baltimore & Ohio was the first one of the eastern truck lines to imitate the example of the Michigan Central in running dining cars out of Chicago. The B & O adopted the new feature [in 1881] and "its business has been greatly stimulated thereby." The Pennsylvania Railroad responded by adding dining cars when its new limiteds began operation between New York and Chicago in 1881.[44] In 1883, the New York Central, faced with the challenge from the Pennsylvania and Baltimore & Ohio railroads, also added dining cars. Service extended into New England in 1884, when the New Haven added dining cars to trains between New York and Boston.[45] It was on these and other eastern railroads—which experienced the heaviest travel, the most trains, and, not coincidentally, the stiffest competition—where trains were eventually equipped with Pullman hotel cars and dining cars in larger quantities than on those in the West.[46] The far western railroads completed the nationwide spread of dining-car service when the Northern Pacific added dining-car-equipped trains in 1887, followed by the Union Pacific in 1890, and the Atcheson, Topeka & Santa Fe in 1891.

ONE RAILROAD'S ROSTER: THE SOUTHERN PACIFIC

While each of the major railroads was unique in the combinations of equipment and services provided their dining-car departments, all could be characterized as large and far-flung networks offering meals in a variety of situations. In addition to dining cars and other food-service cars, these might include station restaurants, resort hotels, steamships and ferries, layover facilities, and bed and board trains for work crews.

An account of the operation of one railroad, the Southern Pacific, demonstrates how extensive such operations were. In 1927, near the peak of dining-car operations nationwide in 1930, Allan Pollok, Southern Pacific's manager of dining cars, hotels, restaurants, and railway clubs, provided these details of his railroad's dining-car department:

Dining cars	140	*The number of meals served in several of these categories in 1926:*	
All-day-lunch cars	26		
Steamship restaurants	20	Dining cars	3,260,000
Hotel restaurants	7	Steamship restaurants	2,243,000
Railway clubs	10	Station restaurants	1,000,000
Club cars	36	Railway clubs	679,000
On-train news agents	73		
Payrolled employees	2,100		

The company operated commissaries for all of these eateries in San Francisco, Oakland, Los Angeles, Portland, El Paso, Houston, San Antonio, and New Orleans. Supplies were also drawn from "foreign" commissaries (those of other railroads) in Ogden, Omaha, and Chicago.

A number of factors contributed to this sporadic but relentless spread of dining cars on trains. There was the increasingly disadvantageous practice of slowing the progress of fast trains to provide meals at station eating houses. There was the indigestion among passengers when such stops were made. There are those who speculate, too, that George Pullman pushed dining cars as part of his ambition to control the creation and movement of all passenger trains. Ultimately, however, it was the competition for passengers that persuaded railroads, one by one, to try dining cars. First-class travelers, when they had a choice, preferred to make their trip on the train line with a diner. But the financial losses associated with diners from the very beginning hindered their widespread adoption until competition among railroads for passengers intensified dramatically. The experience of the transcontinental railroads west out of Chicago illustrates this point. And while the particulars may vary, the same phenomenon appears to have been repeated among the major eastern and north-south railroads as well.[47]

THE KANSAS CITY SOUTHERN:
A REGIONAL CARRIER'S STORY

The Kansas City Southern Railway offered travelers a route "straight as the crow flies" south from Kansas City to Pittsburg, Kansas; Joplin, Missouri; Fort Smith and Texarkana, Arkansas; Shreveport, Louisiana; and Beaumont, Lake Charles, and Port Arthur, Texas. Connecting in Beaumont with the Missouri Pacific's *Sunshine Special*, or trains of the Southern Pacific, passengers could go on to Houston, San Antonio, El Paso, Brownsville, and Galveston, Texas, and to Mexico City. A merger in 1940 with the Louisiana and Arkansas Railway extended KCS service into Dallas and New Orleans. To promote these routes, the KCS named its flagship passenger train *The Flying Crow*. Once service extended to New Orleans, *The Southern Belle* was added to its roster.

Prior to 1928, passengers traveling on Kansas City Southern trains did not have the convenience of taking their meals on board because there were no dining cars. Passengers were, however, offered the opportunity to eat well during scheduled meal stops at designated stations. A 1924 KCS timetable lists such facilities at Joplin, Texarkana, and Shreveport, as well as at Sulphur Springs, Arkansas, and Heavener, Oklahoma. The dining rooms were operated for the railroad by the Van Noy–Interstate Company of Kansas City. Meal stops lasted twenty-five minutes. Very likely the traditional news "butch" was on board the trains as well, selling light snack foods.

On July 15, 1928, with the advent a newly equipped *Flying Crow*, dining service on the railroad became a reality. The first cars to serve meals were operated by the Pullman Company. They were cafe-lounge cars named the *Gulf States*, *Kawmo*, *Oildom* and *Ozarka*. In 1927 the KCS introduced a china pattern no doubt intended for the dinners they planned. A unique and attractive pattern, also named "Flying Crow," it consisted of a white body edged with an orange-red and black band pinstriped in gold and emblazoned with a red-and-black railroad logo. It can be assumed that this china pattern was used on the Pullman cafe-lounge cars, in place of the traditional Pullman pattern of the day, and was certainly used on the new KCS diners when they went into service in 1929.

In 1929, KCS purchased three used thirty-six-seat dining cars from the Pullman Company, numbered them 50, 51, and 52, and placed them in service on *The Flying Crow*. In 1937, a fourth used dining car was purchased from Pullman and numbered 53. Before the new acquisition was placed in service, it and the three cars purchased in 1929 were remodeled into diner-chair cars. Each car could then seat twenty-four in the dining room and thirty-two in the chair section. The addition of air conditioning allowed the railroad to boast, "Kansas City Southern dining cars always have provided the 'extra' in food and service—at moderate prices. New KCS meals are even more enjoyable, served in the cool comfort of delightfully finished coach-diners of newest design and appointments." At the same time, four new light-weight chair cars were delivered by the Pullman Company and, coupled with the "new" diner-chair cars and assigned Pullman sleepers, offered the first air-conditioned service on the railroad. Publicity presented the train as the "New *Flying Crow*–Air Conditioned."

An advertising brochure promoting this new service shows a dining-car table set with a new china pattern. Called "Roxbury," this stock pattern featured a white body with a red floral design. This is the earliest noted evidence of the first use of "Roxbury," leaving one to conclude that in 1937, along with the appearance of the refurbished diners and new chair cars, the "Flying Crow" custom china pattern was retired and the "Roxbury" was installed. The "Roxbury" pattern was used until the end of dining-car service on the KCS in 1969.

An interesting sidelight to the KCS china story appears in a 1940 16-mm color promotional movie entitled *The Southern Belle*. A scene in the dining car shows a waiter serving food at a table. The waiter is clad in a white uniform with light-blue trim. The china on his serving tray and on the table is white with a light-blue border. Could this be evidence of the plates rumored to carry a "Southern Belle" logo and used on the *Southern Belle* for a short while prior to the installation of the "Roxbury" pattern? Because the plates in the movie are almost totally covered with food, it is impossible to determine the presence of a logo. This sort of mystery interests rail fans and china collectors.

The December 1937 issue of *Service*, a publication of the Tuskegee Institute for those in the hospitality industries, reprinted the following account from *Kansas City Southern Magazine*. It tells of the life and work of the railroad's top chef, John Reid: "On November 1, 1894, he became Porter on [car] 96, used by President Stilwell and the other high officials of that day. John proudly recalls his first trip, extending only to Hume, but how proud he was to

In the TEMPO of the TIMES

Southern Belle

A HIGH NOTE in travel comfort between Kansas City and New Orleans, with ALL THE EXTRAS at NO EXTRA FARE! Yes . . . you'll find complete relaxation aboard the SOUTHERN BELLE — in commodious chair cars . . . in deep-cushioned lounges . . . in the delightful observation solarium . . . in the cocktail lounge, or in the diner, where the best in food and service is yours at moderate cost.

The FLYING CROW—another Top Train between Kansas City and New Orleans—also provides daily service to and from PORT ARTHUR, BEAUMONT, LAKE CHARLES and OTHER K. C. S. POINTS.

For reservations, travel information and assistance, or literature describing vacation and recreational centers, romantic New Orleans and other cities and resorts on the KCS-L&A, call your local travel agent, or address.

W. C. CLARK
Passenger Traffic Manager
KCS-L&A LINES
Shreveport, Louisiana

The "EXTRA" in FREIGHT SERVICE too!

Heavier rail . . . improved roadbed . . . high-speed freight engines . . . Diesel-electric switching locomotives . . . speedy highway units—all tools in the hands of an efficient, interested personnel — assure KCS-L&A patrons the fastest, most dependable freight and merchandise service in the territory.

serve the handsome president of the line and the prominent guests aboard. Longer trips followed, during all of which Chef Nance taught Porter Reid how to prepare the appetizing dishes John still makes so expertly. . . . Then, in November 1907, John Reid reached his goal as a Chef. Since then, he has traveled thousands of miles on private cars and has demonstrated his culinary skill to prominent people from many lands and places. 'I became so wrapped up in cooking,' says John, 'that I forgot all about my desire to travel, and instead of seeing the sights, I found more fun in the kitchen.'

"Through the years, John has compiled an extensive card index of recipes, many of his own creation. His recipe for 'spoon bread' has been sought by many folks he has served [see page 338]. . . . Ever on the lookout for new dishes, Chef Reid subscribes to a monthly from the Waldorf-Astoria and watches the magazines and newspapers for improved recipes. 'I love to cook,' he smiles, 'and it seems most folks like my cooking, so what could make a man happier?' . . . John Reid has enjoyed his forty-three years' service on the Kansas City Southern—the only employer he ever had."

In all, from 1929, when it introduced dining-car service, until 1969, when the service was discontinued, the Kansas City Southern at one time or another operated fifteen cars offering food service. This total includes the four aforementioned diners, two of which were converted to diner-lounge cars in 1942. All four were again modernized as diner-lounge cars between 1949 and 1958, then phased off the roster between 1962 and 1970. In addition, three new diner-lounge-observation cars were purchased in 1940 and converted to tavern-observation cars in 1948. Two new thirty-six-seat diners were bought in 1948, and two used diners were acquired from the Illinois Central in 1949. In 1960 the railroad converted four tavern-observation cars it bought from the New York Central into cafe-lounge-observation cars. All were sold or scrapped by 1970. Six other cars were operated by the Pullman Company: four cafe-lounge cars, between 1928 and 1929, and two coach-restaurant-sleepers, briefly in 1940. These latter cars enabled "set-out" service on night trains between Kansas City and Fort Smith, wherein a car would be set out on a siding in Fort Smith at 4:00 A.M., but remain occupied by sleeping passengers until 8:00 A.M., with breakfast service available to those who desired it. Those bound for Kansas City could board their car at 9:30 P.M., be picked up by a through train at 2:00 A.M., and enjoy breakfast service into Kansas City at 8:15 A.M. In addition to Pullman cars, the railroad operated cars built by the Budd Corporation and American Car Foundry. KCS, then, was truly a representative carrier, but on a smaller scale.

(Adapted with permission from material provided by Jack B. Austerman of the Kansas City Southern Historical Society.)

The inside of a Chicago, Milwaukee & St. Paul Railway Dining Car Menu of 1882. (COURTESY OF THE UNION PACIFIC MUSEUM)

The inside of a Chicago, Milwaukee & St. Paul Railway Dining Car Menu of 1882. (COURTESY OF THE UNION PACIFIC MUSEUM)

A Chicago & North Western Railway menu of 1899. (COURTESY OF THE UNION PACIFIC MUSEUM)

The advent of private sleeping berths and provisions for civilized meals enabled women and children to undertake long-distance train travel. In dining cars of the 1880s, such as this one of the Chicago & Alton Railroad, in addition to the ornate chandeliers they might find "potted palms, rubber plants, or other live and flowering plants sitting in elaborate vases in niches along the walls." (COURTESY OF THE ASSOCIATION OF AMERICAN RAILROADS)

Until 1884, meals and hotel accommodations for passengers of the Union Pacific lines were provided at eating houses in Nebraska, Wyoming, Kansas, Colorado, Utah, Idaho, and Montana. In buildings owned by the railroad, but rented to and operated by local vendors on short-term leases, food of varying uniformity and quality was served during scheduled meal stops. As a result of numerous complaints from passengers, and of a survey ordered by the railroad's president, Charles Francis Adams, the decision was made to contract all such services to one company. In November, 1884, Markel and Swobe, operators of Omaha's Millard House, were granted a contract to take full charge of all eating houses and hotels on the Union Pacific. In March 1889, the railroad bought the contract back for $100,000 and thereafter operated all eating houses and hotels along the right-of-way itself.

Meanwhile, for many years the railroads operating west of the Missouri River refrained from using dining cars in their regular trains. Until 1883, the only railroads operating in this vast territory were the Union Pacific's, with through connections on the Central Pacific Railroad, the Chicago, Burlington & Quincy, and the Atcheson, Topeka & Santa Fe. On November 21, 1881, the management of each of these three railroads signed a document whereby:

"It is hereby agreed by and between the Chicago, Burlington and Quincy Railroad Company, the Atcheson, Topeka and Santa Fe Railroad Company, and the Union Pacific Railway Company, that neither party to this agreement shall run regularly on its trains between the Missouri River and Denver any Dining or Hotel cars, with-

The dining car La Rabida, created for the Columbian Exposition. At the close of the nineteenth century, dining car "interiors [were] outfitted in rare woods with stained glass windows and hissing gaslights for illumination." (COURTESY OF THE ASSOCIATION OF AMERICAN RAILROADS)

out first giving the other parties hereto written notice of intention to do so, at least six (6) months in advance of doing so."

To be effective, such an agreement had to be adhered to by all parties. On May 10, 1884, G. W. Holdrege, an assistant general manager of the Burlington, served this notice on his counterparts at the other two railroads:

> Referring to agreement of November 21, 1881, between the Chicago, Burlington and Quincy [Railroad Company], the Atcheson, Topeka and Santa Fe [Railway Company], and the Union Pacific [Railway Company], relative to running dining cars between the Missouri River and Denver. You are hereby notified that the Chicago, Burlington, and Quincy . . . will on November 10, 1884, withdraw from the agreement as provided for in the terms thereof, that is to say, in six months from this date. . . .

The Burlington apparently did not begin dining-car service west of the Missouri on that date, and the Union Pacific and the Santa Fe continued to observe the agreement as one between themselves. But, on May 24, 1886, the Union Pacific notified the Santa Fe that it intended to withdraw from the agreement six months hence. However, Union Pacific Vice President S. R. Callaway pointed out, "At present we have no intention of establishing a general dining-car service on our regular trains."

Cracks in this collusive arrangement began to occur as the number of railroads operating in the West expanded. In 1887, the recently completed Northern Pacific Railway initiated the use of dining cars in its trains to the northern Pacific Coast. This innovation caused such a loss of first-class passengers by the Union Pacific over competing routes that passenger-department officers urgently advised the Union Pacific to follow the Northern Pacific's lead. The crisis was brought to a head when another railroad, the Chicago, Rock Island & Pacific, entered Denver in 1888 and inaugurated the newest vestibule trains through from Chicago, with dining cars included. J. S. Tebbets, Union Pacific's general passenger and ticket agent, pointedly expressed the view of his department's officers in a letter to Assistant General Manager C. S. Mellen on October 20, 1888:

> I beg to call your attention to the following copy of telegram from Mr. Lomax (an assistant general passenger agent):
>
> Denver, October 9, 1888
>
> J. S. Tebbets:
>
> Rock Island road will run vestibule trains very latest pattern between Chicago and Denver, and dining cars to accompany the train entire trip between Denver and Chicago; two trains daily in and out. I think we better arrange with Northwestern Railroad or any line that has got some dining

cars to spare, for dining car service. It has got to come. The Burlington will meet the Rock Island on dining cars, and probably Missouri Pacific. The dining car question cannot be put off much longer.

E. L. Lomax

He continued:

> This seems to me a most important matter. If the Union Pacific is to continue in the future as in the past, to be like a cow's tail, always behind because it belongs there, we can continue to run our trains without dining cars, and I will do my best to get business, but, as you can readily see, at a great disadvantage. We are the pioneer line and ought not to let every one-horse railroad in the country teach us how to do business. With the [Burlington], Rock Island, and the [Santa Fe] from Chicago, and the Missouri Pacific from St. Louis, running through solid trains with dining cars to Denver (for I do not for a moment imagine that the 'Q', Santa Fe, or the Missouri Pacific will not meet the action of the Rock Island), we shall lose our grip on Colorado business; and, once lost, it will be very difficult and expensive to get it back again. I would most earnestly request that the Union Pacific arrange to run dining cars to Denver—I say Denver, but it would be far better, and I strongly recommend it, to put them on for Denver, Ogden, and Portland. Our westbound first class business to Portland makes a shocking showing as compared to that of the Northern Pacific, and the one great reason is the dining car, and, as you so clearly stated recently, 'if the first-class business can be secured by attractive service, this second-class business can be secured without much effort.' I can see this very clearly when I scrutinize the statement of second-class passengers westbound to Ogden points—showing a very small percentage for us, as compared with the Northern Pacific.
> "Can anything be done to get us out of the old rut?

After conferring with Union Pacific President Adams, Vice President W. H. Holcomb telegraphed from Boston on April 26, 1889, to General Manager Thomas L. Kimball, at Omaha:

> If you and Mellen can arrange permanently with Pullman under Association agreement basis for diners, advertise them to go on the fast California train and day Denver train at once. Notify connecting lines that we propose to put on diners and give them the date after you are sure of same.

Accordingly, Kimball gave the competing lines notice of the Union Pacific's intention to establish dining-car service, beginning May 12, 1889. Despite the Burlington's having served notice in 1884 of its intention to withdraw from the 1881 agreement, but not yet having established dining-car service, Burlington's President Charles E. Perkins wrote Union Pacific's Adams on May 6:

The Union Pacific has notified us that beginning May 12 you will run dining cars on your Denver train. I am very sorry for this because it forces us to do the same and increases expenses all round at a time when the reduction of expenses seems so essential. Experience has shown that dining cars cost much more than they come to, when all competing lines use them, and up to the present time we have succeeded in keeping them east of the [Missouri] river. Is there no way of stopping this proposed departure?

Rock Island President R. R. Cable telegraphed Burlington's Perkins:

Some months since[,] I entered into an agreement with your people by which none of us would run dining cars west of the Missouri River except by agreement, or after consultation. I called upon Mr. Stone this morning after having been indirectly advised that the Union Pacific had decided to put on dining cars west of the Missouri River May [12]. Mr. Stone advised me that they had had notice within the last few days from the Union Pacific of their intention to run dining cars, but there was no consultation with the lines interested. He also advised me that your people were thinking of meeting this extravagance brought on by the Union Pacific [Company]. When I made the agreement with your people not to run these cars they told me they had an agreement with the Union Pacific to the same effect. It does not seem to me to be good neighborhood for lines to go off in this way and lead us all into expenditure of money that in my mind is useless. If the Union Pacific persists in running dining cars I would like to join you in making dining service to our patrons west of the Missouri River free, as the loss will be but very little more in that way than to run them for the usual compensation. What have you to suggest in the matter?

Perkins in turn sent a copy of Cable's message to Union Pacific President Adams, adding:

I hope something can be done to stop what certainly looks like wasting money. Cable has not always practiced what he preaches about good neighborhood, but that does not make it any less true, and as between the [Union Pacific] and the [Burlington] it would seem as if there should have been some consultation rather than a very short notice.

Perkins wrote Adams again on May 25:

Experience has demonstrated that dining cars do not pay, and up to this time all parties have cooperated to keep them east of the river. It is said now that your people intend using them and of course that forces us all to do the same thing.

Union Pacific President Adams, in response to this flurry of correspondence and concern, instructed Holcomb to keep the use of dining cars within reasonable limits, but did not reverse his decision. In response to the charge by Perkins and Cable that the Union Pacific's intentions had been made to them on too short notice, Holcomb provided Adams with more facts, themselves enlightening about how the railroads grappled with dining-car operations throughout their history:

Just at the time I came here [November, 1888], the Chicago, Kansas, and Nebraska [Rock Island] line was opened to Denver, with a big flourish and the announcement that it would run vestibule trains. We took no notice of this and consequently the new line was somewhat a gainer by putting on these vestibule trains. I next found that the [Burlington trains] were making quicker time Chicago to Denver than any other line, and this was of course a very strong card in favor of their system. Some time after, we made an arrangement with the Chicago & North Western [Railroad] for a through vestibule train between Chicago and Denver. Since this, our travel has constantly increased. The greatest drawback with our line, being a first-class line in every respect between Chicago and Denver, has been the fact that we did not reach either of our dining stations at a reasonable hour. Our only recourse was to put up more dining stations or put on diners, or see our travel gradually drift away from us again. When the last change in time card came up Mr. Dickinson was sent to Chicago to try and arrange with the other lines [over which we run our trains] for leaving an hour and a half later, and so enable us to make our dining stations at reasonable hours. The North Western consented to this if the other lines would. The other lines refused, politely suggesting to us that if this time did not reach our dining stations we could easily build more. It seemed to me better under the circumstances to put on diners, we being as quick a line as any, and the oldest line, and it was hardly good policy, in my judgment, to let our business get away from us by reason of superior advantages by the other lines.

We have seen a good deal of our Washington Territory and Oregon business drift away to the Northern Pacific by reason of their running dining cars and I think that we have no other course but to give the traveling public as good facilities by our line as connecting lines do, and make good time. . . . We feel slow in agreeing to let our competitors run vestibule trains solid from Chicago to Denver while we did not run vestibule cars and required passengers to change cars at Council Bluffs.

This move was also endorsed by Marvin Hughitt, President of the Chicago & North Western, the Union Pacific's key link for its through trains between Denver and Chicago, when he wired Union Pacific President Adams on May 10, 1889:

In conversation with Vice President Holcomb today regarding the service west of Omaha to enable our respective companies to compete with western roads, I think it would be a mistake not to meet them fully with all facilities offered by them to the traveling public, including dining cars.

Meanwhile, under successive contracts dating back to 1867, George Pullman's Pullman Palace Sleeping Car Company supplied and operated the sleeping cars on Union Pacific trains on a joint ownership basis. In an arrangement known as the Pullman Association plan, the Union Pacific paid seventy-five percent, Pullman twenty-five percent, of the cost of cars including equipment, and the profits or losses were divided between the two parties in the same proportion.

When dining-car service was being considered, Holcomb wrote to Adams on May 13, 1889:

> I understand that I am authorized to put dining-car service on the overland trains to San Francisco and on trains 5 and 6 between Denver and Chicago, making arrangements with Pullman to furnish the dining cars and to operate them under the Association agreement, namely, three-fourths profit or loss to be borne by the Union Pacific and one-fourth by the Pullman company.

> If we secure trackage to Puget Sound, I believe it will also be necessary to put dining-car service on one train between Green River and Tacoma. If this becomes necessary, will ask authority later.

Holcomb wrote Adams again on May 18:

> The Pullman Company's proposition is that they will construct these cars under the Association agreement, at cost. Cost, to include dishes, silverware, china, etc., everything included, not to exceed $15,000 per car. To equip the line with diners from Kansas City to Denver, Omaha to Denver, Omaha to Ogden, and Granger to Portland, will take in all fourteen cars. Our proportion of the cost would be $157,500. The Pullman company would operate them and stand one-fourth of the loss or have for their share one-fourth of the profit, as the case may be.

This recommendation was approved but later, evidently because of some misunderstanding of the terms of their negotiation on the part of Pullman or C. S. Mellen, by whom the matter had been discussed, Pullman declined to go through with the plan on this basis. He would, he said, be willing to build the cars at cost plus ten percent; that he would be willing to operate them for the railroad, the Union Pacific paying all expenses; or, to operate them himself under a guarantee of $4,000 per car.

Pullman's counter-offer was not favored by Union Pacific's Mellen, Kimball, and Holcomb. They now favored the Union Pacific's securing bids from responsible builders, buying the cars outright, and operating them itself with its own people. Perhaps financial limitations led President Adams to reject this alternative, for he instructed Holcomb now to negotiate an arrangement with Pullman for eight dining cars, these to be put in service on the line from Omaha to Portland and from Omaha to Denver.

In the end, Pullman offered to build, own, and operate the dining cars under the same plan as the Association contract, the Union Pacific to pay three cents per mile instead of two cents, the extra cent to go to the Pullman company to meet its proportion of any deficit from operation. This offer was accepted and an agreement executed on August 1, 1889, between Pullman's Palace Car Company and the Union Pacific Railway Company. Signed by George M. Pullman and Charles Francis Adams, the agreement included the three-cents-per mile consideration, with a guarantee of 300 miles per day per car.

In 1894, the Association owned thirteen dining cars. The newly formed Union Pacific Railroad Company, which took over the properties on February 1, 1898, did not continue the Association arrangement with the Pullman company. Pullman's operation of dining cars on Union Pacific's trains was discontinued in 1902.

The technological evolution of dining cars and their acceptance as a fact of life by the railroads was more or less complete. After the invention of the vestibule, innovation in dining-car design and operation slowed. The cars did get bigger. From the original dimensions of sixty feet long by ten feet wide, with an eight-square-foot kitchen, they grew in the 1930s to twin and triple units up to 201 feet long containing kitchens occupying 360 square feet. Air conditioning, also introduced in the 1930s, improved working conditions for the crew and made food preparation more sanitary. It also enhanced consumption, as the cars could be hermetically sealed against outside dust and dirt. After World War II, all-electric kitchens using technology developed for submarines were introduced, beginning on the Illinois Central. But the floor plan of dining cars—containing kitchen, pantry, and eating area—and the relative space devoted to each area, as well as the unique window-and-door arrangement which clearly identified the diner in a train's consist, remained pretty much as originally designed. Crew size and duties, too, remained relatively static. Only the introduction in the 1950s of the domed diners on the Train of the Future and the two-story hi-level cars of the Santa Fe increased the seating capacity, necessitated larger crews, and enhanced the scenic pleasure associated with eating on a train. All these changes have left dining-car service as it is experienced even today.

These passengers enjoy the Milwaukee Road's cuisine on board the Southwest Limited *in 1910.* (COURTESY OF THE MILWAUKEE ROAD COLLECTION OF THE MILWAUKEE PUBLIC LIBRARY)

Menus of the early 1900s from the Big Four: Cleveland, Cincinnati; Chicago & St. Louis Railway; and the Lake Shore & Michigan Southern Railway; the last two eventually part of the New York Central System. (COURTESY OF THE UNION PACIFIC

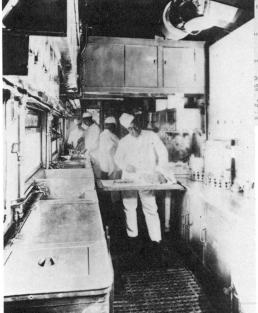

In an eight-foot-by-five-foot kitchen, such as this one on a Louisville & Nashville Railroad dining car, a staff of four cooks prepared as many as six hundred meals a day. (COURTESY OF THE ASSOCIATION OF AMERICAN RAILROADS)

A cutaway view of a heavyweight all-steel dining car of the 1930s, this one from the New York Central's famed Twentieth Century Limited. (COURTESY OF ROSS GRENARD)

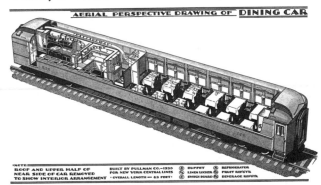

The Baltimore & Ohio Railroad's Martha Washington, *the first air-conditioned dining car, with its tell-tale roof contour. The distinctive window and door arrangement also immediately identified the dining car in a train.* (COURTESY OF THE ASSOCIATION OF AMERICAN RAILROADS)

The standard showpiece, the entry buffet, is apparent in this Milwaukee Road dining car of the 1930s. (COURTESY OF THE MILWAUKEE ROAD COLLECTION OF THE MILWAUKEE PUBLIC LIBRARY)

A dinner chime, many produced by J. C. Deagan, Inc., in Chicago, announced the beginning of midday and evening meals in the dining cars of all but the lowliest passenger trains. A waiter designated by the Steward toured the cars, beginning in the first-class section, to summon passengers by striking the bars in the center, directly over the resonator opening, with a quick blow of the mallet. Many railroads copied the famous NBC notes, G - E - C, when this practice was begun in the late 1930s. The rich, resonant tone thus produced was distinctive, memorable, and, perhaps most important, unobtrusive to those napping in their seats or compartments. (COURTESY OF GREAT NORTHERN RAILWAY COMPANY RECORDS, MINNESOTA HISTORICAL SOCIETY)

Illinois Central Railroad's Shrimp Creole served on china used exclusively on The City of Miami. (COURTESY OF THE ILLINOIS CENTRAL GULF RAILROAD)

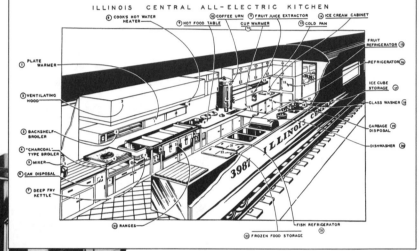

The Illinois Central was the first to adopt the all-electric kitchen after World War II. It employed technology developed during the war for kitchens in the submarine fleet. (COURTESY OF THE ILLINOIS CENTRAL GULF RAILROAD)

The Illinois Central all-electric kitchen, as it was executed and reflecting its submarine origins, enabled the crew to work in greater comfort. (COURTESY OF THE ASSOCIATION OF AMERICAN RAILROADS)

Twin-unit diner, 1930s: When the big twin-unit diners were introduced on overnight trains, one of the units held the kitchen, pantry and the crew's quarters. Such units on daylight-only trains held a lounge in lieu of quarters for the crew. (COURTESY OF THE UNION PACIFIC MUSEUM)

Dome diner 8004: One of ten domed dining cars built in 1955, the lessons learned from EMD's "Train of Tomorrow" were incorporated into the design to make these among the most glamorous and popular dining cars operating on a number of lines through the scenic American west. (COURTESY OF THE UNION PACIFIC MUSEUM)

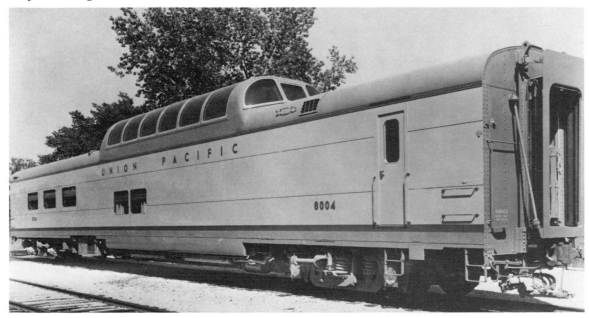

When train-builder EMD created the "Train of Tomorrow" in 1950, it included what many argue is the world's most beautiful dining car, the domed Sky View. *This is the main dining room of the* Sky View *after the Union Pacific took over the operation of the car.* (COURTESY OF THE UNION PACIFIC MUSEUM)

Domed dining area on the Union Pacific's City of Los Angeles. *The popularity of these, the finest seats in the house, is easily understandable. When domed diners were first introduced, a second steward was on board to cater exclusively to those eating in the dome.* (COURTESY OF THE UNION PACIFIC MUSEUM)

Until shortly after the turn of the century, dining cars were not common to all trains. At first, only the fastest and most exclusive trains, the Limiteds, carried a dining car. By the 1890s, secondary carriers, those operating only within a region, began offering lavish dining cars and food. By 1900, "many of the nation's steam-powered all-Pullman name trains provided a quality and diversity of service which rivaled the finest hotels."[48]

Santa Fe Railway's answer to domed cars, a hi-level train, the El Capitan, *compares with Amtrak's Superliners today.* (COURTESY OF THE ASSOCIATION OF AMERICAN RAILROADS)

Dining cars, such as this one on the Chicago, Burlington & Quincy Railroad's Denver Zephyr, *continued to capture, more than three-quarters of a century after they were introduced, the tranquil civility of eating on the train.* (COURTESY OF THE ASSOCIATION OF AMERICAN RAILROADS)

Lucius Beebe, rail fan extraordinaire, measured this development large. "With the advent of the diner," he wrote, "began the golden age of American railroad travel which lasted in mobile glory for nearly three-quarters of a century."[49] By 1914, another railroad enthusiast, Edward Hungerford, was able to pronounce the dining car as having come into its own.

LIFE ON A LIMITED TRAIN

The dining car was not an isolated gem in a string of faux pearls. With the introduction in 1887 of the vestibule, which enabled passengers to pass safely from one car to another, the modern form of the American passenger train was born. No longer a series of cars coupled together, the train became one continuous car.

The transcontinental railroads operated four distinct classes of train, each aimed at a different size wallet. The premier trains—deluxe, first-class, mostly Pullman "Limiteds"—were so named because the number of passengers allowed on board was fixed, and advance reservations were required. Limiteds, like the Union Pacific's streamliner *City of Los Angeles,* whisked passengers between Chicago and Los Angeles in thirty-nine and three-quarters hours, and had sleeping accommodations for 150 passengers and coach seats for an additional 104. A second level of first-class trains, equipped with cars handed down from the railroad's flagship limiteds, were those with historical significance for the railroad and the communities they served. A third category, a mainline fleet of secondary trains made up of both older Pullman equipment and coaches, operated on a slower schedule, made more frequent stops, and held passengers for fewer miles per passenger. Finally, branch-line trains brought passengers to connecting points at mainline stations.

It was the Limited trains which, often for an extra fare, sought to create the aura of a grand hotel. They culminated in the all-room trains introduced in the late 1930s. Every car on such a train was air conditioned, with every room, compartment, and drawing room equipped with individual temperature controls. If one wanted room enough to lie down in privacy, a choice of a single roomette, duplex room, double bedroom, compartment, or drawing room suite was available. Electric lights operated throughout and outlets were available in all dressing rooms and private bathrooms, with the current supplied from the car axle. A pas-

Great Northern Streamlined International Limited. (COURTESY OF GREAT NORTHERN RAILWAY COMPANY RECORDS, MINNESOTA HISTORICAL SOCIETY)

senger could call on the services of a stenographer or secretary, if not already accompanied by one, or those of a concierge or social secretary to, among other things, get theater tickets at one's destination. Service features of the Great Northern's *Oriental Limited,* promoted as "A Chain of Great Hotels on Wheels," included a maid, a manicurist, a hairdresser, a shower bath, and a lounge for women; and a barber, valet, and shower bath for men. Tea was served in the observation lounge. News bulletins, as well as magazines and books, were available in the train's library. Some early trains had on-board publications created specifically for passengers. New York Central's *Twentieth Century Limited* offered riders the opportunity to "extend the business day by one hour" by taking a friend or business associate from Grand Central Terminal in mid-Manhattan as far as Croton-Harmon, where the train stopped to change from electric to steam power—the guest's return trip to the city was free. On the Santa Fe's deluxe *California Limited,* gentlemen travelers received gold-embossed pigskin wallets, and, as the train reached California, ladies were presented with orchid corsages. Dining-car patrons were not exempt from this lavish treatment.

Most Limiteds also had a lounge car, club or parlor car, and an observation car with big windows or, starting in 1945, a dome car with an upper level of seats surrounded by glass. It wouldn't be a surprise to find a piano in the lounge or parlor car. An Illinois Central Railroad special train, carrying the Chicago Cubs to spring training in Tampa in 1916, ran on a roadbed smooth enough to allow the club's president, Charles Weeghman, and manager, Joe Tinker, to play pool on a top-of-the-line Brunswick-Balke-Collender table, with the train at running speed.

Describing life on these trains, French reporter Paul Achard wrote in 1930 of his experience crossing America on the New York Central's flagship, the *Twentieth Century Limited,* and other Limiteds. "The cabins are huge. They are for two persons, seated; they can hold four on the two benches, and there is a folding table which permits of playing bridge; for lying down there are two wide and thick beds. The porters are all black men— dressed in white; tall ebony fellows make up your bed, supply you with ice, serve drinks, put your clothes on coat hangers, your hat in a box, clean your shoes that you place in a small cupboard of which they can open the door from the outside in the morning so as not to wake you up. You need only give a ring and they come with a straw brush to brush your jacket; they go and fetch cigarettes for you at the bar or stamps from the writing room.

The Parlor-Lounge on the International Limited *featured restful and comfortable revolving adjustable parlor chairs. The large myrtlewood sculpture symbolized principal activities and resources of the Pacific Northwest, which this train served.* (COURTESY OF GREAT NORTHERN RAILWAY COMPANY RECORDS, MINNESOTA HISTORICAL SOCIETY)

"Everywhere matches are supplied gratuitously by the company, bearing their mark—and they light each time. Everywhere ashtrays and a net to empty one's pockets. The washstand gives day and night by its three taps cold water, hot water, or iced water to drink, as in the trains a large quantity of ice is used. Do you wish to take a bath? You give a ring and the black man gets a bath ready. Do you wish to read, write? The reading and writing room is supplied with a lot of publications and letterheads showing the name of the company. At every station the 'mail' calls for your letters. Do you wish to send a wire? An employee of the Western Union is always available. A cable sent from New York reached me at Albuquerque, in the middle of New Mexico at the exact time of arrival of the train.

"There is a hairdresser on the train, and a manicurist; the barman who can only give you lemonades, ginger ale, or Coca-cola, sells cigarettes at the same price as anywhere else.

"There is a smoking room, another at the end of the train where the ladies preferably sit and from which, comfortably seated in arm chairs, one can look at the landscape.

"In the dining car meals are served 'a la carte' around large tables. You can find there a great variety of dishes. . . . As soon as you sit down, you get a saucer full of butter and iced water in your glass. Big black hands pass before your face to put the dishes on the table or take them off even though you are putting the fork to the mouth. Service, service.

"Life on board the train is pleasant."[1]

3

AN EXISTENCE ALL ITS OWN

Writer August Menchen observed that from its humble origins as a stagecoach adapted to ride on rails, the passenger car rapidly became a sophisticated, highly refined, and complicated mechanism, one that emerged from its lineage to take on an existence all its own. No type of passenger car better embodied that assertion, nor required greater organization and attention to keep it running effectively, than the dining car. F. M. Graves described it for readers of *Woman's Home Companion* in 1910 as "a remarkably elaborate machinery of detail that produces the apparently simple result of a table, a chair, a waiter, and food."[50] Edwin Kachel added that the "machinery of detail" included "cleaning dishes, polishing silverware, keeping snowy-white linen, supplying cars with merchandise to protect all menus, keeping perishable supplies refrigerated, cooking instructions, preparation of menus, keeping dining cars clean en route, exacting service bulletins, accounting, and the supervision of officials, all executed for one grand result: service."[51] To the list could be added keeping track of how many passengers are boarding and de-training at each terminal, and providing "sufficient victuals to care for their wants [and] to make sure that these foodstuffs can be compactly refrigerated, cooked in a limited space on a moving train, and served hot or cold as the case may be." Among railroad people, it was generally concluded that dining-car service was the most difficult activity in their profession.[52]

When the Pullman Company operated dining cars, up until the early twentieth century, those details were its worry. The dining-car contract called on the company to furnish as many dining cars as the demands of the traveling public required, without any charge to the railroad. On-train employees, including the steward, cooks, and waiters, were hired, trained,

A reporter aboard a Hotel Train in 1867 wrote: "At almost every station our conductor, whose duties included those of commissariat, goes forth on a foraging expedition and lays in stores of whatever delicacies the place affords—trout from some mountain stream, antelope steak, game of all sorts, or such vulgar necessities as eggs and milk."

He continued: "Then there is the frequent process of supplying our kitchen tank with fresh water by a long hose through a pipe in the roof. All of the ice coolers and washing room tanks are filled throughout the train, and the supply of water is plentiful, although in quality not of the best."

and supervised by the company. Pullman was compensated by an extra fare collected from passengers wishing to travel in Pullman equipment, and from revenues generated through the operation of the cars. The railroad, in turn, was compensated by having free use of the cars—in return for which it guaranteed the Pullman Company an exclusive right to furnish such cars for a fixed term, often fifteen years—and by the extra ticket sales generated by trains known to carry a dining car. As the Union Pacific experience demonstrated, these terms were universally negotiable. Nor was the contract mutually exclusive. The Pullman Company could offer similar equipment to competing railroads serving identical cities.

While a similar arrangement worked profitably for both Pullman and the railroads in regards to other equipment, notably sleeping cars, it turned out to be a money-losing proposition for Pullman with dining cars. Un-

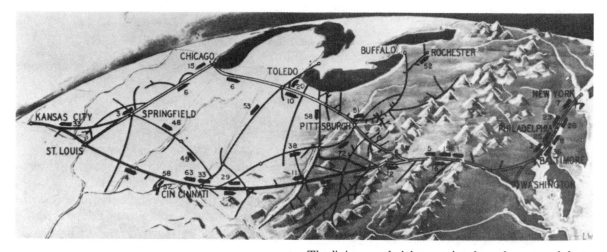

like the sleeping car, which roamed all across America with its crew of one, dining cars, with their crews of ten, tended to work a geographically specific but varied and rigid schedule dictated by the eating habits of train patrons and the intricate schedule of the trains themselves. And, while passengers benefited from a nationwide network of

The dining car schedule was printed on a large spread sheet separated into sections by heavy black lines running across it. The superintendent can tell by the minute where his cars are placed in the system. This is 6:00 P.M. on a weekday evening in 1940 on the Baltimore & Ohio Railroad system. (Illustration by Linn H. Westcott accompanying "Meals Enroute," by Lawrence W. Sagle in January 1941 Trains, *page 7, ©1940. Kalmbach Publishing Co.; reproduced with permission)*

sleeping-car operations that eliminated the need to change trains at major junctions—a through sleeping car, with passengers on board, could be deposited at important interchanges along one train's run and be picked up by another train or railroad and taken to a final destination—dining cars held no such advantage. They were dropped off at some convenient point along a railroad's system, serviced, restocked, and sent back in another direction with a subsequent train on the same railroad. As a result, the Pullman Company discontinued staffing and operating dining cars in 1902, either selling or leasing existing equipment to the railroads affected. This step completed a movement that had begun in the late 1800s at many railroads.

Several other reasons are advanced for the Pullman Company's decision to withdraw from operating dining cars. By the end of the nineteenth century, railroads all over the country realized that excellent food was the most effective way to attract business away from other railroads. But while sleeping-car service by necessity called for standardization, dining-car service offered each railroad the opportunity to establish an identity all its own. A management philosophy that reflected this reality began to take shape. As early as 1883, the Baltimore & Ohio, to answer the administrative challenges posed by evolving dining-car operations, concluded that "as [with] a house divided, so is a railroad company with too many masters." It thus operated under one management throughout, including supervising its own dining cars and dining halls. Such a practice left "one company responsible to the public for every department of business transacted on the road, and the one executive head [to] control all." It also left the railroad free of "foreign" capital and the power attached to it; free to act in the interests of the public without the need to consult others; and eliminated a possible source of resistance to change and innovation.[53]

Thus, the railroads now made their own meals while the Pullman Company's commissary operations continued to tend only the buffet-, club-, and parlor-car patron. So taxing was running an efficient and successful "migratory restaurant" program, and so constant the pressure to limit financial losses while creating the appearance of a smooth and effortless operation, that an entire department evolved at each railroad to handle such responsibilities. Variously named the Dining Car Department, the Dining Car and Hotel Department, or the like, it was headed by a superintendent who reported to the vice president in charge of passenger operations. The superintendent's managerial duties took in the commissary, on-line eating houses and hotels, resorts, and work-train eating facilities, as well as dining-car operations and personnel. His challenge was to overcome the "trials and tribulations of operating a restaurant while rolling down the track at sixty miles per hour or more."[54]

The dining-car department, as one part of a railroad, was comparatively small. Its importance lay in direct ratio not to its size, but to its impact on the traveler. Among experienced travelers, no other feature of passenger-train service was so frequently praised or criticized as the dining car—

At the Union Pacific Railroad Commissary, a cart is loaded ready to take requisitioned items to a waiting dining car. (COURTESY OF THE UNION PACIFIC MUSEUM)

A self-powered truck made handling the dozens of dining cars deposited each day for stocking a little easier by the 1930s. (COURTESY OF THE UNION PACIFIC MUSEUM)

whether comments came in person to the steward, or in writing to the management. "In these circumstances," according to a steward on the New York Central Lines' *Twentieth Century Limited,* "if just one meal came out of this kitchen wrong, you could be sure the offended party would write somebody at the railroad, threatening to travel the next time by another carrier," perhaps on the arch-rival Pennsylvania Railroad's *Broadway Limited.* J. M. Collins, superintendent of the Erie Railroad's dining cars after World War II, believed passengers wanted to "receive the little courtesies and personal attention which make eating on the train such a delightful adventure. [Our] aim is to provide the kind of service that, even if it means losing money, will make a satisfied traveler who will want to ride the line again."[55]

A pleased passenger was thus considered a permanent passenger. And it was axiomatic that, as F. M. Dow of the Illinois Central maintained, "a shipper of freight, all things being equal, will naturally ship over the same line he rides on." For railroading was unique in that a prospective shipper could sample the speed and efficiency of a carrier by becoming part of its cargo, a problem that was not faced by competitive haulers employing ships, trucks, or airplanes (only in the early days of riverboats did companies handle both freight and passengers). The president of one line liked to claim, "There is no way that you can lose or pick up freight customers so fast as by the quality of the meal or the cup of coffee that you provide the traveler."

The needed items were moved into the cars by the crew and each man was responsible for putting up the items within his areas of responsibility. (COURTESY OF THE UNION PACIFIC MUSEUM)

A Union Pacific cook loads frozen chickens into dining car storage. (COURTESY OF THE UNION PACIFIC MUSEUM)

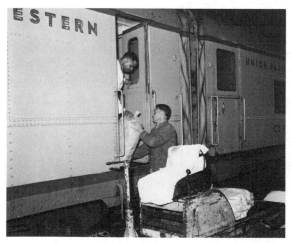

To turn this handicap to advantage, astute railroad executives saw the dining-car as a showcase of efficiency and fine cuisine, an opportunity to demonstrate the services they were trying to sell. Superintendent Norris of the Union Pacific observed: "Since railroad operation must have a 'show window' for prominent display to the public, we believe the most convenient and flexible vehicle for this purpose is the dining-car operation."[56] And if the customary trip of evaluation was marked by a relaxed dinner of braised duck Cumberland or chicken barbecued in a "secret" sauce, or a breakfast featuring Maryland crab cakes, the greater the likelihood that a lucrative freight consignment for the railroad would result. An attentive steward, courteous waiters, and sympathetic chefs were as critical to winning business for the railroads as their sales department.[57]

Showcasing the work of the railroad was but one challenge addressed by the dining car. The other was that of feeding people with a variety of eating preferences. In 1883, *The Railroad Gazette* characterized this as the one great obstacle to universal adoption of dining cars: "They make every passenger live at the rate of a first-class hotel while traveling, or else put up with what he can carry with him."[58] The complaint proved to be unfounded. Just as Pullman had educated people to sleep on trains, so dining cars acquainted all classes, not just the wealthy, with eating while in motion. "We find the public in general demanding dining-car service. The dining car is now a general eating place rather than an aristocratic dining and social center. The old lunch basket is almost a relic and in its place Dad carries a little extra money so the kiddies, and Mother—who wishes and enjoys the experience of being waited on—[can] all go to the dining car to dine. Some of the older stewards probably remember years ago, when they passed through the day coaches making the first call, that passengers would reach down for their lunch baskets. Now, when giving that call, he enjoys the thrill of heading a parade."[59]

The Railroad Gazette, in the same article, called attention to another problem, the solution to which happily proved even less intractable: "By far the larger number of travelers, including nearly all ladies, are ignorant of the art of

These cook's utensils, adapted for use in the dining-car kitchen, were common enough to make it into the Car Builder's Dictionary.
(COURTESY OF SIMMONS-BOARDMAN BOOKS, INC.)

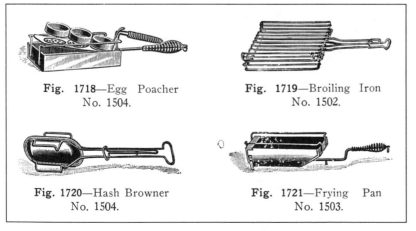

Fig. 1718—Egg Poacher No. 1504.

Fig. 1719—Broiling Iron No. 1502.

Fig. 1720—Hash Browner No. 1504.

Fig. 1721—Frying Pan No. 1503.

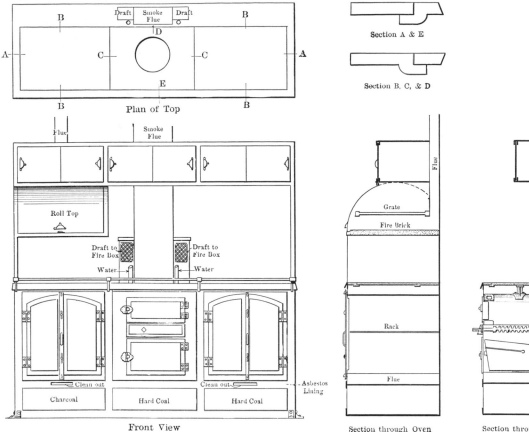

Plan of Top

Section A & E

Section B, C, & D

Front View

Section through Oven

Section through Fire-Box

dining at a restaurant. They are not accustomed to it, and a journey is no time to learn."[60]

While the railroads liked to compare their dining-car service to that in great restaurants and hotel dining rooms, and did so by competing with them successfully in culinary exhibitions and by naming their dining cars after famous restaurants, hotels, and chefs, railroad service differed in a number of ways from the businesses it sought to emulate. Commenting on the intensified nature of the modern dining car, C. H. Shircliffe, superintendent of the Chicago & North Western dining service, said "All the tastes of practically all the people in the United States are brought to its tables, and we must write a bill of fare that will please every passenger, from the most fastidious epicure to the man who has no idea of what he wants or how to order. We have to do this without knowing in advance anything about our guests. A hotel, restaurant, or lunch counter builds up a certain classified patronage to which it caters, but for us every day is an opening with patrons who, in town, would patronize half a dozen different sorts of eating places and a few who rarely eat away from their homes."[61]

This 1916 Stearns Safety Range for dining cars was manufactured by the Stearns Steel Range Company. (COURTESY OF SIMMONS-BOARDMAN BOOKS, INC.)

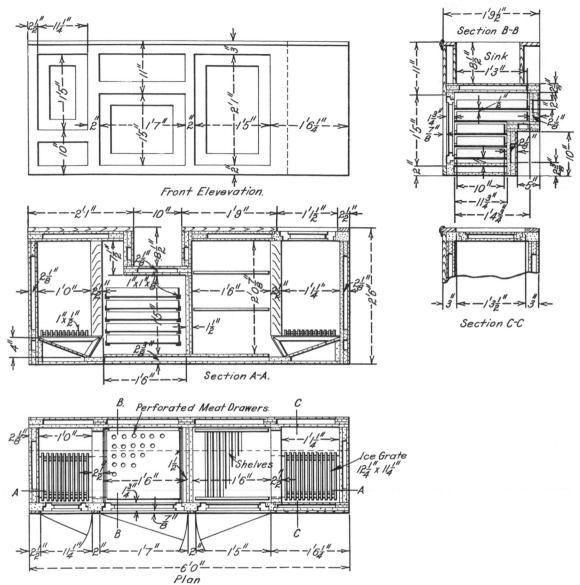

Front Elevation.

Section B-B

Sink

Section C-C

Section A-A.

B. *Perforated Meat Drawers.* C

Shelves

Ice Grate
$12\frac{1}{4}$" x $11\frac{1}{4}$"

A

B C

Plan

A buffet-style refrigerator from the White Enamel Refrigerator Company in 1916.

(COURTESY OF SIMMONS-BOARDMAN BOOKS, INC.)

There were other fundamental differences between dining-car and hotel-restaurant operation which prevented the railroads from achieving the cost efficiencies possible in the latter. On the long run of a transcontinental train, especially one west of Chicago, a dining car had to be stocked with the same perishable commodities found in a hotel restaurant, on the assumptions that the train would be heavily booked with long-distance passengers and that a majority of them would require meals. If this were not the case, then fresh food was transported needlessly for several days and had to be disposed of at the end of the run.

Further, dining-car service, especially during the evening meal, required serving each patron in a shorter period of time than is possible in a hotel. The hotel was likely to have a more favorable seats-to-guests ratio in its dining room than is economically possible on a train. And if the train was full, and all employees worked to insure it was, and the sought-after majority opted to eat in the dining car, then a considerably larger service crew was needed. The demands of those eating had to be met without allowing these patrons to linger too long in their seats and thus create a long wait for others. Hence, a steward, four cooks, and six waiters attended to the needs of not more than thirty-six people at one time when dinner was served in the diner.

A dining car's challenges required efficiency in using supplies and equipment, and maintaining a balance among the types of food service offered passengers. The structure enabling such efficiency was built on the work of the commissary department and on tight schedules for use of dining equipment.

The man in charge of the commissary had to be bonded by a surety company and was held ac-

This six-piece, Union Pacific Dining Combination Server, designed by Silversmiths of International for use on the Railroad's Streamliner fleet in the 1950s, replaced several single service pieces with one item that took up less always-valuable space on the dining car. It consisted of (counter-clockwise) a frame holder and base stand; a liner for soups, desserts, cereals, or hot water or crushed ice; a collar to hold the glass or silver bowls; a silver lid; a glass bowl for fruit cocktails or poached eggs; and, a silver cone for seafood-type cocktails.
(COURTESY OF HOMER H. NOAR)

countable for each item of food, beverage, and tobacco he received. His holdings were inventoried monthly and all that was not assigned to a dining-car steward during that month was to be on hand or otherwise accounted for. Pinkertons and other security personnel were used to uncover fraud. Commissary men knew the menus to be used for a particular trip and thus were able to set out the foods and ingredients in sufficient quantity for a dining car being stocked at the beginning of a trip. O. T. Hall,

Great Northern Railway silver: Extra-heavy silver plate was selected because these items were subjected to constant and continued heavy duty, and were the recipient of daily cleaning and polishing. (COURTESY OF GREAT NORTHERN RAILWAY COMPANY RECORDS, MINNESOTA HISTORICAL SOCIETY)

These Great Northern Railway plates and dishes carry the distinctive "Mountain and Flowers" pattern. (COURTESY OF GREAT NORTHERN RAILWAY COMPANY RECORDS, MINNESOTA HISTORICAL SOCIETY)

Great Northern Railway glassware: A typical railroad dining car had about ten percent of the glassware and a like amount of china broken per trip. (COURTESY OF GREAT NORTHERN RAILWAY COMPANY RECORDS, MINNESOTA HISTORICAL SOCIETY)

Great Northern Railway flatware: Typically, souvenir hunters carried an average of half a dozen pieces of silverware, as well as an occasional $20 menu holder, off a dining car on each trip. (COURTESY OF GREAT NORTHERN RAILWAY COMPANY RECORDS, MINNESOTA HISTORICAL SOCIETY)

The Northern Pacific Railway insured the quantity and quality of its dairy and poultry products with this farm near Kent, Washington. (COURTESY OF GREAT NORTHERN RAILWAY COMPANY RECORDS, MINNESOTA HISTORICAL SOCIETY)

The unrelenting pressure to reduce deficits produced an interesting effect: "We buy only the best of everything," said one superintendent, "because we know that by doing so we are achieving long-run economy. Quality foods keep cost down because there is less waste." If the railroad didn't own farms, its representatives bought from shippers and local suppliers in competition with other railroads and the best hotels and restaurants. (COURTESY OF THE MILWAUKEE ROAD COLLECTION OF THE MILWAUKEE PUBLIC LIBRARY)

superintendent of the Frisco Lines, claimed that, using the law of averages, he could estimate within one chicken or one steak how much food would be consumed in a given number of days. The heaviest dining-car days had to be taken into consideration as well. For one eastern railroad, they were, in order, Friday, Thursday, Sunday, Wednesday, Monday, Tuesday, and Saturday. With vigilance as to the number of Pullman passengers traveling on its trains on those heavy days, the dining-car superintendent could accurately forecast the food items and number of waiters needed for each train. Once eighty first-class passengers were booked onto a train, thought had to be given to adding another dining car to the run. If the number increased much beyond eighty, the superintendent would consider the possibility, after consulting with the operations people, of adding an entire additional train. Should a chef run short of certain items, the steward had to be able to wire ahead and have additional supplies ready at the next terminal or commissary. Or, on railroads such as the Baltimore & Ohio, which had tracks that crossed each other, supplies could be rushed to a junction for later pickup by the train that is short on supplies.

The Union Pacific Railroad's Commissary building in Omaha, Nebraska. (COURTESY OF THE UNION PACIFIC MUSEUM)

The commissary served as the logistical hub of the sometimes far-flung rail empire over which the dining cars moved. Located in the passenger-car service yard not far from head-quarter-city passenger stations, these busy locations could serve as many as thirty dining cars an hour during peak operation. Beginning at 5:30 A.M., and often earlier, the commissary maintained its ritual seven days a week, 365 days a year.

All railroads publicized the work of their commissary departments to their employees. The Great Northern Railway, however, took the unusual step of publishing a booklet just for passengers. Entitled *The Unseen Service*, it spoke for all those working behind the scenes to keep these jewels of the railway's Passenger Department in top form. The following de-

The front office. (COURTESY OF GREAT NORTHERN RAILWAY COMPANY RECORDS, MINNESOTA HISTORICAL SOCIETY)

scription could, with little modification, describe any line's commissary operation:

You accept the chair the dining-car steward holds for you and, folding your napkin across your knees, pick up the menu.

Having chosen the various items which you feel will make a satisfactory meal, you cast about for some means to fill the interval between decision and realization.

At this time it might be interesting to ponder on a service seldom thought of, hardly even known about, the "unseen service," which has made possible the meal you are about to eat.

The cleanly brightness of the dining car is apparent, the spotless linens, the shining silver, the attractive dishes and glasses. You take them as a matter of course, yet they fill you with a certain feeling of satisfaction and your meal is more enjoyable because of them.

To keep the dining cars and their equipment up to the high standard of efficiency and attractiveness required by the Great Northern Railway demands an almost inconceivable amount of detail work—foresight and preparation. This work is handled by the Commissary Department, a most vital, though "unseen service."

Silver service, cutlery, and flat silver. The silver-plate used was manufactured by the best firms in the business, including Rogers Bros. and Meriden Wear. (COURTESY OF GREAT NORTHERN RAILWAY COMPANY RECORDS, MINNESOTA HISTORICAL SOCIETY)

Assembling and checking supplies. (COURTESY OF GREAT NORTHERN RAILWAY COMPANY RECORDS, MINNESOTA HISTORICAL SOCIETY.

At regular intervals, or as often as there is the slightest need, the dining cars are taken off the line and renovated; thoroughly house-cleaned. Before this is done the car is placed alongside the commissary storeroom platform and all dishes, silverware, glasses, kitchen gear, etc., are removed—checked and stored until the time when the car, back from the shops, bright and clean, is ready to resume its run. It is then the duty of the commissary to re-equip.

Equipping a car is a matter of routine, simply supplying a certain number of each article determined by the car's seating capacity, yet extreme care must be used, as the omission of a single article might cause annoyance to some dining-car patron. This would be an unpardonable crime in the eyes of the Great Northern personnel.

The method employed in re-equipping the cars is interesting. Large trucks, operated by men working with skill borne of long practice, are rapidly filled with dishes, cups, pots, pans—everything, in fact, necessary to completely equip a modern restaurant on wheels. The bins in the storeroom from which they draw their supplies remind one of a well-stocked crockery house, except that the attractive pattern is the same on all the dishes. As quickly as they are filled, these trucks are rushed to the platform and unloaded into the dining car's pantry and kitchen. A special room, lined with shelves, and drawers filled with every necessary item of silver service, cutlery, and flat silver, furnish an im-

Shelves of dishes. (COURTESY OF GREAT NORTHERN RAILWAY COMPANY RECORDS, MINNESOTA HISTORICAL SOCIETY)

posing array of articles which are hurried into the car to be polished by the crew. Table linens—white jackets, towels, etc.—are drawn from the linen supplies and stored on board.

All of these operations would seem to involve an almost insurmountable mass of detail, yet compared to the selection of the food supplies they are comparatively simple. The dining-car steward, who is directly responsible for the car and its service, determines the varying quantities of each item. His experience has taught him how the seasons affect appetites and just what percentage of each of the many things with which he must stock his pantry and icebox is eaten by the average traveler. His judgment must be sound. Once the train is under way, there is not a chance for him to run out to the corner grocery to buy some forgotten item or

Linens and jackets. (COURTESY OF GREAT NORTHERN RAILWAY COMPANY RECORDS, MINNESOTA HISTORICAL SOCIETY)

to send over to a neighbor to borrow an egg or a cup of sugar. He is furnished printed lists on which are itemized every article carried in the commissary stores and against each item he checks the quantity he knows he will need for the trip.

The word "Fish" on the menu brings to you a mental picture of flaky white meat, temptingly browned, garnished with parsley and a bit of lemon! To the commissary store-keeper it brings a mental map of the many lakes and streams which line its right-of-way, from which he can obtain, fresh and firm, just the kind of fish he needs. Across one side of his storeroom are built the refrigerators, cooled automatically by the commissary ice machine, each refrigerator a large, cement-lined room with a sign above its heavy, air-tight door to designate its contents. So in the room labeled "Fish" the careful selections from his most convenient source of supply lay like glistening jewels in settings of chipped ice.

Another marked "Meats" is filled with rows of beef, veal, mutton, pork, and poultry. Its shelves stocked with hams, bacon and sausage, wrapped in sealed, airtight coverings—all obtained from the splendid farming regions tributary to the Great Northern Railway. "Dairy"—with its cases of bottled

Sorting soiled linens. Tablecloths survived about twenty trips and were cut down into napkins when they were no longer new enough to cover a table.
(COURTESY OF GREAT NORTHERN RAILWAY COMPANY RECORDS, MINNESOTA HISTORICAL SOCIETY)

milk and cream, crates of eggs, and cartons of butter from the dairy centers of Minnesota and Dakota.

"Fruits–Vegetables"—with its ever-changing supplies in quantities figured so accurately they hardly even pause on their way from the gardens and orchards traversed by the Great Northern from Minnesota to Washington and Oregon, onto the tables of the diners.

The greatest farming, dairy- and cattle-raising regions of the country may be viewed from the dining-car windows. The commissary department chooses and collects the very best of their products and places them fresh and delicious on the diner's tables.

Staple groceries, such as flour, coffee, sugar, salt, etc., are chosen with the same thoughtful care.

As the steward's requisition is filled the articles are placed on the counters of the commis-

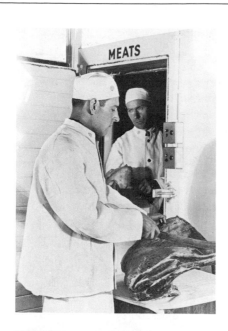

Meat is scored to insure steaks of equal size. Uniform portions kept passengers from complaining because someone across the aisle got a bigger serving. (COURTESY OF GREAT NORTHERN RAILWAY COMPANY RECORDS, MINNESOTA HISTORICAL SOCIETY)

sary storeroom and carefully examined. Everything not already covered is wrapped as a protection against handling and as a sanitary precaution. Looking over these counters loaded with baskets of staple and fancy groceries, one is brought to the realization that here are potential fluffy rolls and muffins, famous Great Northern chicken pies, appetizing salads, tasty omelets and griddle cakes, baked Wenatchee apples and apple pies.

The materials here assembled will make possible many an appetizing meal, from clear consommé and thick soup with their attendant olives, celery, and crisp crackers, to steaming cups of coffee. Everything is included from the breakfast grapefruit to the after-dinner cigar.

Choice Olympian oysters, fresh Columbia River salmon, luscious Wenatchee apples, delicious Minnesota mushrooms, and in season fresh strawberries, raspberries and loganberries from Washington or Oregon, serve as examples of the storekeeper's ability to select and obtain tempting delicacies.

Just outside the commissary building, a small white structure juts from a hillside. Its heavy airtight doors, when opened, disclose a tunnel which slopes gradually downward into a cement-lined room well below the frost line. This is the root cellar in which

Meat locker. (COURTESY OF GREAT NORTHERN RAILWAY COMPANY RECORDS, MINNESOTA HISTORICAL SOCIETY)

Giving the steward a square deal. (COURTESY OF GREAT NORTHERN RAILWAY COMPANY RECORDS, MINNESOTA HISTORICAL SOCIETY)

Bottled goods. (COURTESY OF GREAT NORTHERN RAILWAY COMPANY RECORDS, MINNESOTA HISTORICAL SOCIETY)

A perfect cigar. (COURTESY OF GREAT NORTHERN RAILWAY COMPANY RECORDS, MINNESOTA HISTORICAL SOCIETY)

are stored those large, firm potatoes from Montana and Dakota, for which the Great Northern diners are so famous. Those of you who have lived on farms know how well these underground storage places preserve the so-called root vegetables, such as potatoes, turnips, carrots, and onions. With such a method of preservation, the diners are assured of the very best of these vegetables even in the winter months.

All of the rolls, biscuits, and pies are baked fresh for every meal by the dining-car chefs en route. The bread and those delicious cakes served with ice-cream orders are obtained fresh daily and placed at once in the commissary bread box. Even though they are kept there only the shortest possible time, this bread box is constructed so as to retain all of their original freshness. The bread is covered by sealed, airtight paper wrappings.

It would seem that everything necessary to make a perfect meal has been considered, but there are still two items most important to a large number of people—something to drink and something to smoke. In the commissary a special room with V-shaped bins holds an ample supply of all the best-known brands of ginger ale, rock spring, apollinaris and other mineral waters and soft drinks. Another room, known as the humidor, cement lined and kept at just the proper degree of moisture, is well stocked with favorite brands of cigars and cigarettes.

So it is that everyone's wishes are fulfilled to the last detail.

It is a pity that the commissary is indeed an "unseen service," as its efficiency of operation would be a revelation to any businessman—its shelves, bins, and refrigerators a joy to the housewife.

Your meal is ready.

Perhaps now, back of the smiling waiter who places the steaming tureen of soup before you, you can see that long line of earnest workers bringing you the best fare the land affords, using every method of modern ingenuity to keep it clean and fresh, furnishing the utensils with which to prepare it and the tableware on which to serve it, contributing their efforts toward maintaining the highest standard of service possible, to the end that you may have an appetizing, enjoyable, and satisfactory meal.

(Excerpted by permission from the Great Northern Railway Company records of The Minnesota Historical Society.)

The compact kitchen, with each of the four men working there having an average of only six-and-one-half square feet of work space to himself, required simplicity and efficiency. With so little room in which to carve meat, the task fell to the commissary, which did it in advance. Each single portion of meat was trimmed and wrapped, in the early years in oiled paper, later in waxed paper. Chickens were split in half, and the chops and steaks cut and weighed to a high degree of uniformity before being loaded.

Dining-car supervisors, or inspectors, traveled constantly to taste the food, observe the crew at work, and inspect for violations in standards of cleanliness. They wrote up everything. One checklist included these items:

_____ Silverware polished?
_____ Cruets filled?
_____ Condiment bottle necks and caps clean?
_____ Cleanliness of pantry, floor, and floor racks?
_____ All kitchen appliances clean?
_____ Corrective actions noted?
_____ Menu items prepared to recipe?
_____ Taste of the foods?
_____ Number of meals served in the dining car? As room service?
_____ Speed of service?
_____ Needs of the car to improve service?
_____ People working as per instructions?

Not surprisingly, when an inspector patrolled the trains, crews would pass word along to their colleagues on other trains on the line, often in unique ways. When the inspector got off an eastbound train, say in Cleveland, to board a train going west, the crew of the eastbound train would signal westbound crews by sitting a ketchup bottle in a certain window, or by assigning a waiter to wave a tablecloth or tie a towel to the kitchen door safety bar, or a cook to hold a frying pan at arm's length. Crews on the Pennsylvania Railroad were tipped off to the presence of Superintendent John F. Trout by a cook's standing in an open kitchen door holding a large fish by the tail.[62]

Vigorous inspections occasionally produced equally vigorous attempts to short-circuit them. A Union Pacific inspector, certain in his knowledge that one of his chefs was drinking on the job, tried in vain for years to learn the whereabouts of the chef's potion. At the chef's retirement party, he learned what he wanted to know. The man routinely sunk his bottle in the vat containing the dining car's milk supply, assuring himself of both secrecy and an appropriately chilled brew.

RAILROAD CHINA

With the evolution of dining cars came the development of railroad china, a frequently distinctive pattern of crockery having a railroad's name or logo included in its design. Some of the largest and best-known American pottery firms, including Greenwood, Hall, Jackson, Scammell, Shenango, Sterling, Syracuse, and Walker, as well as international firms such as Germany's Bauscher, France's Haviland, and England's Crown-Staffordshire, created an estimated 300 patterns of railroad china.[1]

Two varieties of railroad china prevailed, "stock" and "custom." Stock patterns, those in current inventory at the manufacturer and available for immediate shipment, saved railroads time and money and were most often used on the secondary trains of the major railroads and throughout the dining cars of railroads with limited dining-car service. Custom patterns were either specific to a railroad (but available for purchase by other non-competing eating houses), or proprietary, and thus protected from sale to anyone other than the railroad. The custom patterns frequently had names as exotic and evocative as those of the trains on which they rode: the Chicago, Burlington & Quincy's "Black Hawk," the Milwaukee Road's "Galatea," the Illinois Central's "Coral."

Railroad china was designed and manufactured to be durable and practical. An advertisement for Syracuse China in 1927 claimed that "concealed in each graceful piece is strength to resist the shocks and strains which china inevitably meets under the extraordinary conditions encountered in dining cars." To maintain stability at table, it had to be heavy, and of a low profile, to create a low center of gravity. When streamlined trains, with their narrower cross-section for increased speed, were introduced in the 1930s, tables narrowed too. Dining-car superintendents turned to the china manufacturers to create a plate that would take up less table space but still provide a seven-inch well for food. The result was the Syracuse "econo-rim"® plate, in which the rim was trimmed back to half its original width, but with the plate's footwell left unchanged. Other manufacturers referred to their designs as narrow-rimmed plates. Shortly thereafter, Bill Dolphin, the Milwaukee Road's dining-car superintendent, designed the non-spill coffee cup. Known as the Dolphin cup, it resembled any other cup on the outside, but had a little lip around the inside top which acted as a breakwater. When a sudden movement sent the coffee toward the customer's lap, the waves struck the lip and were broken.[2] Concern over spillage may have been exaggerated, however. A steward on the Illinois Central's *Panama Limited* at the time pointed out, "you can place a pair of sugar tongs on end in one of the diners and they will remain standing until you knock them down."[3] The ride of the trains was that smooth.

Breakage, however, was still common. Typically, waiters as a crew were allocated some dollar allowance for breakage each month. For example, in 1910 the New York Central granted twenty dollars per month. Damage in excess of that amount was deducted equally among the waiters from the crew's pay. The theft of china, as well as of accompanying flat and hollow silverware (all beautiful vacation souvenirs), was also substantial.

At the peak of rail-passenger service, it was not uncommon on a railroad's premier trains—the Union Pacific's *City of Streamliners*, for example, or the New York Central's *Twentieth Century Limited*—to have a china pattern created specially for an individual train. Arguably the most distinctive of these was the Santa Fe's "Mimbreno" pattern, introduced in 1936, which was copyrighted and used exclusively on the *Super Chief*.

Sante Fe's "Mimbreno" china design goes back nearly a thousand years, to 1100–1200 A.D., when the Mimbres Indians occupied southeastern Arizona and southwestern New Mexico. In the Mimbres Valley, during the Pueblo III period, an unusual type of pottery was developed unique to that part of the world.

The pottery of the Mimbres was usually black on white. However, some red-on-white designs were found, often on the same bowl. Distinctive stylized life-form painting was often expressed on open-bowl interior backgrounds. Beautiful and artistic geometric designs were also used, many of them conveying highly complex arrangements of triangles, frets, scrolls, and zigzags, carried out in alternating black and white areas. Mountain sheep, birds, fish, insects, frogs, rabbits, deer, and humans all were shown in an animated manner despite a basically rectilinear style.

A bowl was "killed" by breaking a hole in the bottom of the vessel. After a hole was made, the bowl would be placed over the head of a dead person at burial, allowing spirits to enter and leave the corpse freely. Mimbres pottery, an outstanding product of the Southwest, depicts cultural relationships of the early peoples of the region.

A second version of "Mimbreno" china had its origins in the mid-1930s, when the Santa Fe was developing and designing its new, deluxe, all-Pullman train between Chicago and Los Angeles, the *Super Chief*. Philadelphia architect Paul F. Cret, designer S. B. McDonald, and Santa Fe Advertising Manager Roger W. Birdseye planned the interior decor. From the outset, the designers decided to use an Indian motif throughout the train. This included the dining car. Elizabeth Coulter, a 35-year veteran of the Fred Harvey system, designed the china and silver. Her designs were based on concepts suggested by the characters in the pottery of the Mimbres Indians.

Chicago's Dearborn Station was the location for the inaugural run of the *Super Chief* on May 12, 1936. On board the new dining car was the updated and beautiful "Mimbreno" china. "Mimbreno" has been called the oldest of all railroad china, as its design concept, as noted, went back nearly a thousand years.

Mimbreno China, each of its thirty-nine red-on-buff pieces carrying a different Indian pictograph, was purchased at least once and sometimes twice a year from Chicago's E. A. Hinrichs and Company for use on the Super Chief *exclusively,* (COURTESY OF RICHARD W. LUCKIN)

(Unless otherwise noted, this article was adapted, with generous consent, from Richard W. Luckin's *Dining on Rails: An Encyclopedia of Railroad China.* Golden, CO. RK Publishing, 1990).

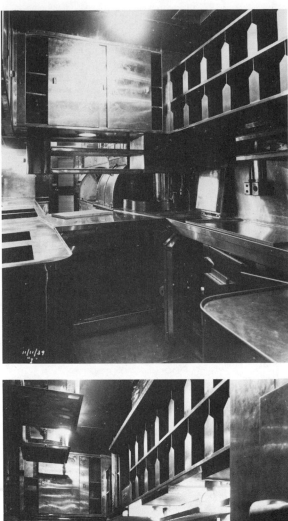

For unobtrusively establishing a model of equipment-use efficiency while maintaining a noteworthy level of complete dining service, arrangements the Pennsylvania Railroad made for its dining cars west of Pittsburgh are exemplary. Its method for shuttling about the twelve cars assigned to the territory in 1892 were typical of most rail-

The dining car is a unique piece of rolling stock. It has appeared virtually unchanged from its inception in 1868 through today's Amtrak Heritage equipment. Here is the general arrangement of a pantry on a Milwaukee Road car of 1939, where waiters did their own set-ups and dishes. (COURTESY OF THE MILWAUKEE ROAD COLLECTION OF THE MILWAUKEE PUBLIC LIBRARY)

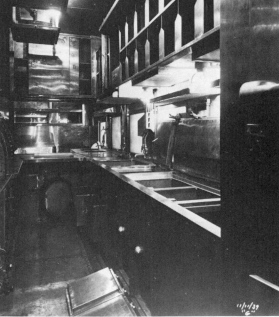

The kitchen arrangement looking toward pantry. In 1914, Ben Loomis, a chef on one section of the Twentieth Century Limited, *offered a visitor a tour of his domain. It measured but four feet by fourteen feet and was occupied by four men producing upwards of 120 meals for any one of four sittings, three times a day. "Against the thin partition that separates the kitchen from the long, narrow, public passageway that runs alongside it, is the range, also long and narrow, and equipped with ample grilling facilities. Over this are the water tanks and the brightly scoured pans in a row; across from it a working counter. Under this counter are bins, containing potatoes and other foodstuffs that are not harmed by short exposures to kitchen heat. Adjoining this are sinks and ice-boxes—many of the latter. Some of these are given to perishable vegetables, another to cream and milk, still another for fish, a fourth to poultry and meats. . . . It takes a ton and a half of ice to stock the refrigerator of his car. 'We've got to have plenty for everybody.' (Loomis) explains, as he throws up the cover of his meat refrigerator. It is clean, and after the fashion of the kitchen itself, efficient to the last degree."* That kitchen technology, too, was slow to change after the 1880s is evident from the accompanying photographs, taken aboard a Milwaukee Road dining car in 1939. *Hungerford, E. "Eating on the Train." Harper's Weekly. (March 21, 1914), 12–4.* (COURTESY OF THE MILWAUKEE ROAD COLLECTION OF THE MILWAUKEE PUBLIC LIBRARY)

roads from then until such extensive operations ceased in the 1960s and 1970s. On the *New York and Chicago Limited,* departing Chicago at 5:00 P.M., one car would be sent out with the train. After serving dinner, the car would be left off in Fort Wayne, Indiana, at 8:50 P.M., and be picked up by the westbound train the next morning to serve breakfast before arriving in Chicago at 9:45 A.M. Meanwhile, three cars out of St. Louis were assigned to trains numbered 20 and 22, to and from New York. The dining car for this train would leave St. Louis at 8:10 A.M., serve three meals, and be deposited at Newark, Ohio, at 9:25 P.M. It would be picked up for the return trip by the westbound train at 5:55

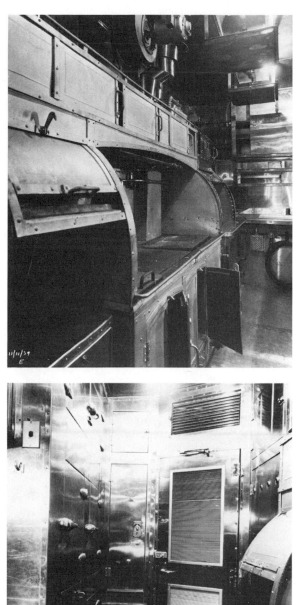

The coal stove and oil range. Note the railing to prevent pots and utensils from being tossed on the floor when the train rounded a curve. (COURTESY OF THE MILWAUKEE ROAD COLLECTION OF THE MILWAUKEE PUBLIC LIBRARY)

Kitchen ice boxes and storage. (COURTESY OF THE MILWAUKEE ROAD COLLECTION OF THE MILWAUKEE PUBLIC LIBRARY)

One who was adept at opening a valve or bringing up a gauge "just so" was clearly called for among the innards of a dining-car kitchen. This is the hot water heater underneath the steam table. (COURTESY OF THE MILWAUKEE ROAD COLLECTION OF THE MILWAUKEE PUBLIC LIBRARY)

Unloading meat from refrigerator. Typically, the commissary shopkeeper solicited bids each month from an approved list of suppliers for the foodstuffs needed on the dining cars in the coming months. With contracts awarded, the shopkeeper, using requisitions received from his stewards, then needed only to notify the supplier of the quantities needed for a day's operation. The requisitioned food and other supplies arrived shortly thereafter.
(COURTESY OF THE UNION PACIFIC MUSEUM)

A.M., to arrive in St. Louis at 7:00 P.M. The second and third cars were used when it was necessary to add a second or third section to the train for the trip, in the event of equipment delays elsewhere that could impact a very tight schedule, and to allow for a longer end-of-run layover for cleaning. Another pair of dining cars was assigned to a one- or two-section train leaving Chicago at 10:45 A.M. The car(s) would be left in Alliance, Ohio, at 9:20 P.M. and picked up for return to Chicago at 4:00 the next morning to serve breakfast and lunch before reaching Chicago again at 3:00 P.M.

By far the most elaborate schedule was that prepared for the six cars assigned to trains numbered 4, 6, 8, and 11, which typically spent five days out on an assigned run. Six cars were necessary because of the frequent need to run multiple sections on these trains, which were some of the railroad's finest, to meet passenger demand. The schedule, beginning when the cars left Chicago, went like this:

Leave	Chicago	Train #8	3:15 P.M.
Arrive	Fort Wayne, IN		7:45 P.M.
Leave	Fort Wayne	Train #4	5:15 A.M.
Arrive	Alliance, OH		2:10 P.M.
Leave	Alliance	Train #6	3:15 P.M.
Arrive	Altoona, PA		10:40 P.M.
Leave	Altoona	Train #11	5:40 A.M.
Arrive	Richmond, IN		7:25 P.M.
Leave	Richmond	Train #6	7:15 A.M.
Arrive	Pittsburgh		5:50 P.M.
Leave	Pittsburgh	Train #9	7:10 A.M.
Arrive	Chicago		9:30 P.M.

After laying over for nearly forty-one hours for cleaning and backup duty on any of the Pennsylvania's trains out of Chicago, a car was returned to service on the next train out. A clue to the pace for the car and its crews can be seen in the fact that the out-of-service stopovers were short and a car on this run served three meals a day every day of the run.[63]

Most are familiar with the short musical verse, "dinner in the diner, nothing could be finer." But dining cars gave birth to other song and verse. Less familiar, perhaps, but nonetheless published somewhere along the mainline of railroad literature of the time, were these poems. The first celebrates the box lunch:

Dining de Luxe

The modern streamlined diners
    Trimmed in silver, glass, and chrome,
Are well prepared to cater
    To the traveler far from home.
But recollections haunt me,
    With their own nostalgic charm,
Of lunches Aunt Jo packed for
    My return trip from the farm.

Now here's your railroad ticket
    And be sure to hold it tight,
And when you reach the city
    Please remember, dear, to write.
And just in case you're hungry
    And should like a bite of lunch,
I've fixed a little snack on
    Which I thought that you could munch.

I packed it in a shoe box
    And it's really not a lot,
But mind that you don't tip it,
    For that apple pie is hot.
It's next to the tomatoes,
    Freshly picked; and in that jar
Is buttermilk; it's filling
    When you're traveling so far.

There are powdered sugar doughnuts
    Made especially for you,
A liver-sausage sandwich
    And a big banana, too.
Some chocolate-frosted cupcakes
    And a pickled hard-boiled egg,
A slice of raisin pound cake
    And a nice fried chicken leg.

And don't you talk to strangers,
    Keep your feet off of the seat,
Your hands inside the window
    And your shoes and stockings neat.
Remember what I told you
    About holding to your grip?
And eat that lunch all up, for
    Ninety miles is quite a trip.

Marie Hotson[1]

Dining-car patrons on the Texas & Pacific Railroad found a Grace–Before Meals prayer-card on their tables. Each offered three prayers, one Roman Catholic, one Protestant, and one Jewish. The four-page menu on the *Leland*, the dining car assigned to the Chicago & North Western's *North Western Limited* in 1896, reminded diners that the experience they were about to enjoy was suitable for royalty:

A flying palace that outshines
    The splendor of great Kublai Kahn
Rich with the woods of the Orient
    And cunning handiwork of man,
Stored with the rarest of old wines
    And foods of dainty nourishment—
King Luxuries' winged caravan,
    The North West Limited.[3]

The experience of getting to the dining car is the concern of this contribution:

Dining Car Forward
A Poetical Shimmy in Nine Stanzas Through Twelve Cars

Last Call for dinner—
Rise from your seat.
Sink back gracefully—
Then repeat.
Start for the diner—
Right and left sway,
Meet fat lady in the
Narrow way.
One step forward,
Then two steps back—
Shove her in the wash room,
All clear track.
Train starts to lurching—
Down on all fours.
See funny names on the
Vestibule doors.
Meet hungry fellow—
He says "Hey!

Going to the dining car?
T'other way!"
Reverse your engines.
Feeling pretty sore.
See the silly people—you
Saw before.
Trip over baby—
Land on your ear.
Smell chops a-burning—
Diner's near.
Dodge past a waiter—
Train takes a loop—
Put steadying hand in
Someone's soup.
Sit next to lady
Whose husband has gone—
Order an oyster cocktail—
Party's on!

Fairfax D. Downey[2]

Patrons, too, praised the dining cars. This, from Strickland W. Gillilan, appeared in the January 1904 issue of the Baltimore & Ohio Railroad's on-train magazine, *The Book of the Royal Blue:*

In the Dining Car

I dreamed I'd delectably dined with the gods,
Had crammed down Olympian fodder in wads;
    I dreamed I had quaffed on the nectar they serve
    That thrills every fiber and steels every nerve;
But, waking, my memory's sweeter by far—
I've eaten the grub in a dining car!

No restaurant meal with a trunk hinge for steak,
No coffee like that which the lunch counters make,

No bread made of alum, no butter of grease,
No codfish of very unrecent decease,
　　No flies in the flapjacks one's hunger to bar—
Nay, none of these things in the dining car.

Instead there are biscuits that melt in your mouth,
Good coffee as hot as July in the South,
　　Some milk that is neither diluted nor blue,
　　A tenderloin steak you can really chew,
Some French-fried potatoes—that cook is a star
Who hustles the grub in the dining car!

Some kick on the price they compel you to pay—
I've figured it out in a different way;
　　And when I've been starved by the lunch-counter crowd,
　　Have suffered in restaurants smellfully loud,
I feel I am paying too little by far
For genuine food in the dining car.[4]

No sooner had the Southern Pacific introduced a quick-lunch car on its San Francisco-to-Bakersfield route in 1914, than it too was immortalized:

Quick Lunch on the Fly

When you're traveling to Los Banos, Dos Palos, or Gustine,
On any of the stations that are strung along between,
　　You get a sandwich egg,
　　Or a storage chicken leg,
While you're speeding through the valley of the San Joaquin.

All aboard for Alameda, waiter, bring on a ham-on-rye,
All out for Goshen Junction, how's the huckleberry pie?
　　You can have a roll or muffin,
　　Or a slice of veal with stuffin'
While the locomotive's puffin through Madera on the fly.

Change cars for Sacramento, have some sugar in your tea;
Next stop is Modesto, cottage cheese and cream for three;
　　You can eat from Niles to Ceres,
　　At a pace that never wearies,
And a little coin will feed you from Fernando to the sea.

W. H. James[5]

Cliff Trembly shared these one-liners with patrons of his railroad in the company publicity magazine, *The Great Northern Goat*, named for the railroad's logo:

- The Goat feels at home with the kids in the diners.
- One doesn't feel like a martyr when the steward leads him to the steak. (Not our steaks, at least.)

- Did you ever notice the frieze in our dining cars? No? Ice cream.
- You pay as you leave in the dining car, but we've noticed folks don't leave very much. Food, we mean.
- You wouldn't call a waiter intoxicated, would you, just because he gets tips, see?
- We specialize in sea food in our diners. We'll say you see food there.
- The chef may not know much about clothes, but he can dress a salad to perfection.
- "Well," said the oyster as it slid down a diner's throat at Summit, "I certainly never expected to end my days at the crest of the Rockies."
- They are feeding goat's milk to the children but the Goat don't mind that in the least, for she intended it for the kids all the time.
- You can have your grapefruit in the morning or in your lap, whichever you prefer.
- Our pancake batter has Babe Ruth beaten a mile.
- Our Commissary Department stands back of every meal, except cornmeal.[6]

Finally, for those working the Chicago, Milwaukee, St. Paul & Pacific's dining-car department, this anthem:

Milwaukee Porters' and Waiters' March Song

The Milwaukee of railroad fame
    Has always stood the test
For Service it has made a name
    Because it is the best.
The passengers that go its way
    And many of them do—
Do not regret the price they pay
    For such a loyal crew.

CHORUS:
Milwaukee Porter and Waiters
    We want the public to know us
As you journey on your way
    We will serve you night and day.
When in our cars do not worry
    For to your call we will hurry.

The Milwaukee electrified
    Its employees, true and tried.
When o'er the mountain side you climb
    Up on the Great Divide
Sweet melodies of song will chime
    From those with whom you ride.
So smooth and easy without smoke
    No cinders in your eye—
A Porter or a Waiter's joke

    As on your way you fly.

                        T. J. Sadler[8]

Thanksgiving on the Dining Car

By Sidney Warren Mase

It is Thanksgiving day, and I
    Am many miles away from home;
But yet I do not grieve or sigh
    Because it falls my lot to roam.
Here all my wants are satisfied,
    And there is naught my joy to mar,
With such a feast as they provide
    Thanksgiving on the dining car.

Of course I miss the wife and kids,
    And wish that they were here with me;
But hapless circumstance forbids
    That I may share their company.
And so to this Thanksgiving treat
    I turn, and though I'm miles afar
From home, I'm sure I couldn't beat
    This dinner on the dining car.

I gaze upon the passing scene,
    Which like a moving picture glides
The while I dine, and all serene
    A festal air of joy presides.
I'll say the dinner sure is prime,
    And so I thank each lucky star
I'm here this blest Thanksgiving time
    And dining on the dining car.

And if again I'm forced to be
    Away from home Thanksgiving day,
I'll have the folks along with me
    And joy will then have perfect sway.
Here one may dine in utmost bliss,
    As many here about me are,
And like I'm also dining this
    Thanksgiving on the dining car.

(COURTESY OF THE UNION PACIFIC MUSEUM)

The railroad's efficient use of equipment allowed for fewer dining cars and crews, but nonetheless, railroads maintained a competitive train *and* meal schedule, and reduced the cost associated with each train's operation by lessening by some 100 tons the load hauled at every opportunity.

If anything, the scheduling got more complex as train travel increased. The New York Central alone at one time ran eighteen trains daily along the corridor between New York and Chicago. The most popular of them often had more than one section, each section a complete train, for a given run. For example, the *Twentieth Century Limited,* the premier train on the schedule, routinely had three or four complete trains making a daily dash west to Chicago while an equal number of sections made the trek eastward to New York—the peak point a day when nine sections left Chicago for New York. For that train alone each day, the dining-car superintendent had to have ready and equipped in each city three or four of the company's best dining cars. They were cut out of their respective trains at Buffalo and sent back on the next run.

ARTICLES	Unit of Measure	On Hand from Last Trip	Supplied at	Supplied at	Supplied at	Supplied at	Supplied at	Supplied at	Supplied at	Supplied at	On Hand at End of Trip	Consumed	Value Consumed During Trip	Value On Hand at End of Month
Forward														
Veal, Leg	Lb.													
", Loin	"													
Fresh Fruits & Vegetables														
Apples, Baking														
", Cooking														
", Table														
Apricots	Lb.													
Artichokes	No.													
Asparagus														
Avocados	No.													
Bananas														
Beans, Lima	Lb.													
", String	"													
", Wax	"													
Beets														
Berries, Black	Box													
", Cran														
", Goose														
", Huckle	Box													
", Logan	"													
", Rasp, Blk.	"													
", ", Red	"													
", Straw	"													
", Young	"													
Broccoli	Lb.													
Brussels Sprouts	"													
Cabbage														
Carrots														
Cauliflower														
Celery	Bch.													
Cherries, Pie														
", Table														
Chives	Bch.													
Corn, Green	No.													
Cucumbers	"													
Dates	Lb.													
Egg Plant	No.													
Forward														

ARTICLES	Unit of Measure	On Hand from Last Trip	Supplied at	Supplied at	Supplied at	Supplied at	Supplied at	Supplied at	Supplied at	Supplied at	On Hand at End of Trip	Consumed	Value Consumed During Trip	Value On Hand at End of Month
Forward														
Endive	Lb.													
Figs	"													
Garlic	"													
Grape Fruit	No.													
" "	"													
Grapes	Lb.													
Leeks	Bch.													
Lemons	No.													
Lettuce	"													
Limes	"													
Melons, Cantaloupe	"													
", Casaba	"													
", Honey Dew	"													
", Persian	"													
", Water	"													
Mint	Bch.													
Mushrooms	Lb.													
Okra	"													
Onions, Dry	"													
", Spring	Bch.													
Oranges, Juice	No.													
", Table	"													
Oyster Plant														
Parsley	Bch.													
Parsnips														
Peaches														
Pears														
Peas, Green	Lb.													
Peppers, Green	"													
Persimmons	No.													
Pineapples	"													
Plums														
Potatoes, Baking	Lb.													
", Chips	"													
", Cooking	"													
", New	"													
", Sweet	"													
Pumpkin														
Radishes	Bch.													
Romaine														
Rhubarb														
Forward														

And when these trains reached Grand Central Terminal, the metropolitan hub for all the New York Central's trains, the scheduling got even more harried. Some cars had to be sent to Mott Haven yard for washing and cleaning, others were to be switched from one train to another in the terminal, and cleaned during the process of making up trains in the station. "The equipment of one train may be put on six other trains, and this does not occur by magic. Not all Pullmans are of a style suitable for every train. Somebody must know which is which and how to get them where they belong. Diners of course must be provisioned and switched as well as other cars and all must be kept out of the way of incoming and outgoing trains—no small job—particularly when it is understood that during twenty-four hours about 600 trains enter and leave Grand Central Terminal, often with as many as five trains arriving within three minutes. A day in December 1929 showed 854 trains gliding in and out in twenty-four hours."[64]

The steward was accountable for supplies and consumption: In a booklet of as many as twenty-one pages such as this, the steward itemized everything taken on his car when it was stocked at the commissary before a trip. A record of all articles sold was entered on the sheet from the meal orders, crew's meals, and the like, then, when the car reached "home," another inventory was made and all articles that had not been sold were to be on hand. (COURTESY OF HOMER H. NOAR)

To satisfy the various demands for food on such trains, other types of food-service cars were assigned to supplement the dining car. For most first-class trains, this meant a consist that included a dining car, a cafe car, and a buffet car. The Baltimore & Ohio's reasons for such scheduling were typical, as shown in this description of its service on the Royal Blue Line between Washington, Baltimore, Philadelphia, and New York:

"Of the twenty trains between the capital and the metropolis, fourteen have dining cars. Beginning with the first train eastward from Washington at 7:05 A.M., which carries the through sleeping cars from St. Louis, Cincinnati, Cleveland, and Pittsburg[h], breakfast is served à la carte, i.e., you order what you desire from the card and pay for what you get. This is desirable, as Baltimore is reached in forty-five minutes, Philadelphia in two hours more, while New York is reached in time for passengers to dine or lunch at their hotel at the noon hour. The next Blue Line train leaving Washington at 8:30 is after the breakfast hour, and it arrives in New York also in time for service at [a] hotel; this train, therefore, is supplied only with buffet in the parlor car. All of the trains which follow touch either the noon or evening dining hours and are therefore supplied with dining cars serving meals à la carte or table d'hote, as the class of travel demands. The one, three, and five o'clock trains are particularly popular with businessmen, and each of these trains have cafes as well as diners. These cafes are attractive in their bohemianism. Travelers and especially businessmen consume the entire time between the cities over their lunches and cigars in the cafe. The cars are made attractive in their plain polished hardwood fittings with movable chairs and tables.

The *Royal Limited*, which leaves both Washington and New York at 3:00, is the most complete daylight train in the country. Not only is it Pullman throughout, but is provided with [an] observation parlor for ladies and observation buffet smoking car for gentlemen; also with a regular dining and cafe car—the cafe serving à la carte and the dining car, table d'hote—as is the rule where dining and cafe cars are on the same train.

The return service from New York is conducted under almost exactly similar arrangements.

The through trains between New York, Pittsburg[h], Chicago, Cincinnati and St. Louis are provided with splendid dining-car equipment the entire distance, which generally includes three dining cars from terminal to terminal."[65]

At its peak, the extent of railway dining-car service in the United States was enormous, perhaps best demonstrated by operating figures for a single year. The Bureau of Railway Economics, using available data from member railroads and estimates of operations on other lines, reported in 1924 that as many as 50 million meals were served annually.[66] Among the major items comprising those meals were 8 million pounds of beef, taken from a "herd" of 70,000 cattle (remembering that only the choicest cuts

RAILROADS OPERATING DINING CARS

The following, a 1921 membership roster of the American Association of Dining Car Superintendents, gives an idea of how extensive dining-car operations were within the railroad system. However, it is difficult to compile a definitive list for one particular point in time. For example, one list naming the railroads with distinctive china patterns—a clue that dining cars were operated—mentions sixty-three railroads not on the list below. Such patterns, could, of course, have been for use in those railroads' private cars. Or, by 1921, some of those railroads may have phased out their dining cars, or employed the services of the Pullman Company or another caterer.

Atcheson, Topeka & Santa Fe
Atlantic & West Point
Atlantic Coast Line
Baltimore & Ohio
Boston & Albany
Boston & Maine
Buffalo, Rochester & Pittsburgh
Canadian National
Canadian Pacific
Chesapeake & Ohio
Chicago & Alton
Chicago & Eastern Illinois
Chicago & North Western
Chicago, Burlington, & Quincy
Chicago Great Western
Chicago, Indianapolis & Louisville
    (Monon)
Chicago, Milwaukee & St. Paul
Chicago, North Shore & Milwaukee
Chicago, Rock Island & Pacific
Chicago, St. Paul, Minneapolis & Omaha
Cleveland, Cincinnati, Chicago & St. Louis
Colorado & Southern
Cuban Railway

Delaware & Hudson
Delaware, Lackawanna & Western
Denver & Rio Grande Western
Duluth, Missabe & Northern
Duluth, South Shore & Atlantic
El Paso Southwestern System
Erie Railroad
Frisco Lines
Grand Trunk
Grand Trunk Pacific
Great Northern
Illinois Central
International & Great Northern
Lehigh Valley
Los Angeles & Salt Lake
Louisville & Nashville
Michigan Central
Minneapolis, St. Paul & Sault Ste. Marie
Missouri-Kansas-Texas
Missouri Pacific
Nashville, Chattanooga & St. Louis
New York Central
New York, Chicago & St. Louis
    (Nickel Plate Road)
New York, New Haven & Hartford
Norfolk & Western
Northern Pacific
Oregon Short Line
Pennsylvania Railroad
Pere Marquette
Philadelphia & Reading—Central Railroad of
    New Jersey
Pullman Car Lines
St. Louis Southwestern (Cotton Belt)
Seaboard Air Line
Southern
Southern Pacific
Texas & Pacific
Union Pacific
Virginian
Wabash
Western Pacific

went to the cars). It would take a freight train thirty miles long, made up of more than 3,500 cattle cars, to transport the cattle to market, demonstrating one way in which the dining car produced business for railroads and shippers alike. An additional 2 million pounds of ham, 1.75 million pounds of lamb chops, and 4.5 million pounds of other varieties of meat made up red-meat consumption. A million fish, weighing 4.5 million pounds, were served. A like number of chickens were also eaten. The cost of meat alone approached $7 million in 1923.

Other commodities were consumed in similar amounts. It took 6,000 acres of farm land to yield the 16 million potatoes served. An indeterminate number of tons of fresh vegetables, berries, and small fruits were bought from truck gardens and farms around the nation. Farmers also sold 135,000 bushels of wheat to dining-car departments, which turned them into 2.25 million loaves of bread and 60 million rolls. A large portion of the 2.5 million pounds of butter consumed was no doubt used on these bakery items.

Among the numerous and varied fruits consumed, apples from the Pacific Northwest predominated. It took 4,000 apple trees a full year to yield the 20,000 barrels of apples consumed. Other favorites were oranges, with 3.25 million eaten, and grapefruits, at 1 million eaten, both fruits from Florida and California. Satisfying the sweet tooth of riders required 3.25 million pounds of sugar; enough, the Bureau of Railway Economics assured, to create a wall of one-pound bags ten feet high and eight miles long.

Back at the farm, 165,000 hens labored all year to produce the 25 million eggs used for all purposes. As many as 4,000 cows also worked day and night to deliver 6 million quarts of milk and cream for the dining cars. These 200,000 cubic feet of liquid were capable of floating the ocean steamship *Leviathan*. And they do not include the dairy ingredients used to make the 900,000 quarts of ice cream dining-car patrons bought.

Served with all of this food were the results of brewing 2 million pounds of coffee beans and steeping 500,000 pounds of tea. Of the known costs, in addition to the red meat, fish, poultry, bread and butter totalled $2.25 million, fruit $1.5 million, and coffee and tea, $800,000.

No figures are available on the amount of water consumed, but it too usually involved an expense. Transcontinental trains traveled widely and through territory with water of varying, often questionable, quality. A chef on the Cotton Belt Line's dining car 240 out of Memphis refused to take on water at Pine Bluff, Arkansas, complaining that it was of a red color that offended patrons when served in the glass (and, presumably, offended him by damaging the flavor of his concoctions). Frequently, therefore, the trains carried bottled water in the dining car. The Baltimore & Ohio offered its own Deer Park Spring Water exclusively on the trains, the Chicago & North Western featured Waukesha Table Water, while the Chicago, Burlington & Quincy served Denver Artesian Water. Even a secondary carrier, the Lake Shore & Michigan Southern Railroad, made passengers aware via the menu that it used only water from "Hudson, Michigan's celebrated springs."

In 1924, the same year the above figures were reported, a new standard dining car cost approximately $50,000. Typically, the car contained a fully equipped kitchen, comfortable seating arrangements for as many as forty-two people, and heating, lighting, and ventilating apparatus. Bringing space efficiency to a high art, the dining car was stocked with 1,000 dishes of various sizes and purposes (from butter plates to finger-bowls), 300 pieces of glassware, 700 pieces of often custom-designed silverware, and 900 linen tablecloths with 1500 matching napkins—the Gulf, Mobile & Ohio, for one, required seven pieces of linen be set up at every table in its dining cars: a table pad, a large table cloth, a small top cloth, and four napkins, with the top cloth and napkins changed after every seating.[67] And there had to be enough food to feed 400 people three meals a day. A staff of four chefs, six waiters, and a steward insured satisfactory service.

One anonymous but reportedly well-managed Midwestern railroad of the time presented these figures on the per-person-served (as opposed to per-person-on-board) cost of key items:

- laundry, four cents
- crew salaries, forty cents
- fuel consumption to pull the car and ice to cool it, five cents
- other pertinent items of expense *excluding* food, depreciation, upkeep, and portable items such as kitchen utensils, linen, silverware, china, and glassware, twenty-seven cents.

Other costs of operation included printing the menus and repairing theft, where costs ranged from replacing silver creamers—in at least one case it included the cream—to restocking pencils. On the Erie Railroad, more than 700 pencils each week were carried away from its sixteen dining cars.

Not surprisingly, dining cars nearly always operated at a loss. Harry Norris pointed out that "dining cars [are] the only business I know of in which the net loss is in inverse ratio to an increased gross business that [it] may enjoy."[68] Before the age of cost accounting, that discrepancy could be overlooked because the men running the railroads had confidence in the good-will value derived from offering their patrons the best of everything at a very modest price. Greater and greater deficits were urged on commissary departments, resulting in some outrageous examples of gastronomic good fortune. On the New York Central as late as 1907, a dollar at

In the 1920s, the place to be seen, for aspiring bathing beauty contest winners and others, was in the kitchen of named-train dining car. (COURTESY OF THE MILWAUKEE ROAD COLLECTION OF THE MILWAUKEE PUBLIC LIBRARY)

breakfast would buy either fresh fruit, a baked apple, a choice of oatmeal or shredded wheat; followed by Lake Superior whitefish, broiled or salted mackerel, tenderloin or sirloin steak, ham or bacon, mutton chops, sausages, or broiled chicken on toast with fried mush; eight styles of eggs and six of potatoes; a wide assortment of breads, wheat or buckwheat cakes, preserved fruit, or marmalade; and coffee, cocoa, milk, or English breakfast tea.[69] One rumor has it that Fred Harvey, already accused of gustatory opportunism for cutting his pies in four rather than seven pieces, fired one of his dining-car managers on the Sante Fe Railway for losing only $500 a month and replacing him with a man willing to quickly "up" the deficit to $1,500 a month—a feat which earned the new man a promotion to general superintendent.[70]

Operating dining cars at a loss was a problem to which there seemed no solution. Regardless of his railroad or the time during which he spoke, the second-most-frequent remark made by an employee—after lauding his railroad's dining-car service as second to none—concerned how much money was lost with each meal served. Rising costs—of food, labor, constructing and outfitting a car, and scheduling to assure the cars would be on the right trains at mealtimes—all contributed to these losses and increased relentlessly. So in 1937, for example, while the average meal check on the diners of the Pennsylvania Railroad was $1.24, the cost to the railroad per meal that year was $1.61, creating losses of more than $1 million. By 1949 they had increased to more than $4 million yearly, with wage increases contributing greatly to the growing deficit. By 1954, for every dollar of dining-car revenue taken in by all railroads of the nation, they were actually spending $1.44. The 1,400 diners in service in 1957 grossed a revenue of $62 million, and ran up a deficit of $29 million on the year. Only with the cancellation of numerous trains in the late 1960s did the deficits decline.[71]

Nevertheless, it was apparent from the beginning that railroads running dining cars on their trains were much better patronized than those that did not. An article in the *Chicago Tribune* as early as February 14, 1882, reported that the Chicago & North Western had to add dining cars on its trains from Chicago to Council Bluffs, Iowa, to compete with the Chicago, Burlington & Quincy and the Rock Island Line. The piece concluded, "The running of dining cars is not a profitable arrangement, as far as direct receipts are concerned, and on most lines the expenses are greater than the income. Yet the indirect gain from the earnings of the dining cars is very great, as it advertises the roads and brings them increased business."[72] In 1891, when railroads west of Chicago were trying to agree to raise the price of American Plan meals from seventy-five cents to a dollar, *The Railroad Gazette* reported that, while the fact that practically every road was losing money on dining-car service was the best argument for such a move, there was little likelihood such an increase would ever occur. For the railroads, low-cost meals in the cars was the favored method of advertising.

And so the railroads absorbed the losses for the sake of building their freight and passenger business. The Northern Pacific's general manager represented the prevailing school of thought when he wrote in the company's 1890 annual report that the cost of dining service should be considered a necessary expense of the passenger department, and only the results of the department as a whole should be considered when estimating the monthly or annual profits. The losses accumulated by dining-car departments were either literally or figuratively charged off to advertising.

A fictitional steward of the Missouri Pacific Lines explained it to passengers this way in the 1927 booklet *Our Dining Service*: "The Missouri Pacific Railroad Company has built up a standard of service surpassed by no other railroad. It could save money, from one point of view, by cutting costs here and there, but at the same time it would cut down the standard of its service which eventually would react against the prosperity of the lines. This railroad, you know, has but one thing to sell—service—and it invests heavily to build and maintain the highest character of service possible. Now the dining service is just as important as the locomotives or passenger cars, as far as the quality of the service is concerned—therefore the railroad company provides the best foods available and the highest character of service in its diners. . . . If the railroad charges prices high enough to 'break even' it would be far above the prices prevailing in the better hotels and restaurants throughout the country—this cannot be done, because the railroad desires to give a service equal, or superior, to hotel and restaurant service, meeting (or frequently beating) hotel and restaurant prices."[73]

The dining cars weren't without their critics. Foremost among them were those within the industry who decried the losses. Charles Frederick Carter spoke for them in an article aptly entitled, "The Brutal Truth About Dining Cars" in *The New York Central Lines Magazine* of September 1927. He accused railroad management of promoting passenger travel when it wasn't necessary, with the result that:

The Great American Ambition is to save up money enough to go somewhere.

The idea in going somewhere is to get something good to eat.

If they get it they will go again.

On these three cardinal principles the dining-car service on American railroads is predicated. Without the hopeful note in this creed of the passenger department there would be no dining-car service.[74]

Carter blamed Pullman and the Chicago & Alton Railroad (which, he gloated, was then in receivership) for introducing dining cars and asserted it was ambition, not business sense, that led to their creation. "Success was so immediate and so marked in providing passengers with comfortable sleeping quarters that Pullman thought he could go a step further and offer complete hotel service on wheels. . . . Unfortunately, the Chicago & Alton [became] so enamored of those first dining cars that it acquired an interest in them and later took over the dining cars altogether, thus establishing a deplorable precedent."[75]

Moralists had things to object to as well. Great Northern steward W. E. Meagher could recall stories from "the early days of Montana, where men were real he-men; days when cowboys would board the train with spurred boots and the dining car, especially between meals, was a social hall for the painted ladies" who served "these rough but lonesome cowboys."[76] Such goings-on, surely done with the bought or silent consent of the train crew, outraged the moralists among the passengers.

Another source of irritation was the practice of serving drinks to dining-car guests. In an appeal to railroad "boards of directors and high officials . . . most prominent in Christian work," Andrew Stevenson, himself a prominent railroad official of twenty years' standing, wrote in the *New York Observer* of April 11, 1912, that "railroads have allowed the habits and selfishness of the few to govern the health, enjoyment, and the comfort of the great majority of their patrons" by making them tolerate the "tobacco fiends" and dine in "the barrooms conducted by the transportation companies of this country." And he offered proof:

No other road in the country makes its dining-car patrons quite so conscious of the fact that they are in a barroom as does the New Haven road. No Christian man would take his children—no, not even his wife—into the dining car on the *Merchant's Limited* out of Boston or New York at 5:00 in the evening. Why they call the man in charge the conductor instead of the bartender is difficult to understand. By actual observation seventy-two percent of his time was taken on one evening recently in opening bottles and serving liquor to twelve percent of the passengers in the dining car.

The Wabash road, too, was singled out for condemnation after Mr. Stevenson's experience on its noon train out of Decatur, Illinois, en route to Chicago:

> There were fourteen passengers altogether in the (buffet parlor) car, including three ladies, whom it was easily to be seen were women of the most refined tastes and habits. There were two girls of seventeen or eighteen, evidently returning home from college. The rest were a [mixed] class. One man and a woman commenced ordering drinks. Within an hour both were under the influence of liquor and what transpired was a disgrace to American civilization.... we all had to be subjected to their coarse, vulgar, suggestive talk. Supposing one of the girls had been the daughter of the president of the Wabash road, what would she have thought?[77]

DINER DAWDLERS

The average passenger took an hour and ten minutes to eat, necessitating a combination of efficiency, luck, and occasionally, action by fellow passengers, to enable three sittings per table for each meal served.

And finally there was the interminable waiting in line for a seat in the diner to vex passengers and stewards alike. "Possibly dining-car officials are compelled to add to their menus the long-course dinners because of the demands from the public. But on a dining car, with its congested working space, limited number of employees, and limited seating capacity, the course dinner does halt and slow up service. Passengers probably want and enjoy the table d'hote meal with the exception of those who are in line, waiting. A course dinner with the average traveler is not enjoyed at home, and to have such a thing on a train with a continual panorama of scenery unfolding itself through the car window, is so rare a treat that those dining simply will not give a considerate thought to the poor, hungry, impatient fellow waiting."[78]

World War II challenged the railroads with a number of new operating circumstances. Vast numbers of men and women had to be carried over great distances, frequently under the cloak of secrecy. Service personnel and their supplies were to be given the right of way. Returning wounded had to be carried quickly, softly, and comfortably to hospitals specializing in the type of wound each suffered, the railroads assuring the government that battle victims would be moved immediately without regard for other traffic.[1] The resulting heavy traffic backed up branch lines and created delays on mainlines. Train crews often worked twelve-to-sixteen-hour stints and ended their day in a location that lacked boarding facilities. For civilians, travel was curtailed to only the most essential. The availability of railroad equipment was limited and labor was in critically short supply.

To feed the hundreds of thousands of troops and other passengers on their trains, dining-car departments had problems of their own to solve. Key personnel were called away to duty—seven Great Northern chefs, with a combined fifty-three years experience on *The Empire Builder*, went at one time to work in the kitchen of a unit in the Railway Grand Division of the Military Railway Service in North Africa, where former Great Northern employees made up all but two or three of its one hundred men.

Food supplies, including those distributed to railroad dining-car departments, were rationed. As the war progressed, meat especially became more difficult to obtain. Military riders were to be served meat for each of their three daily meals; perhaps bacon for breakfast, hamburger for lunch, and roast beef for dinner. Civilians had to observe one meatless meal a day. By the end of the war, many railroads were serving only fish, turkey, and lamb as meat items.

On top of the difficulties imposed by rationing and scarcity was the dramatic increase in ridership. It was not uncommon to have 600 or more people, military and civilian alike, on board regularly scheduled trains which during the Depression era may have carried only 200 passengers. By 1944 the Pullman Company was "carrying out mass troop movements with half its fleet of sleeping cars and carrying more passengers in the other half than the entire fleet carried in peacetime."[2]

(COURTESY OF THE ASSOCIATION OF AMERICAN RAILROADS)

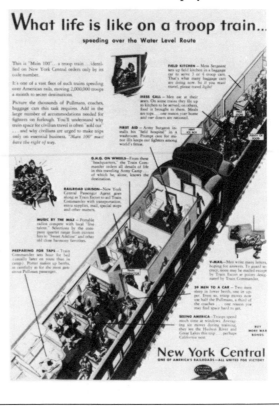

The generally followed procedure for transporting troops was to handle small parties on regular trains and move large contingents as special troop trains. Either way, railroad equipment and personnel were stretched to their fullest capacity. The Southern Railway, which served an average of 70,000 meals a month in 1939, was by the end of 1943 serving a monthly average of 350,000 meals. Chefs in the six by thirteen-and-a-half-foot kitchens of the New York Central's dining cars averaged 7.3 meals every minute during all of 1942. This volume required eight or ten sittings at mealtime in place of the usual three in peace time.[3]

As with the trafficking procedures, small groups of GIs were fed in the dining cars; larger groups were more likely served military style. "Eating on troop trains is a novel experience," wrote E. L. Holmes, an Illinois Central passenger agent who frequently served as troop escort to trains operating over his railroad's track. "The troops have meals prepared in 'kitchen cars.' Army gas ranges or wood stoves are assembled in baggage cars and each meal is prepared and the food either passed through the train, or the men pass the serving tables in the kitchen car and return to their seats. The kitchen car is a favorite spot just before retiring hour, as there is usually a pot of hot coffee on the stove."[4] It was not uncommon for troop trains to have 1,200 men on board. Kitchen cars could feed them in fifteen minutes.

The extremes in work duration and service rendered by employees during the war are illustrated by one episode during the winter of 1942–1943. The dining-car crew of *The Creole,* the Illinois Central's daily train between Chicago and New Orleans, wound up on assignment in

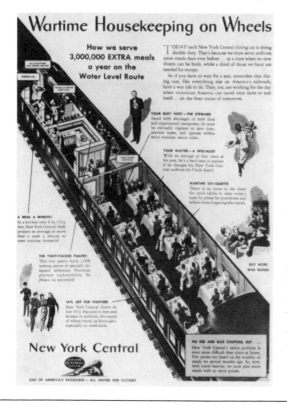

continuous service for twenty-one days, with no time off except the regular eight-hour sleeping period at night. The situation was far from exceptional, as a crew might get in from a run only to find special orders assigning their dining car to a troop train or to an unexpectedly overloaded train in need of an additional dining car, or learn they were assigned to substitute for a dining-car crew that was out of sequence for such reasons.[5]

And what surprises a trip might hold. Steward W. J. Ryan started his crew out on one run along the Illinois Central's mainline, busy for connecting soldiers with fourteen of the nation's largest wartime encampments, and received orders to serve an additional one hundred soldiers boarding down the line. He wired ahead for supplies, sped up service to his train's regular patrons, then had the waiters set up for and cooks get busy on one of the prescribed "military meals." When the train got to the pickup point, 200 men

(COURTESY OF THE ASSOCIATION OF AMERICAN RAILROADS)

boarded. They consumed ten gallons of fruit cocktail, one hundred pounds of chicken, one hundred pounds of potatoes, ten gallons of green peas, sixty heads of lettuce, thirty pounds of tomatoes, two gallons of french dressing, sixty loaves of Pullman bread, and similar quantities of dessert and beverages—for lunch.[6]

To supplement the regular dining-car accommodations, which became taxed beyond capacity, many railroads set up platform canteens at various stations. In a throwback to the "twenty minutes for dinner" eating house, GIs were offered sandwiches, fruit, doughnuts, and beverages while their train was serviced. Three such facilities on the Illinois Central's mainline between Chicago and New Orleans (Jackson, Mississippi; Fulton , Kentucky; and Champaign, Illinois) used 270 loaves of bread, forty-seven meat loaves, twelve bricks of cheese, and sixty-eight gallons of coffee each day to satisfy demand.[7] These in turn were supplemented by groups such as the Victory Mothers Club of Carbondale, Illinois, which served home-made sandwiches and beverages to troops passing through on the trains.

Not surprisingly, the war years were the only time in their history that many railroads made a profit on dining-car service. In 1943, on passenger revenues of $1,652,867,962, all railroad dining departments combined reported spending only $1.01 to collect $1.00 in revenue. The only year close to that previously was 1918, another war year, when it cost $1.07 to earn $1.00. In 1940, the last full year prior to the impact of World War II, dining-car expenses overall were $1.48 for each $1.00 taken in.[8]

North Platte, Nebraska's railroad canteen: North Platte, Nebraska's famous railroad canteen served more than six million GI's while trains stopped there during World War II. (COURTESY OF THE UNION PACIFIC MUSEUM)

4

DINING-CAR PERSONNEL

He who gets
And never gives
May long exist
But never lives

EDWIN KACHEL, STEWARD
GREAT NORTHERN RAILWAY

I f the commissary was the hub for a far-flung dining-car network, and an "unseen service" accounted for its flawlessness, the dining-car crew was what translated dining on the train into a memorable experience for passengers. Crewing was not a "star" system, but one of teamwork, calling for a high level of efficient cooperation among eight to fifteen men who worked in a small, hectic, moving space. Edwin Kachel compared it to playing a game of football: "Give me seven good courteous waiters in the line, the pantryman acting as center, all executing as one unit making yardage for service. Seven strong [blocking] waiters and a ground-gaining chef as fullback with his assistants running perfect interference, in properly timed sequence."[79]

Raleigh Mull of the Missouri-Kansas-Texas Lines (Katy), in 1954 the first dining-car steward to win the coveted Annual Railway Progress Employees Award, paid tribute to this teamwork in his acceptance speech when he gave personal attention to "the men who make me look good." His comments offer a glimpse of the men behind the service[80]:

"Waiter Earl Anderson, with the Katy some thirty years, originator of the famed 'Roquefort Dressing à la Earl' featured on Katy dining cars [see page 321], World War I veteran, leisure-time fisherman.

"Waiter Tom Johnson, native of San Antonio, with Katy some twenty-eight years; Johnson's imposing appearance has adorned several pieces of advertising promotional literature. In his spare time, he is a dog fancier and dotes on his thoroughbred cocker spaniels.

"Waiter John Brown, twelve-year Katy man, father of three children; Brown's an avid baseball fan, and is perhaps best known for his unfailing good nature.

"Waiter Eldridge Lott, twelve years with the railroad; father of six youngsters, an eager and willing Methodist Church worker, leisure-time pianist 'interested in music of all kinds.'

"Chef Willie Smith, famed up and down the system for his pastry-making abilities; Smith is happiest fashioning the ultra-tasty little 'morning coffee' doughnuts that Katy patrons relish so much, or bringing to perfection another specialty of his—Katy Apple Pie; he's been with the road thirty-one years.

"Second cook William Hadley, native of Stringtown, Oklahoma, Chairman of the Executive Board of the Hotel and Restaurant Employees and Bartenders' Union, deacon in the First Baptist Church of San Antonio, twenty-nine years with the Katy.

"Third cook Nelie Washington, a twelve-year Katy veteran, unceasingly cheerful and cooperative, ardent softball fan; mechanical minded, one of his greatest delights is tinkering with friends' automobiles."

The evolution of the crew and its duties dates from the early practice, when eating houses were the custom, of a brakeman's querying the passengers as to their intention to eat and—for the better run establishments—their food selection. This information he turned over to the conductor, who then wired it ahead to the trackside concessionaire. When food was first served on the train itself, then, it fell to the conductor to manage that additional part of his train's operation. But as the popularity of dining cars spread, as their use increased and as their menus became more complex, as passengers became more exacting, and as receipts and expenses began to fluctuate regardless of the amount of business done due to theft or mismanagement, it became clear the dining car needed its own manager. The position of steward emerged, and required a man who could systematize the work and show "clearly the distribution of all supplies and the results therefrom."[81] And, of course, there was a need for someone on board that knew how to cook for upwards of forty people at one time, a professional familiar with working in a restaurant kitchen. Meanwhile, the brakeman had to be replaced by someone skilled in serving the needs and wishes of people taking their meals—and more suitably dressed for such activity.

Ultimately, as the size and complexity of the dining car increased, the size of its crew came to be determined by balancing the productivity of the

cooks against the ability of the waiters to accommodate the workload. An executive of the Chicago, Burlington & Quincy said, "Our kitchen employees in number must balance with the waiters in the dining room." If a kitchen worker were added, the "weight" would favor the kitchen, creating a shortage of waiters to handle the output. An imbalance favoring waiters would result in their standing about waiting for action from the kitchen. Such calculations were further complicated by the need to factor in anticipated business—light, medium, or heavy—on individual runs. For crewmen, especially less senior employees, the uncertainty over being assigned to a train produced anxiety sometimes accompanied by a sense of humor. A waiter on the Pennsylvania Railroad reported his dream on the matter to Maynard A. Ingram, the executive charged with balancing that railroad's dining-car crews against the number of passengers traveling on any given day: "You was dead, and some of us waiters were the pallbearers. Just as we were taking you up the church steps, your corpse sat up in the coffin and said, 'Boys, there is too many of you on this coffin. Lay a couple off. Six of you can carry me to Glory just as easy as eight can.'"[82]

The crew of the dining car on a first class train of the Baltimore & Ohio Railroad in the 1920s graphically depicts why labor costs were the largest single item in a list of dining car expenses.

But from such needs and considerations the standard crew for a six-section 36- or 48-seat dining car evolved to include a steward, a chef, three cooks, and six waiters. Extending these eleven men-per-car over an entire railroad produced a sizable group of employees. In 1941, the Baltimore & Ohio and its subsidiary, the Alton, operated forty-two large 36-seat dining cars, eight 30-seat cars, eighteen cafe-parlor cars, four cafe-club cars, eleven lounge cars, and nineteen reclining-seat cars with dining facilities, for a total of 102 cars on which food and drink were available for purchase. To operate these cars, the railroad employed 45 stewards, 194 cooks, and 322 waiters.[83]

As the size of dining cars grew, so did the size of the crew. A twin-unit, domed, or hi-level diner required one or two stewards, as many as nine waiters, a permanent pantryman, and perhaps five cooks.

The racial composition of these crews has enabled some to argue that dining cars were among the first integrated workplaces in America. Railroads with a long history of racially mixed crews can make such a claim.

Throughout most of the history of the position, the steward was a white man, often from Europe, always with a background in restaurant management. Chefs and cooks were often mixed, but also occasionally of one race or the other. In 1921, a poll of dining-car superintendents found twelve railroads using white cooks and fifty-one using "coloreds." The New York Central's superintendent said he used "white cooks West, and in the East we use the colored cooks."[84] Yet another variation saw white chefs but black cooks. In waiters, the railroads nearly universally sought "men with black skins and white habits." All these men worked long hours together in close quarters. On those railroads with either long runs or a shortage of dining cars, the crew then slept in the dining car, breaking down the tables and converting the space into sleeping quarters. This unsanitary, not to mention unpleasant, practice continued into the 1940s, when dormitory facilities were added in space taken from a baggage or lounge car.

Why was the work so predominantly the province of black men? Writing in 1917, Joseph Husband, in *The Story of the Pullman Car* observed, "The Pullman Company is today the greatest single employer of colored labor in the world." He continues, with a candor marked by a combination of ego, ignorance, and naivete, that such labor is "trained as a race by years of personal service in various capacities, and by nature adapted faithfully to perform their duties under circumstances which necessitate unfailing good nature, solicitude, and faithfulness. . . . The reputation of the company depends in a large measure on the character of its employees, and particularly in those concerns which render a personal service to the general public is it necessary that the standards of the employees be exceptionally high. Such standards of personal service cannot be quickly developed; they can be achieved only through years of experience and the close personal study of the wide range of requirements of those who are to be served." That this writing may reflect the thinking of Pullman himself is supported by the fact that much of the content of Husband's book echoed a Pullman promotional booklet prepared for the 1893 Columbia Exposition. Further, there is within Husband's book enough frequently repeated praise of Pullman as "a man of genius, vision, untiring energy, etc.," to mark it as a company-sponsored paean to its founder.[85]

Another theory offered on the predominance of black employees, especially as dining-car waiters, is that among all others working in the food-service industry of the time, even recent immigrants, dining-car service was scorned. This was because the waiter of a dining car performed more than one task. He was a waiter, but he may also have been the busboy, the pantry cleanup man, or the one designated to clean silver. Such practices occurred in the kitchen as well, where at a minimum the fry cook also did dishes. Such crossover job duties, which included chores often relegated to unskilled workers in hotels and restaurants, were considered beneath the station of restaurant help.

On many railroads, attention was paid not just to the race of the crew member, but to the fine points of his coloration. Several railroads boasted of their rule that the black men employed on their dining cars "must be of the same shade of color, and as near the same size as possible, in every car." On some other railroads, the desire to convey uniformity in the waiters' appearance reached further insensitive depths. A steward for the New York Central reported that on his railroad's best trains, "Down at headquarters they try to put the same kinds of niggers in a squad. Medium mulattoes go in one car, tall blacks in another. It sort of helps dress the car in a uniform fashion."[86]

A less harsh explanation for blacks working on dining cars in such large numbers lies in the fact that, for many who worked on the railroad in any capacity, the most frequent means of securing a job was through friends who worked for a railroad and knew it to be hiring. Such a procedure, occurring in an America that was legally segregated and more prejudiced than today, would explain the continuation of the practice if not its inception. And because promotion came through current employees' bidding on a seniority basis for jobs at a higher level, once a man got a job with a railroad, he tended to stay.

And there were a number of attractive reasons why men wanted to work on the railroad. The pay was comparatively good. For those skilled in work on the dining car there was job security and the chance to earn extra income through tips and by assignment to private cars and special trains. There was the opportunity to travel. Perhaps most important, there was "the pass," a card entitling the railroad employee, and often his family, to free or reduced-fare travel on the employing line and on most others as well.

In hiring and supervising dining-car workers, health and sanitation were primary concerns. Railroads operated under the prevailing sanitation guideline that ninety percent of communicable diseases could be transmitted by food. Each prospective employee was first thoroughly examined for general health and such defects as a wart on the hand or part of a finger missing, which could ruin one's prospects for a job as a waiter. Once employed, regular health inspections—on some railroads monthly, but more often every two, three, or six months—helped protect passengers from even the remote possibility of contagion. Medical facilities in the commissary—the New York Central's commissary included a com-

plete emergency room—served to examine cooks and waiters and to treat injured workers.

New men were then trained thoroughly before joining a crew on a train. For Illinois Central Superintendent N. L. Patterson, it was important that "every member of the dining-car crew [be] trained to remember that the most personal thing about a guest is his appetite."[87] "Service doesn't just happen. . . . stewards must be educated in ordering, their orders checked by the commissary, and both stewards and waiters trained to quick, efficient service and the fact they will have to cater to moods as well as appetites of passengers, some of whom have never eaten in a dining car before."[88] Complaints were not tolerated. Two complaints from patrons, unless the complainer was known as a grouch, meant a man would be out looking for a new job. Classroom instruction covered all procedures to be followed throughout the dining car for the duration of its assignment to a train. Special emphasis was placed on an indoctrination on the standards of cleanliness of person, food, and equipment in effect on the employing railroad. Advanced training took place in old dining cars converted for classroom use and parked near the headquarters' commissary. Cooks and waiters alike were drilled in all aspects of food service under simulated dining-car operating conditions.

A class of Illinois Central cooks observe the art of carving in a simulated dining car that is their classroom. Employees had to go through three four-hour class sessions in the dining-car department's "school on wheels" before they made their first run, regardless of their experience elsewhere. (COURTESY OF THE ASSOCIATION OF AMERICAN RAILROADS)

Training continued on the road. Posters such as those proclaiming "This Month's Sanitation Pointers" were distributed, covering the proper handling of dishes, glassware, and silver; the protection of foods; control of flies and insects; the proper use of equipment; the washing and sanitizing of utensils; the care of personal health, and the like. Instruction cars toured the system to acquaint the men with new procedures, standards, and menu items. John Crawford, some of whose recipes are found on pages 223-229, became a traveling chef for the Illinois Central and was responsible for teaching new tricks and recipes to fifty-five students scattered across that line's 6,500-mile system.

Training for cooks was marked by rigid inspections, constant supervision, continual menu-planning, and increasingly skilled selection of quality foods. To perform well enough to succeed as a chef took determination. One's career began as a "fry cook," with actual cooking experience limited to simple fry dishes. A promotion introduced the aspirant to vegetable dishes and the frying not delegated to the fry cook or limited to the chef. Only when a man became skilled in preparing all the dishes of the railroad, including baking and pastry-making, did he become a chef. It often took as many as a dozen years to be adequately trained to serve as a dining-car chef, and that rapid a climb assumed no obstacle, such as unavailable positions. Texas & Pacific Chef Eddie Pierce was noteworthy for his meteoric climb to the top rung—in just three years.

More than one superintendent emphasized that what counted most in the intricate task of operating their dozens of moving restaurants was discipline. Clean and rigid rules, accompanied by swift and certain punishment for infractions, they would say, were all that kept a machine made up of dozens of stewards and hundreds of cooks and waiters from breaking down. The division of labor paralleled this thinking.

The steward ran the dining car. As a result, he had a number of duties to perform. He had to order the proper supplies; be able to make out both a table d'hote and an à la carte menu; judge portions as legitimate; render courteous and proper service in a businesslike manner; dispense information on train schedules, connections, and hotel or entertainment prospects at a moment's notice; compute checks, count money, and make change; tabulate and report on the financial and gastronomic details of his trip; and promote fairness and maintain discipline among his crew—all with propriety, precision, and a neverending smile. Regular patrons came to expect the steward to know the cut, thickness, method, and time for broiling their steaks. Many railroads provided the steward with uncirculated currency with which to make change, complicating the money-handling.[89] And when he was between meals in the dining car, he was often called on to serve tea to the ladies passing time in the Pullman lounge car.

From passenger railroading's earliest days, rail-roads sought the services of leading chefs to create menu items for their dining cars. As early as 1842, for example, the renowned Mr. Barnum of Baltimore's City Hotel prepared meals for the Baltimore & Ohio Railroad's "refectory cars." The Union Pacific acquired its early recipes from the St. Francis Hotel in San Francisco. The Southern Pacific publicly em-phasized the role of Paul Reiss as their super-vising chef, and he and his recipes were fea-tured in national magazines of the 1920s. The recipes commissioned by the Chesapeake & Ohio for its post-World War II trains were the work of Michael DeZutter, a chef famous at the Chrysler Club. The work and creations of these men were promoted through the dis-tribution of recipe booklets and cards to pas-sengers, and by providing recipes and profiles to employee magazines and the leading food and women's service magazines of the day. No chef was more famous, even before he joined a railroad, than George Rector. Retained as Di-rector of Dining Car Cuisine in the fall of 1928 by the Chicago, Milwaukee, St. Paul & Pacific Railroad, Rector brought with him a lifetime of accomplishment and international stature as a restauranteur and chef.

George Rector was noted for his French cuisine, but took pride in his family's dis-tinctly American roots and success. His

*Mr. Geo. Rector
Director of Cuisine
The Milwaukee Road*

The finishing touch to fine service

**Dinner
by RECTOR**

Everybody knows of George Rector!

Readers of the Saturday Evening Post fol-lowed him weekly through the delightful chapters of "The Girl from Rector's" and "A Cook's Tour".

Countless Americans—and distinguished persons from other lands—have happy re-collections of his reign at Rector's, for years the brightest spot on brilliant Broadway. His fame is world-wide; his skill and genius hailed wherever the mastery of cuisine is concerned.

Mr. Rector now is director of The Milwau-kee Road's newly-created department of cuisine. A departure in dining car service— the acquisition of the master hand to direct cuisine. Yet not surprising on The Milwau-kee Road where dining cars command the best and where 656 miles of electrification, silent roller bearings, coil spring mattresses and a host of other features contribute to the comfort and pleasure of our patrons.

The **MILWAUKEE**
ELECTRIFIED OVER THE
ROCKIES TO THE SEA **ROAD**

Through advertisements such as this, the Milwaukee Road promoted its acquisition of George Rector as Director of Cuisine. (COURTESY OF THE MILWAUKEE ROAD COLLECTION OF THE MILWAUKEE PUBLIC LIBRARY)

grandfather founded "the famous Frontier House," which catered to French, English, and American woodsmen and trappers, as well as Indians, along the Niagara River in 1845. The business was moved to Lockport, New York, along the Erie Canal, where his father, Charles, was born. Charles worked as a caterer for Pullman in Chicago after the Civil War. George would claim his father had been in charge of the first Pullman dining car to go coast to coast as part of the three-week-long Boston Board of Trade excursion to California in 1877, on a train actually made up of hotel cars.[1]

Charles subsequently opened a restaurant in Chicago in 1884, and another in New York in

1889. It was in New York, at Rector's, Broadway, where son George's fame grew. A frequent traveler to Europe, George was sought after by cafe owners in Paris and Vienna. He wrote regularly for the *Saturday Evening Post* and compiled a number of popular cookbooks, eventually earning the Cordon Bleu and membership in La Societe des Cuisiniers de Paris.[2]

Upon joining the Milwaukee Road, Rector set to work instructing its chefs. He organized a school in a specially fitted instruction car and demonstrated there and in the commissary in Chicago how to carry out "recipes that only he is capable of executing properly." The railroad's publicity claimed for Mr. Rector that he was "the most distinguished man in the world in his particular line of endeavor" and that his restaurant was famous "without a rival during its long period of existence," then gleefully pointed out that "he is applying his genius to an entirely different field." Passengers were assured that "every week Mr. Rector will place a few of his choicest preparations on the regular menu, and you will be sure to find that a tomato is no longer just a humble solanaceae on the Milwaukee Road dining cars."[3]

The impact George Rector had on ridership was apparent and appreciated along the route of the Milwaukee Road. In a speech before the Seattle Chamber of Commerce in 1929, he acknowledged this when he proclaimed that, instead of lamenting the loss of two Rector restaurants to prohibition, people had cause for celebration as, now, sixty Rector's were open for business—all inside the dining cars of the Chicago, Milwaukee, St. Paul & Pacific Railroad. Loud applause from the audience dramatically demonstrated the importance of food to the trains and of the trains to the cities. The comment also supports the claim that dining cars were the nation's first fast-food chains.[4]

Even after Rector left the Milwaukee Road sometime in the 1930s, the line continued to serve his dishes and to distribute his 1928 self-published book, *The Rector Cookbook,* with the reminder "Compliments of the Milwaukee Road." Here is found the rationale motivating

railroad managements throughout America to lure the best chefs to work for their dining-car departments: "The difference between a good chef and a famous chef lies in the individuality of his dishes; and the difference between a good train and a famous train lies in the individuality of its service. . . . Care in the perfection of details is the chief 'ingredient' in our recipe for making the Milwaukee Road trains famous."

George Rector imparts his "secrets of the culinary art," acquired here and abroad, to the chefs of the Milwaukee Road for use in the railroad's dining cars. (COURTESY OF THE MILWAUKEE ROAD COLLECTION OF THE MILWAUKEE PUBLIC LIBRARY)

The steward attending to patrons of a forty-eight-seat diner on the streamliner City of St. Louis. (COURTESY OF THE ASSOCIATION OF AMERICAN RAILROADS)

The steward was often the bartender, and so had to be familiar with mixed drinks. He had to keep track of where along the line a drink or a meal was ordered and consumed. Such things determined which state collected the liquor or sales tax. If a traveler ordered his meal and ate it while his train was still in Arizona, he was charged Arizona's sales tax. But if he still had a sip of coffee left after crossing into California, he enriched that state's coffers. The steward also had to keep track of boundaries separating "wet" states from "dry." In the latter, it was necessary to lock and seal the liquor supply so that no one could get at it.

All of this while suffering the hardships associated with the work: long hours, heat, fatigue, and the need to deal with the hard-to-please. A steward on the Santa Fe's *Chief* and *Super Chief* described the extremes this last might reach. The man, a regular passenger, had seven rules he made known to all who served him: 1) Don't call him by his name; 2) Have the waiter appear at his table promptly at 5:00 P.M. to present the menu; 3) Serve him his meal exactly thirty minutes later; 4) Bring all his dishes, from soup to dessert, at one time; 5) Let him eat alone at the last table-for-two in the car—positively no one is to sit opposite him; 6) The waiter is to neither stand too close by nor watch him eat; and 7) His bread is to be toasted on one side only.[90]

In such a position, perception was one key to a steward's success. If, by his behavior, a patron demonstrated he was unfamiliar with dining-car meals—on the Boston & Maine "it was the practice to put a slice of lemon in the finger bowls, and it was by no means an infrequent experience to see a patron calmly put sugar in the bowl and drink the 'lemonade'"[91]— the steward must watch over him, guide him to his seat, lay the right spoon before him just as he needs it, and perform other kindly acts to avoid or relieve nervousness or embarrassment, or perceive when a patron simply wants to be left alone with his thoughts.[92]

Experience and a proper attitude were the other prerequisites for success. Men with experience in clubs and hotels, who had worked as waiters, headwaiters, and stewards, and who could cater to the most fastidious gourmand, were eagerly sought for the position. On attitude, one influential steward remarked, "I tried to make my attitude toward the traveling public like the attitude a host would have in his own home." Greet them cordially. Give the ladies the most comfortable chairs. Place ashtrays near the men. Serve a lunch as nicely as your facilities allowed. Say "So soon?" to those who wish to leave early. "The more unexpected their calls were the more you would appreciate their coming, for they came out of desire and not invitation."[93]

The Chef, meanwhile, is the "'Captain of the Kitchen' and is head of all kitchen employees on the train," declared R. W. Burford, superintendent of dining-car service on the Texas & Pacific Railroad. From his position "in the hole" by the serving window through to the pantry, the chef's constant attention was on food preparation, "be it boiling, broiling, frying, stewing, sautéing, blanching, braising, basting, roasting, baking, or what not, until the food has passed from the raw material through the various stages of the culinary art to choice appetizing dishes properly garnished and ready for the waiters' service."[94] In addition, the chef was to make the soups, salads, and sauces; carve raw and cooked meats; bake pastries and breads; and run the broiler when preparing fish, steaks, chops, or poultry.

"If there is any 'trick of the trade' at all, it's with spices. A good cook has a 'nose for seasoning.' Every top chef I know is an expert at seasoning foods," said Chef Pierce of the Texas & Pacific. "The training and years of experience combined to give the impression that the chefs, and others working under his supervision in the kitchen were 'natural born cooks.'" For Pierce, interest in cooking began early. Born in College Station, Texas, he was a frequent playmate of the children of Texas A & M University's future president, Frank Bolton. "When Mrs. Bolton would go out, she would ask me to mind her cooking; to add this or that, turn the fire down or off at a certain time. I was curious. I often ask[ed] Mrs. Bolton about cooking. She was the person who started my interest in it."

The second cook, from the opposite end of the kitchen, was the chef's assistant. He was to take care of short orders, such as cooking pancakes; sausage, ham and bacon; eggs and omelets; and stews. He often cooked the simpler entrees; baked breads, pastries, and desserts; and assisted in operating the broiler. He was also expected to assist the third cook and, during the off hours, clean and maintain the range and broiler. At the commissary, the second cook helped check out groceries and supplies, as-

"The first cook, nearest the pantry window, is the absolute monarch of his spotless, swift-moving little domain." C. H. Shircliffe, Supt., Dining and Parlor Car Service, Chicago & North Western Railroad. (COURTESY OF GREAT NORTHERN RAILWAY COMPANY RECORDS, MINNESOTA HISTORICAL SOCIETY)

Item #2 among thirty-six pages of the Southern Pacific Company's General Instructions Covering Service by Waiters in Dining and Café Cars reminds waiters: "Before each meal announcement waiters should make a check of their personal appearance. . . . Put on a clean and fresh coat and apron before each meal. If they become soiled during serving of [a] meal, make a change with as little delay as possible." This Great Northern Railway waiter is modeling the uniform designed specifically for those working on The Empire Builder.

sisted the pantryman load them onto the car, then put away what went into the kitchen.

For the third cook, on trains which operated overnight, the day started at 4:30 A.M. when he was in the kitchen to start the fires. The rest of the crew joined him at 5:00 A.M. His duties as cook included preparing cold foods, such as cereals; side dishes, such as baked apples, toast, and vegetables; and general frying. Standing between the second cook and the chef, he arranged side dishes on the plate before it went forward to the chef for the main item, and lent a hand to the fourth cook as necessary.

Standing next to the chef, the fourth cook's main task was to wash the dishes, pots, pans, and kitchen utensils, and clean up the kitchen floor. Approximately 1,000 dishes of all kinds had to be washed during a single meal by this one man at a sink less than two feet square. He peeled potatoes and took care of the fires, then disposed of the ashes and garbage. On occasion, he helped the third cook complete his duties.

Describing his work, Chef George Fulton of the B & O said, "You had to be an acrobat to work in the dining-car kitchen. Your legs would go one way and your stomach the other from the movement of the car, but you had to maintain your concentration. Quite often you'd be working on fifteen to thirty dinner or breakfast orders at one time, and you had to hold onto your wits. We were out to make the [passengers'] meals aboard the B&O memorable, and if a passenger complained, which was seldom, he was given a new order. We worked all the time. If we weren't preparing for meals we were cleaning the car, since the health department kept a close eye on our dining cars which, I believe, were the cleanest in the railroad business."[95]

He was helped by an intimate knowledge of the roadbed he traveled so frequently. The sway of the train and the feel of the track told crew members where they were. "When we hit the Reading crossover at Bound Brook, New Jersey," Chef Fulton said, "I knew I had forty-five minutes to finish up whatever meal we were serving. Going into Cincinnati there are twenty-three tunnels, and when we began whistling and blowing, I knew I had to have certain things finished. It's something you get used to."[96]

THE LANGUAGE OF DINING-CAR PERSONNEL

One of the most picturesque aspects of dining-car lore is the strange and unique language employed by those who worked the cars. Often a code to enable communication with each other to the ignorance of those outside the service, it is also a perfect example of how jargon can offer succinct summary. Expressions applied to passengers, to the equipment, to each other, and to the food.

The Passengers:

a cook's load: a train with very few people on board, fewer yet of whom ate in the dining car.

crew's portion: a double order of food.

for Nellie: on some railroads, another name for room service.

going upstairs: when a waiter goes to serve food someplace other than in the dining car, either room service or to pass through the coaches with a tray of sandwiches and beverages.

a lamb's tongue: a generous tip, usually anything from one dollar up.

the hard way: a signal from the waiter to the steward on how to make change for a troublesome passenger. If fifty cents in change was due, the steward would give the victim a fifty-cent piece, practically forcing the customer to leave the whole fifty cents as a tip.

the easy way: when the steward would leave a quarter, two dimes and a nickel as the fifty-cent change for cooperative passengers.

snake: someone who doesn't leave a tip, as in, "That snake bit me," or "The snakes are eating me up tonight."

bread: a signal that a woman was around.

cake: the opinion that the woman is extra fine.

whole wheat bread: a woman of light brown coloring.

white bread: a white woman.

burnt toast: an ugly woman or one who is very black.

The Equipment:

feed box or pie wagon: a dining car.

struggle buggy: an old dining car.

smoke wagon: a dining car in a train pulled by a steam locomotive.

flat: a dining car that is completely filled.

forty-eight flat and standing: all forty-eight seats in a modern diner were filled and other customers were waiting.

a deuce: table for two.

a large: table for four.

flattened out: a waiter whose deuce and large were filled with customers.

top table: the table section nearest the pantry.

bottom table: the table section furthest from the pantry.

the dresser: the kitchen counter where vegetables were prepared and added to the plates.

the hole: the opening between the kitchen and the pantry where orders were handed to the chef and food was passed to the waiters.

watching television: doing dishes in a dishwasher with a glass window.

the dog house: the main refrigerator, where beef was stored.

tin can: buffet-parlor cars.

eyes: the block signals that control train movements.

possum belly: an area under the dining-car floor where extra coal for the stove, or bedding for the crew, was carried.

The Personnel:

attention please: an expression waiters used to warn other waiters they were about to come through with a full tray.

the captain: the train's conductor.

gone up a tree: A waiter flustered and making errors. This one was immortalized by a training film, "Don't Go Up a Tree," for waiters.

doggie: a waiter who is not feeling well and is, thus, dragging his chain.

gold-bricking: taking some time off.

greased: to get paid.

get my rug beat: to get a hair cut.

being put on the boss's desk: a waiter who has been written up by the steward for some violation.

switch: a warning one waiter would issue to another to stop talking, because someone was listening.

soup run: being assigned to handle a nearby run on a buffet-parlor car, serving soups, sandwiches, coffee, and the like.

tubbing: what a waiter who refuses to share his tips is doing.

one-stepping: the unique shuffle used by waiters to slide around the three sides of the pantry to pick up bread, butter, and other finishing details of their service. Adapted from traffic cops dodging traffic, it enabled waiters to alternately come in and to go out of the pantry, and to keep out of each other's way while still moving continuously.

upstairs man, or **swing man:** a waiter put on heavily traveled trains at mealtime, he did not serve food but generally made himself useful by changing linen, clearing tables, filling water glasses and butter dishes, and the like.

mule: the waiter assigned to also clean up the pantry or do other dirty work, usually the newest man in the car.

pearl-diver: the fourth cook, whose duties included washing the dishes and pots, pans, and kitchen utensils.

Mr. Green: the newest man on a crew, also referred to as "young blood."

THE FOOD:

stump: an economy meal.

AP yellow-capped and hot: hot apple pie with cheese.

society grass: salad.

hog's hips and cackleberries: bacon and eggs.

nervous Liz: gelatin.

poor boy: a ham sandwich. A "poor boy walkin'" was a take-out ham sandwich.

shorty white-capped and juicy: strawberry shortcake with whipped cream.

And lest it be concluded that such language was limited to those working on dining cars, consider this exchange at a station eating house:

A timid-looking little man took a seat at the counter of a railroad eating house and ordered ham and eggs. He looked bewildered when the waiter turned his face toward the kitchen and yelled vociferously, "A mogul with two headlights!" A second later the little man said: "Beg pardon, sir, but I'd like to have those eggs turned over." "Blanket the headlights!" yelled the waiter. An engineer next took his seat at the counter. "Wheat cakes and coffee for mine," he said. "Running orders!" yelped the waiter briskly, and turned to confront the next one. "A beefsteak, well done," said the latest arrival. "A hot-box, and have it smoking!" was the information given to the cook. "Some scrambled eggs, please," piped an old lady with trepidation. The waiter turned around and yelled: "Wreck 'em on the mainline!" A boomer brakeman noisily set down his lamp and mounted one of the stools. "Let's see yer switch list," he commanded. "Gimme a couple of battleships and a pan of Murphys on the mainline and a string of flats on the siding," he ordered. It was the waiter's turn to look mystified. "Cut the cowcar off the Java train," continued the boomer, "and switch me a couple of life-preservers for a consolidation, and as it's a long drag to the next feed tank, you better fill the auxiliary to its full capacity." "Say," interrupted the biscuit shooter, "I've only been here a week you left me behind at the first stop." "Excuse me," apologized the boomer, "I thought you were an old head. Gimme a couple of pork chops and some fried potatoes, and a side order of wheat cakes. Then, for the second course, you can bring me a cup of black coffee and some doughnuts. Fill up the lunch basket, too, because it's a long drag to the next hash factory. Put the coffee in the bottom and fill the upper deck with sandwiches and pie." "I got you, Steve," replied the waiter.[6]

Waiters, too, learned tricks that made it look easy for them to walk gracefully down a narrow aisle in a swaying car, carefully balancing a heavily loaded tray. "Well, try it some time," said Boston & Maine waiter James E. "Jimmy" Binns. "It takes long years of practice to do that. The best waiter in the biggest hotel in the country would be lost if he tried to work in a diner. . . . Every muscle is ready to act, involuntarily, whenever anything threatens to throw us off balance. And even when a passenger, passing through the car, bumps against us unexpectedly, we are prepared for it. Just walking through a car [going through] a curve at sixty miles an hour is more than some people can accomplish; but we've got to do it with a heavy tray in our hands, or keep our balance when we're pouring coffee into a patron's cup. You simply learn how, that's all; I can't tell you how it's done."[97] He would also inaudibly alert others to his presence. As he faced a table, he spread his feet apart, and, with an imperceptible move, pressed his weight into the tabletop. He learned to pour from a stretch, so the dramatic gesture of rising the coffee pot high above the cup while pouring actually improved accuracy.

The duties of the dining-car waiters were spelled out, often on a printed schedule posted in the pantry. Each man had specific duties to perform and was held to strict account in performing them. Typical of those duties are these from the Illinois Central Railroad:[98]

The first, or chief, waiter was also known as the pantry man. He ran the pantry and thus was responsible for the care and storage of the milk, cream, ice cream, butter, bread, cheese, and any fruits or vegetables used as relishes. He made sure the dry stores—salt, pepper, sugar, and other condiments—were ready for immediate use by all the waiters. In the pantry, the waiters placed their orders with the chef and received their dishes. Here, drinks, salads, and bread platters were prepared and garnishes and other finishing touches applied to the meals before service. In the pantry also, there being no extra hand, each waiter washed his own dirty salad and bread dishes and replaced them in their racks. In addition to insuring the pantry items were ready for the other waiters, the chief waiter waited on the first compartment, the two tables nearest the pantry.

The second waiter served the second compartment, but also cleaned the large silver hollow ware, kept the buffet gleaming and properly decorated, mopped the walkway along the kitchen, took care of orders going to the cars (unless there was an "upstairs" man on board), and helped inventory and maintain supplies.

The third waiter waited on the six or eight people eating in the third compartment and took care of the linen, replacing tablecloths, tabletops, and napkins, and counting, bagging, and tagging dirty linen to be left off at points along the line for return to the laundry. He also looked after any curtains or drapes and saw to it the breads were kept warm.

The fourth waiter attended to the fourth compartment and sorted and polished the silverware and returned it to its storage compartment. He swept the carpeting, dusted, and took care of general cleaning.

A fifth waiter worked the fifth compartment and cleaned and filled the salt and pepper shakers, sugar bowls, and vinegar and oil cruets or salad-dressing containers.

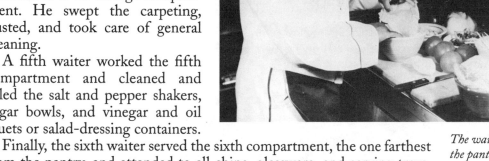

The waiter's duties in the pantry. (COURTESY OF GREAT NORTHERN RAILWAY COMPANY RECORDS)

Finally, the sixth waiter served the sixth compartment, the one farthest from the pantry, and attended to all china, glassware, and serving trays, cleaned and brightened the dining compartment's center aisle, and kept the refrigerated storage bins at his end of the car clean.

Restauranteur George Rector felt the waiters deserved the highest acclaim. "Praise the dining-car waiter," he said a few years after leaving the Milwaukee Road as director of cuisine. "He turns out a wonderful job compared to other waiters. He has no service table, no omnibus, he works in small quarters and does all well."[99] W. F. Ziervogel, superintendent of dining and parlor cars for the Missouri Pacific Railroad, backed the work of all his men with the observation that, "it is a pretty generally accepted fact that no other employees of a railroad, with the possible exception of conductors, enjoy such intimate contact with the traveling public as do we of the dining-car service."[100] It was estimated that W. E. Meagher, in the thirty-five years he spent in the capacity of dining-car steward on the Great Northern, came into contact with over a million guests.[101] As a result, it was not uncommon for regular patrons of trains or routes to know the dining-car crew by name. More noteworthy, such patrons often sought out particular crews as part of their travel plans. The key, of course, was either the steward, known for his ability to manage a crew—"I need a bedroom on *The Texas Special* to St. Louis," a San Antonio passenger agent for the Missouri-Kansas-Texas Lines reported hearing often, "anytime of the week is fine, just so long as it's a day when Raleigh Mull is in charge of the diner."[102]—or the chef, known for his specialty concoctions or his ability to "personalize" standard menu items.

"Service Second to None"

More than one steward or chef claimed his dining car offered "service second to none." Just how good did that mean the service had to be aboard dining cars? These three incidents offer a clue.

First, from Paul Reiss, supervising chef of the Southern Pacific dining-car system in 1926: "One morning last spring a man stepped into a dining car on the *Overland Limited.* Everything about his appearance smacked of precision, and the first words he spoke were quite in keeping with the general impression:

'Steward, I wonder if your chefs know how to boil a three-minute egg?' he asked as he took a seat. 'I'm very, very particular. If my eggs are boiled thirty seconds longer than three minutes they are spoiled for me.'

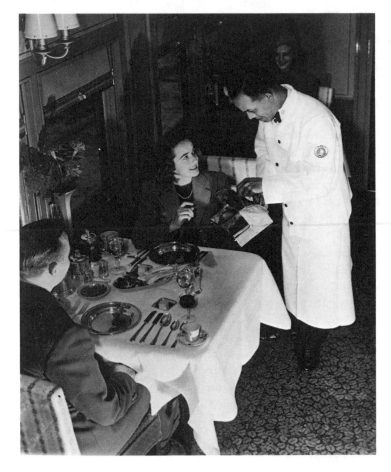

The proper methods of serving the public were often as Emily Post said they should be.
(PHOTOGRAPH BY WILLIAM BULL, COURTESY OF GREAT NORTHERN RAILWAY COMPANY RECORDS, MINNESOTA HISTORICAL SOCIETY)

'I'll guarantee you absolute satisfaction,' said the steward, 'provided you will tell me where you live.'

'Why, I live in San Francisco.'

The steward handed the man an order card. 'When you write down the three-minute eggs, underscore them,' he said. 'I'll speak to the chef.'

In due time the waiter took the order card. 'I want the eggs first,' the passenger said. Four minutes went by and the man called the waiter to his table.

'Where are the three-minute eggs?' he asked.

With a quick 'Yessir' the

waiter rushed to the kitchen. But he returned, without the eggs. 'Up in this country it takes five minutes for a three-minute egg!' he explained.

'What! Send the steward here!'

The steward was right there in three or four strides.

'What's this waiter trying to do, kid me?' demanded the passenger. 'He says it takes five minutes for a three-minute egg!'

'It does,' said the steward. 'That's why I had you underscore your order, so I could identify it. Let me explain: Look here on this timetable and see where we are. Just leaving Summit, California. Notice the elevation of Summit, 7,018 feet. We're coming down all the time now, and at present we're about 6,800 feet up. Now, down in San Francisco where you live, the boiling point is about 212 degrees, because San Francisco is practically at sea level. But up here, where the atmosphere is lighter, the boiling point is only about 199 degrees! So, you can see, it takes longer to boil a three-minute egg here than it does in San Francisco.'"[1]

Next, from William B. Plummer, a passenger aboard the *Twentieth Century Limited*, who wrote *Gourmet* in 1963 to refine a point made in an earlier article about dining service on that train: "My complaint," wrote Mr. Plummer, "is that you did not mention my favorite steward by the name of Burns. You also failed to mention one of the longtime specialities of the *Century* diners, which was lobster Newburg on toasted cornbread. The reason I bring this up is to exemplify the service that the *Century* used to perform. One night I got on the train and wanted this special lobster, but it wasn't on the menu. So I spoke to Burns about my problem and pointed out that there was cold lobster on the menu so that the chef at least had a starting point. Burns said it would be arranged but that it might take a little time. So I had a drink and waited for some minutes, when Burns finally came back and reassured me that it was in the works but would take a few minutes longer. So I had another drink and waited a bit, and ultimately Burns came back with the lobster Newburg on toasted cornbread and apologized for the delay. It seems that while they had the lobster, there was no cornbread in the galley so they had been forced to make a pan of fresh cornbread, cook it, and then toast an appropriate amount in order to fill my order."[2]

Finally, this account from the Illinois Central Railroad of the experience of a little girl traveling with her family on the railroad's Chicago-to-Miami *Floridian* in 1930: "Tomorrow's my birthday," she confided to a ticket agent as her father was buying the family's tickets for Florida. The next day at luncheon on the *Floridian*, suddenly there appeared a huge birthday cake with ten candles on it. "Why, even the railroad knows I'm ten," she exclaimed in delighted amazement. The fact that the ticket agent had a daughter, as did the dining-car steward, prompted them to arrange for the extra attention that made this trip memorable for the youngster.

The hazards of working in a small space, in close proximity to others, with sharp, hard, and/or hot materials, while moving at the rate of sixty miles-per-hour in circumstances given to sudden changes, are apparent in this picture of cooks at work. (COURTESY OF THE MILWAUKEE ROAD COLLECTION OF THE MILWAUKEE PUBLIC LIBRARY)

Of all people working on a passenger train, indeed, of trainmen in general, the dining-car crew worked longer hours, often 6:00 A.M. to midnight, and covered more mileage than all the rest. It is not altogether surprising, then, that they occasionally performed at less than peak efficiency. What is surprising is that injuries did not appear to result in the proportion one might expect from the combination of a hazardous workplace, intense demands, and long hours that made up the crew's environment.

Injuries suffered were, for the most part, to be expected among workers in eating establishments. In a three-year period, the New York, New Haven & Hartford Railroad recorded thirty-nine injuries. Among the eight burn victims were four burned by grease, including a second cook whose sleeve caught on a ladle in hot grease, causing the grease to pour over his right hand and induce second-degree burns. The other four burns resulted from spills, including one on a fourth cook whose feet were burned when a pot of hot soup fell from the board. Rough starts and stops or sudden swaying injured five, including a waiter thrown so badly off balance that his right arm went through a window, severely cutting his wrist. Another thirteen people experienced cuts caused by such things as dishes breaking, knives slipping or falling, or, in one case, a coffee pot exploding. A cook, pulling a basket of supplies through the side door of a dining car, strained his back, one of three such injuries. Fractures included an ankle broken from missing a step while de-training and a left hand broken by a falling broiler. Two men experienced puncture wounds, one when a nail protruding from the floorboard went through the ball of his foot, the other when a broken hook penetrated the middle finger on his right hand. Other incapacitating injuries included three sprained ankles (two on one man who slipped getting off the car) and a bruised hand and knee. One unfortunate fourth cook struck his left thumb on a lobster shell, causing a cut which became infected. And, from a hazard perhaps unique to those working around dining cars, a commissary employee was temporarily disabled when a several-hundred-pound piece of ice being loaded into the roof of the dining car slipped off and struck his right leg.

Data from the Texas & Pacific Railroad for the same period places dining-car injuries within the context of injuries to railroad employees in general. In an eight-month period, the personal-injury record in the Dining Car Department, as one of twenty departments reporting, was:

DATE	RANK	# OF PERSONAL INJURIES	# OF REPORTABLE INJURIES	RATIO MAN-HOURS
12/45	16	8	4	49.14
1/46	5	2	0	0.00
2/46	7	4	2	14.27
3/46	7	5	1	15.38
4/46	7	4	1	16.39
5/46	5	1	0	0.00
6/46	4	2	1	18.38
7/46	5	4	2	34.66

In the execution of their duties, the men and women of each railroad's dining-car department strove to deliver an unforgettable experience for the passenger. When the varied and complex duties attached to each facet of the operation were assembled as a whole, when one witnessed the run of a dining car, one couldn't help but be impressed. "If the system is perfect," Illinois Central Superintendent Patterson said, "everything will run smoothly."

On returning from a run, the dining car is removed from its train and taken to the commissary. All perishable foods are removed and an inventory is taken of what is left on board. The crew cleans the kitchen, and, if the task wasn't completed earlier, washes the dishes, and polishes every piece of silver. The car is then hauled to the passenger yard, where a cleanup crew washes its exterior down and cleans and scrubs the inside. If, however, it needs to be overhauled or repaired, the car is delivered to the commissary to have all food items, china, kitchen and eating utensils, and linens removed. Then it is taken to the yard and stripped, worked on, and inspected. The trucks and wheels on which the car rides are especially carefully inspected, as their proper functioning assures a ride smooth enough to cook a souffle and prevents the jumps and sways those dining find so inconvenient. When cleaning or an overhaul is completed, the car is ready to be placed back into service.

Meanwhile, as the car sits at the commissary, the steward completes his lengthy supply report to show how much food—staples, canned goods, and perishables—was consumed on the just-completed trip and how much breakage or equipment damage occurred. From this, if the car is not to be shopped for overhaul or repair, a requisition the size of a full sheet of newspaper is made out showing how much of each of the several hundred items is needed to bring the car's materials and supplies back up to the requirements called for by the menu. It is the task of the steward who will take over the car on its next run to complete a similar request for perishable items.

"As Marked As That For Furnacemen"

If passengers described their experience in dining cars in a range from "splendid" to "superior," those working in the cars, especially the men in the kitchen and pantry, no doubt used terms extending to the other extreme of the spectrum. Consider a 1915 survey by the director of the Division on Occupational Diseases of the United States Public Health Service, entitled "Report of Industrial Health Hazards." He investigated working conditions on four nearly identical railway dining cars from three manufacturers. The director backed up his claim that "the chief hazard was the exposure to extreme heat. . . . as marked as that for furnacemen or mill hands employed in an iron and steel works," by noting the following hellish conditions:

> The temperature is favored by a number of factors. First, there are hot stoves and ovens extending along one side of the narrow kitchen for a distance of twelve feet, and heated

by coal, coke, or charcoal. These are equipped with heat-confining hoods, which come down about to the level of the head or a little lower. Up beneath the hoods are located shelves for warming purposes. Second, the spaces between the stoves and the sinks, tables and cabinets opposite are so narrow—only a matter of about three feet—that three men are kept very close to the main source of heat. Third, the roof overhead is practically full of obstructive piping and two long horizontal tanks, one containing hot water, which was not covered with insulation or other protective covering, and consequently helps to add in the heating of the quarters. The other is a cold-water tank which, however, from its close proximity to the other tank, and location of the ovens, usually gets hot, and further helps to radiate heat. Fourth, where the roadbeds are at all dusty, it is necessary to keep the windows practically closed, and on account of railway smoke. The same applies to the narrow window ventilators in the roofs. It was also stated that orders were issued prohibiting the opening of the door into the vestibule. This was due to several reasons, such as the liability of passengers to mistake the entrance into the kitchen for the entrance into the dining cars, the desire for privacy for the workers, and the liability of theft, etc. In one instance the door contained a screened window which helped a little in promoting ventilation, but it was too small and placed too high, it being on a level with the head. Otherwise the vestibule was closed up solidly. Fifth, the window spaces, which were on one side only, when open were so small, narrow, and high placed that they would admit but very little air, and the screen meshing used was so fine that this also hindered greatly. It was also pointed out that in the case of a wreck these men were likely to be caught in quarters from which they could not escape, because of the jamming of the only doorway present and the fact that the window openings were too small for a man to get out of. Sixth, a turn in the kitchen required from two to four hours, according to the number of dining-car 'calls' and the number of passengers to be served. During this time all workers were constantly busy and usually there was considerable hurry, so that respites were few. Seventh, workers were under orders not to leave the kitchen during these 'turns.'

It can be seen from the above that all these factors combine to render the exposure to high temperature in a crowded and air-stagnant space very great. Workers, (both colored and white), made great complaint as to the heat, which in addition to profuse perspiration, (which was literally pouring from all of them), caused suffusion and heat dermatitis on the face and skin of the arms, and bloodshot eyes, and unquestionably affected the eyesight, particularly of the chief cook, who necessarily had his face toward the oven the greater part of the time. Wearing of protective eyeglasses was impractical because of soiling with perspiration, smoke, and steam. In one kitchen a thermometer, which the investigator carried, registered 135 degrees, at the level of the head and in the position which the cook occupied. Perspiration also dropped constantly from the arms, face, and head to whatever was below, oftentime including the food being prepared. The impossibility of taking a bath after each 'turn,' and the wearing of sweaty underclothes out in the draft afterwards, were both arch health hazards.

When a dining car is again assigned to a train, notice is sent to the commissary along with the steward's requisition for the perishable and nonperishable items needed to protect his menus for the trip. A commissary crew fills the requisition, picking and placing enough packaged and canned goods to last for a round trip in cases and hampers. Perishable foods—meats, fruit, vegetables, dairy products—are loaded in special watertight hampers and packed in ice. Not until an hour before train departure time is the meat ground to assure freshness. Supplemental supply points in station restaurants along the way stand ready to replenish any stocks running unexpectedly low, one reason why railroads continued to operate station-stop eating houses after dining cars were introduced. As a last resort, the steward is empowered to buy needed foods at local grocery stores. The mark of the efficient crew, however, is to avoid these latter alternatives.

Four or five hours before departure, the car is moved to the commissary. The steward, chef, and pantryman arrive at about the same time to find their requisitioned supplies awaiting them. The steward checks with the passenger department to learn how many passengers are holding tickets, then makes any needed last-minute adjustments in his requisition. Now, with a clerk on one side of the commissary counter and the steward on the other, the order is double-checked to be sure it is complete. The steward signs for the order and it is loaded onto a string of four-wheeled carts and towed by a small tractor to the car.

The rest of the crew reports to find women from the housekeeping department washing down the car's walls and windows, mopping the tile floor, wiping the tables and chairs, and vacuuming the carpet. The car's crew adds the finishing touches to bring the car's cleanliness to its peak. They then help transfer the arriving supplies to the pantries, cabinets, closets, and ice boxes of the car. They are briefed by the steward regarding aspects of the run: expected dignitaries and celebrities, special groups that will be on board, and, on the trains with an experienced crew that works as a unit, any special problems reported from the previous trip.

The car is picked up, placed in its train, and moved into the station to soon take on passengers. As this is going on, the cooks begin their work, roasting meat, baking bread, preparing vegetables and desserts. This enables concentration, once the train is under way, on cooking specific dishes to order, and allows for such incidentals as the occasional passenger who may come on board with game.

The third waiter places mats on the tables and the others help, following with tablecloths and napkins. The second waiter follows, arranging the table's setup, and the fourth waiter finishes by placing the silverware. The pantryman places a fresh bunch of daffodils in each of twelve silver vases and takes them to the tables. A last check by the crew insures that the garbage cans have new liners, the floor is spotless, and their uniforms are unblemished.

In the station, a department inspector comes on board to examine the car and the train's conductor comes through to see that everything is right. For a line's premier trains, a standby dining car awaits to replace any car found wanting. With less than an hour until departure, everything is in readiness. The crew takes a break, sipping coffee before the arrival of passengers launches them on a five-hour work shift.

Even before the train is clear of its originating station, the dining car is apt to be serving patrons. Passengers may board and send the porter to their room with their bags while they head directly to the dining car for a late lunch, as the train sets out, slowly picking up speed. Since the early 1900s, trains with first-class sections accepted advance reservations for dinner. The steward passes through the train, beginning in the Pullman sections, and asks passengers for their preferred seating times. Most trains offered three seatings: 5:00, 6:00, and 7:00 P.M. To ease crowding, some trains offered a "chef's special," a limited menu to be served from 4:15 to 5:00 P.M. Each passenger stated his preference and got a slip with the assigned time, table and seat number on it. Then, when he or she walked into the dining car, a seat was waiting and dinner was served without delay.

Meals in the dining car are often promoted by a waiter in sparkling white coat and apron sent out with pasteboard signs to be hung on a nail at the forward end of each car. One sign announces, "Meals are now being served in the dining car attached to this train. Order what you want. Pay for what you order." In case passengers were sleeping, reading, or gazing out the window during this performance, the waiter returns later to announce the meal and to hand out a neatly printed menu of the day's fare.[103]

As meals are served and patrons move out of the dining cars, the third waiter quickly replaces the linen, the table's waiter arranges the place settings, and the steward ushers another group to their seats. To those who haven't booked a reservation earlier, he hands menus, meal order forms, and pencils. Meanwhile, if the waiter's uniform has become soiled, he goes to the linen closet for a clean coat. He arrives with water for the new diners and offers coffee. The steward returns and collects their reservation tickets or reviews the orders each has written on the meal order form. He tears the top copy off and delivers it to the chef while the waiter returns to memorize the details on the copy left at the table. Passing through the pantry, he assembles the salads and bread basket and returns to the table.

The steward mixes any alcoholic beverages ordered. When the meals are "up," they too are delivered promptly to the table. The attentive waiter knows precisely when to clear the table and deliver dessert. The steward arrives discreetly to collect payment and the diners move on, perhaps to the lounge, to allow the ritual to begin anew.

This rhythm continues throughout each meal at each seating for all the meals to be served while the dining car is accompanying the train. At the evening meal, the last passenger departs at 8:30 P.M. Then the train's crew, the conductor, car attendants, Pullman porters, and brakeman, as well as the dining-car crew, settle down to eat. By 10:00 P.M., their having finished, the car is cleaned, appropriate items secured, and shut down for the night.

Activity to service and restock the car continues throughout the trip. At the first large terminal after a meal, as the train glides to a halt, the fourth cook opens the kitchen door to the passageway and the door across it to the outside and empties the garbage into cans placed on the platform for that purpose. A train servicer pushes a two-wheel enclosed buggy beneath the diner's sink disposal to capture refuse from it. Other train servicers are busy loading ice into the chill boxes and holding receptacles. The sixth waiter gets ice for his refrigerated areas and restocks them. The pantry man ices and salts the ice-cream holding bins and packs the ice down tight. Still another servicer climbs up on the car's roof to fill the large overhead water tanks. With the fourth cook back aboard and the servicers de-trained or clear of the track, the doors are once again secured as the train imperceptibly inches forward on its way.

At longer stopovers where the engine receives service or the schedule calls for a delay, the steward, chef, and pantryman will rush to the commissary, if one exists there, to gather needed food and supplies, complete and sign a requisition, tear off and retain the steward's copy, then load the items onto a pushcart and return to the train. The rest of the crew may run through a service tunnel into the station, out of sight of the passengers, to call their families or buy some needed personal items. All return in time to restock the car.

At night, to retire, the crew members break down the tables to form berths, string drapes to attain privacy from any passengers who may wander through during the night, then draw their bedding out of the linen closet under the buffet or from the "possum belly" under the floor of the car, and make their beds. At 4:30 A.M., the third cook awakens to start the fire in the range and begins brewing coffee. At 5:00 A.M., the others awake, break down their beds, dress, and set to work. The cooks prepare breakfast biscuits, breads, and pancake batter, meats, and hot cereals. The waiters straighten the dining compartment. At 6:00 A.M., the early risers among passengers enter the dining car. Normally, breakfast lasts until 10:00 A.M. and is followed by lunch from 11:30 until 2:00 P.M. Two or three hours later, dinner is again offered. The pace continues, with little interruption, until after the last evening meal is served. On the premier transcontinental trains, especially the *Twentieth Century Limited* and the *Chief* and *Super Chief,* the New York-to-Hollywood connection, the kitchen is open twenty-four-hours a day for special requests and partying passengers.

This routine is maintained throughout the round trip or until the car reaches its prearranged intermediate destination. Dining cars seldom accompanied their assigned trains throughout a trip. Instead, they would be added to the train's consist only long enough to serve the customary meals spanned by a portion of the trip. Then, at an interchange, a switchman comes into the vestibule, disconnects the curtains, and closes the endgates on each end of the car. A switch engine gently cuts it off the train and sets it on a waiting track nearby. The crew cleans and reprovisions the car, then relaxes or sleeps until the car is picked up by another train that will make use of it while at the same time delivering it back to its city of origin or to its next dropoff location. If they can determine how many passengers are planning to eat once the car is cut back into a train, preparations can commence in the kitchen so that passengers can enter the car and be served as soon as it is attached to the train.

In this way, the crew, often spending more time with each other than with their families, put the crowning touch on the work of the dining-car department. Said one crew member, "Being out on the road like that was quite an experience when you think about it." That many did "think about it" is apparent from the memories the activity created.[104]

5

A Postscript

O n May 1, 1971, the National Railroad Passenger Corporation, Amtrak, took over the operation of most of America's intercity passenger trains, including their dining cars. Only the Denver & Rio Grande Western, the Rock Island, and the Southern railroads continued to run their own trains, and all of those were either canceled or turned over to Amtrak by 1983. This transition, from an exhausted and often bankrupt system of independently operated passenger trains more akin to those of the 1840s than those of the 1940s, to a new national passenger railroad system, put to death a desperately ailing industry that had been born and had grown, flourished, attained grandeur, and then withered in barely more than 125 years. Railroad passenger service, and dining-car service particularly, had been sent reeling.

First it was ravaged by the Great Depression, which cut ridership, forced economy meals for those on board, and, through layoffs, left the most senior (meaning oldest) men to work on the trains while tossing the next generation of chefs out of work early in their careers. Then it was hit by World War II, which called to duty the few crewmen with experience remaining—the Great Northern, for example, lost a chef with twenty-eight years' experience—and resulted in curtailed service availability, the often last-minute loss of a seat, crowded trains, rationed food and meatless meals, and shorthanded crews. By 1946, patrons had gone nearly fifteen years without benefit of full-service rail travel accompanied by a dining experience in the grand manner offered by the Limiteds of the 1920s.

Changed travel habits, such as the increased use of automobiles and the growth in passenger air travel, when added to the recent memory of poor service, accelerated the erosion of train ridership. In 1929 the Illinois Central, for example, had provided passenger service on practically every mile of its trackage—over more than 6,500 miles. In the early 1920s, the *Official Guide* listed more than 400 separate Illinois Central passenger trains. In the 1930s and later, the local trains on branch lines were slowly discontinued. After World War II, nearly all trains were intercity carriers, not local, with an average Illinois Central passenger train being of about ten cars. By 1952 passenger service was available on less than half of the system, covering just over 3,000 miles. In 1962, the number of passenger trains had been reduced to fewer than thirty and one, the *Panama Limited*, was one of the three remaining all-Pullman trains operating in America.[105]

Too, the railroads no longer operated as the plush bonanzas they had been in the late 1800s. Now in stiff competition for riders with cars, buses, and airplanes, they also could not afford to charge off to advertising the large losses dining-car operations inflicted. While the dining cars nearly always lost money, such losses had been trivial when compared to overall revenues created by passenger operations. But, with commodity prices soaring and labor costs also pushing upward, railroads in the 1950s could no longer afford to merely absorb the deficit imposed by dining cars.[106]

To try to serve and keep its clientele, railroads initially responded with uncharacteristic creativity, placing emphasis again on the details, large and small, they were famous for observing. Massive investments were made by virtually all the major intercity railroads in completely new streamlined trains, offering all the latest Pullman innovations, pulled by the most pow-

---

Form 2191-B

3 72—300

UNION PACIFIC RAILROAD COMPANY

Time Filed _____ M

TELEGRAM

```
JRF Salt Lake
ROB WPC JBG WJG JR FMY Ogden          Omaha - May 1, 1971
FJC WEM EEK Green River
JRJ AEH JFB DRR GMF WAB AWR WEH RFD CEB Cheyenne
AJW JEG JSW North Platte
EPM HHL CWJames JRH JH HHN KTC HWG RKA Omaha
Tower YdMaster Davenport St Omaha c/o CRR
OAD GA CED FDA FDB Omaha
OAD On Line
Joint all:

     Psgr trains:

     No. 18 GR today 2 cars. Last train No. 18.

     No. 106 GN abt 40"L 8 cars incl ex coach GR 1 GrRiver. Last
train No. 106.

     No. 104 OG abt OT 16 cars incl ex slpr 1049 Omaha, ex slpr 1046
Chgo. No Pick up NoPlt. Last No. 104

     No. 112 not run.

     No. 10 CY this PM 6 cars incl dorm lge 6103 & cafe lge 5007
KC. Last No. 10.

     No. 9 CY abt OT 8 cars incl DH slpr Pacific Union DH UP coach
5483 Los Angs. Last No. 9.

     No. 103 NO abt 15"L 19 cars incl ex coach 1018-1019-1020 Oak,
2 DH UP coaches LA. P/U CY from No. 9 DH slpr Pacific Union DH
coach 5483 LA. P/U GR from yard DH cafe lge 5016 LA. Last No. 103.

     No. 105 GR this PM 8 cars incl from yard ex coach Port. Last
No. 105.

     Amtrak No. 102 due Ogden May 2nd 9 cars incl 1 dorm, 2 coaches,
dome lge SP 3604, Silver Cup, Silver Diner, 2 slprs and Silver
Solarium.

                         J. Bowen  JCT  81 5am
```

With one telegram, over one hundred years of the Union Pacific's famed passenger trains were brought to a halt (note: "Last No. 18" etc. at the end of all but the final entry) as Amtrak took over passenger train operations on May 1, 1971.

(COURTESY OF HOMER H. NOAR)

Efforts to bring eating on the train within reach of more travelers included these two adaptations. A lunch counter car on the Denver Zephyr. (COURTESY OF THE ASSOCIATION OF AMERICAN RAILROADS)

A coffee shop-lounge on the Great Northern. (COURTESY OF THE ASSOCIATION OF AMERICAN RAILROADS)

erful diesels, and featuring eye-catching color schemes inside and out. Among the small details, the Texas & Pacific, for example, in 1947 began sending dining-car attendants through the coaches at 10:00 A.M. and 3:00 P.M. offering "coffee on the house." In 1950, the Milwaukee Road introduced the Tip Tap Top Diner aboard the *Pioneer Limited,* its overnight flyer between Chicago and Minneapolis-St. Paul. Beginning at 10:00 P.M., an hour before the train's 11:00 P.M. departure, passengers could board and enjoy a late snack. The menu, called "For Pantry Prowlers," included piping-hot onion soup (thought to be conducive to sound sleep), scrambled eggs, and a club sandwich. Similar steps were taken by the score, each a customized approach to serving the passengers of specific trains.

And some railroads still held out at maintaining high-quality dining-car service, continuing to believe that food service was one of the best advertisements possible for railroad travel. The Baltimore & Ohio, the Chicago, Milwaukee, St. Paul & Pacific, the Northern Pacific, the Union Pacific, and the Chicago & North Western, at costs ranging from $1.47 to $1.87 per dollar of sales, struggled to build and satisfy ridership in part through fine dining. Some, especially the Union Pacific, continued to do so up until Amtrak's inception.[107]

This approach is kept alive today by some carriers, including Amtrak, which operates full dining cars on many of its intercity trains, by operators of such private trains as the American European Express, in large measure an overnight movable feast, and by the growing number of private trains devoted exclusively to dining, such as the Napa Valley Wine Train.

But as train travel declined, and the dining car's good-will value diminished, the cars in general service became progressively less ornate and opulent as the years passed. The Santa Fe introduced a cafeteria car on its

California Limited in 1953. The Pennsylvania Railroad in 1954 instituted the Automatic Cafe Bar Car, which included a seventeen-foot standup bar on one end, coach seats on the other end, and in the center, an automatic restaurant where vending machines dispensed sandwiches, candy bars, juices, ice cream, milk, coffee and cigarettes.[108] The B&O began allowing the use of frozen vegetables in the mid-1950s. Budget meals were introduced at a lunch-counter car on the Illinois Central's overnight limited, the *City of Miami,* in1960.

The financial "other shoe," cost-cutting, included the reasonable—the Pennsylvania Railroad rendered its own lard from scraps gathered by the commissary's butchers—and the stingy—New York Central train crews, once able to eat from the passenger menu, were made do with ground meat and frankfurters instead. Worn-out table linen was cut into napkins or used as dustcloths. There were now paper plates, napkins, and doilies. Dining cars had three and not six waiters to hurry a reduced variety of now lower-quality foods to passengers. Menus were kept in effect longer, increasing the likelihood that if you were a regular passenger you would eat the same foods for two or three weeks at a time. A sudden increase in the cost of a menu item could result in changes, as in 1953, when the Pennsylvania Railroad removed grapefruit, a staple, after prices rose from $4.50 to $15 a case.[109] Other "reforms" included making dinner plates smaller so the shrinking portions looked larger, and replacing the resplendent white uniforms of cooks and waiters with green coats which, it was pointed out, could be sorted more easily to launder, and which certainly didn't have to be washed as frequently.

For a majority of passengers on a majority of trains, the economy measures stripped much of the color, tradition, and atmosphere from the experience of riding the train, not to mention that of eating a meal in the dining car. It simply was no longer the memorable experience Tom Scott of the Pennsylvania Railroad had intended it to be in 1854 when he introduced meals to the passengers of his railroad at the Logan House in idyllic Altoona.

If, however, the vast network of elegant, high-speed, long-distance, full-service Limited trains became the industrial equivalent of the dinosaurs in their rapid and complete disappearance, they have left a few fossils to remind us of their existence. Among them is the concept of compact, efficient kitchen design. In the late 1800s, before the advent of interior designers, a home's builder dictated the room's design. The economic class that could afford extra-fare Pullman service, and could spend the equivalent of a worker's average daily wage for a meal in the dining car, had as members those who could build a custom home. And these travelers, so taken with the interiors of Pullman's cars, "rode on a train and then went home and 'did likewise.'"[110] By the 1920s, as the apartment began to supplant the farmhouse as home, kitchen designers looked "for inspiration to an analogous example of the efficient utilization of space, the galley of the railroad dining car."[111]

Some attribute the American habit of bolting down food, often on the run, to the ways in which railroads fed those who rode them. Historian Daniel J. Boorstin, in *The Americans: The National Experience,* writes of the "'lunch counter,' offering both rapid service and enough discomfort to discourage the customer from lingering over his meal, [as] a by-product of railroad travel."[112] Waverly Root, in *Eating in America,* concurs, pointing out that "later its name would become even more brief: quick lunch."[113] In fact, the Southern Pacific did introduce a dining car it called the quick-lunch car early in the 1900s. The influence of this new method of eating, on moving land-based public conveyances, even extended to less mobile restaurants. The word "diner," originating in the early 1800s as a reference to one who dines, quickly if somewhat controversially came to apply to the unique car catering to the hunger of train passengers. So widespread and popular did the term "diner" become—it is now used almost exclusively to refer to the eating establishment and not the eater—that numerous immovable restaurants were built to resemble a dining car.

The story of Bisquick, "a new product which revolutionized American eating habits," originated on a Southern Pacific train connecting Portland with San Francisco. Carl Smith, an executive with one of General Mills' companies, entered his dining car late one evening in November 1930 and was astonished to find placed before him almost immediately a plate of oven-hot fresh biscuits. Inquiring how these could be produced on such short notice, Smith learned from the chef that he blended lard, flour, baking powder, and salt together and placed it in the ice chest for later use, thus saving valuable time during meal service. At a time when there were no mixes for cakes, rolls, or muffins, and breads were started from scratch, Smith had the presence of mind to recognize the commercial possibilities of such an idea. Work in a General Mills lab made a similar blend, one which would retain leavening power and yet not spoil when stored on the grocer's or housewife's shelf. Work in the marketing department gave it a name, "bis, for biscuit, and quick, to give the tongue a twist around the second syllable that resulted, all at once, in a pun, a tribute, and an absolutely unforgettable trade name."[114]

The innocuous square loaf of bread found on grocery shelves all over America today and generally known as "sandwich bread," is referred to in the trade by its original name, the Pullman loaf. Baked in square, straight-sided bread pans with a cover to insure a top identical to the other three sides, more of these loaves could be stored in the tight space of a dining car kitchen than could loaves with beveled sides and a rounded top.

While not developed by a railroad or a dining-car department, the compressed sawdust log available everywhere fireplaces are found was nonetheless intended for use there. Known as presto-logs, they were introduced by Weyerhauser under a patent granted on February 12, 1935. The Dining Car and Hotel Department of the Union Pacific was among those approached to test their usefulness. The railroad operated trains loaded with hundreds of passengers across the Rocky Mountains in winter. Faced with the real threat of a train becoming snowbound and thus possibly of having the electricity generated for the kitchen curtailed or lost altogether if the locomotive ceased operation, management's interest in such an alternative fuel was high. Two such logs in the large kitchen stove gave off a smokeless and nearly ashless fire that produced great heat for about two hours. Eventually, the dining cars of the Union Pacific alone consumed a boxcar load, nearly 16,000 artificial logs, each week.

Finally, there is the nonspecific but certain influence dining cars had on the development of the fast-food industry. Two clear similarities to today's fast-food restaurants existed. First, there was the strict adherence to prescribed recipes, portions, and standards of service, all intended to insure the predictability of food quality and crew behavior throughout a vast system. J. M. Collins, superintendent of dining cars for the Erie Railroad, expressed the philosophy pointedly and in a manner every fast-food restaurant manager in the 1990s would recognize: "A passenger who liked the roast beef au jus and tossed salad he had on number 5 out of Jersey City wants to have the same quality and taste the next time he travels, though next time may find him going from Chicago to Jamestown."[115] Second, there was the large number of outlets. On a given day and time, as many as 150 "restaurants," the dining car roster of a single large railroad, might be serving meals to passengers. At the peak of such service, no other hotel chain, steamship line, or restaurant chain could claim to have as many meal-service facilities in operation serving uniformly outstanding dishes.

None of these contributions, of course, answers the remaining question: "What was it about dining on a train that made it such a memorable experience?"

Railroad dining clearly met humorist H. F. Ellis's rule applied to eating while in motion: "The motion must be apparent and it must be forwards—movements up and down, and to an even greater extent sideways or circular movements, are worse than useless." He observed three other

The dining cars of the Union Pacific consumed sixteen thousand pressed sawdust logs (one boxcar load) per week. (COURTESY OF THE UNION PACIFIC MUSEUM)

reasons why consuming food on a train was superior to consuming it on other means of transportation. First, the scenery was both visible and changed with appropriate rapidity, qualities not to be obtained from a ship's or airplane's porthole. And there was a miraculous quality to the service of a freshly prepared four-course meal from the confines of a dining-car kitchen that could not describe the work of a crew in a ship's galley or the food served aboard airplanes. Finally, the desire to eat did not altogether disappear at the critical moment, as it could with the sight of food at sea or in the air.[116]

The answer, too, can be found in the romance associated with travel, what Mark Twain described as "an exhilarating sense of emancipation from all sorts of cares and responsibilities." For many, that feeling was magnified when undertaken on a transcontinental train. Accompanied by uncommonly great-tasting food, served in remarkably elegant settings, highlighted by vivid, colorful, often spectacular scenery unfolding outside a large window, the whole was greater than a sum of the parts.

Another explanation sees the mystique's origin in a then-common childhood experience, that of watching the high-speed flyers pass through, an attraction so strong that a judge in Mississippi daily adjourned court long enough to go to the window and watch the *Panama Limited* pass the courthouse. Jan Clayton, the Campbell Soup Company's commentator in commercials on *Lassie* in the 1950s, described her youthful yearning to eat in the dining car this way: "There was a continental railroad not far from where we lived, and in the early evenings I could see the passengers at dinner in the brilliantly lighted dining cars. Everything looked so gay, so festive, so romantic, that I wanted almost more than anything in the world to be eating with that happy crowd. I never see a train rushing through the night that I don't want to be aboard, and I never pass up the chance to eat dinner in one of those lovely dining cars."

Anyone who was in that dining car, lingering after a satisfying meal to watch the landscape roll by, would support Ms. Clayton's enthusiasm for dinner in the diner. Wayne Johnston, quotable longtime president of the Illinois Central, asserted that "one of the pleasures of riding a train is the opportunity it affords for dining in style." Even its name, the "dining car," conjures images of elegance, grace, and good food. The unglamourous label "restaurant car" was used early, dropped, then used again later, but only to describe reduced services. Attempts at cost-saving brought cars with such names as the luncheonette, buffet, club, parlor, and lounge car into use. None of these evoke the sense of civilization one expects of the experience of "dinner in the diner."

Novelist Herman Wouk asserts that "American railroads are capillaries of mechanized civilization threading through the wilderness." A trip along any mainline would confirm his belief. If railroads carried industrial America's life blood, it often coursed along through industry's back yards. A meal in the dining car helped transcend these surroundings, as when one writer recalled "the special elegance of . . . the starched napery, the heavy silver, all while the train stood briefly in a drab street of industrial Troy [NY]." For many, the dining-car meal and surroundings surpassed anything available to them in the cities that were their destination. Only major end terminals—New York, Chicago, Los Angeles, or the like—had notable restaurants. The rest had "beaneries," "greasy spoons," and "slop houses."

A short, dramatic, violent episode during the Civil War, known as "the Great Locomotive Chase," was planned around a meal stop. On April 12, 1862, at 6:00 A.M., the conductor of the express train from Atlanta to Chattanooga announced twenty minutes for breakfast at Big Shanty, twenty-nine miles north of Atlanta. Big Shanty was not a station but only the Lacy Hotel, a little freight shed, and a Confederate camp. As was the custom, the train stopped beside the hotel, whose dining room served meals for passengers and trainmen. While the crew and most passengers were in the Lacy Hotel eating breakfast, their Western & Atlantic Railroad mixed train, pulled by the locomotive the *General,* was commandeered by eighteen disguised Union soldiers and two civilians, all of whom had been passengers on the train. A planned race north, destroying right-of-way en route, was foiled by a tenacious Confederate train crew which set out after the *General* almost immediately. When captured, the two civilians were tried and hanged, as were six of the soldiers. The rest of the soldiers were imprisoned until March 17, 1863, then exchanged for southern prisoners.[117]

The widespread integration of trains into the fabric of people's lives during this period insured a similar role for the dining cars. Thomas Edison, in addition to his experience with the Logan House in Altoona, sharpened his skills as a businessman when, at the age of twelve, he was a news butch for the Grand Truck Railroad. Horatio Alger created an American hero of a train boy working on the Erie Railroad, and Robert

Louis Stevenson did the same for one on the overland route to the Pacific. Ernest Hemingway married Martha Gelhorn while en route from Sun Valley, Idaho, to New York in the Union Pacific Railroad dining room in Cheyenne, Wyoming. Former U. S. Supreme Court Justice Thurgood Marshall worked on the dining cars of the Baltimore & Ohio Railroad.

In fact, work as a waiter or porter was often a stepping stone for the brightest young African-American men to overcome the closed traditional doors to advancement. A Pullman Company porter, speaking at Dartmouth College on March 25, 1924, reported that thirty percent of all black doctors were ex-porters. The writer Wright Morris tells of his father's making a living for a while selling eggs to the Union Pacific commissary. Celebrities "taking the *Century* and the *Chief* to the coast"—that is, the New York Central's *Twentieth Century Limited* from New York to Chicago and the Santa Fe's *Super Chief* from Chicago to Los Angeles—were often seen in publicity photographs shot in the dining car.

A publicist for the Northern Pacific Railway asked, "Where else . . . can one find that joyous combination of movement toward a goal, food in a pleasing variety, ineffably delightful scenery, service fit for a reigning monarch, and a feeling of intimacy that is totally at odds with time and place?"[118]

A final explanation, offered, appropriately enough by a veteran steward, Ike Greenberg of the *Panama Limited*, goes like this: "On land you kill time to eat, but on a train you eat to kill time. . . . When a fellow goes into a restaurant or hotel dining room his main idea is to finish as quickly as possible and get on to something else. . . . Now, on a dining car a passenger has all the time in the world, and nothing to do with it. He goes into the diner in just the opposite frame of mind. He wants something fine to eat and wants to lose himself in it. That is true dining." For Greenberg, the effect this phenomenon had on the digestive system and the perceived effectiveness of a meal was obvious.[119]

SECTION TWO

The Railroads and Their Cuisines

A meal in the dining car was second only to the departure of the train in significance to travelers. It was, perhaps, the most memorable dining experience available to Americans of the day. Those fortunate enough to live where trains stopped occasionally rode the train solely to eat. Richard Ford of St. Paul, Minnesota, was one of these fortunates. In the 1920s, four different railroads offered competing trains between Chicago and the Twin Cities. At that time, Ford wrote his brother, "the Chicago, Milwaukee, St. Paul & Pacific pulled into St. Paul . . . about six in the evening and then took a long time for oiling, checking brakes, and making the twelve-mile haul to Minneapolis. I would get on, go into the diner, have a seven-course dinner for a dollar, and get off at Minneapolis an hour later full of good vittles."[120]

Such meals featured menu items that were made of fresh, natural, and locally available ingredients. The Baltimore & Ohio, reflecting its Tidewater origins, was influenced by Southern plantation cooking. In a further attention to detail, passengers on B & O trains from the Midwest enjoyed freshwater fish from the Great Lakes while westbound passengers were served saltwater fish from the Chesapeake Bay. The Union Pacific hunted for four years before it found, in a little valley in Utah, just the right kind of raspberries. Double cream to serve with them was loaded at the Omaha commissary. The Southern Pacific found what it considered the best prunes at a ranch in California, which became its exclusive source. Such "finds" were purchased in quantities that could be staggering. It was not uncommon for the Fred Harvey organization to purchase an entire boatload of Dover sole, or take an entire season's catch of whitefish from Lake Primrose in Canada.[121]

Eating habits, of course, were different when dining-car service reached its peak. Americans of the late nineteenth and early twentieth centuries ate three meals a day: breakfast, followed in three hours by a large luncheon meal called dinner, and four hours after that the evening meal, or supper. And travelers of the day had a choice of food and drink available that is unknown today. The menu on the dining cars of the Chicago & North Western's Omaha train offered thirteen different entrees, six kinds of game, and a choice of twenty-five desserts. The meal cost seventy-five cents.[122]

In an age when caloric intake was not a consideration, a typical dinner menu might offer sirloin, tenderloin, porterhouse, or venison steak, prairie chicken, snipe, quail, golden plover, blue-winged teal, woodcock, broiled pigeon, mallard, widgeon, canvasback or domestic duck, wild turkey, veal, mutton, chicken, roast pork, sixteen relishes, eleven clam and oyster dishes, five fish dishes, fifteen kinds of bread, as well as many soups.[123] On the Union Pacific, the steaks as late as the 1950s weighed one pound each, down from a high of two and three-quarter pounds each in the 1890s. In either era, a person ordering steak was shown a tray with three choices, rare, medium, or well done. Second helpings of anything on the menu were free, on the Union Pacific and elsewhere.

The standards for food quality and service were so high that one veteran steward, writing in 1937, was able to conclude that "the culinary art has shown less progress [in the past fifty years, when compared with other improvements in dining-car service] as there were excellent chefs of the old school years ago. Such progress as has come to dining-car service [recently] is rather due to closer supervision, more discipline, improved kitchen facilities, artistic appointments and modern equipment."[124]

During 1952, the thirty-seven member-railroads of the American Association of Railroad Dining Car Officers served 37,827,633 meals. In all, America's railroads served 80 million meals that year.[125] But statistics only hint at the greater impact of the stylish twelve-wheeled marvels of efficiency and comfort on the memories of the men and women who encountered them while traveling. Such memories recall fine food served in a setting today found only in expensive restaurants, of fresh-cut flowers adorning a table covered with crisp white linen, and of thick and heavy plates, set down among napkins, silverware, and crystal glassware and accessories. Presented here are more than three hundred of the best foods from the greatest trains to run in America.

INSTRUCTIONS AND ADMONITIONS: DOING IT RIGHT!

As early as 1883, the Chicago and North Western Railway Company was distributing a twelve-page booklet entitled *Regulations for the Guidance of Conductors, Cooks, and Waiters of the Dining Cars* to dining-car crews. Then, as later, each crew member had to sign an acknowledgment that "I have read and understand the rules and agree to conform to the same." Loss of the manual or a failure to turn it in when leaving the service resulted in its cost being recovered from the employee's wages.

From such a brief beginning evolved extensive books of several hundred pages in length, describing everything from requisitions and supplies to charts of appropriate fruits and vegetables "of the season"; tables labeled "Approximate Quantities of Food Supplies to Order Per Servings Shown"; illustrations of how to carve beef, poultry, and fish; and recipes for the railroad's menu items. The manuals included instructions for all personnel on operating the dining car, setting it up for service, and preparing and presenting the food.

Such instruction often went into considerable detail. The Union Pacific, for example, offered these specifics on how silverware should be arranged on its various trains:

Silverware Setup: Streamliners and Standard Trains

BREAKFAST MEAL
> One fork to left of napkin
> One table knife to right of napkin; cutting edge to napkin
> One dessert spoon adjacent to knife
> Two teaspoons adjacent to dessert spoon

LUNCH AND DINNER MEALS
> Two forks to left of napkin
> One table knife to right of napkin
> One bouillon spoon adjacent to knife
> One butter knife adjacent to bouillon spoon
> Two teaspoons adjacent to butter knife
> Waiter to bring dessert spoon with entrees requiring this service

DOME ROUND TABLES AND DOME DUCES
> Flower vase adjacent to window
> Menu holder adjacent to vase
> Cube (or indiv. pack) sugar bowl adjacent to menu holder to right when viewed from aisle
> Salt and pepper shakers or coaster; salt facing aisle; pepper facing window
> Granulated sugar bowl to left, adjacent to menu holder
> Water pitcher on large round tables facing kitchen

DOME FOUR'S AND GOLD ROOM
> Flower vase adjacent to window and wall of gold room
> Menu holder adjacent to vase

Granulated sugar bowl towards window and wall of gold room
Cube (or indiv. pack) sugar bowl in center of table facing aisle
Salt and pepper shakers between bowls, salt to right
Water pitcher on dome large tables facing stairway

ALL 48 SEATERS
Flower vase adjacent to window
Menu holder adjacent to vase
Sugar bowls in center of table
Cube or individual pack sugar bowl facing aisle
Granulated sugar bowl facing window
Salt and pepper coasters between bowls, salt to right
Water pitcher on to right of aisle facing kitchen

(COURTESY, UNION PACIFIC RAILROAD COMPANY)

In some instances, a rationale for the insisted-upon behavior was provided. These comments, from the *Atlantic Coast Line Food Service Manual,* give an indication of the level of perfection expected of dining-car crews:

BACON
While it is realized that in heavy trains it will be hard to broil bacon to order, nevertheless the system of dumping one or two pounds of bacon in the frying pan, allowing it to fry with the net result that about ten to fifteen per cent will break, curl up, and look messy when served, must be stopped. Hereafter on heavy trains chefs will place ready sliced bacon neatly on baking pan, cook partially in the oven to break the grain of the meat, and finish on the broiler. Bacon thus cooked will look more appetizing, will not crumble or curl, will show better on the plate, and will repay you in better percentage for the extra effort.

VEGETABLES
Too little attention is paid to the preparation, service, and seasoning of vegetables. All vegetables should be thoroughly washed in cold water before cooking. This is important, as vegetables while they are growing, come in contact with fertilizers and sprays used against insects.

Use only as much water in cooking as is absolutely necessary to prevent burning, so that vegetables will absorb all the moisture and help prevent their valuable mineral salts and vitamins from escaping. Cooking in this manner also helps vegetables to retain their color and taste.

Cook vegetables in as short a time as possible, do not overcook. It is important, of course, that vegetables are cooked sufficiently so that they are not served half done.

Do not prepare large quantities at one time, but stagger the cooking of vegetables during the meal period so that the late as well as early dining-car patrons will be served vegetables which are freshly cooked, colorful, and palatable.

Stewards and chefs will be held accountable for the proper preparation and seasoning of all vegetables.

NEW HAVEN SALAD PLATE SPECIAL

13-AJ-11

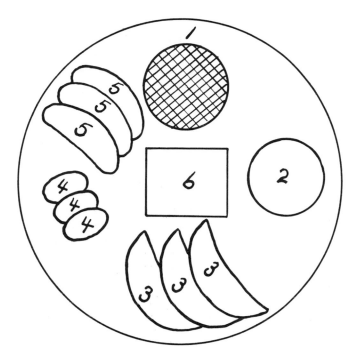

LINE PLATE FOR LETTUCE

1 Pineapple, cut in cubes (1 slice)

2 Fig (1)

3 Grapefruit or melon sections (3)

4 Dates (5)

5 Orange sections (6)

6 Cream cheese (1 cake)

Perhaps some prize for step-by-step instructions should go to the Pullman Company for these 1939 requirements to serve just one of the more than thirty drinks described in *Commissary Instructions: Broiler-Buffet-Club and Lounge Car Service*. The company even distinguished between serving domestic and imported ales.

TOM COLLINS

1. Ask guest if bottled water is desired. If not, serve syphon seltzer.
2. Arrange setup in buffet; place on bar tray: individual bottle of gin; bottled water standing upright (or syphon seltzer); glass (No. 12, 14 oz.); cap knife; bottle opener; bar spoon; and paper cocktail napkin. Attendant should carry clean glass towel on his arm with fold pointing toward his hand while rendering service.
3. Place juice of ½ lemon in glass (No. 12).
4. Add 1 teaspoonful sugar in glass (No. 12).
5. Stir until thoroughly dissolved. Add one red cherry.
6. Put in glass (No. 12) containing mixture, finely chopped ice—⅔ full.
7. Proceed to passenger with above setup.
8. Place bar tray with setup on table (or etc.).
9. Place paper cocktail napkin on table in front of passenger.
10. **Present individual bottle of gin to passenger, displaying label, strip tax stamp, and Goldy seal, by holding bottle on sides between index finger and thumb.**
11. **Open individual bottle of gin with cap knife in presence of passenger, pointing neck of bottle away from passenger; wipe top of bottle with clean glass towel.**
12. Pour contents of individual bottle of gin into glass (No. 12).
13. **STIR BRISKLY WITH BAR SPOON TO THOROUGHLY MIX INGREDIENTS.**
14. Fill glass (No. 12) with bottled water or syphon seltzer. (If bottled water is used, present bottle to passenger and open in presence of passenger, pointing neck of bottle away from passenger; wipe top with clean glass towel before pouring.)
15. Stir lightly with bar spoon and return bar spoon to bar tray.
16. Place glass (No. 12) containing drink on paper cocktail napkin; wipe bar spoon with clean glass towel and place alongside of drink.
17. Remove bar tray with equipment not needed by passenger.
18. If bottled water is used, do not remove bottle until drink is finished.

Most commissary instructions ended with this announcement: "Any employee of the dining cars disobeying any of the foregoing rules is liable to reduction of salary or dismissal, as the superintendent may decide; and in entering the service, does so with this understanding."

(PREVIOUS PAGE)
The New Haven Railroad food service manual illustrated exactly how to serve nearly seventy salads. Under the heading "Fermented Liquors and Wines," ten pages of history, serving customs, and qualities, spelled out in similar detail how these items were to be served. (COURTESY OF MARC AND FAITH FRATTSIO)

SOME STANDARD RECIPES, INSTRUCTIONS, AND SUBSTITUTIONS

The recipes that follow sometimes call for certain basic ingredients or steps. To avoid listing them repeatedly, preparation instructions for these items are provided here.

BOUQUET GARNI (NEW HAVEN)

Unless components of the bouquet garni are specified otherwise within a recipe, follow these directions. A twelve-inch square piece of cheesecloth and a few inches of string are needed each time.

a few sprigs parsley	pinch, thyme
½ carrot, cut lengthwise	¼ bay leaf
1 leek, white	2 whole cloves
sprig of celery	sprig of marjoram

Place spices in cheesecloth square, tie with string and use as directed.

CONSOMMÉ (UNION PACIFIC)

This recipe may be used in making all varieties of consommé.

BEFORE YOU BEGIN
You'll need: large stock pot, sheet of cheese-cloth, Chinese strainer
Preparation time: 4 hours (beginning with cooled stock)
Yield: about 2½ quarts

1 lb. beef trimmings, chopped	1 bay leaf
1 carrot, cut fine	3 whole cloves
1 onion, quartered	3 whole allspice
2 Tbsp. celery, sliced	1 small clove garlic, crushed
2 Tbsp. green pepper, diced	1 cup tomatoes, diced
3 sprigs, parsley	12 cups rich beef stock, cooled
6 eggs, shell and all*	

* While the railroad's recipes called for eggs, shell and all, you can safely use whites only.

In a large stock pot, mix beef trimmings, carrot, onion, celery, green pepper, and parsley. Add eggs, shell and all, bay leaf, cloves, all-spice, garlic, and tomatoes. Add beef stock and slowly bring to a boil. Reduce heat and simmer for 3 hours. Do not stir after it starts to simmer. Strain through cheesecloth spread over Chinese strainer. When cold, remove fat from top and use as directed.

COOKED RICE

BEFORE YOU BEGIN
You'll need: small saucepan
Preparation time: 30 minutes
Yield: 2 cups

2 cups water	1 Tbsp. butter
¼ tsp. salt (optional)	1 cup enriched long-grain rice

Place water, salt, and butter in a small saucepan over high heat. Add rice and bring all to a boil. Reduce heat to medium-high and allow to cook, uncovered, until rice has absorbed moisture, about 25 minutes.

CREAM SAUCE (FRED HARVEY)

BEFORE YOU BEGIN
You'll need: 2-quart saucepan, 1½-quart saucepan, double boiler, strainer
Preparation time: 30 minutes
Yield: 2 cups

½ cup butter or chicken fat	3 cups whole milk
½ cup flour	1 cup chicken stock

In the 2-quart saucepan, make a roux using butter and flour and bring to a light brown color, about 2-3 minutes. Meanwhile, combine milk and chicken stock and heat just to boiling.

Pour hot milk/stock mixture slowly into roux, stirring constantly with a whisk to prevent lumps. Cook over low heat for 30 minutes. Strain into the top of preheated double boiler, place a dab of butter on top to prevent crust from forming, and set aside until needed.

DEMI-GLACE

Demi-glace is a rich thin brown gravy made from concentrated meat stock that has been highly seasoned with an assortment of vegetables, spices and seasonings. Note: Knorr® makes a demi–glace sauce mix which yields 1¼ cups per package.

BEFORE YOU BEGIN
You'll need: 2-quart saucepan, fine strainer
Preparation time: 1½ hours
Yield: 2 cups

2 cups Espagnole	pinch, curry powder
3¼ cups beef stock	3 Tbsp. Madeira

In the saucepan, combine Espagnole (see recipe this page), beef stock, and curry powder. Bring to a boil, reduce heat, and allow to simmer until reduced to one-third of its original volume. Remove from heat and stir in Madeira. Put mixture through a fine strainer two or three times before serving.

DESSERT PIE CRUST
(BALTIMORE & OHIO)

BEFORE YOU BEGIN
You'll need: medium mixing bowl, pastry blender, rolling pin
Preparation time: 15 minutes (plus one hour if prepared on a hot day)
Yield: dough for top and bottom pie crust or 6 individual pies

1 cup flour	½ Tbsp. butter, melted
½ Tbsp. powdered sugar	1 tsp. milk
pinch, salt	1 tsp. heavy cream
¼ cup shortening	½ cup ice water, as needed

In a bowl, mix together with a fork the flour, sugar, and salt. Cut shortening in with a pastry cutter until coarse (pealike). Continue mixing, gradually adding butter, milk, and heavy cream. Add just enough ice water to make dough medium-soft. On hot days, let dough set in the refrigerator for 45–60 minutes to chill through. Sprinkle some flour over dough and onto a flat surface. Roll dough to ⅛-inch thickness, then carefully remove to pie pan.

ESPAGNOLE
(CHICAGO, BURLINGTON & QUINCY)

Espagnole is used as a base for a number of flavorful sauces cited later. It was prepared in quantity by the commissary for later use in the dining cars. A quick substitute can be made in this manner: for each cup of Espagnole called for, melt 1 tablespoon of butter over medium heat and add 1 tablespoon of flour to make a brown roux; add 1 cup of heated beef stock and add 1 tablespoon of tomato paste; stir to mix well; bring to a boil and reduce heat and simmer for 1 hour to blend flavors and thicken sauce.

BEFORE YOU BEGIN
You'll need: small skillet, 8-quart roasting pan, 8-quart stock pot; several 12-inch square pieces of cheesecloth
Preheat oven to 400 degrees
Preparation time: 14 hours
Yield: 4 quarts

2 veal shin bones or equivalent	pepper
	2 bay leaves
paprika	4 whole allspice
2 Tbsp. clear fat, melted	1 clove garlic, diced
	½ cup flour
2 cups carrots sliced thin	1 28-oz. can whole tomatoes
2 cups sliced onions	6 quarts beef stock
salt	(approximately)

Cut meat into small pieces and crack shin bones. Place the meat and bones in the roasting pan, dust with paprika, and drizzle melted fat over all. Place in oven and brown well, about 1 hour. Add dry vegetables, dust with salt and pepper, add spices, cover, and return to oven for 30 minutes. Now dust everything with flour and return to oven uncovered until flour is browned. Remove and place in stock pot. Add tomatoes and stock sufficient to nearly fill the stock pot. Bring to a boil, reduce heat and let simmer for 10 to 12 hours. Add salt and pepper to taste. Strain well through cheesecloth and store in refrigerator until used as directed. To attain rich brown color, it is important that meat, bones, and flour be properly browned.

MAYONNAISE

A number of the salad dressings presented call for starting by making a mayonnaise by whipping raw egg yolk, cold oil, vinegar, salt, and dry mustard together for an extended period of time (anywhere from 10 to 30 minutes). When such a step is called for, you may substitute commercial mayonnaise in an amount equal to the combined volume of the egg yolk(s), oil, vinegar, and seasonings used in the recipe. Such a substitution will better enable reducing the yield of the recipe if so desired.

MEAL DISH PIE CRUST
(COTTON BELT ROUTE)

BEFORE YOU BEGIN
You'll need: medium mixing bowl, pastry
   blender, rolling pin
Preparation time: 15 minutes (plus one hour if
   prepared on a hot day)
Yield: dough for top and bottom pie crust or 6
   individual pies

2 cups flour	¾ cup lard or butter,
pinch, salt	room temperature
pinch, white pepper	3–5 Tbsp. cold milk
pinch, sugar	

In medium mixing bowl, lightly stir flour, salt, pepper, and sugar together. Cut lard into dry ingredients with a pastry blender until well mixed and coarse (pealike). Sprinkle in cold milk, one tablespoon at a time, and mix with a fork after each addition until pastry just holds together. Shape pastry into a ball with hands. If you are cooking on a hot day, wrap pastry in waxed paper and refrigerate 60 minutes before continuing. Divide pastry in half and shape each piece into a ball. On a lightly floured surface, using a lightly floured rolling pin, roll one ball of dough into a ⅛-inch thick circle. Use a knife or scissors to cut dough to size and shape sufficient to line pie pan or individual baking dishes, allowing a 1-inch overhang of dish edge. Fill crust as recipe directs. Roll remaining dough for top crust in the same manner. Trim to ½ inch beyond edge of baking dish. Pinch or fold overhanging dough surfaces together. Cut two or three slices in each top crust to vent steam. Bake according to recipe instructions.

PEELING TOMATOES FOR SALADS

Bring a saucepan of lightly salted water to a boil. Meanwhile, use a sharp knife to cut a shallow X in the bottom of each tomato. Using a slotted spoon, lower each tomato individually into the boiling water. Hold it there for 15 seconds, then transfer it to a bowl of iced water. When the tomato has cooled, gently pull the skin away.

RICH STOCK

A rich stock is one which has been reduced to three-quarters of its original volume by slow simmering. Start with the type of stock called for (chicken, beef, fish, etc.), bring to a boil, reduce heat, and let simmer until reduced.

ROUX

A roux is used to thicken sauces. It is a cooked mixture of equal amounts of butter and flour, unless specified otherwise by the recipe. Begin with a skillet or saucepan of suitable size. Over medium heat, warm the butter or its equivalent (margarine, chicken fat, lard, etc.) until melted. Stirring constantly with a whisk to avoid lumps, gradually add the flour. When all flour is added, continue stirring and cooking mixture until it is of the desired color. For white sauce, cook roux 2 to 3 minutes until it just begins to take on a light golden color. For brown sauce, simmer roux 5 to 10 minutes longer, until of a light brown color. When the proper color is obtained, use as called for by the recipe. When adding a liquid to a roux, the liquid should be warmed. Add slowly, stirring constantly.

SHRIMP FOR COCKTAILS, MILWAUKEE ROAD STYLE

BEFORE YOU BEGIN
You'll need: 3-quart saucepan
Preparation time: 1¼ hours
Yield: mixture sufficient to cook one pound of
    shrimp

tops of one bunch celery	**½ tsp. salt**
1 carrot, cut in 1-inch slices	**⅛ tsp. pepper**
	pinch, paprika
1 small onion, quartered	**1 bay leaf**

Add all ingredients to 2 quarts of cold water. Bring water to boil, reduce heat, and slow boil for 1 hour. Place shrimp in mixture, cover tightly, and cook until shrimp are tender, exactly 6 minutes. Remove from heat immediately, drain and rinse in cold water. Pick shrimp out of cooked vegetables, shell and devein, and keep refrigerated until ready to serve.

6

THE ATCHESON, TOPEKA, AND SANTA FE RAILWAY SYSTEM

BAKED HAM WITH LLEWELLYN SAUCE

This sauce is suitable for baking with ham prepared by any method (see pages 219, 268, 269, or 294 for baked ham recipes).

BEFORE YOU BEGIN

You'll need: roasting pan, medium saucepan, strainer
Preheat oven to temperature called for to bake the ham
Preparation time: 30 minutes plus baking time
Yield: 1 quart sauce

2 oranges	½ cup white vinegar
1 lemon	½ cup flour
6 bay leaves	3 cups water
12 cloves, whole	1 cup tomato puree
12 whole allspice	1 5-lb. fully cooked ham
¼ lb. sugar	1 cup claret wine

Squeeze the juice of the oranges and lemons into a roasting pan. Add rinds of 1 orange and the lemon, broken in pieces. Mix next eight ingredients together in roasting pan. Following the recipe for the ham you've chosen, place ham in roasting pan with the mixture and bake for length of time indicated. Remove when cooked through. Strain remaining liquid from roasting pan into saucepan. Over medium heat, add claret wine and stir to mix well. Simmer uncovered until mixture is warmed through. Place a small amount of sauce on meal plate, arrange a serving of sliced ham over sauce, then add a generous spoonful of sauce on top.

BRAISED DUCK CUMBERLAND

As this recipe by Chef Joseph Stoesser of the Super Chief *demonstrates, the call to dinner was often a call to a superior meal, not just food. The sauce alone has won raves from epicures.*

STUFFED DUCK

1	5–6 lb. duck	¼	cup butter
	salt and pepper	½	tsp. salt
3	Tbsp. butter	1	large celery stalk
¼	cup onion, chopped fine	1	large carrot, whole
1	cup rice, uncooked	1	small onion
2 ½	cups chicken broth	1	cup water

Sprinkle cavity of duck with salt and pepper and wipe to cover. For stuffing, melt butter in the 1-quart saucepan over medium heat and sautéed chopped onion until tender. Add rice and continue cooking until rice turns yellow. Meanwhile, bring chicken broth to a boil. To sautéed onion/rice mixture, add broth, ¼ cup butter, and salt. Cover and simmer until moisture is absorbed by rice, about 30 minutes. Stuff and truss duck and place on a wire rack in roasting pan, breast up. Add celery, carrot, whole onion, and water. Place in oven and bake 25 minutes per pound (about 2½ hours), basting occasionally.

SAUCE

1	tsp. flour	¼	tsp. English mustard
1	cup duck or chicken stock	1	tsp. Worcestershire sauce
1	large navel orange	1	Tbsp. currant jelly
⅓	cup Burgundy wine		dash, cayenne

Remove baked duck from roasting pan, place on a platter, and keep warm. Drain excess fat off remaining liquid. Sprinkle flour in pan, stirring constantly to mix. Meanwhile, in a small saucepan, heat duck stock and add to drippings, stirring constantly. Simmer for 20 minutes, stirring occasionally. Peel orange and remove white membrane from peel. Cut the peel into narrow strips and place in small saucepan with water to cover. Bring peel and water to a boil and continue boiling for 5 minutes. Drain peel strips and add to hot mixture. Add wine, mustard, Worcestershire sauce, jelly, and cayenne and heat through. Meanwhile, separate orange into sections, removing all white membrane. Place the duck on a serving platter. Arrange orange sections in two rows over the duck. Ladle a few spoonfuls of sauce over the duck and serve remaining sauce with individual portions.

CHEESE TIDBIT

Something tasty to serve guests while they await dinner.

6 slices white bread, each ⅛-inch thick	3 oz. ham, finely diced
3 oz. butter, at room temperature	1 Tbsp. butter
½ lb. American cheese, grated	4 egg yolks, lightly beaten
1 tsp. English mustard	white bread crumbs to coat

Trim crusts from bread slices. Place soft butter in a small bowl and add cheese, mustard, and ham and mix well. Apply cheese mixture ¼-inch thick on three bread slices. Top with remaining bread slices and cut each sandwich into eighths in wedge shape. Heat the 1 tablespoon butter in large skillet over medium-high heat. Dip wedges in lightly beaten egg yolks, then bread crumbs. Sauté in butter until golden brown, 1 to 2 minutes per side, turning once. Serve warm.

BEFORE YOU BEGIN

You'll need: small bowl, large skillet
Preparation time: 30 minutes
Yield: 24 portions

HUNGARIAN CHEESE DUMPLINGS

1 lb. dry cottage cheese	½ tsp. salt
4 eggs, slightly beaten	1 cup fresh bread crumbs
12 Tbsp. flour	4 Tbsp. butter

Put cottage cheese through a ricer. Add beaten eggs. Stir well, then add flour and salt and mix until smooth. Form the mixture into balls the size of a large walnut. Meanwhile, bring 2 quarts water and a pinch of salt to a boil. Reduce heat to a gentle boil and drop in cheese dough. Cook 20–25 minutes. When done, remove with slotted spoon and drain off all water. Meanwhile, in a small skillet over medium heat, melt butter and sauté fresh bread crumbs until nicely browned. Sprinkle buttered bread crumbs over dumplings and serve hot.

BEGIN YOU BEGIN

You'll need: ricer or masher, mixing bowl, 3-quart saucepan, small skillet
Preparation time: 45 minutes
Yield: 6 servings

HUNGARIAN BEEF GOULASH
WITH POTATO DUMPLINGS

HUNGARIAN BEEF GOULASH

1 clove garlic, minced	1½ lbs. lean beef,
½ tsp. salt	cut into 2-inch pieces
4 oz. butter	1 cup water, as needed
1½ lbs. onions, chopped	salt to taste
1½ Tbsp. Hungarian paprika	

In a small bowl, mash garlic and salt into a puree. Melt butter in a large skillet over medium-high heat. Sauté onions to a golden brown. Add garlic/salt mixture and paprika and mix well. Add meat. Reduce heat to medium, cover, and cook for 1½ hours, stirring frequently to prevent meat from sticking. Once or twice, add water in ½-cup quantities as needed to keep goulash moist. Season to taste.

POTATO DUMPLINGS

2 lbs. potatoes, grated	2 egg yolks, lightly beaten
3 Tbsp. flour	flour to coat dumplings
1 tsp. cornstarch	2 cups stale bread crumbs
pinch, nutmeg	¼ cup butter
pinch, salt	

In 4-quart saucepan, bring 3 quarts water and 1 teaspoon salt to a slow boil. Meanwhile, in a large bowl, mix grated potatoes, flour, cornstarch, nutmeg, and salt. Add egg yolks and mix thoroughly. Place about a quarter cup of flour in a dish. Form dumplings the size of a golf ball and roll in flour to coat. Drop dumplings into slow-boiling water, cook uncovered for 10 minutes. Remove dumplings with a slotted spoon and drain. Meanwhile, melt butter in medium skillet, add bread crumbs and stir while heating until browned. Roll drained dumplings in bread crumbs. Serve alongside goulash. NOTE: If first dumpling falls apart in boiling water, add flour to dumpling mixture just until dumplings hold together water.

LOBSTER AMERICAINE

BEFORE YOU BEGIN

You'll need: 1-quart saucepan, small skillet, wire whisk
Preparation time: 1 hour
Yield: 1 serving

This creation of Chef Carlos Gardini on board the Super Chief *reflects the food-consciousness of the celebrities and business and social leaders who frequented this luxury all-room train. So recognizable and noteworthy were many of the train's riders that the railroad offered them dining privacy in the Turquoise Room, with a long menu of dishes such as this.*

1 2-lb. lobster, boiled	2 Tbsp. flour
3 Tbsp. butter	¼ cup fish or lobster stock, boiling
1 Tbsp. minced celery	2 Tbsp. white wine
1 tsp. minced carrots	2 tomatoes, peeled and chopped
1 tsp. minced leeks	dash, salt
1 tsp. minced shallots	dash, pepper
½ garlic clove, minced	dash, cayenne pepper
2 Tbsp. cognac	1 Tbsp. butter

Remove lobster meat from shell and cut into pieces 1 inch thick, saving brain. In a 1-quart saucepan over medium heat, melt 3 tablespoons butter and sauté minced vegetables several minutes, taking care not to brown. Add lobster meat and minced garlic and continue to sauté for 5 minutes. Add cognac and set aflame. When flame subsides, blend flour in with a whisk to make a roux. Add boiling broth, stirring constantly, and continue to heat until smooth and slightly thickened. Add wine and tomatoes. Season to taste. Cook over low heat for 20 minutes. In a small skillet, melt 1 tablespoon butter, mix in brain, and heat through, then add to lobster mixture. Serve at once.

MOUNTAIN TROUT AU BLEU

BEFORE YOU BEGIN

You'll need: fish pan, large skillet, large saucepan, medium mixing bowl, strainer
Preparation Time: 1 hour
Yield: 1 serving

Stewards, when asked if the trout was really fresh killed, were known to turn to the table's waiter and quip, "Bring the fish to our guest's table to be killed." Nowhere is it recorded that this was actually done, which leaves as a mystery whether it was possible or for effect only. It was not uncommon for guests to ask that trout be "dressed" for eating, in which case the waiter would remove the head and the tail, split the fish down the side lengthwise, gently open it up, remove the entire bone structure, and lay the sides back together.

1 10-inch mountain trout	2 cups court bouillon

Use a fresh-killed trout. Remove entrails, leaving head and tail on. Be careful not to remove the slime covering the trout, as it is important to the flavor of this dish. Place trout in fish pan and set aside. Meanwhile, prepare court bouillon and pour over trout to cover. Return pan to burners, reduce heat to slow boil and cook for 10–12 minutes. Remove trout from pan and serve with drawn butter and horseradish cream.

COURT BOUILLON

2 cups fish stock	3 whole cloves
1 onion, sliced	2 Tbsp. vinegar
1 bay leaf	juice of ½ lemon

Bring fish stock to a boil. Add onion, bay leaf, cloves, vinegar, and lemon juice. Stir to mix, reduce heat and simmer 30 minutes. Strain before using.

HORSERADISH CREAM

½ cup heavy cream	two drops white vinegar
1 tsp. sugar	1 tsp. freshly grated horseradish

Combine all ingredients and mix thoroughly. Keep refrigerated.

NEW CORN CHOWDER, SOUTHERN STYLE

The key to this delicious soup is to gently scrape the kernels off the corn cob with a table fork so the skins remain on the cob, leaving you with only the fresh pulp.

BEFORE YOU BEGIN

You'll need: 12-inch square of cheesecloth, large saucepan, small bowl
Preparation time: 1½ hours
Yield: 8 servings

4 sprigs parsley	½ cup onions, chopped fine
1 leek	½ cup celery, chopped fine
½ carrot, cut lengthwise	4 cups chicken broth
1 stalk celery, 1-inch slice, including leaf	¾ cup raw potatoes, diced
¼ bay leaf	1½ cups peeled tomatoes, chopped
pinch, sage	pinch, cayenne pepper
pinch, thyme	½ cup heavy cream
2 thick slices bacon, diced	1 tsp. cornstarch
1 cup new corn pulp	

Use cheesecloth to make a bouquet garni of parsley, leek, carrot, celery, bay leaf, sage, and thyme, and set aside. In a large saucepan over medium heat, first soften bacon, then add corn, onions, and celery and sauté until tender, about 5 minutes. Add chicken broth, potatoes, tomatoes, and bouquet garni. Bring to a boil, reduce heat, and slow boil for 1 hour. Remove bouquet garni. Add cayenne pepper. Meanwhile, using fingers, dissolve cornstarch in heavy cream at room temperature. Add cornstarch/cream mixture to soup and stir until heated through.

ST. FRANCIS SEAFOOD SALAD DRESSING

An excellent base for a cold seafood salad made up of chopped white fish or shrimp, crabmeat, lobster, etc.

BEFORE YOU BEGIN

You'll need: small mixing bowl
Preparation time: 15 minutes
Yield: 2 cups

½ cup chili sauce	pepper to taste
½ cup mayonnaise	1 green pepper, finely chopped
2 Tbsp. white wine vinegar	2 stalks celery, finely chopped
4 Tbsp. olive oil	4 scallions with tops, finely chopped
salt to taste	1 hard-boiled egg, finely chopped

In a bowl, mix the first six ingredients. Add the green pepper, celery, and scallions and combine thoroughly. Chill until ready to serve. When serving, mix dressing with seafood. To serve, top a bed of lettuce with a slice of tomato, pour on the seafood salad, and sprinkle chopped egg over the salad.

STUFFED ZUCCHINI ANDALOUSE

BEFORE YOU BEGIN

You'll need: 3-quart saucepan, medium mixing bowl, baking pan
Preheat oven to 350 degrees
Preparation time: 1 hour
Yield: 6 servings

This specialty of Chef Carlos Gardini, when he manned the kitchen on the Super Chief, *calls for leftover ham and beef, demonstrating that dining departments used foodstuffs to their fullest. The simple yet elegant serving was able to satisfy a wide variety of tastes and pocketbooks.*

6 small zucchini	½ clove garlic, minced
2 Tbsp. fine-chopped onion	1⅓ cups soft bread crumbs,
3 Tbsp. chopped mushrooms	piled lightly
3 Tbsp. chopped green pepper	2 Tbsp. beef broth
⅓ cup chopped tomato	dash, pepper
¼ cup chopped cooked ham	dash, salt
¼ cup chopped cooked beef	

In 3 quarts of boiling, unsalted water, cook whole zucchini for 5 minutes. Carefully remove zucchini from water, remove stem, and cut in half lengthwise. Remove pulp, taking care not to break skins, and combine it with remaining ingredients. Mix thoroughly, adding broth only as needed to moisten sufficiently to loosely bind mixture. Spoon generous portions of the mixture into zucchini shells. Place on ungreased baking pan and bake for 30 minutes.

TOASTED HOT MEXICAN SANDWICH SANTA FE

BEFORE YOU BEGIN

You'll need: large bowl, baking sheet
Preheat oven to broil
Preparation time: 30 minutes
Yield: 6 servings

You'll need an appropriate white toasting bread (see page 173) cut into half-inch slices to complete this open-faced sandwich. Serve with Mexican cole slaw (see page 192) and/or potato salad (see page 171) and sliced tomato.

1 lb. cooked roast beef, diced fine	¼ lb. Swiss cheese, diced fine
4 hard-boiled eggs, chopped fine	½ cup mayonnaise
4 green chilies, parboiled, diced fine	1 tsp. lemon juice
½ cup pimentos, diced fine	½ cup chili sauce
1 celery stalk, diced fine	8 drops Tabasco sauce

Warm both sides of bread under the broiler before topping with the sandwich spread. Place diced cooked beef, hard-boiled eggs, green chilies, pimento, celery, and Swiss cheese in a bowl. Add mayonnaise, lemon juice, chili sauce, and Tabasco sauce. Mix thoroughly and spread generously on bread slices. Place on baking sheet and put 5 inches under preheated broiler. Toast until topping is lightly browned and bubbly.

7

THE ATLANTIC COAST LINE RAILROAD

CHICKEN MULLIGATAWNY SOUP

2 Tbsp. butter
2 onions, diced
½ green pepper, diced
½ cup rice, uncooked
½ Tbsp. curry powder
¼ cup flour

2 qts. chicken stock
pinch, cayenne pepper
salt to taste
1 cup chicken, cooked and diced
1 cup tart apples, peeled and diced
juice of one lemon

BEFORE YOU BEGIN

*You'll need: 3-quart saucepan, 2-quart saucepan, whisk
Preparation time: 45 minutes
Yield: 8 servings*

In the 3-quart saucepan over medium heat, melt butter and braise onions, green pepper, and rice until onions are tender. Stir frequently to avoid browning the rice. Add curry powder and stir. Add flour and make a roux, then cook for 10 minutes. Meanwhile, bring chicken stock to a boil and slowly pour into cooked vegetables, whipping constantly until boiling and smooth. Add cayenne pepper, salt, and diced chicken. Stir and simmer until rice is done. Finish by adding the apples and lemon juice. Simmer until apples are tender.

CREAM OF LIMA BEAN SOUP

4 14½-oz. cans lima beans, drained
1 carrot, diced
1 onion, sliced
1 qt. ham stock

½ cup butter
½ cup flour
4 cups milk, warmed
4 Tbsp. butter

BEFORE YOU BEGIN

*You'll need: 2-quart saucepan, strainer, 3-quart saucepan
Preparation time: 45 minutes
Yield: 8 servings*

In the 2-quart saucepan, combine lima beans, carrot, onion, and ham stock. Bring to a boil, reduce heat, and simmer until beans and other vegetables are soft. Force mixture through strainer or use blender to puree. Meanwhile, in 3-quart saucepan over medium heat, make a roux of ½ cup portions of butter and flour. Slowly stir hot lima bean puree into the roux. Add milk, bring just to boiling point, add 4 tablespoons butter in small pieces, and stir until melted and mixed well.

BAKED FILLET OF SOLE
WITH SPANISH SAUCE

BEFORE YOU BEGIN

*You'll need: baking
dish or pan, large
skillet, small skillet
Preheat oven to 350
degrees
Preparation time:
30 minutes
Yield: 4 servings*

*This is but one of many fresh seafood favorites of passengers of the Atlantic Coast Line.
For a lighter topping on a fillet main course, the railroad also featured easy-to-prepare
Sole Cubanese: Place 1 pound of fillets in a baking dish, top each serving with two thin
slices of tomato, sprinkle on one-quarter cup each of finely chopped onion and green pepper, salt to taste, pour on a small amount of melted butter, and bake at 350 degrees for
twenty minutes.*

1	lb. fresh fillet of sole	½	cup mushrooms
2	Tbsp. butter	1½	cups stewed tomatoes
¼	tsp. paprika	½	tsp. sugar
½	cup sliced onions		salt to taste
½	cup green peppers	1	Tbsp. butter, melted

In a large skillet over medium heat, melt the 2 tablespoons butter and blend in
paprika. Add onions, green peppers, and mushrooms and sauté until soft, about
5 minutes. Add stewed tomatoes, stirring until mixed thoroughly. Stir in sugar
and salt. Cover and let simmer until thick, about 20 minutes. Meanwhile, arrange
fillets skin side down in baking dish, brush on the 1 tablespoon of melted butter,
and place in oven for 15 minutes. Ladle hot sauce onto fillets just before serving.

＊━☀☒☀━＊

SEAFOOD COCKTAIL SAUCE

BEFORE YOU BEGIN

*You'll need: small mix-
ing bowl
Preparation time:
1¼ hours (including
minimum standing
time)
Yield: 2 cups*

*For tastes that run to hair-raising, perspiration-inducing, breathtaking heat, this recipe
won't disappoint. Waiters quipped that they'd have to see how angry the chef was on a
given day before they could describe how hot the cocktail sauce had gotten. To produce the
desired degree of "heat," adjust the amount of each ingredient accordingly.*

1½	cups tomato catsup	½	cup horseradish
	juice of 1 lemon		generous dash Tabasco sauce
2	Tbsp. Worcestershire sauce		salt to taste

Combine all ingredients and mix thoroughly. Refrigerate at least one hour before
serving; overnight if possible.

BAKED PORK CHOPS WITH NOODLES CREOLE

BEFORE YOU BEGIN

*You'll need: large
heavy skillet, baking
pan, 2-quart
saucepan, whisk
Preheat oven to 300
degrees
Preparation time:
1 hour
Yield: 6 servings*

2 Tbsp. cooking oil
  salt and pepper to taste
  flour to coat
1½ lbs. (6-12) pork chops
2 Tbsp. butter, melted
4-6 Tbsp. water

4 Tbsp. butter
1 qt. cooked egg noodles,
  drained
1 cup Creole sauce
  chopped parsley

In a large heavy skillet, heat cooking oil to hot. Meanwhile, season both sides of the pork chops with salt and pepper, pass lightly in flour, then fry in hot, shallow oil until well browned on both sides, about 4 minutes per side. Place pork chops in baking pan, sprinkle with melted butter and water, then place in oven for 20 minutes, basting occasionally to keep moist. Meanwhile, in a clean skillet over medium heat, melt butter and sauté cooked and drained egg noodles, taking care not to let stiffen or brown. Add Creole Sauce and heat to let get very hot. To serve, place one or two pork chops on heated individual plate, noodles Creole alongside, and chopped parsley sprinkled over noodles.

CREOLE SAUCE

¼ cup butter
2 onions, chopped fine
1 green pepper, minced
4 stalks celery, chopped fine
1 clove garlic, minced
¼ cup sifted flour

2 cups diced tomatoes with juice
1 cup tomato puree
¼ cup mushrooms, sliced
1 bay leaf
  salt and pepper to taste
1 tsp. chopped parsley

In 2-quart saucepan over medium heat, melt butter and sauté onion, green pepper, and celery for 4 minutes. Add garlic and continue to sauté one more minute. Add sifted flour, stirring constantly to make a roux. Add tomatoes, tomato puree, mushrooms, bay leaf, salt, and pepper. Bring just to a boil, reduce heat, and simmer for 30 minutes, stirring occasionally. Add chopped parsley.

BROWN BETTY WITH FRUIT SAUCE

BREAD PUDDING

1 **loaf slightly stale white bread**	1 **tsp. cinnamon**
4 **cups cooking apples, peeled and sliced**	3 **Tbsp. butter,**
¾ **cup sugar**	3 **Tbsp. butter, melted**

Butter baking pan thoroughly and set aside. Break bread loosely into small cubes. Spread a layer of bread cubes over the bottom of baking pan. Cover with a layer of sliced apples, sprinkle ¼ cup sugar over all, season with cinnamon and dash of nutmeg, and top with a dot of butter. Repeat until pan is filled, finishing with bread. Drizzle melted butter evenly over top of completed pudding assembly. Bake until nicely browned and heated through, about 30 minutes. Cut into portions, place on serving dish, and cover with fruit sauce.

FRUIT SAUCE

1 **Tbsp. cornstarch**	1½-inch **stick cinnamon**
¼ **cup cold water**	**juice of 1 lemon**
1 **cup pineapple juice**	¼ **cup diced peeled apples**
1 **cup peach juice**	¼ **cup diced pineapple**
½ **cup sugar**	¼ **cup diced orange**
¼ **cup maple syrup**	¼ **cup diced peaches**
2 **whole cloves**	1 **Tbsp. seedless raisins**
pinch nutmeg	

Dissolve cornstarch in cold water and set aside. Place pineapple juice, peach juice, sugar, and maple syrup in 2-quart saucepan and bring to a boil. Add cloves, nutmeg, cinnamon stick, and lemon juice. Reduce heat and simmer. Add dissolved cornstarch, stir to mix, and continue cooking until thickened slightly. Meanwhile, in large bowl, mix diced fruits well. While syrup is still boiling, strain it over the mixed diced fruit and add raisins. Return to saucepan over low heat to heat through. Cover, remove from heat, and allow to cool before serving over bread pudding. NOTE: Sugar quantity given applies if natural, unsweetened fruit and juices are used. If canned or preserved fruits and juices are used, less sugar will be needed.

CREAM SCONES

2 cups flour
4 tsp. baking powder
2 tsp. sugar
¼ tsp. salt
4 Tbsp. butter, softened
2 eggs
⅓ cup heavy cream
sugar to taste

BEFORE YOU BEGIN

You'll need: medium mixing bowl, small mixing bowl, pastry blender, large cookie sheet
Preheat oven to 400 degrees
Preparation time: 1½ hours
Yield: 12 scones

Mix, then sift the dry ingredients. Work in the butter with pastry blender until coarse. Before beating eggs, retain 1 teaspoon of egg white for an egg wash. Beat eggs well and add to dry ingredients. Add cream and mix dough thoroughly. Wrap dough in waxed paper and place in refrigerator for 1 hour before proceeding. Toss dough on a floured board, pat and roll to ¾-inch thickness. With sharp knife, cut in squares or triangles and brush with egg wash made of reserved egg white diluted with 1 teaspoon water. Sprinkle with sugar, place on ungreased cookie sheet, and bake 15 minutes.

CUBAN SANDWICH, YBOR CITY STYLE

"Cuban" bread, a short French-style loaf, could also be called "Continental" bread because of its ready availability in Spain, Portugal, and Italy.

1 14-inch loaf Cuban bread
¼ oz. butter, softened
1 oz. baked ham, thinly sliced
¾ oz. turkey breast, thinly sliced
2 ¼-oz. slices hard salami
2 pickle chips
1 slice Swiss cheese

BEFORE YOU BEGIN

You'll need: bread knife, baking sheet
Preheat oven to 200 degrees
Preparation time: 15 minutes
Yield: 1 sandwich

Cut loaf of bread crosswise into 7-inch lengths. Split each piece lengthwise through the center. Spread top slice of bread with soft butter. On bottom slice, prepare sandwich by first covering the bread with baked ham. On top of the ham place white meat of turkey. On top of turkey, place 2 salami slices. Place 1 pickle chip on each piece of salami. Cover each with slice of Swiss cheese, (half of a full slice). Close sandwich, place on baking sheet, and put in oven. Heat until bread is hot but not dried out. Serve hot.

FRICASSEE OF LAMB WITH DUMPLINGS

BEFORE YOU BEGIN

You'll need: 3-quart saucepan, 2-quart saucepan, strainer, large mixing bowl, sifter, two-level steaming pot
Preparation time: 1½ hours
Yield: 8 servings

2 lbs. lean lamb, cut in 1-inch cubes
½ bay leaf
1 cup carrots, diced
1 cup onions, diced
1 cup celery, diced
¼ cup butter
¼ cup flour
2 cups lamb stock
1 egg yolk, lightly beaten
1½ cups cooked peas
¼ tsp. celery salt
⅛ tsp. white pepper

Place lamb cubes in the 3-quart saucepan with cold water to cover, add bay leaf, and bring to a boil. Reduce heat and simmer until nearly tender, about 1 hour. Remove from heat, drain and wash off meat. Place lamb back in clean pot and cover with fresh cold water. Add diced carrots, onions, and celery. Bring to a boil, reduce heat, and simmer until meat and vegetables are tender but firm, about 30 minutes. Meanwhile, in 2-quart saucepan, make a roux of the butter and flour. When lamb and vegetables are done, strain off and retain the broth. Add 2 cups of broth to the roux, stirring constantly. Continue cooking 5–6 minutes to thicken. Meanwhile, in large bowl, beat egg yolk to a light lemon color. Slowly stir thickened broth into the egg yolk, mix well, and return sauce to saucepan. Do not allow the sauce to boil after the egg is added. Sauce should be thick enough to adhere to the meat. Return meat and vegetables to the sauce and simmer for a few minutes until heated through. Serve in a casserole with dumplings on top. Pour some sauce over dumplings and sprinkle with chopped parsley.

DUMPLINGS

2½ cups flour
2 Tbsp. baking powder
½ tsp. salt
2 eggs
1 cup of milk, approximately

Sift flour, baking powder, and salt together into a mixing bowl. Make a depression in the center and break eggs into it. Add milk gradually, while stirring, to make a stiff batter. Using a two-level steaming pot (or a colander placed over a large saucepan half-filled with boiling water), drop ½ tablespoonful of batter evenly over bottom of steaming platform. Cover and steam about 5 minutes. Keep cooked dumplings warm until ready to use.

ORANGE MARMALADE PUDDING

12 slices 1-day-stale bread	¼ tsp. salt
6 cups milk	1 Tbsp. lemon juice
6 egg yolks	1½ cups orange marmalade
¾ cup sugar	at room temperature

BEFORE YOU BEGIN

You'll need: 2-quart saucepan, large mixing bowl, 9" x 9" baking pan, electric beater, small mixing bowl
Preheat oven to 350 degrees
Preparation time: 1½ hours
Yield: 6 servings

Butter the baking pan well and set aside. Toast bread lightly, cut into 1-inch squares, place in baking pan, and set aside. In the saucepan, scald the milk. Meanwhile, in a large bowl, beat egg yolks to a light lemon color and add sugar. Very slowly, pour the scalded milk into egg-sugar mixture, beating constantly. Add salt and lemon juice and stir until mixture is smooth. Pour mixture over toast squares and allow to stand 15 minutes. Bake until a fork placed in center of pudding comes out clean, about 40 minutes. Remove from oven and increase oven temperature to 425 degrees. Meanwhile spread top of pudding generously with orange marmalade, taking care not to damage pudding. Cover with meringue, return oven to brown, about 10 minutes. Serve warm or cold.

MERINGUE

6 egg whites	½ cup sugar

Beat egg whites until frothy. Continue beating while gradually adding sugar and beat until stiff.

POTATO SALAD

6 new potatoes, boiled	⅓ cup celery, chopped
¼ tsp. salt	⅓ cup dill pickle, chopped fine
⅛ tsp. white pepper	3 hard-boiled eggs, chopped fine
2 Tbsp. sugar	¼ cup pimento, chopped fine
⅓ cup white vinegar	1 cup mayonnaise
1 tsp. parsley, chopped fine	

BEFORE YOU BEGIN

You'll need: large saucepan, large mixing bowl
Preparation time: 1 hour (plus several hours to chill)
Yield: 12 servings

Begin with all ingredients at the same (room) temperature. Place potatoes in water to cover and boil with skins on until cooked but not softened, about 15 minutes. When done, remove from water, cool, peel, and dice in small cubes. In large mixing bowl, season diced potatoes with salt and pepper. Add sugar and vinegar, mix well, and let marinate for 30 minutes. Then add parsley, celery, pickle, hard-boiled eggs, pimento, and mayonnaise. Mix well and season further to taste. Moisten further, if desired, by adding vinegar blended with salt and sugar to taste. Refrigerate several hours before serving to allow flavors to penetrate and blend.

VARIATIONS: FRENCH TOAST AS SERVED ON FIVE RAILROADS

A predominantly male ridership, in a time when dietary health concerns were not voiced, assured beefsteak its perennial place as the most popular food item on dining-car menus of transcontinental trains. Aside from the quality of the cut, however (where the Union Pacific, with its ready access to the stockyards at Omaha, Nebraska, surely prevailed), distinction could only be established with cosmetics. Thus, the Cotton Belt Route topped its steaks with a pimento cut to the distinctive shape of its logo, and the Union Pacific—leaving nothing to chance—served its steaks with a large fried onion ring, unique for its coating of potato flour and potato meal.

In meeting the demand for the second-most-requested item, apple pie, the railroads played up whatever apple of the season was grown by their shippers. Beyond that rather important distinction, only a pie's crust and toppings could differ, as the nutmeg sauce that topped Fred Harvey's French apple pies and the sweet pastry crust of the Baltimore & Ohio Railroad attest.

It fell, then, to French toast to become the most popular menu item that was both common to the various railroads, yet creatively distinctive. And as the samples below demonstrate, chefs responded with some dazzling variations on the classic formula of stale bread soaked in an egg-and-milk wash, then fried. These frequently requested recipes were distributed to patrons to share with others, giving special meaning to the concept of "word-of-mouth" marketing. The Northern Pacific Railway went so far as to develop a flavorful bread used for its French toast, one suitable for use with all the recipes provided.

(COURTESY OF THE ILLINOIS CENTRAL GULF RAILROAD)

TOAST BREAD (NORTHERN PACIFIC)

BEFORE YOU BEGIN
You'll need: large mixing bowl, medium mixing bowl, two 8" x 4" bread pans
Preheat oven to 375 degrees
Preparation time: 2½ hours
Yield: 2 loaves

2 pkgs. active dry yeast	1 Tbsp. dry malt
3 Tbsp. sugar	2 Tbsp. shortening
¾ cup warm water	5–5½ cups all-
1½ cups warm milk	purpose flour
1 Tbsp. salt	

In large bowl, combine yeast with sugar and warm water and let stand for 8–10 minutes. Add milk, salt, dry malt, and shortening. Mix at low speed until blended. Add 3 cups of flour and beat thoroughly. Using a wooden spoon, gradually stir in enough of remaining flour to make a moderately stiff dough. On floured surface, knead dough until smooth and elastic. Place in greased bowl, turning to grease top. Cover and let rise until doubled, about 40 minutes. Punch down dough, divide in half, and let rest for 10 minutes. Form loaves and place in the greased bread pans. Let rise again until doubled, about 35 minutes. Bake for 40 minutes.

For the best French toast, allow bread to become stale by storing in a paper bag at room temperature for 2–3 days. If bread is still moist when sliced, expose each side to air for up to an hour before using. Slice as directed by the individual recipes.

NORTHERN PACIFIC FRENCH TOAST

BEFORE YOU BEGIN
You'll need: shallow dish, large skillet
Heat oil for frying to hot
Preparation time: 20 minutes
Yield: 1 serving

2 slices bread	¼ tsp. salt
2 eggs, slightly beaten	¼ tsp. cinnamon
½ cup milk	butter or shortening
1 Tbsp. sugar	to fry

Cut bread into 1½-inch slices and cut slices in half diagonally. Mix eggs, milk, sugar, salt, and cinnamon well in a shallow dish. Dip bread into mixture. Fry it in a little butter or shortening until golden brown on both sides. Serve hot with topping of your choice.

SOO LINE SPECIAL FRENCH TOAST

BEFORE YOU BEGIN
You'll need: deep fryer, shallow dish
Preheat frying oil to hot
Preparation time: 30 minutes
Yield: 1 serving

2 slices bread	2 oz. sugar
1 egg, well beaten	oil for deep frying
pinch, salt	
3 oz. light cream	

Cut bread in ¾-inch slices and cut slices in half diagonally. In a shallow dish, make a batter of well-beaten egg, salt, cream, and sugar. Dip bread in batter and fry to a golden brown in hot, deep fat. Remove and drain. Sprinkle with fruit, maple syrup, or honey and serve immediately.

PENNSYLVANIA RAILROAD
FRENCH TOAST

BEFORE YOU BEGIN
You'll need: electric mixer, mixing bowl, large
    skillet, paper towels
Heat oil for frying to hot
Preparation time: 30 minutes
Yield: 4 servings

8 slices white bread, cut ⅜ inch thick	1½ cups milk
	pinch, salt
2 oz. butter, at room temperature	3 Tbsp. powdered sugar
6 Tbsp. strawberry preserves	1/4 tsp. vanilla or cinnamon
3 eggs	oil for frying

Spread one side of 4 slices of bread with butter.
Spread one side of the other 4 slices of bread
with preserves. To make sandwiches, press well
together a buttered slice of bread onto a slice
spread with preserves. Trim crust carefully and
cut each sandwich into four triangles. In a mixer, beat eggs and sugar well together for at least
10 minutes. Add salt, milk, and vanilla or cinnamon and beat well again. Lay small sandwiches in this mixture, carefully turning them
over to soak well. Drain on paper towels. Fry in
a very little hot oil. Remove when of nice gold-
en brown color and drain. Dust with powdered
sugar and serve hot with maple syrup.

FRENCH TOAST,
UNION PACIFIC STYLE

BEFORE YOU BEGIN
You'll need: shallow bowl, large skillet
Heat oil for frying to hot
Preparation time: 15 minutes
Yield: 1 serving

2 slices white bread	1 Tbsp. clarified butter
2 eggs	
2 Tbsp. light cream	1 Tbsp. lard
	powdered sugar

Cut two slices of bread ¾-inch thick and trim
crust. Cut diagonally, making four triangular
pieces. Beat eggs and cream together well. Dip
bread triangles in mixture and fry until golden
brown in hot butter and lard. Serve hot and
well drained. Top may be sprinkled with powdered sugar if desired.

FRENCH TOAST À LA SANTA FE

*This special and renowned recipe, perhaps the best
French toast of them all, was perfected by Fred Harvey chefs in 1918 for the Santa Fe Railway's dining
cars. It produces a puffy, golden brown delicacy. The
Santa Fe Railway dining-car service, at its peak,
provided nearly 1 million breakfasts a year. This
item perennially topped the "most popular" list.*

BEFORE YOU BEGIN
You'll need: small mixing bowl, whisk, 12-inch
    cast iron skillet, paper towels, baking sheet
Preheat oven to 400 degrees
Preparation time: 20 minutes
Yield: 2 servings

2 slices white bread, cut ¾ inch thick	2 eggs
	pinch, salt (optional)
½ cup light cream	½ cup cooking oil

Place cooking oil in skillet, heat to hot. Meanwhile, cut each bread slice diagonally to form
four triangles, and set aside. In small bowl,
combine eggs, cream, and salt and beat well.
Soak bread thoroughly in egg/cream mixture.
Fry soaked bread in hot oil to a golden brown
on both sides, about 2 minutes per side. Lift
from skillet to clean paper towel and allow to
absorb excess cooking oil. Transfer to baking
sheet and place in oven. Bake 4–6 minutes, until bread slices have puffed up. Serve sprinkled
with powdered sugar and cinnamon and apple
sauce, currant jelly, maple syrup, honey, or preserves, and bacon, ham, or sausage if desired.

8

THE CANADIAN NATIONAL RAILWAYS

STUFFED CALF'S LIVER

2 lbs. calf's liver
2 Tbsp. bacon drippings

2 cups brown sauce
1 small onion, diced

BEFORE YOU BEGIN

*You'll need: baking
pan, skewers, small
skillet, small bowl*
*Preheat oven to 350
degrees*
*Preparation time:
2½ hours*
Yield: 8 servings

Begin with a single chunky piece of liver. Wash and dry. Make a deep cut near-ly the entire length of the liver, beginning at thick end. Fill the cut pouch with stuffing (below). Skewer cut in liver closed and rub upper side with bacon drip-pings. Put liver in baking pan, pour brown sauce (see page 156) all around, and bake uncovered for 2 hours. Baste every 12 minutes with sauce in pan. Mean-while, in a small skillet, melt 1 tablespoon bacon drippings over medium-high heat. Add diced onion and fry, stirring occasionally, until well browned (about 10 minutes). To serve, place liver on serving dish, strain sauce all around, and garnish with fried onions.

STUFFING

½ cup cold cooked ham, chopped
½ cup stale bread crumbs
½ small onion, finely chopped
1 Tbsp. finely chopped parsley

2 Tbsp. beef stock
1 egg, beaten
salt and pepper to taste

Mix ham, bread crumbs, onion, and chopped parsley. Apply enough beef stock to moisten. Add beaten egg, season with salt and pepper, and mix well.

✦ ⊰◈⊱ ✦
CHICKEN À LA STANLEY

BEFORE YOU BEGIN

*You'll need: 6-quart
stewing pot, small
skillet, strainer,
1-quart saucepan,
large skillet
Preparation time:
1 hour
Yield: 4 servings*

1	3–4 lb. broiling chicken	1	cup chicken stock, warmed
½	cup butter	2	Tbsp. butter
1	medium onion, sliced	2	Tbsp. flour
1	bay leaf	½	cup heavy cream, warmed
¼	tsp. salt	¼	cup butter
⅛	tsp. white pepper	2	ripe bananas, sliced
	pinch, ground mace		flour to coat

Cut chicken into suitable serving-sized pieces. In the 6-quart stewing pot over medium heat, melt the ½ cup butter, then add chicken pieces, onion, bay leaf, salt, pepper, and mace. Cover and cook for 10 minutes. Add chicken stock, cover, and simmer until cooked, about 30–45 minutes. Meanwhile, in a small skillet over medium heat, make a roux of 2 tablespoons each of butter and flour. Then, remove chicken from pot. Slowly stir roux into stock and allow to thicken. Strain sauce into 1-quart saucepan, add cream, stir to mix and heat through. Meanwhile, in a large skillet over medium-high heat, melt the ¼ cup butter. Drag banana slices in flour to coat, then fry in hot butter, turning once. To serve, arrange chicken pieces on a platter, cover with cream sauce, and garnish with fried bananas.

✦ ⊰◈⊱ ✦
CHICKEN BROTH, SOUTHERN STYLE

BEFORE YOU BEGIN

*You'll need: 3-quart
saucepan
Preparation time:
1 hour
Yield: 8 servings*

2	cups chicken meat, uncooked	¼	tsp. curry powder
2	Tbsp. butter		salt to taste
1	small onion, minced	¼	tsp. cayenne pepper
1	green pepper, shredded	1	cup lima beans
1	Tbsp. flour	1	cup sweet corn
2	qts. chicken stock, warmed	1	cup okra, sliced

Cut chicken meat into small pieces. In a the saucepan over medium heat, melt butter and, stirring occasionally, sauté chicken with onions and green peppers until meat is cooked through and vegetables are tender but not browned, about 8 minutes. Add flour, stirring constantly. Then add hot chicken stock. Add curry powder, salt and cayenne pepper. Bring to a boil, reduce heat, and slow boil 45 minutes. Skim residue, if any, and add lima beans, corn, and okra. Simmer until added vegetables are tender and heated through.

FISH CHOWDER

BEFORE YOU BEGIN

You'll need: 3-quart saucepan, 2- quart saucepan, 1-quart saucepan, large skillet with cover
Preparation time: 1½ hours
Yield: 8 servings

1 medium haddock
3 large potatoes, diced
3 slices salt pork, diced
1 large onion, diced
1 clove garlic, diced

2 Tbsp. butter
4 Tbsp. flour
2 cups milk, warmed
2 Tbsp. finely minced parsley
salt and pepper to taste
Worcestershire sauce to taste

Remove all white flesh from haddock and dice in 1-inch squares. Remove eyes from head of haddock, washing latter thoroughly. Place haddock head and bones, in 3-quart saucepan with 6 cups of water. Bring to a boil, reduce heat, and allow to simmer for 1 hour. Strain and retain 1 quart of liquid. Meanwhile, in lightly salted water to cover, cook diced potatoes until soft, about 10 minutes, then set aside in cold water. Using a covered skillet over medium-high heat, braise salt pork, onion, and garlic without browning. Put butter in a 2-quart saucepan over medium heat and when melted, add flour, stirring constantly. Pour heated milk on fish stock, stir to mix, then add to butter and flour, stirring briskly until smooth. Add fish squares, onion, salt pork, and garlic. Drain and add potatoes. Season to taste with salt, pepper, and Worcestershire sauce, stir to mix, and simmer until fish is tender, about 15 minutes. Serve hot.

CHEF'S RICE SALAD

BEFORE YOU BEGIN

You'll need: large mixing bowl
Preparation time: 30 minutes
Yield: 6 servings

1½ cups cooked rice
1 cup finely chopped celery
2 Tbsp. finely chopped green onion
2 Tbsp. finely chopped parsley
2 Tbsp. olive oil
4 Tbsp. white vinegar
2 Tbsp. mayonnaise
salt and pepper to taste
1 cup finely diced lettuce

1 cup finely chopped watercress
6 hard-boiled eggs
3 medium tomatoes
24 asparagus tips
12 cucumber slices
6 ¼-inch green pepper rings
½ cup mayonnaise
paprika
chopped parsley

Cook rice (see page 153), taking care that it remains firm and easily separable. In a bowl, mix rice with celery, green onions, parsley, olive oil, vinegar, mayonnaise, and seasonings. Add lettuce and watercress and mix lightly. To serve, place a mound of rice mixture on a bed of lettuce. Arrange around or over each serving: 1 egg cut in quarters; half of a tomato cut in thirds; 4 asparagus spears, 2 on each side; 2 slices of cucumber; 1 green pepper ring, cut in half; 1 generous spoon of mayonnaise; and a dash of paprika and chopped parsley.

GOLDEN PUDDING WITH RICH ORANGE SAUCE

BEFORE YOU BEGIN

You'll need: large mixing bowl, sifter, electric beater, 8" x 8" baking pan, 1-quart saucepan, grater, juicer, small bowl
Preheat oven to 350 degrees
Preparation time: 1 hour
Yield: 8 servings

2 cups flour	1 cup milk
¼ lb. butter, room temperature	⅛ teaspoon salt
1 cup sugar	½ tsp. vanilla
2 egg yolks	1 tsp. baking powder

Grease baking pan and set aside. Sift flour 4 times and set aside. Cream butter and sugar well. Add egg yolks and whip until creamy. Add milk, sifted flour, salt, and vanilla, mixing until light and smooth. Stir in baking powder. Pour into baking pan and bake for 60 minutes, or until knife inserted in center comes out clean. Cut into 2-inch squares and serve with Rich Orange Sauce.

RICH ORANGE SAUCE

1 orange, juice and rind	pinch, salt
1 cup boiling water	1 bay leaf
¼ cup sugar	2 Tbsp. cornstarch
2 Tbsp. butter	2 Tbsp. cold water

Grate rind and squeeze juice from orange. In a 1-quart saucepan, blend all ingredients except cornstarch and cold water. Bring to a boil, reduce heat immediately, and simmer for 10 minutes. Remove bay leaf. Dissolve cornstarch in cold water and stir into mixture. Simmer until creamy. Serve warm.

GRAHAM ROLLS

BEFORE YOU BEGIN

You'll need: large mixing bowl, 2-quart saucepan, electric beater, spatula, large bowl and cloth towel to cover, 2 large cookie sheets, small bowl
Preheat oven to 400 degrees
Preparation time: 3½ hours
Yield: 24 rolls

5¼ cups (1½ lbs.) graham flour	¼ cup butter
7–8 cups (2 lbs.) flour	6½ Tbsp. molasses
4½ tsp. salt	1 egg, well beaten
2 pkgs. active dry yeast	1 Tbsp. milk
1 qt. water	

In a large bowl, combine 1 cup each of graham flour and white flour, salt, and yeast. In a 2-quart saucepan, combine water and butter and heat to 120–130 degrees. With mixer on low speed, gradually beat butter/water liquid into dry ingredients. Increase mixer to medium speed and beat two minutes, clearing sides of bowl with spatula. Continue beating and add molasses and ½ cup graham flour and beat for 2 more minutes. Stir in remaining graham flour and enough white flour to make a soft dough. On a lightly floured surface, knead dough until smooth and elastic, about 10 minutes. Place in large greased bowl, turn once to grease top, then cover with cloth and place in warm spot to rise until dough is doubled and will recede to the touch, about 1 hour. Punch dough down, fold edges over, and turn dough over in bowl. Let dough rise again by about one-half, or for 30 minutes. On a lightly floured surface, cut dough in half, then divide each half into 12 pieces. Shape into balls and place 2 inches apart on greased cookie sheets. Cover with cloth and let rest 15 minutes. Brush tops with wash made of beaten egg and milk. Bake until golden brown, about 10 minutes. Cool on wire rack and serve warm.

MEAT SAUCE FOR SPAGHETTI

3 Tbsp. olive oil	1 Tbsp. chili powder
1 lb ground beef	2 tsp. basil leaves, ground
1 lb. ground pork	½ tsp. ground cloves
1 onion, minced	3 bay leaves
½ green pepper, minced	2 cups chicken stock
3 cloves garlic, mince	½ tsp. salt
5 cups crushed tomatoes	¼ tsp. cayenne pepper
¼ cup tomato paste	

BEFORE YOU BEGIN

*You'll need: large skillet, 4-quart saucepan, 6-quart sauce pot
Preparation time: 2½ hours
Yield: 2 quarts*

Heat olive oil in a large skillet over medium-high heat. Add beef, pork, onion, green pepper, and garlic and sauté until browned, about 10 minutes. With slotted spoon to drain off fat, place sautéed ingredients in the 4-quart saucepan. Add remaining ingredients and mix well. Slowly bring to a boil, reduce heat, cover, and simmer for two hours.

SPLIT PEA SOUP

1 lb. split green peas	1 stalk celery, sliced
2 qts. chicken stock	2 Tbsp. flour
½ lb. salt pork	¼ cup water
3 medium carrots, peeled and sliced	salt and pepper to taste
2 large onions, chopped	

BEFORE YOU BEGIN

*You'll need: 6-quart saucepan, large bowl, colander, sieve
Preparation time: 2 hours (after soaking peas overnight)
Yield: 8 servings*

Soak split peas overnight in cold water to cover. Drain peas well and place in the saucepan. Add stock, salt pork, carrots, onions, and celery, and bring to a boil. Reduce heat and slow boil for 1 hour. When soup is done, dissolve flour in water and stir paste into the soup to thicken and prevent settling. Remove the pork and cut into small dice. Meanwhile, force the rest of the soup through a fine sieve into a clean saucepan. Bring puree to a boil, season to taste, add the pork, and heat through. Serve with croutons.

---◆—⊫◆⊠—◆---

SOUFFLÉ ROTHSCHILD

2 cups crushed macaroon cookies
2 cups ripe bing cherries, pitted
2 cups sponge cake cut into 1-inch cubes

1 recipe Sabayon sauce
2 Tbsp. currant jelly
1 recipe meringue

Lightly grease a soufflé pan. Fill with alternate layers by first evenly distributing crushed macaroons, then pitted cherries, then sponge cake cubes. Pour hot Sabayon sauce over the layered ingredients and allow to filter through. Place in oven for 10 minutes. Remove from oven, place currant jelly on top, and cover with meringue. Return to hot oven and bake until browned, about 10–15 minutes. Serve without sauce.

SABAYON SAUCE

4 egg yolks
¾ cup sugar

juice of 1 lemon
½ cup sherry wine

In a small bowl, beat together well, egg yolks, sugar, and lemon juice. Pour into top pan of double boiler over simmering water and cook, stirring constantly with a whisk, until thickened enough to adhere to the whisk. Remove from heat and continue stirring constantly while slowly pouring in the sherry wine.

MERINGUE

2 egg whites
4 Tbsp. sugar

½ tsp. vanilla

Beat egg white until stiff but not dry. Gradually add sugar and continue to beat until stiff peaks form and hold. Add vanilla and beat only long enough to mix.

BEFORE YOU BEGIN

You'll need: 2-quart soufflé pan, small mixing bowl, electric beater, double boiler, whisk, medium mixing bowl
Preheat oven to 350 degrees
Preparation time: 45 minutes
Yield: 8 servings

---◆—⊫◆⊠—◆---

TOURTIERES (CANADIAN PORK PIE)

2-crust meal pie-pastry recipe
1½ lbs. ground pork
1 medium onion, minced
1 clove garlic, minced (optional)
½ tsp. salt

⅜ tsp. celery salt
⅜ tsp. ground cloves
⅜ tsp. cinnamon
¾ cup water

Make pie pastry (see page 154), line pie pan with one portion, set all aside for use later. In the saucepan over medium heat, brown the ground pork lightly. Add all remaining ingredients, mix well, and cook for 20 minutes. Pack pork mixture into pie pan and cover with top pastry, sealing edges and putting 2–3 slits in the top for steam to escape. Place in oven and bake until crust is golden brown, about 40 minutes.

BEFORE YOU BEGIN

You'll need: 8-inch pie pan with 1-inch sides, 2-quart saucepan
Preheat oven to 450 degrees
Preparation time: 1 hour
Yield: 4 servings

9

THE CANADIAN PACIFIC RAILWAY

CANADIAN PACIFIC YELLOW PEA SOUP

½ lb. whole yellow peas
¼ lb. salt pork, thickly sliced
1 large carrot, peeled and sliced
1 medium onion, chopped
1 stalk celery, chopped
2 quarts hot water

BEFORE YOU BEGIN

You'll need: 6-quart pot, small skillet
Preparation time: 3 hours
Yield: 8 servings

Wash peas well in cold water. In a pot over medium heat, render some fat from the salt pork and sauté the carrot, onion, and celery until tender. Add hot water, slowly at first, then peas, bring all to a boil, and boil for 1 hour. Remove pork and vegetables and continue boiling until peas are thoroughly cooked, adding water, if necessary, to bring to required consistency. Wash salt pork, allow to cool, then dice small. In a small skillet over medium heat, slowly fry until crisp, drain all fat off, and serve in soup like croutons.

COCONUT ROCK

2 egg whites	**1 lb. coconut, shredded**
1 cup sugar	

Grease baking pan all around, dust with flour, and set aside. Beat egg whites to meringue consistency. Continue beating and add sugar. When thoroughly combined, add coconut and beat long enough to mix well. Spread on the greased pan and bake 30 minutes, until hard. Cool and break to serve.

+—ᴇ◊ᴈ—+

CREAM VIRGINIA SWEET POTATO SOUP

4 sweet potatoes	**½ tsp. salt**
2 Tbsp. butter	**2 egg yolks, well beaten**
1 onion, chopped	**1 cup milk, warmed**
2 stalks celery, sliced	**1 cup heavy cream, warmed**
2 Tbsp. flour	**1 Tbsp. butter**
3 cups chicken stock, warmed	

Peel and quarter sweet potatoes. In a 1-quart saucepan, bring to a boil cut-up sweet potatoes in enough water to cover and cook until tender, about 25 minutes. Drain well, set aside ¼ of one potato for garnish, and mash remaining potatoes well. Meanwhile, in another clean 1-quart saucepan over medium heat, melt 2 tablespoons butter and sauté onions and celery until tender, about 5 minutes. Stirring constantly, add flour to make a roux and let simmer 3–5 minutes. Do not brown. Slowly stir in chicken stock and add salt, bring to a boil, reduce heat, and simmer 30 minutes. Meanwhile, in a large bowl, beat egg yolks until smooth. Stir in warmed milk, then cream, and whisk until smooth. Stirring constantly, strain stock/vegetable liquid into cream mixture. Return to a 2-quart saucepan over medium heat and add mashed sweet potatoes. Stir with a whisk to mix well and heat through. Dice retained ¼ sweet potato and, in a small skillet over medium heat, sauté in 1 tablespoon of butter until browned. Sprinkle fried/diced sweet potato over soup for garnish.

FISH AU GRATIN, ITALIAN STYLE

BEFORE YOU BEGIN

You'll need: large skillet, small skillet, broiling pan, 9" x 13" baking dish, 1-quart saucepan
Preheat oven to broil
Preparation time: 45 minutes
Yield: 6 servings

2 lb. fish fillets
2 Tbsp. olive oil
3 cups Italian sauce

½ cup grated Parmesan cheese
½ cup fine bread crumbs
2 Tbsp. butter, melted

Use sole, orange roughy, or similar fish. Place fillets on broiling pan skin side down. Lightly coat the fillets with oil and place 5 inches under broiler element. Broil until fish is white but not flaking, about 6 minutes. Turn fillets, taking care not to separate. Return to broiler for 5 minutes. Remove to a baking dish. Cover with Italian sauce. Sprinkle grated cheese and bread crumbs over all. Drizzle melted butter on top and place in a 350-degree oven until bubbly, about 20 minutes. Garnish with chopped parsley.

ITALIAN SAUCE

2 cups demi-glace
1 cup tomato sauce
2 Tbsp. butter, melted

2 Tbsp. finely chopped onion
¼ tsp. cayenne pepper
   juice of 1 lemon

In a 1-quart saucepan over medium heat, melt butter and sauté onions until lightly browned. Add demi-glace (see page 154) and tomato sauce (see following recipe or substitute 3 cups of a favorite red pasta sauce). Season with cayenne pepper and lemon juice. Bring to a boil, reduce heat, and simmer for 5 minutes before using.

FRIED FISH, ORLY STYLE

2 lbs. fresh cod fillets
pepper
juice of 1 lemon

1 Tbsp. finely chopped parsley
1 recipe frying batter
4 cups tomato sauce

In a large skillet, bring 1 inch of cooking oil to hot. Season fish fillets to taste with pepper, lemon juice, and chopped parsley. Dip in frying batter and fry in hot oil until golden brown, turning occasionally. Serve with tomato sauce poured over.

FRYING BATTER

2⅔ cups sifted flour
½ tsp. salt
4 tsp. baking powder

2 eggs, well beaten
1⅓ cups milk

Sift flour before measuring. Add salt and baking powder and sift again. Add well-beaten eggs and milk and stir to mix. Batter should be just thick enough to coat fish. Add milk if too thick; add flour if too thin.

TOMATO SAUCE

2 Tbsp. butter
1 small clove garlic, diced fine
2 carrots, peeled and diced fine
1 small onion, peeled and diced fine
1 stalk celery, julienne
1 sprig thyme

½ bay leaf
2 Tbsp. flour
2 cups tomatoes, chopped
2 cups chicken stock
2 tsp. sugar

In the saucepan over medium heat, sauté garlic in butter until nicely browned. Add carrots, onion, celery, thyme, and bay leaf and mix well. Cover, reduce heat to low, and simmer for 20 minutes. Then add flour, stirring constantly. Add tomatoes and chicken stock. Bring to a boil, reduce heat, and simmer to thicken, about 1 hour. Add sugar and stir to dissolve. Strain before using.

LEMON OR ORANGE MERINGUE PIE

juice of 6 lemons or oranges	¼ tsp. salt
4 oz. cornstarch	1 lemon or orange rind, grated
12 egg yolks	5 cups boiling water
¾ lb. sugar	2 Tbsp. butter

BEFORE YOU BEGIN

You'll need: two 9-inch pie tins, 2-quart saucepan, electric mixer, medium mixing bowl, whisk
Preheat oven to 400 degrees
Preparation time: 1 hour (using baked pie crusts)
Yield: 2 pies

Prepare baked dessert pie crust for two pies (see page 154). Juice lemons or oranges and dissolve cornstarch in juice. In a medium mixing bowl, beat egg yolks well until light-lemon in color. In the saucepan, stir in sugar, salt, grated rind of either lemon or orange, and cornstarch dissolved in juice. Mix well. Add boiling water, stirring constantly, and bring all to a boil. Remove from heat. Stirring constantly, add ½ cup of hot mixture to beaten egg yolks. Slowly pour egg mixture into sauce, whisking rapidly to avoid lumps. Return to medium-high heat stirring constantly until mixture thickens (do not boil). Remove from heat and stir in butter until it melts. Fill pie shells with mixture, cover with meringue, dust with sugar and place in oven for 10 to 15 minutes to color.

MERINGUE

6 egg whites	½ Tbsp. vanilla
¾ cup sugar	

Beat egg whites until frothy. Continue beating, gradually adding sugar, until mixture begins to stiffen. Add vanilla and beat until well mixed. Use as directed.

PARISIENNE POTATOES

8 large new potatoes	½ bunch chopped parsley
3 Tbsp. butter	

BEFORE YOU BEGIN

You'll need: 2-quart saucepan, large heavy iron skillet, melon baller
Preparation time: 45 minutes
Yield: 6 servings

In the saucepan, bring potatoes to a boil in water to cover and cook until just about tender, about 15 minutes. Drain and allow to cool. Remove a thin slice of skin lengthwise to allow access to pulp. Use a melon baller to cut in medium round balls. In a large heavy iron skillet melt butter over medium heat. Brown potato balls in melted butter, turning frequently to brown all around (take care not to break potatoes). Serve sprinkled with chopped parsley.

ROAST QUEBEC CAPON, CANADIAN PACIFIC STYLE

BEFORE YOU BEGIN

You'll need: roasting pan with rack, 2 yards string, meat themometer, 1-quart saucepan, small saucepan, double boiler, whisk
Preheat oven to 325 degrees
Preparation time: 3 hours
Yield: 4 servings

1 6-lb. capon
6 thin slices salt pork
   flour
1 onion, quartered
1 carrot, cut in 1-inch slices

3 stalks celery, cut in 1-inch slices
¼ cup drippings
¼ cup flour
2 cups chicken stock, heated

Clean, wash, and drain capon. Lightly salt cavity and tie legs as for roasting a chicken. Cover breast and leg joints with thin strips of salt pork. Tie around with string to keep pork in place and dust all over with flour. Place bird on its side on a wire rack in roasting pan and bake, basting frequently. Turn over after 1 hour. Insert thermometer, taking care that it not rest on bone, and continue cooking until done (internal temperature 180 degrees), about another 1½ hours. At the same time, add onion, carrot, and celery to roasting pan drippings. When bird is cooked, make a gravy by removing vegetables and skimming fat from drippings. In a 1-quart saucepan, make a light roux of drippings and flour. Slowly add in hot chicken stock, stirring constantly. Bring to a boil, reduce heat, and allow to simmer until thickened, stirring constantly. Carve capon and place on a platter. Cover with gravy and garnish with sprigs of watercress. Serve bread sauce in sauceboat.

BREAD SAUCE

2 cups milk, scalded
1 tsp. salt
⅛ tsp. white pepper
1 medium onion, in 4 slices

8 whole cloves
⅔ cup fresh bread crumbs
1½ Tbsp. butter
1½ Tbsp. heavy cream

In a double boiler, bring milk to a scald and stir in salt and pepper. Add onion slices studded with 2 whole cloves each, and bread crumbs. Heat for 20 minutes. Remove onion, add butter and cream, and smooth with a whisk before serving.

SMALL TENDERLOIN, CANADIAN PACIFIC STYLE

½ Tbsp. butter
4 9-oz. steaks
4 slices bread

8 strips bacon
2 cups mushroom sauce
chopped parsley

BEFORE YOU BEGIN

*You'll need: large skillet, medium skillet, 1-quart saucepan
Preparation time: 20 minutes
Yield: 4 servings*

In a large skillet, melt the butter over medium heat. Place steaks in skillet and cook until done, turning occasionally. Meanwhile, trim bread crusts and toast. Cook bacon to desired degree of doneness. To serve, mask toast with mushroom sauce, place steak atop, and add bacon strips placed crosswise on steak. Add chopped parsley.

MUSHROOM SAUCE

2 cups demi-glace
¾ cup sliced mushrooms

1 Tbsp. butter

In a 1-quart saucepan over medium heat, melt butter and sauté mushrooms until tender. Stir in demi-glace (see page 154) and heat through. Use as directed.

THOUSAND ISLAND DRESSING

3 egg yolks
2 cups salad oil
½ cup white vinegar
½ bottle chili sauce
1 bunch chives, chopped

3 hard-boiled eggs
2 pimentos, chopped
½ green pepper
paprika to taste
salt to taste

BEFORE YOU BEGIN

*You'll need: large mixing bowl, sealed storage container
Preparation time: 45 minutes
Yield: 1 quart*

Beat egg yolks until of light lemon color. Continue beating as you slowly alternate adding oil and vinegar. Continue beating for approximately half an hour, until a smooth and well-blended mayonnaise forms. Now, slowly stir in chili sauce and mix well. Meanwhile, chop together chives, hard-boiled eggs, pimentos, and green pepper until very fine. Add paprika and salt and mix well. Stir mixture into mayonnaise. Refrigerate at least 1 hour before serving. Cover and refrigerate unused portion.

VENISON SAUTÉ CHASSEUR

*Like their American counterparts covering the vast and rugged Northwest, the Canadi-
an railroads offered game dishes, a reminder of the tradition of stocking cross-continen-
tal dining cars with foods virtually foraged from the territory being traversed.*

1 **lb. venison, cut into 1½ inch cubes**	½ **cup onions, chopped fine**
2 **Tbsp. butter**	½ **cup diced salt pork, fried**
1 **qt. Chasseur sauce**	½ **cup thin sliced mushrooms**

In a large pot, melt butter over medium-high heat. Add venison cubes, a few at
a time, and sauté until browned on all sides. Remove pieces as they brown. When
all venison pieces have browned, reduce heat to medium and return meat to pot.
Stir in Chasseur sauce and slowly bring to a boil. Reduce heat to low, cover, and
simmer until meat is tender (about 2½ hours), stirring occasionally. Meanwhile,
separately in small skillet(s) using 1 tablespoon of butter each time, sauté onions
until browned and mushrooms until tender, and fry salt pork until crisp. To serve,
place a portion of meat and sauce in individual serving dishes and garnish with
onions, salt pork, and mushrooms.

CHASSEUR SAUCE

2 **cups finely chopped mushrooms**	1 **cup tomato sauce**
4 **shallots, chopped fine**	1 **Tbsp. butter, creamed**
8 **Tbsp. butter**	6 **Tbsp. butter**
1 **cup white wine**	¼ **cup chopped herbs (equal**
1 **qt. beef stock**	**amounts tarragon, chervil,**
	and parsley)

In a 3-quart saucepan over medium heat, melt 8 tablespoons butter and sauté
finely chopped mushrooms and shallots until tender. Add white wine and simmer until mixture is reduced by half. Then add stock and tomato sauce and simmer again until reduced further by a third. Add creamed butter and boil for 2
minutes. Add remaining 6 tablespoons butter and chopped herbs and heat
through. Use as directed.

Dinner in a dining car was the result of careful planning. It took efficient purchasing and close coordination for a railroad to bring the right foods to the right trains at the right times. The planning started with the menu. To create it, the dining-car department's superintendent juggled a number of factors. To remain aware of changing trends in passenger eating habits, for example, he reviewed each train's meal tickets to learn what was ordered most often. In this way, he could populate his menus with things people liked and at the same time keep costs and waste to a minimum.

The varied tastes of the different individuals on board his trains also had to be considered. B.J. Bohlinder, manager of dining service for the New York Central System, said, *Twentieth Century Limited* passengers order smoked turkey, lobster thermidor, and other dishes that they would eat in a nightclub or at the Waldorf-Astoria. Some of these dishes and their special sauces would be un-acceptable to men

The attractive design of menus was in part intended to induce passengers to take them and not the silver or china as a souvenir of the trip. When shared with family and friends, they became advertisements for the railroad and its dining car service. (COURTESY OF THE UNION PACIFIC MUSEUM)

accustomed to simple unseasoned foods."[1] It was axiomatic that those dining "in the cars" wanted pretty much the same simple, wholesome dishes to which they were accustomed at home. As one superintendent put it, "If there are as many different tastes as there are men and women, it is also true that many people like the same thing, and equally true that few people like the same combination." And H. A. Butler, a dining-car superintendent with more than thirty-five years of service, was not alone when he considered the different tastes in the various regions through which his trains traveled. "Northerners like their marmalade rather tart, while southerners prefer it sweet. Southerners also like heavy, syrupy coffee, which Northerners won't stand for."[2]

Equally important were the railroad's shippers whose goods were to be featured. It would

be beyond embarrassment if that large Arkansas cantaloupe grower were on board and discovered his melons weren't promoted when "in season." The Union Pacific, for one, began its menu planning around the new fruits and vegetables just coming into season, a list of which was supplied the superintendent ten days prior to their arrival in the commissary by his storekeeper.

Planning had to provide for the possibility of a train's running out of the ingredients for one or two items before it completed its trip, a problem especially for the trains connecting Chicago to the West Coast. Railroads solved this problem by creating a basic menu that could safely be prepared well in advance, and adding a foldover featuring special dishes, such as Roast Spring Chicken with Cream Gravy. If the chicken was consumed, its foldover was replaced with one promoting a roast-beef special. Another solution had the steward, right on the train, print inserts of the day's specials on small squares of colored paper. These could be reprinted if an item had to be deleted.

Other menu-planning objectives included insuring that passengers did not look at the same menu on two separate trains. Management did not want the passenger on today's Kansas City–Denver run to have the same choices on the Denver–Portland portion of his trip tomorrow.

Even the weather was taken into consideration. With the advent of hot weather, the tomato stuffed with crab or chicken salad had to be replaced with, say, a fruit platter and special dressing or a tossed salad with shredded ham and smoked tongue, accompanied by the railroad's house dressing.

All of these factors pressured the dining-car superintendent to make the right choices. After all, the variety of dishes and the way in which they were served was the measure by which a railroad's management was judged. The public image of an entire railroad was closely tied to the fame of its special trout or French toast.

The degree of flexibility passengers had in making menu selections changed over the years. The original practice, called the American Plan, saw a fixed price cover an entire meal. An example is this breakfast menu offered in 1882, when seventy-five cents could buy the following in its entirety:

BILL OF FARE

English Breakfast Tea—French Coffee—
Chocolate—Ice Milk

BREAD
French Loaf—Boston Brown Bread—
Corn Bread—Hot Rolls—
Dry, dipped, cream toast

BROILED
Tenderloin Steak, plain or with mushrooms—
Spring Chicken—Mutton Chops—
Veal Cutlets—Sirloin Steak—
Sugar-Cured Ham
Game in their Season—Oysters in their Season

FRIED
Calf's Liver with Bacon—Country Sausage—
Trout

EGGS
Fried—Scrambled—Boiled—Omelets—Plain

RELISHES
Radishes—Chow Chow—
French Mustard—Currant Jelly—
Walnut Catsup—Mixed Pickles

VEGETABLES
Stewed—Fried and Boiled Potatoes

FRUITS
Apples—Oranges[3]

The rising costs of commodities, especially as World War I approached, made this approach—also known as table d'hote—impractical. Already, railroads had raised the price of

table d'hote meals on their flagship trains to $1.50, both to increase the prestige of the train and to reduce losses.

By 1916, though, dining on most American trains was from an à la carte menu. Furnishing meals "by the card" began on the Lehigh Valley in 1894. The menu indicated that a full dinner could be had for one dollar, but those wishing a lighter meal could have a simple lunch for from thirty to sixty cents. A sandwich with boiled eggs and tea or coffee was fifty-five cents, and stewed oysters cost forty cents.[4] The practice brought those who formerly carried a lunch box to the dining car instead, with nine out of ten patrons expressing great satisfaction with the à la carte plan.[5] The Chicago, Burlington & Quincy introduced "from the card" dining at the same time, and it reported, "The result, in brief, is that the number of customers is much larger than before, the gross receipts somewhat larger, and the expenses about the same." Hidden in these numbers is "the fact that the expenses do not increase with the number of customers [illustrating] the fact that service

constitutes a very large share of the cost of running a dining car."[6]

The à la carte menu posed the greatest challenge for the crew. Simultaneously preparing meals for twenty-five or thirty people on short notice in confined quarters on a tight three- or four-seating schedule was difficult at best. To impose on the crew the need to respond to orders for randomly selected dishes in various combinations magnified the stress under which they worked. And making their selection à la carte had a demonstrated tendency to slow down the passengers as well, a continuous curse for the steward and those waiting to eat.

Table d'hote meals still remained on the menu, to be served when time permitted and when circumstances provided the desirability of a multi-course meal. The à la carte system was used where the time was short between cities, especially in the East, and where light meals, such as breakfast and luncheons, were preferable.

10

THE CHESAPEAKE & OHIO RAILWAY

BACON AND POTATO OMELET

BEFORE YOU BEGIN

*You'll need: 1-quart
saucepan, large skil-
let, medium mixing
bowl, slotted spoon,
paper towels, omelet
pan
Preparation time:
30 minutes
Yield: 8 servings*

3 medium new red potatoes	1 Tbsp. freshly chopped parsley
12 strips bacon	24 eggs

Cut potatoes in ⅛-inch square dice. Place diced potatoes in boiling water until tender, about 3–5 minutes, drain well, then plunge in cold water and set aside. Cut bacon across in ⅛-inch strips and fry over medium heat to desired degree of doneness. Drain bacon, retaining drippings. In a bowl, combine bacon and parsley. Return skillet with bacon drippings to stove at medium-high heat. Drain potatoes well and fry in bacon drippings until golden brown. Use a slotted spoon to lift potatoes to a clean paper towel to drain, then add to bacon and parsley. Meanwhile, for each omelet, beat 3 eggs well, put in lightly buttered omelet pan. When omelet is firm, add a portion of the bacon/potatoes/parsley mixture, fold, and serve hot.

COLE SLAW, MEXICAN STYLE

BEFORE YOU BEGIN

*You'll need: large mix-
ing bowl, shredder
Preparation time:
30 minutes (plus 1
hour to chill before
serving)
Yield: 8 servings*

1 medium head white cabbage	1 medium onion, chopped fine
2 small green peppers	2 Tbsp. parsley, chopped
⅔ cup mayonnaise	salt and pepper to taste
1 oz. white vinegar	16 strips pimento

Quarter cabbage head, remove the core, and shred very fine. Quarter green peppers, remove seeds, and shred very fine. Combine cabbage and green pepper. Add mayonnaise, vinegar, onion, salt, pepper, and chopped parsley. Mix thoroughly and chill. To serve, place a leaf of lettuce on a salad plate, one serving of cole slaw in center of lettuce, and top with crossed strips of pimento.

CHESAPEAKE BAY FISH DINNER

BEFORE YOU BEGIN

You'll need: 9" x 13"
baking dish, small
saucepan, 1-quart
saucepan, 6 shirred-
egg dishes, 2-quart
saucepan, fine
strainer
Preheat oven to 350
degrees
Preparation time:
1 hour
Yield: 6 servings

6	4–6 oz. flounder fillets	18	Parisian potatoes
18	oysters	1½	cups cream sauce, warmed
¾	cup onions, chopped fine	18	small boiled white onions
¼	cup lemon juice, strained	1	Tbsp. chopped chives or
	salt and pepper to taste		freshly chopped parsley
1	cup boiling water		

Butter a baking pan and place fish in it. Distribute oysters evenly over the fish. Sprinkle chopped onion, lemon juice, salt, and pepper over fish and oysters. Pour boiling water over all, place in oven and bake for 5 minutes. Meanwhile, boil potatoes in salt water until just firm. Remove fish from oven, carefully lift fish and oysters to a platter and keep warm, retaining juice in a 1-quart saucepan. Heat juice just to a boil, reduce heat, and simmer to reduce by half. Now blend in hot cream sauce and again bring to a boil. Add chives and season to taste. Heat onions in a small saucepan with water to cover. To serve, place single fish portion in shirred-egg dish, arrange 3 oysters over fish, place 3 onions to one side and 3 potatoes on the other side. Pour cream sauce over all and serve very hot.

CREAM SAUCE

¼	cup lard	2½	Tbsp. flour
¼	stalk celery, sliced thin	2	cups milk
½	small onion, sliced thin		salt and white pepper to taste
1	bay leaf		

In a 2-quart saucepan over medium heat, melt lard and add onion, celery, and bay leaf. Sauté until tender without allowing to brown. Stirring constantly, add flour and cook very slowly for 4–5 minutes. Meanwhile, bring milk to a boil. Add boiling milk, stirring constantly. Increase heat, and stir well until all comes to a boil. Reduce heat and slow boil for 15 minutes. Strain through fine strainer without pressure.

CREAM OF CARROTS SOUP

½ cup lard (or cooking oil)
2 medium onions, sliced
2 stalks celery, sliced
1 lb. carrots, sliced
2 bay leaves
   pinch, thyme
1 clove garlic, chopped fine

1 cup flour
2 qts. hot water
¼ cup chicken stock
1 cup light cream, warmed
1 Tbsp. butter
   salt and white pepper to taste

In a large pot over medium heat, melt lard. Add onion, celery, carrots, and sauté until tender, then add bay leaves, thyme, and garlic. Stir to mix. Reduce heat to medium-low, cover pot, and slowly sauté mixture well without browning. Add flour, stirring constantly, and cook for 2 minutes. Slowly add hot water and chicken stock, and bring all to a boil. Reduce heat and slow boil for 35 minutes. Strain, retaining liquid, and puree vegetables in blender or food processor. Return pureed vegetables to liquid, add hot cream and butter, and reheat as necessary without bringing to a boil. Season to taste and serve hot.

CURRIED VEAL

½ cup lard
3 lbs. veal, boned,
   cut in 1½-inch squares
2 medium onions, diced small
2 cloves garlic, crushed and chopped
3 bay leaves
1 tsp. thyme
1 tsp. salt
½ tsp. pepper

3 Tbsp. curry powder
3 cups canned whole tomatoes
4 cups water
1 tsp. chicken bouillon
¼ cup grated coconut
5 Tbsp. cornstarch
¼ cup cold water
1 cup apple sauce

Melt lard in an oven-proof pot over medium heat. Add veal and brown lightly on all sides. Add onion, garlic, bay leaves, thyme, salt, and pepper and blend well. Stir in curry powder and simmer to allow sauce to blend well, about 20 minutes. Add tomatoes, water, chicken bouillon, and coconut. Season further to taste. Bring to a boil, cover, and place in oven until meat is done, about 1 hour. Meanwhile, dissolve cornstarch in cold water. Stir cornstarch and apple sauce into curried mixture and continue to simmer two minutes. Remove bay leaves and skim off all fat. Serve over steamed rice (see page 153) with chutney (see page 271).

CURRY OF LAMB MADRAS

BEFORE YOU BEGIN

You'll need: 3-quart saucepan, 1-quart saucepan, 1-quart casserole, cotton cloth
Preheat oven to 225 degrees
Preparation time: 3 hours
Yield: 4 servings

1 Tbsp. lard
1 lb. boned shoulder or chuck of lamb, cut in 1½-inch squares
1 medium onion, diced small pinch, crushed thyme
1 bay leaf salt and pepper to taste
1 heaping tsp. curry powder
½ cup clove garlic, chopped
¼ cup canned whole tomatoes
¾ cup hot water
1 Rome Beauty apple, peeled and diced
1 Tbsp. grated coconut
⅓ tsp. cornstarch
1 Tbsp. cold water

In a 3-quart saucepan over medium-high heat, melt lard. Add lamb and brown well on all sides. In order, add onion, thyme, bay leaf, salt, pepper, and curry powder. Stir and simmer for 4 minutes. Add garlic and simmer 1 additional minute. Add tomatoes and water and bring to a boil. Stir in apple and coconut. Cover and cook until lamb is done tender, about two hours. Skim off all fat and remove the bay leaf. Add cornstarch diluted in 1 tablespoon of cold water. Season further to taste. Serve with Indian-style rice and chutney (see page 271).

INDIAN-STYLE RICE

1 cup long-grain white rice
2 cups water
salt to taste

Thoroughly wash rice in cold water. Pour rice into salted boiling water and cook for 12 minutes. Wash in hot water until most of the starch is removed, drain, and pour into 1-quart casserole lined with a clean cloth. Cover with edges of cloth, place in 225 degree oven for 15 minutes. Rice should be nice and dry when served.

FRENCH-STYLE PEAS

BEFORE YOU BEGIN

You'll need: 2-quart saucepan, small skillet
Preparation time: 30 minutes
Yield: 6 servings

Reflecting the postwar era during which the C&O introduced this item, the railroad's cooking manual advised chefs that this recipe could also be made with frozen peas and precooked onions. When this method is used, add onions to peas when almost cooked.

6 strips bacon, cut into ¼ inch-wide dice	3 Tbsp. sugar
	pinch, pepper
12 small white onions, peeled	1 tsp. chicken bouillon
½ head Boston lettuce, cut in coarse julienne strips	2 cups water, or enough to cover
	3 Tbsp. flour
1½ lbs. green peas	2 Tbsp. butter
1 tsp. salt	

In the saucepan over medium heat, fry bacon slowly until half done. Add onions and lettuce, stir, and let simmer for 5 minutes. Then add peas, salt, sugar, pepper, chicken bouillon and water to cover. Continue to cook slowly until peas are heated through and done to the desired degree of firmness. Meanwhile, in a small skillet, make a roux of the butter and flour. Add roux to peas and bring to a boil. Remove from heat and stir once before serving. Sprinkle with fresh chopped parsley.

+ ═◆═ +

IRISH LAMB STEW

BEFORE YOU BEGIN

You'll need: large pot, colander, large mixing bowl, 6-quart covered pot
Preparation time: 1 hour
Yield: 8 servings

3 lbs. boned shoulder of lamb, cut in 1½-inch cubes	pinch, ground thyme
	2 cloves garlic, crushed
2 medium onions, sliced	salt and pepper to taste
8 medium potatoes, sliced	2 Tbsp. freshly chopped parsley
2 bay leaves	

Fill a large pot with enough water to cover lamb. Bring water to a boil, add meat and boil for 5 minutes. Remove immediately and drain well in colander. Put meat back in the pot and add onions, potatoes, bay leaves, thyme, garlic, salt, and pepper. Cover with cold water. Bring to a boil, reduce heat, and slow boil until meat is done, about 1½ hours. Skim off fat and serve stew with hot dumplings sprinkled with chopped parsley.

DUMPLINGS

4⅓ cups Bisquick®, approximately	2 Tbsp. freshly chopped parsley
4 eggs	1 gallon water
2 tsp. salt	2 Tbsp. chicken bouillon
½ cup milk	

In mixing bowl, combine 4 cups Bisquick®, eggs, salt, milk, and parsley, and blend well. Add Bisquick® and mix just until mixture holds together. Meanwhile, in 6-quart pot, add chicken bouillon to water and bring to a boil. Reduce to a slow boil and drop in one generous tablespoonful of batter per dumpling. Cook for 10 minutes uncovered, then cover and cook for 10 more minutes, or until dumplings are done through.

OYSTER BISQUE

4 Tbsp. butter	½ cup onion, chopped fine
2 Tbsp. flour	1 cup celery, chopped fine
1 qt. boiling milk	2 tsp. paprika
salt and white pepper to taste	fresh chopped parsley
12 oysters (1 cup), chopped coarse	

BEFORE YOU BEGIN

You'll need: two 2-quart saucepans, one 1-quart saucepan
Preparation time: 45 minutes
Yield: 4 servings

In a 2-quart saucepan over medium heat, make a light roux of 2 tablespoons each of butter and flour. Add boiling milk and mix well. Add salt and pepper and simmer for 15 minutes. Meanwhile, place chopped oysters in a 1-quart saucepan with their own juice to cover. Over medium heat, warm until oysters begin to curl, remove from heat, and set aside. In another 2-quart saucepan over medium heat, melt 2 tablespoons butter and sauté onion and celery until tender. Add paprika and simmer for 2 minutes. Add oysters in juice to the onion, celery, and paprika mixture. Strain the light cream sauce into the pot and mix thoroughly, but do not boil. Adjust seasoning to taste and serve hot. Garnish with parsley.

WELSH RAREBIT

Serve this tangy treat hot over crisp white toast and a slice of cooked Canadian bacon.

3 Tbsp. butter	1 tsp. Worcestershire sauce
1 lb. sharp cheddar cheese, shredded	½ cup ale
½ tsp. dry mustard	2 eggs, slightly beaten
½ tsp. salt	

BEFORE YOU BEGIN

You'll need: double boiler, grater/shredder, small bowl
Preparation time: 30 minutes
Yield: 4 servings

Melt butter in double boiler over slowly boiling water. Add cheese and cook until melted. Stirring constantly, add in order the dry mustard, salt, Worcestershire sauce, ale, and beaten eggs. Continue to stir until mixture becomes thick and heated through.

---◆▨◆ ▣◆▨ ◆---

YORKSHIRE PUDDING, C&O STYLE

1½ cups flour
3 eggs
2½ cups milk, warmed

salt and pepper to taste
pinch, ground nutmeg
3 Tbsp. roast beef drippings

Place flour in a mixing bowl and add eggs. Slowly add hot milk, stirring constantly to make a smooth batter. Add salt, pepper, and nutmeg, and mix thoroughly. When the roast beef is within 40 minutes of being done, pour drippings from cooking roast beef into a heavy skillet and heat well over medium-high heat. Pour batter into skillet and place in oven. Place a grill across the skillet and place roast beef over batter. Allow the drippings of the roast beef to run through the grill and over the batter. The timing of this is important. If the roast beef is small, it should be withdrawn when cooked and the pudding allowed to remain in oven until done. Cooking time of this Yorkshire pudding is about 40 minutes in a 400-degree oven.

11

THE CHICAGO, BURLINGTON & QUINCY RAILROAD

BAKED LIMA BEANS

Dry fruits and vegetables were important to a railway's commissary department. They were easy to store, saved space, and had a long shelf life. This mildly spicy side dish makes good use of a dining car-staple vegetable and is an excellent accompaniment to the Illinois Central's Shrimp Creole (page 228). Precede the meal with cole slaw from the Missouri Pacific (page 233) and end it with a Hot Strawberry Sundae from Fred Harvey's restaurant (page 300).

1 lb. dry lima beans	salt and pepper to taste
¾ lb. salt pork	2 Tbsp. brown sugar
½ cup chopped onion	2 Tbsp. prepared mustard
1 cup potato, peeled and cubed	

BEFORE YOU BEGIN

You'll need: large bowl, large saucepan, small mixing bowl, small skillet, 9" x 9" baking pan
Preheat oven to 350 degrees
Preparation time: 2 hours (plus soaking beans overnight)
Yield: 8 servings

Soak lima beans overnight in cold water. (NOTE: beans will absorb approximately two-and-one-half times their volume in water and swell to nearly three times their dry size during soaking; allow liquid and bowl space for the expansion.) Drain beans and wash well, removing skins that have soaked loose but leaving in place those which remain on the beans. Place beans in a large saucepan, fill with cold water to cover, and bring to a boil over medium-high heat. Reduce heat, cover, and simmer about 30 minutes. Remove cover. Add salt pork and continue to simmer 40 more minutes. Add onions and potatoes, season with salt and pepper, and continue simmering another 30-40 minutes, until beans are soft but not mushy. Meanwhile, combine brown sugar and mustard and blend to a paste. Remove salt pork and cut into small cubes. In a small skillet over medium heat, melt a little fat removed from the pork and sauté salt pork cubes until golden brown. Add salt pork and sugar/mustard mix to simmering beans and stir to mix thoroughly. Pour all into baking pan and place in oven to bake until an even brown, approximately 20 minutes. Remove and serve in individual dishes.

BAKED INDIVIDUAL STEAK AND KIDNEY PIE, BURLINGTON STYLE

BEFORE YOU BEGIN

You'll need: 2-quart saucepan, small bowl, medium skillet, small saucepan, 4 individual casseroles
Preheat oven to 450 degrees
Preparation time: 3½ hours
Yield: 4 servings

1½ Tbsp. bacon drippings
¼ cup flour
1 Tbsp. salt
½ tsp. pepper
1½ lbs. beef tenderloin, cut into 1-inch cubes
1 Tbsp. chopped onions
1 cup beef stock

2 large carrots, diced
2 large white potatoes, diced
flour to thicken
½ lb. veal kidney
1 Tbsp. butter
1 Tbsp. parsley, chopped fine
1 meal pie pastry recipe

Melt bacon drippings in a 2-quart saucepan over medium heat. In a bowl, stir flour, salt, and pepper together. Dredge beef with flour/seasonings mixture, then add beef and onion to hot drippings and brown lightly, turning often. Add stock, cover, reduce heat and simmer. Add just a little stock from time to time to keep moist. After 1½ hours, add carrots and one potato and continue cooking for a few minutes until vegetables begin to get tender. Stirring constantly, sprinkle in enough flour to make medium-thick brown sauce. Cover and continue cooking slowly until meat and vegetables are very tender. Peel, dice, and boil remaining potato in a small saucepan with salted water to cover until nearly done, about 15 minutes. Drain and place in cold water and set aside. Meanwhile, remove fat and skin from veal kidneys and cut them into ½-inch pieces. In a skillet over medium-high heat, melt butter and sauté veal kidneys until well done, about 3 minutes. Add the kidneys and butter in which they were sauteed to the beef. Stir well together, and add freshly chopped parsley. To finish, place a few diced boiled potatoes in the bottom of individual casseroles, then fill with the stew. Cover with meal pie-pastry (see page 155), slit crust to allow steam to escape, and brush top with egg wash. Place in oven and bake until crust is browned, about 15 minutes. When stew is prepared as instructed, sauce will have a nice brown color and be medium thick, meat will be brown and tender, and vegetables done but not cooked to pieces.

BAKED STUFFED TOMATO

BEFORE YOU BEGIN

You'll need: 1-quart saucepan, large skillet
Preheat oven to 400 degrees
Preparation time: 1 hour
Yield: 6 servings

6 medium tomatoes
rice jambalaya to fill

½ cup bread crumbs
2 Tbsp. melted butter

Cut the top from tomato, and carefully remove pulp, leaving a ¼-inch wall. Stuff cavity with Rice Jambalaya. Top with fresh bread crumbs and drip melted butter over lightly. Bake for 10 minutes.

RICE JAMBALAYA

2 cups boiled rice	¼ clove garlic, minced
2 Tbsp. butter	½ cup tomato puree
½ cup cooked ham, diced	½ cup chicken stock
¼ cup diced onion	salt and pepper to taste
½ green pepper, diced	½ cup cooked shrimp, diced

Cook rice (see page 153). Meanwhile, in a large skillet over medium heat melt butter and sauté ham until heated through. Add onion, green pepper, and celery, and sauté until tender, about 10 minutes. Add garlic for the last minute. Add tomato puree, chicken stock, salt, and pepper. Stir to mix thoroughly, then simmer until heated through. Pour over boiled rice. Add shrimp and stir to mix. Use as stuffing for baked tomatoes or green peppers.

BANANA BLANC MANGE

6 Tbsp. cornstarch	2 tsp. vanilla
4 cups milk	2 Tbsp. orange juice
¾ cup sugar	1 tsp. grated orange rind
¼ tsp. salt	3 bananas, peeled and sliced
4 egg yolks, slightly beaten	½ cup whipping cream
4 egg whites	4 maraschino cherries

BEFORE YOU BEGIN

You'll need: small bowl, large double boiler, large mixing bowl, electric beater, medium mixing bowl
Preparation time: 30 minutes
Yield: 8 servings

In a small bowl, dissolve cornstarch in 1 cup cold milk and let stand. In the top of a double boiler, scald 3 cups milk. Stirring constantly, add dissolved cornstarch and cook for 20 minutes, stirring occasionally. Meanwhile, in a large mixing bowl, stir sugar and salt together and combine with slightly beaten egg yolks. Add some of the scalded liquid to the egg/sugar mixture, stirring until smooth. Add the rest of the hot liquid, stirring constantly. Return mixture to double boiler and cook 5 minutes, stirring constantly. Remove top of double boiler from hot water and place in a pan or bowl of cold water. While it cools, beat egg whites stiff. When liquid is cool, fold in beaten egg whites. Add vanilla and orange juice. Stir in orange rind and banana slices. Serve in individual dishes topped with whipped cream and a half maraschino cherry.

BRAISED ROLLED CALF'S LIVER
EN CASSEROLE, BURLINGTON STYLE

BEFORE YOU BEGIN

*You'll need: medium
bowl, shallow bak-
ing pan, 2-quart
saucepan
Preheat oven to 400
degrees
Preparation time:
45 minutes
Yield: 8 servings*

2 lbs. calf's liver, cut in ¼-inch slices	2 tsp. parsley, finely chopped
¼ lb. bacon, diced	2 eggs, well beaten
¼ lb. mushrooms, chopped	salt and pepper to taste
¼ lb. chopped onions	2½ slices bacon
½ cup bread crumbs	1 qt. mushroom sauce

Remove membrane and any veins or blood clots from liver. In a medium bowl, combine chopped bacon, mushroom pieces, chopped onion, bread crumbs, chopped parsley, well-beaten eggs, salt, and pepper, and mix well. Spread this mixture over slices of calf's liver. Roll up and place in shallow baking pan. Place ¼ slice of bacon over each roll and cook in hot oven 20–25 minutes. Remove from oven, pour mushroom sauce over, cover, and keep hot until ready to serve. Sprinkle with chopped parsley before serving.

MUSHROOM SAUCE

2 cups sliced mushrooms	juice of 1 lemon, strained
3 Tbsp. butter	1 tsp. chopped parsley
2 cups Espagnole sauce	2 Tbsp. sherry wine
2 cups tomato sauce	salt and pepper to taste

Melt butter in saucepan over medium heat and sauté mushrooms until tender, about 10 minutes. Add Espagnole sauce, tomato sauce, lemon juice, chopped parsley, sherry, salt, and pepper. Bring just to boil, reduce heat and simmer to thicken slightly, about 10 minutes.

COLORADO MOUNTAIN TROUT *ZEPHYR* STYLE

BEFORE YOU BEGIN

*You'll need: 12-inch
skillet, small bowl,
small plate, warmed
serving platter,
1-quart saucepan,
egg slicer
Preparation Time:
45 minutes
Yield: 2 servings*

This quick favorite of Zephyr passengers exemplifies the tasty regional fare the railroads needed and wanted to serve patrons. Meals such as mountain trout from the Colorado Rockies, served aboard a train between Denver and Chicago as the mountains slid by outside the large, clean window, were a typical allure of eating on a train.

2 mountain trout fillets, ½–¾ lb. each	flour to coat
1 tsp. salt	3 Tbsp. butter
½ tsp. pepper	juice of ½ lemon
milk sufficient to dip trout	1 tsp. chopped parsley

Melt butter in a large skillet over medium-high heat. Meanwhile, season both sides of each trout fillet with salt and pepper, dip in milk, and roll in flour. Quickly fry trout in butter, allowing 4–5 minutes for each side. Remove to heated platter. Pour browned butter over trout, sprinkle with lemon juice and parsley. Garnish with sprigs of parsley, julienne potatoes, and a lemon wedge.

JULIENNE POTATOES IN BUTTER

4 medium new potatoes	2 Tbsp. butter
salt and pepper to taste	

Place potatoes in the saucepan with water to cover and bring to a boil. Cook until potatoes are tender, about 25 minutes. Drain and remove skin. Cut Julienne shape (small strips) using egg slicer to first cut one way, then turn and cut the other way. Season to taste, arrange on serving plate, and top with a pat of butter.

+—◄▣◊▣►—+

FRIED APPLES

BEFORE YOU BEGIN

4 tart apples	2 Tbsp. butter
2 Tbsp. bacon drippings	1 cup brown or white sugar

You'll need: large covered skillet, slotted spoon or spatula
Preparation time: 30 minutes
Yield: 8 servings

Wash and remove core from apples, but do not remove skin. Cut each apple into 12 wedge-shaped slices. In a large skillet over medium heat, melt bacon drippings and butter together. Add the apple wedges and sauté for about 15 minutes without cover, carefully turning once. Sprinkle lightly with sugar, cover, and continue cooking, turning several times until browned well. When properly prepared, apples will have a nice brown color and be tender (not cooked to a mush) and have a sour-sweet taste.

+—◄▣◊▣►—+

OLD-FASHIONED BUCKWHEAT CAKES

BEFORE YOU BEGIN

½ cup warm water, heated to 110 degrees	½ tsp. salt
½ oz. dry yeast	½ cup milk
4 cups buckwheat flour	½ Tbsp. baking soda
¼ cup molasses	1 Tbsp. water
2 oz. melted butter	flour if needed

You'll need: large mixing bowl, two small bowls, pancake griddle
Preheat pancake griddle to hot
Preparation time: 30 minutes (plus overnight for dough to set up)
Yield: 24 pancakes

In a small bowl, dissolve yeast in warm water (100–110 degrees). Meanwhile, add enough water at room temperature to buckwheat flour to make soft spongy dough. Add dissolved yeast to dough, stir to mix, cover loosely, and let stand overnight. Before using, add molasses, melted butter, salt, and milk, and beat well together. If batter is too thin, sift a little flour over and stir to mix. Let batter rise 10 or 15 minutes before using. Last, add baking soda dissolved in 1 tablespoon lukewarm water and mix well into batter. Pour batter onto hot griddle to form 6-inch pancakes. Cook until top of each is full of tiny bubbles and bottom is browned. Turn once to brown other side. Serve with hot maple syrup.

POTAGE ALEXANDRINA

3 qts. chicken stock, warmed		¼ tsp. white pepper
1½ Tbsp. butter		dash, ground mace
1½ Tbsp. shortening		2 cups cooked chicken breast, diced
1 medium onion, sliced thin		1 medium onion, minced
2 stalks celery, sliced		2 stalks celery, minced
2 carrots, sliced		2 carrots, minced
¼ cup flour		2 Tbsp. parsley, minced
2 qts. milk, warmed		1 Tbsp. butter
½ tsp. salt		

In the 4-quart saucepan over high heat, bring chicken stock to a boil. Reduce heat and simmer until reduced to 2 quarts. Meanwhile, in a 6-quart saucepan over medium heat, melt butter and shortening. Add onion, celery, and carrots, cover, and braise until tender but not browned, about 10 minutes. Stirring constantly, add flour to make a roux. Reduce heat to medium-low and cook roux about 5 minutes. Stirring constantly, slowly add hot chicken stock and hot milk. Simmer until thickened, at least 30 minutes. Season to taste, strain into a clean 4-quart saucepan, and add chicken. Meanwhile, starting with fresh onion, celery, carrots, and parsley, mince fine or run through grinder to make paste. Melt 1 tablespoon butter in a medium skillet over medium heat. Sauté minced vegetables until tender, about 5 minutes. Using a slotted spoon, remove vegetables to soup, mix well, and heat through.

SHERRIED FRUIT COCKTAIL

1 cup pineapple, diced small	1 cup peach, diced small
1 cup orange, diced small	1 cup pear, diced small
1 cup grapefruit, diced small	6 maraschino cherries
1 cup apple, diced small	

Place diced fruit in a container. Add sherried syrup and stir to mix all well together. Refrigerate at least 1 hour before serving. Serve the fruit in sherbet glass, garnished with a maraschino cherry.

SHERRIED SYRUP

1 cup water	¼ cup sherry wine
1 cup sugar	

In a small saucepan, dissolve sugar in water and bring to a boil. Boil 5 minutes. Add sherry and stir to heat through. Simmer to thicken, about 10 minutes. Let cool before using.

SWEETBREADS À LA FINANCIERE

BEFORE YOU BEGIN

*You'll need: two 2-
quart saucepans,
large skillet, 4 indi-
vidual serving
casseroles, small
saucepan
Preparation time:
1 hour
Yield: 4 servings*

1 lb. sweetbreads
1 tsp. salt
1 tsp. lemon juice
   salt and pepper to taste
2 Tbsp. butter

flour to coat
4 slices white bread, toasted
2 cups sauce Financiere
2 Tbsp. parsley, chopped fine

Place sweetbreads in cold water 30 minutes, drain, and remove skin and gristle. In a 2-quart saucepan, bring water to cover sweetbreads to a boil. Stir in 1 teaspoon salt and the lemon juice. Add sweetbreads, boil for 15 minutes, then drain and cool. Melt butter in a large skillet over medium-high heat. Season sweetbreads with salt and pepper, roll in flour, and sauté in butter until well browned. To serve, remove crust. Place in individual casseroles and cover with sauce Financiere. Sprinkle with freshly chopped parsley.

SAUCE FINANCIERE

½ cup consomme
2 cups Espagnole sauce
½ cup Madeira wine
¼ cup mushroom catsup

½ cup mushrooms, finely chopped
2 Tbsp. pitted green olives, diced
   salt and pepper to taste

In a small saucepan, simmer ½ cup consommé to reduce by half. Then, in a 2-quart saucepan over medium heat, warm Espagnole sauce (see page 154). Stir in reduced consommé, Madeira wine, mushroom catsup, finely chopped mushrooms, and green olives. Heat through and use as directed.

On Christmas day, the railroads tried doubly hard to be hospitable hosts to those who found it necessary to travel away from home and miss the festivities associated with the holiday. On this occasion, in addition to their regular menu, a traditional Christmas dinner was offered. Along with the usual thought given to taste and eye appeal, these dinners often featured surprising twists on conventional foods.

The meal's centerpiece, of course, was the turkey. These customarily weighed in at fourteen pounds apiece, took almost five hours to roast, and, of course, were cooked on board so they could be delivered fresh and hot when passengers wanted them. On Christmas day, 1951, the Pennsylvania Railroad alone served 3,500 roast-turkey dinners across its system. The dinner presented here, capturing the spirit of unconventional preparation from among nine different railroads, will serve six.

Chef David Lowe of the Southern Pacific's San Joaquin Daylight *prepares to carve one of the delicious turkeys he prepared for his train's holiday diners. An oven in a dining car could typically hold six turkeys weighing an average of 24 pounds apiece.*
(COURTESY OF THE ASSOCIATION OF AMERICAN RAILROADS)

MENU

BEVERAGE
• Horse's Neck (the Pullman Company)

APPETIZER
• Poinsettia Salad *Merchants' Limited*
(New Haven)

ENTREE
• Roast Turkey with stuffing
(Chicago, Burlington & Quincy)
• Cape Cod Cranberry Relish (New Haven)
• Puff Potatoes (Southern Pacific)
• Sweet Potato Puffs (Pennsylvania)
• Buttered Beets (Union Pacific)
• Carrots Vichy (Chesapeake & Ohio)

DESSERT
• Cranberry Pie (Alaska)
• Pumpkin Pie (Missouri Pacific)

HORSE'S NECK

1 lemon	12 oz. ginger ale

Peel the entire lemon, spiral fashion, in one piece. Place a single ice cube in a tall 14-ounce glass. Arrange the lemon peel inside the length of the glass, with one end draped over the rim of the glass. Fill glass with pale, dry or imported ginger ale. Stir slightly with spoon, taking care not to dislodge lemon peel. Serve at once.

POINSETTIA SALAD MERCHANTS' LIMITED

BEFORE YOU BEGIN
You'll need: saucepan to boil the tomatoes before peeling
Preparation time: 15 minutes (after tomatoes are peeled)
Yield: 6 servings

6 medium tomatoes	¼ tsp. salt
6 Tbsp. cream cheese	(or to taste)
3 tsp. heavy cream	⅛ tsp. pepper

6 egg yolks hard boiled and crumbled fine	6 slices iceberg lettuce, ½-inch thick French dressing to suit

Peel the tomatoes (see page 155) and chill before using. Meanwhile, combine cream cheese, cream, salt, and pepper and stir until smooth. Then, cut each tomato into eight sections from top to bottom, but do not sever at the base. Fold back eight tomato "petals" to form a flower, leaving center pulp intact. Put cream cheese/cream mixture on center pulp. Sprinkle cheese with sifted egg yolk to represent yellow center of flower. To serve, place a leaf of iceberg lettuce in a salad bowl, and top with a slice of lettuce and a tomato poinsettia. French dressing can be served on the side (see page 267).

POULTRY STUFFING

This stuffing, sufficient for a fourteen-pound turkey, should finish moist and very light, not heavy and soggy.

BEFORE YOU BEGIN
You'll need: large oven-proof mixing bowl, large skillet, baking dish (optional)
Preheat oven to 350 degrees
Preparation time: 45 minutes (plus roasting time for turkey)

12 cups day-old bread crumbs	1½ tsp. poultry seasoning
1½ cups chicken stock	¼ tsp. salt
⅓ cup minced bacon	⅛ tsp. pepper
⅓ cup minced raw ham	⅓ cup chopped parsley
¾ cup onions, finely minced	2 eggs
½ cup celery, diced	1 Tbsp. milk
1 turkey liver, chopped	

Place bread crumbs in mixing bowl and moisten well with rich chicken stock as needed, taking care not to make soggy. In a skillet, sauté minced bacon and ham over medium heat until done, about 5 minutes. Add onions and celery.

Sauté until vegetables are soft, but not brown. Remove gall bladder from the turkey liver and chop fine. Add turkey liver to the vegetables and meat and continue to cook for a few minutes. Remove from heat, stir into bread crumbs, and mix thoroughly. Add poultry seasoning, salt, pepper, and parsley. Beat eggs with milk and pour into the dressing mix. Stir all together well. To use to stuff a turkey, first bake stuffing in 350-degree oven 20 minutes, then stuff bird. To use alone, place stuffing in well-greased baking pan, add sufficient stock to moisten, sprinkle a little drawn butter on top, and bake in 350-degree oven for 35–50 minutes.

CAPE COD CRANBERRY RELISH

BEFORE YOU BEGIN
You'll need: meat grinder, medium bowl with
    lid
Preparation time: 15 minutes (plus 2 or more
    hours to stand and chill)
Yield: 1 quart

1 lb. cranberries	1 large red apple,
1 large orange,	unpeeled
unpeeled	2 cups sugar

Wash and drain cranberries. Cut orange into wedges to fit meat grinder, then remove any seeds. Core apple and cut into wedges for meat grinder. Put cranberries, orange wedges, and apple wedges through grinder. Add sugar and mix well. Cover and chill at least 2 hours before serving.

PUFF POTATOES

BEFORE YOU BEGIN
You'll need: 2-quart saucepan, colander, baking
    sheet
Preheat oven to 400 degrees
Preparation time: 1 hour
Yield: 6 servings

1 qt. (6 medium) mealy	salt to taste
white potatoes	2 oz. butter

3 egg yolks	flour for dusting
pinch, nutmeg	egg and milk wash

Butter baking sheet and set aside. Peel and cut potatoes evenly. Place in saucepan and cover with boiling water, add salt, and return to boil, cooking until done, about 20 minutes. Drain well and return saucepan on stove to thoroughly dry potatoes. Mash potatoes. Add butter, egg yolks (one at a time, mixing well after each), and nutmeg. Put potatoes on lightly floured pastry board. Dust with flour, roll into long strip, flatten to about 1 inch wide, and cut into finger-length pieces. Set on buttered baking sheet 1 inch apart, brush with milk and egg, and bake until nicely browned, about 10 minutes.

SWEET POTATO PUFFS

BEFORE YOU BEGIN
You'll need: medium mixing bowl, rolling pin,
    small cookie sheet
Preheat oven to 400 degrees
Preparation time: 45 minutes
Yield: 6 servings

1 egg yolk	6 large marsh-
2 cups cold, cooked	mallows
mashed sweet potatoes	1 cup crushed
2 Tbsp. butter, melted	rice flakes
½ tsp. salt	
(or to taste)	

Butter cookie sheet and set aside. In mixing bowl, beat egg yolk slightly. Add mashed sweet potatoes, butter, and salt. Mix thoroughly. Divide mixture into 6 portions. Roll each portion between sheets of waxed paper to flatten into the shape of a pancake. Place one marshmallow in center of each. Carefully pull potato mixture up around marshmallow, leaving a small opening on top. Roll the sweet potato balls in crushed rice flakes. Place on a buttered cooking sheet. Bake 15 minutes. Serve hot.

BUTTERED BEETS

BEFORE YOU BEGIN
You'll need: 1-quart saucepan
Preparation time: 15 minutes
Yield: 6 servings

3 cups cooked beets	1 Tbsp. butter
¼ tsp. salt	1 Tbsp. white vinegar
⅛ tsp. white pepper	1 Tbsp. butter, melted

Drain beets, placing liquid in saucepan. Add salt, white pepper, 1 tablespoon butter, and vinegar. Dice beets, add to liquid, and bring just to a boil. Reduce heat and simmer until heated through, about 5 minutes. Serve using a slotted spoon, draining off all liquid first. Drizzle melted butter over beets just before serving.

CARROTS VICHY

BEFORE YOU BEGIN
You'll need: 1-quart saucepan
Preparation time: 15 minutes
Yield: 6 servings

1½ lbs. carrots, sliced	½ tsp. instant
½ tsp. salt	chicken bouillon
¼ tsp. pepper	½ Tbsp. freshly
1 Tbsp. sugar	chopped parsley
1 Tbsp. butter	

Place first six ingredients in a large saucepan and add just enough water to cover. Stir to mix. Bring to a boil. Reduce heat and slow boil, uncovered, until carrots are done to desired tenderness, about 10 minutes. Liquid should be almost evaporated. When serving, sprinkle with the chopped parsley.

CRANBERRY PIE

BEFORE YOU BEGIN
You'll need: 2 quart saucepan, 9-inch pie tin
Preheat oven to 350 degrees
Preparation time: 2½ hours
Yield: 1 pie

1¼ cups sugar	2 cups cranberries
2 Tbsp. flour	1 tsp. vanilla
¾ cup water	1 two-crust dessert pie
⅔ cup seeded raisins	pastry

In saucepan, combine sugar and flour. Add water, raisins, and cranberries, bring to a boil, reduce heat, and simmer for 10 minutes. Remove from heat and cool to room temperature. Stir in vanilla. Pour mixture into an unbaked 9-inch pie crust shell (see page 154) with a rim, and cover with a lattice top. Bake for 40–50 minutes until crust is brown. Cool before serving.

PUMPKIN PIE

Enhance the unique flavor of this regional specialty with a dollop of whipped cream.

BEFORE YOU BEGIN
You'll need: large mixing bowl, two 9-inch pie tins, electric beater
Preheat oven to 375 degrees
Preparation time: 1½ hours
Yield: 2 pies

1½ cups sugar	1 tsp. pumpkin spice
1½ ozs. butter, softened	pinch, salt
½ cup light cream	1 2½-lb. can
1 cup milk	pumpkin
4 whole eggs	1 2-crust dessert pie
¼ cup molasses	pastry

In large mixing bowl, combine sugar, butter, cream, milk, eggs, molasses, spice, and salt, and beat thoroughly. Add pumpkin. Continue beating until very smooth. Fill two pie tins lined with unbaked dough (see page 155). Bake until knife inserted into pie at least 1 inch from the crust comes out clean, about 45–60 minutes.

12

THE CHICAGO, MILWAUKEE, ST. PAUL, AND PACIFIC RAILROAD

BAKED PEAR CRUNCH WITH LEMON SAUCE

1 Tbsp. cornstarch
4 cups granular sugar
1 cup pear juice
4 16-oz. cans pears, halves or slices

¼ tsp. salt
1 tsp. cinnamon
9 cups corn flakes
¼ lb. butter, melted

In a small saucepan, combine cornstarch and 1 cup sugar. Stir in pear juice and bring to a boil, stirring constantly until thickened. Meanwhile, pour canned pears, including syrup, into the 3-quart saucepan over medium heat, and stir in salt and ½ teaspoon cinnamon. When thoroughly heated, add the pear juice/sugar glaze and 2 cups sugar and stir until dissolved and heated through. Place in 9" x 13" baking dish, making the layer one inch thick (excess liquid can be discarded). Meanwhile, crush the corn flakes and mix well with ½ teaspoon cinnamon, and one cup of sugar and melted butter. Sprinkle over pears and bake at 350 degrees until golden brown and the pears are well cooked, about 20 minutes. To serve, place a small portion of lemon sauce in dessert dish and place pear crunch on top. Do not pour sauce over.

LEMON SAUCE

1 egg yolk
1 cup granulated sugar
1 Tbsp. cornstarch
⅛ tsp. cinnamon
1 cup cold water

1 tsp. grated lemon rind
juice of one lemon
1 Tbsp. butter
yellow food coloring

Beat egg yolk slightly in a medium mixing bowl and set aside. In a small saucepan, stir together the sugar, cornstarch, cinnamon and cold water. Slowly bring to a boil, stirring constantly, and cook until clear and thickened. Stir in the lemon rind and lemon juice. Stirring constantly, pour hot mixture over beaten egg yolk. Return mixture to saucepan and heat one minute (do not boil). Add butter to melt. Add yellow food coloring, one drop at a time, until of desired color.

CHICAGO, MILWAUKEE, ST. PAUL & PACIFIC FUDGE

½ cup chopped walnuts
1 cup granular sugar
½ cup brown sugar
3 Tbsp. grated chocolate

3 Tbsp. butter
½ cup milk
½ tsp. vanilla
¾ Tbsp. light cream

BEFORE YOU BEGIN

You'll need: 1-quart saucepan, 8" x 8" baking pan
Preparation time: 30 minutes (plus several hours to cool)
Yield: 64 1-inch squares

Butter the baking pan, sprinkle generously with chopped walnuts (shredded coconut may be substituted), and set aside. In the saucepan, combine white and brown sugar, chocolate, butter, and milk. Bring to a boil and allow to slow boil until a drop hardens when placed in cold water. Remove from heat and stir in vanilla. Gradually add cream, stirring constantly, until mixture is creamy. Pour into buttered pan and allow to cool. When cooled, cut in 1-inch squares to serve.

CRABMEAT OLYMPIA HIAWATHA

This recipe is also suitable for chopped shrimp or lobster.

1 lb. fresh crabmeat, cooked
1 stalk celery, chopped fine
1 green onion, chopped fine
pinch, chervil, chopped fine
pinch, parsley, chopped fine
1 tsp. tarragon vinegar

4 Tbsp. mayonnaise
dash, curry powder
2 cups lettuce, shredded
8 large pitted olives
4 dill pickles, cut in fantails
4 sprigs watercress

BEFORE YOU BEGIN

You'll need: medium mixing bowl
Preparation time: 15 minutes
Yield: 4 servings

Clean and pick over crabmeat to remove any bits of bone or shell. Place in mixing bowl with celery, onion, chervil, parsley, tarragon vinegar and mayonnaise. Sprinkle over a very small quantity of curry powder. Mix well together. To serve, line a salad plate with a bed of crisp lettuce, torn or shredded. Place crab mixture on center. Decorate each serving with 2 large pitted olives, a dill pickle, and crisp watercress.

DUTCH MEAT LOAF

BEFORE YOU BEGIN

*You'll need: large bowl,
shallow baking pan,
small bowl, baster*
*Preheat oven to 350
degrees*
*Preparation time:
1 hour 45 minutes*
Yield: 8 servings

1½ lbs. ground beef
1 cup fresh bread crumbs
1 medium onion, chopped
4 oz. tomato sauce

1 egg, lightly beaten
1½ tsp. salt
¼ tsp. pepper

In a large bowl, lightly mix ingredients together and form into a loaf. Place in shallow pan and bake for 1½ hours. Meanwhile, make the sauce and immediately pour over meat loaf in oven and continue baking. Add any remaining sauce when baking reduces quantity of sauce in baking pan.

SPECIAL SAUCE

½ cup. tomato sauce
1 cup water
2 Tbsp. white vinegar

2 Tbsp. prepared mustard
2 Tbsp. brown sugar or molasses

In a small bowl, combine all ingredients and stir until thoroughly mixed.

MASHED SQUASH *OLYMPIAN*

BEFORE YOU BEGIN

*You'll need: steamer,
1-quart saucepan,
potato masher or
ricer*
*Preparation time:
30 minutes*
Yield: 6 servings

2 acorn squash
⅓ cup fresh orange juice
4 Tbsp. butter

½ tsp. salt
¼ tsp. pepper

Pare squash, remove seeds and strings, then quarter it. Cut quarters in 1-inch slices and place in covered steamer over boiling water until tender, about 15 minutes. In the saucepan, mash cooked squash thoroughly. Over medium heat, add orange juice, butter, salt, and pepper and stir to mix. Heat through and serve hot.

PORK SAUSAGE AND SWEET POTATOES

BEFORE YOU BEGIN

*You'll need: large
saucepan, potato
masher or ricer,
small bowl, small
saucepan, 1-quart
casserole*
*Preheat oven to 350
degrees*
*Preparation time:
1¼ hours*
Yield: 4 servings

4 sweet potatoes
2 Tbsp. butter
½ tsp. salt

2 eggs, well beaten
¼ cup light cream, heated
1 lb. ground sausage

Butter a 1-quart casserole and set aside. Wash sweet potatoes thoroughly and place in large saucepan with water to cover. Bring to a boil and cook until potatoes are tender, about 25 minutes. Drain, peel, and mash potatoes. Add butter, salt, well-beaten eggs, and heated cream. Beat or whip to make light and fluffy. Place potatoes in buttered casserole. Shape ground sausage into 4 patties and press each into potatoes. Place in oven and bake until sausage is nicely browned and done, about 30–45 minutes.

RICHMOND CORN CAKES

This recipe is especially recommended to accompany roast beef and is best served piping hot with butter.

1 **cup flour**	½ **Tbsp. sugar**
1 **Tbsp. baking powder**	½ **cup milk**
½ **tsp. salt**	¾ **cup whole corn kernels**
2 **eggs**	

Butter muffin pans generously all around and set aside. Sift together the flour, baking powder, and salt. In a large bowl, beat eggs well until of lemon color. Add sugar, milk, and corn and mix thoroughly. Add sifted ingredients and stir just until well mixed. Drop mixture by generous tablespoonsful into buttered muffin cups. Place in oven until lightly browned, about 20 minutes.

BEFORE YOU BEGIN

You'll need: muffin pans, medium bowl, sifter, large bowl
Preheat oven to 350 degrees
Preparation time: 30 minutes
Yield: 18 cakes

SCALLOPED BRUSSELS SPROUTS

4 **cups Brussels sprouts**	3 **Tbsp. flour**
5 **Tbsp. butter**	1½ **cups milk, scalded**
1½ **cups celery, diced**	1 **cup fresh bread crumbs**

Remove wilted leaves from sprouts and soak in cold water to cover. Cut a shallow X on the bottom (stem) end of each sprout. Cook, uncovered, in lightly salted boiling water to cover until tender-crisp and still bright green, about 7 minutes. Drain. Meanwhile, in a large skillet over medium heat, melt 3 tablespoons butter, add celery, and sauté for 2 minutes. Stirring constantly, add flour to form a paste. Gradually pour in scalded milk, stirring constantly. Add the sprouts, stir to mix, and turn into a 1½-quart baking dish. Meanwhile, in a small skillet, melt 2 tablespoons butter and sauté bread crumbs until lightly browned. Cover sprouts with buttered crumbs. Place in oven and bake until bubbly, about 10 minutes.

BEFORE YOU BEGIN

You'll need: 2-quart saucepan, 1½-quart casserole, large skillet, small saucepan, small skillet
Preheat oven to 425 degrees
Preparation time: 30 minutes
Yield: 8 servings

SCRAMBLED CODFISH RECTOR

BEFORE YOU BEGIN

*You'll need: medium
mixing bowl, large
skillet
Preparation time:
20 minutes
Yield: 2 servings*

1 cup salted or fresh codfish	2 cups milk
4 eggs	1 Tbsp. butter

Wash salted codfish in cold water and soak overnight to remove enough salt to make it edible. If fresh codfish is used, do not soak overnight. Tear or shred the codfish with a fork; do not cut with a knife. Melt butter in a large skillet over medium heat. Meanwhile, beat eggs well. Gradually add milk and shredded codfish to beaten eggs. Turn mixture into buttered skillet and cook over medium heat until the eggs and codfish are set, stirring occasionally. Do not allow eggs to become hard and dry. Garnish with crisp parsley and toast triangles.

STUFFED ONIONS

BEFORE YOU BEGIN

*You'll need: large
saucepan, 9" x 13"
baking dish, small
saucepan, 2-quart
saucepan, meat
grinder or blender
Preheat oven to 350
degrees
Preparation time:
1 hour
Yield: 6 servings*

6 large Bermuda onions	1 tsp. beef bouillon
2–3 cups veal forcemeat	¼ Tbsp. butter
6 thin slices fat salt pork	salt and pepper to taste
1 cup brown stock	

Peel onions and scoop out part of the inside, leaving an approximately ¼-inch wall. In a large saucepan, bring sufficient water to cover onions to a boil, add onions, and boil for 6 minutes. Remove and drain. Stuff each onion with veal forcemeat. In the baking dish, place the 6 slices of fat salt pork and put 1 stuffed onion atop each. Pour brown stock (see page 155) around onions and place in oven. Bake until onions are soft, about 35 minutes. Remove onions to a serving dish and keep warm. Strain the stock into a small saucepan over medium heat and skim off all fat possible. Add beef bouillon, butter, and salt and pepper to taste. Stir to mix and heat through. Pour over onions to serve.

VEAL FORCEMEAT

½ lb. veal	1 cup milk
½ tsp. salt	⅛ tsp. mace
¼ tsp. pepper	3 Tbsp. butter
1 cup dry bread crumbs, crusts removed	2 egg whites, beaten stiff

Chop and pound veal, then force through meat grinder or use blender to form 1 cup of veal puree. Add salt and pepper and mix. Meanwhile, mix bread crumbs, milk, and mace in a 2-quart saucepan over medium heat, bring to a boil, and slow boil until a smooth paste forms, about 10 minutes. Remove from heat and add butter, veal puree, and stiff-beaten egg whites. Stir until mixed thoroughly. Use as directed.

SUPREME OF CHICKEN WASHINGTON

A favorite of travelers in the upper Midwest, this specialty was the most popular dinner item from the kitchens of Milwaukee Road dining cars. Serve the chicken on a platter set in a bed of sauce Supreme with sauce poured over and with artichoke hearts warmed in butter. Top the artichoke hearts with a bouquet of hot asparagus tips and strips of pimento. Garnish with watercress or a sprig of parsley.

BEFORE YOU BEGIN

You'll need: medium skillet, roasting pan, small saucepan, 1-quart saucepan, whisk, small skillet or pan with cover, small bowl
Preheat oven to 325 degrees
Preparation time: 3½ hours
Yield: 4 servings

4 lb. roasting chicken	salt to taste
2 Tbsp. butter	pepper to taste
1 small green pepper, sliced	1 large carrot, sliced
2 Tbsp. diced pimento	1 medium onion, sliced
2½ cups whole kernel corn, drained	

Wash chicken, including cavity, and dress for baking. In a large skillet over medium heat, melt butter and sauté green pepper until soft. Add pimento and corn, preferably 3 or 4 ears of fresh corn cut from the cob. Season to taste and simmer for 5 minutes. Stuff the chicken, close the opening, and place in roasting pan on a bed of sliced carrots and onions. Place in oven and roast for 2½–3½ hours, basting frequently, until browned and tender.

SAUCE SUPREME

½ cup sliced mushrooms	2 Tbsp. flour
3 Tbsp. butter	salt to taste
1 cup chicken broth	white pepper to taste
2 Tbsp. butter	1 egg yolk

In a covered pan or skillet over medium heat, braise mushrooms in 1 tablespoon butter until tender; set aside. In a small saucepan, bring chicken broth to a boil. Meanwhile, in a 1-quart saucepan over medium heat, make a roux of 2 tablespoons butter and flour and cook until lightly browned, about 5 minutes. Add the boiling chicken stock a little at a time, whipping constantly, until a medium-thick cream sauce results. Season with salt and white pepper. Remove from heat. Meanwhile, in a medium bowl, beat egg yolk to lemon color. Add thickened broth and whip well. Return to a clean saucepan over medium heat. Add sliced mushrooms and stir until mixed and heated through.

13

THE GREAT NORTHERN RAILWAY

ANNA'S HOT-STUFF SAUCE

BEFORE YOU BEGIN

You'll need: large
bowl, linen towel or
sack, 3-quart sauce-
pan
Preparation time:
1 hour
Yield: 3 quarts

8 **cups green tomatoes**	1¼ **cups cider vinegar**
2 **Tbsp. salt**	½ **cup water**
1 **stalk celery, diced**	1 **cup brown sugar**
3 **large white onions, diced**	1½ **red (hot) peppers, diced**
1½ **green peppers, diced**	

Chop tomatoes fine, sprinkle with salt, stir well, and let stand 20 minutes. Add celery, onions, and green peppers and mix well. Put vegetables in a clean flour sack or linen cloth or towel and squeeze very dry, retaining liquid in the saucepan. Add vinegar, water, and brown sugar, bring to a boil, and keep at a rolling boil for 10 minutes. Put in the pulp mixture from the bag/cloth and continue cooking at brisk boil for 10 minutes. Stir in red peppers and remove from heat.

CHICKEN LOAF

BEFORE YOU BEGIN

You'll need: 2-quart
saucepan, small
bowl, small mixing
bowl, electric beater,
9" x 5" loaf pan,
1-quart saucepan
Preheat oven to 350
degrees
Preparation time:
1 hour
Yield: 6 servings

2 **cups scalded milk**	⅛ **tsp. white pepper**
¼ **cup butter**	3 **egg yolks, lightly beaten**
3 **egg yolks, lightly beaten**	2 **cups cold cooked chicken,**
¾ **cup shredded wheat crumbs**	**diced fine**
¼ **cup biscuit crumbs**	2 **Tbsp. chopped parsley**
1 **tsp. salt**	3 **egg whites, beaten dry**

Butter loaf pan generously all around and set aside. In the saucepan, scald milk, add butter, shredded wheat and biscuit crumbs, salt, and pepper, and cook 3 minutes. Remove from heat. In a small bowl, stirring constantly, slowly add ¼ cup hot mixture to lightly beaten egg yolks. Return beaten egg mixture to the saucepan. Add chicken and parsley and mix all well. Fold in dry-beaten egg whites and turn mixture into buttered loaf pan. Bake until firm, about 45 minutes. Remove from oven and let stand 5 minutes. Turn out of loaf pan onto platter, cut in ¾-inch slices, and serve two to a platter, with sauce poured over.

SAUCE

2 Tbsp. butter	½ tsp. salt
2 Tbsp. flour	⅛ tsp. paprika
2 cups chicken stock, warmed	

In a 1-quart saucepan over medium heat, make a roux of the butter and flour. Slowly stir in hot chicken stock. Continue stirring and add salt and paprika. Reduce heat and simmer 10 minutes before serving.

CHICKEN PIE, GREAT NORTHERN STYLE

3 4½–5 lb. stewing chickens	½ cup heavy cream
1 onion, sliced	salt to taste
1 bunch parsley	4 large potatoes
1 sprig sage	8 large fresh mushrooms, diced
4 heaping Tbsp. flour	16 strips bacon
2 Tbsp. butter	pastry dough for 2 pies
3 egg yolks, well beaten	

In a large stew pot, cover chickens with cold water. Add onion slices, parsley, and sage. Slowly bring to a boil over medium heat, then simmer until meat is about ready to fall from bones, about 1–1½ hours. Separate meat from bones, retaining white meat. Continue to simmer stock until reduced by approximately one-third, then allow to cool. Skim fat off top and mix with 4 heaping tablespoonsful of flour and 2 tablespoonsful of butter, then set aside to use as a binder. Meanwhile, remove cold stock to the 2-quart saucepan and add well-beaten egg yolks and rich cream and stir to mix. Season to taste. Then, over medium-high heat, heat again, stirring continually. Do not boil. Add the binder and strain thoroughly. Meanwhile, make meal pie pastry sufficient for 2 pies (see page 155) and refrigerate. Boil potatoes in skins until nearly tender, about 15 minutes. Allow to cool, then remove slice of skin lengthwise sufficient to allow access with melon baller. Make 32 potato balls and set aside. Dice mushrooms fine, then sauté with bacon until they are tender and bacon is crisp. Crumble bacon. To finish, place 4 potato balls in individual 2-cup casseroles or baking dishes. Add 3 slices of chicken breast and a portion of diced mushroom and bacon. Fill dish with sauce described above. Roll out pie pastry moderately thick, trim to fit, then cover casseroles, sealing edges all around. Bake until crust is a rich brown color, about 20 minutes. Serve hot en casserole.

CREAM OF CAULIFLOWER SOUP

BEFORE YOU BEGIN

*You'll need: small
saucepan, 1-quart
saucepan, 1½-quart
saucepan, 2-quart
saucepan, sieve
Preparation time:
1 hour
Yield: 6 servings*

1 medium cauliflower	4 cups milk, hot
4 Tbsp. butter	1 cup light cream, hot
2 slices of medium onion	1 Tbsp. butter
1 leek, sliced	1 tsp. salt
4 Tbsp. flour	¼ tsp. cayenne pepper

Remove leaves from cauliflower and trim, separating stems from flowerets. In a 1-quart saucepan with water to cover, boil flowerets until tender, 5–10 minutes, drain well, and set aside. Meanwhile, in a 2-quart saucepan over medium heat, melt 4 tablespoons butter and braise onion and leek until tender, about 10 minutes. Continue simmering slowly and add flour, stirring constantly. Add stems of cauliflower and hot milk and bring to a boil. Reduce heat and slow boil until cauliflower is tender, about 15 minutes. Strain heated mixture well through a sieve and return to a clean 2-quart saucepan. Add hot cream and 1 tablespoon butter. Season with salt and cayenne pepper. Cut boiled flowerets into small pieces and add to soup and heat through. Stir to mix well before serving.

GINGERBREAD CRUMB PUDDING WITH BUTTERSCOTCH SAUCE

BEFORE YOU BEGIN

*You'll need: 9" x 13"
baking dish, large
mixing bowl, elec-
tric mixer, 1½-
quart saucepan
Preheat oven to 350
degrees
Preparation time:
1½ hours
Yield: 12 servings*

4 eggs	½ tsp. cinnamon
2 cups milk	½ cup butter, melted
1½ cups sugar	1 lb. loaf stale raised
1 tsp. ginger	white bread, grated
1 cup molasses	

Butter baking dish thoroughly and set aside. In a large mixing bowl, beat eggs until of light lemon color. Continue beating and gradually add milk, sugar, ginger, molasses, cinnamon, and melted butter. Mix well. Add grated bread and stir until well mixed. Pour mixture into buttered baking dish and place dish in a pan filled with hot water to within 1 inch of the top of the pudding dish. Place in oven and bake 1 hour, or until knife inserted in the center comes out clean. Spoon pudding into a serving dish and top with butterscotch sauce.

BUTTERSCOTCH SAUCE

4 Tbsp. cornstarch	1 heaping tsp. powdered
½ cup cold water	cocoa
1 Tbsp. sugar	5 drops vanilla extract
2½ cups water	4 Tbsp. butter
1¾ cups sugar	

Dissolve cornstarch in cold water and set aside. In the saucepan over medium heat, melt 1 tablespoon of sugar until browned to a golden color. Add water and remaining sugar, bring to a boil, and continue to boil for 3 minutes. Add cocoa, vanilla extract, and butter. Stir to mix and simmer to a glaze. Slowly add cornstarch to boiling liquid and simmer until thickened.

—⊷—⊨◈⊨—⊶—

GREAT NORTHERN BAKED HAM

1 raw ham to suit	sugar as needed
2–3 tsp. sugar or heavy molasses	bread crumbs as needed
white vinegar as needed	whole cloves

Start with ham at room temperature. Wash thoroughly in warm water and wipe dry, then soak overnight in cold water to cover the entire ham. Drain off soaking water and re-cover with fresh cold water. Add sugar or heavy molasses to the water. Bring water to boil and let the ham boil slowly for a total of 20 minutes per pound. When ham is fully boiled, remove skin, taking care not to tear the fat. Place in a baking pan and rub the ham, first with sugar and then with vinegar. Next roll the ham in fine bread crumbs and sugar to cover. Spike the ham with whole cloves spaced 2 inches apart. Place in a clean roasting pan, insert thermometer to center while avoiding the bone, and bake uncovered until internal temperature reaches 150 degrees, about 1 hour.

SWEET SAUCE FOR BAKED HAM

2 lemons	1 cup currant jelly
2 oranges	1 cup raisins
2 cups water	2 cups Espagnole sauce
1 cup sugar	

Juice the lemons and oranges, then retain the peel. In a 2-quart saucepan, combine water, sugar, currant jelly, and lemon and orange juice and mix well. Add raisins. Bring all to a boil and continue boiling to reduce until fairly thick. Strain, then work the sweet sauce into an equal amount of Espagnole sauce (see page 154). Continue to simmer until finished, when sauce is smooth and as thick as cold syrup. Meanwhile, place the orange and lemon peel in boiling water for 5 minutes. Remove, shred, and sprinkle as a garnish over the finished sauce. Serve very hot.

GREAT NORTHERN DOUGHNUTS

BEFORE YOU BEGIN

You'll need: large mixing bowl, electric beater, rolling pin, doughnut cutter, slotted spoon, deep fryer
Preheat 4 inches of clean salad oil in deep fryer to 370 degrees
Preparation time: 1½ hours
Yield: 36 doughnuts

6 cups flour	3 eggs
2 cups sugar	½ tsp. cinnamon
1 tsp. nutmeg	2 cups milk
1 tsp. salt	3 Tbsp. lard, melted
1 Tbsp. baking powder	

In a large mixing bowl, combine 1 cup flour and remaining ingredients. Mix at a low speed to form a smooth dough, constantly scraping side of mixing bowl clean. Increase speed to medium, continue scraping bowl side, and beat 1 minute more. Add remaining flour and stir to form a stiff dough. Refrigerate dough 1 hour before continuing. On a well-floured surface, roll dough out to ½-inch thickness. Flour doughnut cutter and cut to shape, re-rolling dough and cutting trimmings until all dough is cut. Fry doughnuts in the hot oil three or four at a time. As they rise to the surface, turn frequently until they reach a golden brown color. Cool on a paper towel before serving.

GREAT NORTHERN ENGLISH BEEFSTEAK PIE

BEFORE YOU BEGIN

You'll need: 4-quart saucepan, 6 individual casseroles
Preheat oven to 400 degrees
Preparation time: 2 hours
Yield: 6 servings

3 Tbsp. butter	1½ lbs. flank of beef, cut in ½-inch squares
¼ lb. salt pork, diced	¼ cup flour
2 slices bacon, diced	1 cup beef stock, heated
3 carrots, sliced	2 potatoes, boiled and diced
1 large onion, chopped	salt and pepper to taste
1 bay leaf	2 tomatoes, peeled and diced
4 whole cloves	1 meal pie pastry recipe
1 small clove garlic, minced	

Melt butter in the saucepan over medium heat. Add diced salt pork and bacon, carrots, onion, bay leaf, and cloves. Cover and braise slowly for 20 minutes. Add garlic for last 2 minutes. Then add the beef, cover, and stir frequently to prevent burning. Cook until meat is nearly tender, about 20 minutes. Sprinkle flour over contents and allow to brown and to absorb moisture. Add hot beef stock, stir, and cook 15 minutes. Add boiled and diced potatoes, season with salt and pepper to taste, and stir to mix and heat through. Place equal portions in individual casseroles, sprinkle in tomatoes, and cover with pie dough rolled thin and sealed over edges. Cut three 1-inch slits in each dough topping to allow steam to escape. Place in oven and bake to a golden brown, about 20 minutes.

GREAT NORTHERN SPECIAL DRESSING

pinch, salt
pinch, dry mustard
1 Tbsp. white vinegar
1 egg yolk
1 cup pure olive oil, very cold
  juice of one lemon
1 tsp. Worcestershire sauce
1 tsp. chili sauce

2 oz. Roquefort cheese,
  crumbled fine
1 small pickled beet, chopped fine
¼ of a hard-boiled egg white,
  chopped fine
⅛ green pepper, chopped fine
1 tsp. paprika

BEFORE YOU BEGIN

You'll need: small bowl, medium mixing bowl, airtight storage jar
Preparation time: 30 minutes (plus 1 hour to chill before serving)
Yield: 1 pint

Dissolve salt and mustard in vinegar and set aside. Beat egg yolk until of a light lemon color. Continue beating and add olive oil, one drop at a time at first, then slowly increasing quantity. When mixture begins to thicken, slowly add the lemon juice and vinegar/seasonings mixture. When mayonnaise forms, stir in Worcestershire sauce and chili sauce. Add Roquefort cheese, pickled beet, egg white, green pepper, and paprika. Mix thoroughly and refrigerate in airtight container before serving.

POTATO ROLLS

1 lb. white russet potatoes
2 pkgs. dry yeast
2 lbs. flour

4 Tbsp. butter
1 tsp. salt
2 cups milk (approximately)

BEFORE YOU BEGIN

You'll need: 1-quart saucepan, large bowl, masher, thermometer, cloth cover, three 12-cup muffin tins
Preheat oven to 400 degrees
Preparation time: 4 hours
Yield: 36 rolls

Peel potatoes and place in the saucepan with water to cover. Boil potatoes until tender, about 25 minutes. Meanwhile, in a large bowl, combine dry yeast and flour. Drain potatoes and return to saucepan to mash with butter. Add salt and milk sufficient to make a soft batter. Over low heat, heat batter to 120–130 degrees. Add heated batter to the dry ingredients and mix into a light dough, adding more milk if necessary. On a lightly floured surface, knead dough until smooth and elastic, about 10 minutes. Place in large greased bowl, turn once to grease top, cover, and place in a warm location. Let dough rise until doubled, about 1 hour. When light, knead it over again, cover, and let rest 15 minutes. Then divide dough into small round cakes and place them in slightly buttered muffin tins. Cover and put them in a warm place to rise until doubled, about 1 hour. Bake in oven until well browned, about 20–30 minutes. When rolls are done, wash the tops lightly with a little water and cover them with a clean towel to keep them soft.

BEFORE YOU BEGIN

You'll need: large stew pot, 12-inch square cheesecloth and string to tie
Preparation time: 4 hours
Yield: 8 servings

━◆━

REINDEER MULLIGAN, HUNTER STYLE

When the Great Northern Dining Car Department introduced reindeer meat onto its menu, it promoted this and other featured dishes with a little booklet that explained: "The reindeer, as now raised in Alaska, is a domesticated animal; has nothing of the wild animal taste—the meat is finer in texture than beef and decidedly more tender— this explained by the fact that the reindeer is a docile animal, seldom exerting itself to the extent of providing ordinary exercise—therefore he grows fat and soft. Reindeer meat has [the] juiciness of beef with delicacy of flavor unequalled by beef or venison. Reindeer meat is a happy medium between wild game and domestic meats." This recipe, the booklet let it be known, "was furnished by an old hunter."

2 lbs. reindeer meat, cut in 2-inch squares	2 large onions, quartered
2 cups rutabaga, cut in 2-inch squares	salt to taste
2 cups carrots, cut in 2-inch slices	6 whole peppercorns
2 cups potatoes, cut in 1-inch cubes	4 bay leaves

Reindeer meat should be taken from the neck, shanks, and parts of the shoulder, and be cut in uniform pieces about 2 inches square. Place meat in large stew pot with water to cover. Bring to a boil, reduce heat, and let simmer about 30 minutes. Then add rutabaga and continue to simmer for 15 minutes. Add carrots, potatoes, onions, and salt. Place peppercorns and bay leaves in small cheesecloth bag, tie, and place in stew. Cover and continue to simmer until meat is tender, about 2½ hours. Serve with dill pickles.

14

THE ILLINOIS CENTRAL RAILROAD

BAKED DEVILED CRABMEAT

Panama Limited *patrons enjoyed this regional favorite, made from a recipe developed in the Illinois Central dining-service training kitchen. The dinner menu offered juice or a home-made soup, salad with Illinois Central Dressing, and their own Potatoes Romanoff. Add Baked String Beans with Mushrooms (see page 314) and Corn Hoe Cakes (see page 347) for a classic railroad dinner.*

(see page 314) (see page 347)

1 lb. crabmeat	¼ tsp. thyme
2 Tbsp. butter	½ tsp. salt
1 large onion, minced	¼ tsp. cayenne pepper
1 large green pepper, diced	1 Tbsp. Worcestershire sauce
1 clove garlic, minced	3 hard-boiled eggs, minced
4 slices white bread,	juice of ½ lemo
broken into coarse crumbs	4 Tbsp. butter, melted
water to moisten	

BEFORE YOU BEGIN

You'll need: large skillet, 4 individual shallow casseroles, small skillet
Preheat oven to 350 degrees
Preparation time: 45 minutes
Yield: 4 servings

Clean and pick over crabs to remove any bits of bone or shell. In a large skillet over medium-low heat, melt butter and sauté onion and green pepper for 10 minutes, adding garlic for the last minute. Break bread into crumbs and moisten lightly with water. To the sautéed onion/green pepper mixture, add thyme, salt, cayenne pepper, Worcestershire sauce, eggs, bread crumbs, crabmeat, and lemon juice. Mix all ingredients carefully to avoid breaking up the crabmeat. Heat through, stirring occasionally. Meanwhile, melt butter in small skillet. Divide crabmeat mixture into individual shallow casseroles and pour 1 tablespoon melted butter over each. Bake for 10 minutes.

---◆─ ▆◆▆ ─◆---

ATHENS PARFAIT

This dessert was among the many specialties of chef J. E. Crawford. It was a favorite among patrons of his dining car aboard the Seminole Limited.

1 pt. heavy cream, whipped stiff	**1 cup light corn syrup**
8 egg yolks	**1 tsp. vanilla extract**

Whip cream and refrigerate for use later. In a small bowl, beat egg yolks until of a light lemon color. Gently stir in syrup. Pour mixture into double boiler and cook over low heat. Stir constantly until mixture thickens sufficiently to coat the spoon. Turn into large bowl, add vanilla extract, and beat with a whip until cool. The mixture will then be very light. Add whipped cream, stir lightly together until thoroughly mixed, and turn into the mold. Place mold in freezer for 4 hours before serving. This parfait can be varied by replacing the vanilla with 2 ounces of chocolate, melted and smoothed, or other flavorings.

---◆─ ▆◆▆ ─◆---

BACON AND EGG SOUFFLÉ

This recipe, created by Chef Charles Meyers for patrons of his dining car on the Seminole Limited, *is a testament to the smooth ride aboard Limited trains. Meyers, typical of many on-train employees, served as chef at the Central Station dining room in Chicago for two years before joining the Illinois Central.*

12 egg whites	**12 egg yolks**
salt and pepper to taste	**12 strips bacon, cooked**
12 Tbsp. (6 oz.) heavy cream	

Butter baking pan all around and set aside. Beat the egg whites to a stiff light froth. Mix in salt and pepper. Pour the mixture into the buttered baking pan. Make 12 evenly spaced dips in egg whites with a small ladle. Place 1 tablespoonful of heavy cream into each dip. Upon each spoonful of cream, gently drop 1 whole yolk, being careful not to break the yolks. Place in oven and cook 10 minutes or until golden. Meanwhile, cook bacon to desired doneness. Cut baked souffle into six portions of 2 yolks each and serve hot with 2 strips of bacon on the dish.

CANAPÉ LORENZO

BEFORE YOU BEGIN

You'll need: two small saucepans, baking tray, 2-inch biscuit cutter
Preheat oven to 350 degrees
Preparation time: 45 minutes
Yield: 12 servings

Another unique creation from the kitchen of Chef J. E. Crawford aboard the Seminole Limited:

1	cup crabmeat, cooked	2½	Tbsp. Swiss cheese, grated
2	Tbsp. butter	1	cup chicken stock, hot
1	slice onion, chopped fine		salt to taste
2	Tbsp. flour		cayenne pepper to taste
1	Tbsp. milk, warmed	12	2-inch circles bread, toasted
2½	Tbsp. Parmesan cheese, grated		watercress

Clean and pick over crab to remove any bits of bone or shell. In a small saucepan over low heat, melt 1 tablespoon of the butter and sauté chopped onion without browning. Stir in 1 tablespoon of flour and cook until thickened without browning. Stir in hot milk and Parmesan and Swiss cheeses. Cook just long enough to soften cheese. Remove from heat and let cool, then form into 12 balls. Next, in a small saucepan over medium heat, make a roux of 1 tablespoon each of butter and flour. Slowly stir in hot stock and crabmeat. Cook until slightly thickened, stirring occasionally. Season with salt and cayenne pepper. Meanwhile, prepare circles of toasted bread. Cover each with a layer of thickened crab mixture and in the center of each place a ball of cheese. Put in oven for 5 minutes. Serve with watercress.

CLAM CHOWDER MID-AMERICA

BEFORE YOU BEGIN

You'll need: small skillet, 3-quart saucepan, small saucepan
Preparation time: 45 minutes
Yield: 8 servings

The Illinois Central, known as the "Main Line of Mid-America," adapted this delicacy from the Eastern seaboard for patrons of its dining cars.

¼	cup salt pork, diced	½	cup white potatoes, diced
½	cup onions, chopped fine	1	tsp. salt
1	1-lb. can chopped clams in juice	½	tsp. white pepper
1	cup water	2	Tbsp. butter
1	cup chopped tomatoes	1	Tbsp. flour
2	cups milk		parsley, chopped fine

In a small skillet over medium heat, fry the salt pork until brown, then remove from drippings and place in the 3-quart saucepan. In salt pork drippings, sauté onion until soft, but do not brown. Remove onions from drippings and add them to salt pork in saucepan. Add chopped clams, clam juice, water, tomatoes, and milk. Bring to a boil and skim off any fat. Add potatoes and seasoning. Simmer until potatoes and pork are tender, about 25 minutes. Meanwhile, in a clean small skillet over medium heat, make a roux of butter and flour and stir into the chowder. Allow to thicken by simmering another 10 minutes, stirring frequently. Do not allow to boil. Serve hot with chopped parsley sprinkled over.

FRUIT UPSIDE-DOWN PUDDING

The experienced Illinois Central traveler knew to pass up the ice cream and other more common desserts if this treat was on the menu. Originally created for the Panama Limited, *it came to be served on the other "name" trains as well. Passengers were reminded that if they served it at home, the generous dab of real whipped cream was obligatory, or "Don't say it's from the IC, thank you!"*

1½ cups flour	½ tsp. vanilla extract
1½ tsp. baking powder	½ cup chopped walnuts
¼ tsp. salt	½ cup brown sugar, light or dark
¼ cup butter, melted	¾ cup fruit cocktail, drained
¾ cup granular sugar	¼ cup maraschino cherries, chopped
1 egg, well beaten	½ pint whipping cream, whipped
¾ cup milk	

In a large mixing bowl, sift flour, baking powder, and salt together. Add melted butter, sugar, egg, milk, vanilla extract, and chopped walnuts, and beat until smooth. Next, butter bottom only of the baking pan. Sprinkle brown sugar evenly over the butter. Spread fruit cocktail over butter/sugar coating and sprinkle with maraschino cherries. Pour the batter over the fruit. Bake until knife inserted in center comes out clean, about 1 hour. Remove from oven and immediately turn upside-down on a serving board or platter. Allow pan to remain over pudding a few minutes so the brown-sugar mixture can run down over the pudding. Cut into portions and serve each with a dollop of whipped cream.

CURRIED LOBSTER

Noted for his fine pastries, chef A. G. Ferguson joined the Illinois Central in 1903 after stints with the Crescent News and Hotel Company and the Pennsylvania Railroad. He also served on the private car Zamora *of the Waters-Pierce Oil Company. This outstanding concoction delighted patrons of the Illinois Central's western lines.*

2 1–2 lb. American lobsters, cooked	½ cup light cream
¼ lb. cooked ham, diced	1 tsp. flour
⅛ tsp. cayenne pepper	1 tsp. curry powder
½ tsp. salt	2 cups boiled rice
½ cup lobster or chicken stock	

Remove the cooked lobster meat from the shells. Place the lobster meat and ham in the saucepan. Add cayenne pepper and salt. In a small bowl, mix stock and cream together, pour over the meat, and stir to mix. Put mixture on medium heat until bubbly, reduce heat, cover, and let simmer for about 1 hour. In a small dish, place 1 tablespoon of the hot stock, then add in the flour and curry powder, stirring constantly until smooth. Stir curry powder/flour mixture back in to the saucepan and cook 3 minutes longer. Serve on a bed of boiled rice (see page 153).

ILLINOIS CENTRAL SALAD DRESSING

While noteworthy on a lettuce and tomato salad, any tossed salad can be dressed with this, one of the most famous of the Illinois Central's fine foods. The only recipe carrying the railroad's name, it was developed after much experimentation by the railroad's chefs and was prepared fresh on each train.

BEFORE YOU BEGIN

You'll need: medium mixing bowl, 1-quart storage container
Preparation time: 45 minutes
Yield: 1 quart

2 Tbsp. celery, chopped fine
2 Tbsp. green pepper, chopped fine
1 tsp. green onion, chopped fine
2 Tbsp. dill pickle, chopped fine
2 Tbsp. pimento, chopped fine
2 hard-boiled eggs, chopped fine
2 cups mayonnaise
1 cup chili sauce

Place celery, green pepper, green onion, dill pickle, pimento, and egg in mixing bowl and mix thoroughly. Add mayonnaise and stir well. Add chili sauce and stir well. Store in a cool place. Serve on fresh garden salads.

OLD-FASHIONED RAISIN PUDDING

Here is a simple and fitting conclusion to a good meal. This raisin pudding has an old fashioned flavor that made it a favorite with patrons on the Illinois Central trains, as well as with those in its Chicago Central Station restaurant.

BEFORE YOU BEGIN

You'll need: large mixing bowl, 8" x 8" baking pan, 1-quart saucepan
Preheat oven to 350 degrees
Preparation time: 45 minutes
Yield: 8 servings

¾ cup flour
¼ cup granular sugar
1 tsp. baking powder
½ cup raisins
¼ cup milk
1 cup brown sugar
1 cup water
2 Tbsp. butter
whipped cream (optional)

Butter the baking pan all around and set aside. In mixing bowl, stir together the flour, granular sugar, baking powder, and raisins. Slowly add milk, beating constantly until smooth. Spread batter mix in the bottom of the baking pan. In saucepan, mix brown sugar, water, and butter and bring to a boil. Remove from heat and pour over the batter while hot. Bake for 30 minutes. Let stand 10 minutes before serving. Serve as is or top with a dollop of whipped cream.

＋◆ ⊠◆⊠ ◆＋

POTATOES ROMANOFF

BEFORE YOU BEGIN

*You'll need: small and
medium bowls, 2-
quart baking dish
Preheat oven to 350
degrees
Preparation time:
1 hour
Yield: 4 servings*

*Done Illinois Central style, this classic old-world creation is suitable as a savory side
dish to meat, fish, or fowl.*

2 **cups white potatoes, cooked and diced**	1 **small clove garlic, minced**
1 **tsp. salt**	¼ **cup American cheese, diced**
1 **cup small-curd cottage cheese**	**pinch, paprika**
1 **cup sour cream***	2 **Tbsp. butter, melted**
2 **Tbsp. scallions, minced**	**sprig of parsley**

**½ cup half-and-half and ½ teaspoon fresh lemon juice may be substituted for sour
cream, if desired*

Butter the baking dish all around and set aside. In a small bowl, sprinkle potatoes with salt. In medium bowl, combine cottage cheese, sour cream, scallions,
and garlic. Fold in the potatoes. Pour mixture into baking dish. Top with American cheese, and sprinkle lightly with paprika and melted butter. Bake 15 minutes, until thoroughly heated and lightly browned on top. Serve hot, topped with
parsley.

＋◆ ⊠◆⊠ ◆＋

SHRIMP CREOLE

BEFORE YOU BEGIN

*You'll need: 2-quart
saucepan, colander,
3-quart saucepan,
molds for rice (op-
tional)
Preparation time:
1 hour
Yield: 4 servings*

*Combining the best of French cooking and the colorful flair of Spanish ideas, New Or-
leans-style Creole recipes were a specialty of Illinois Central chefs. This masterpiece won
praise from patrons and the media alike. The recommended meal consisted of fruit cocktail, fresh green beans, Corn O'Brien, hush puppies, a chocolate sundae, and coffee.*

STEP ONE: THE SHRIMP

2 **lbs. jumbo shrimp (about 40)**	1 **Tbsp. salt**
4 **whole allspice**	1 **stalk celery, broken in two**
¼ **tsp. cayenne pepper**	1 **Tbsp. white vinegar**
1 **bay leaf**	

In the 3-quart saucepan, place enough water to cover shrimp and stir in allspice,
cayenne pepper, bay leaf, salt, celery, and vinegar. Bring to a boil. Meanwhile,
wash shrimp in cold water. Add shrimp to the boiling mixture, cover, and cook
at the boil for 6 minutes. Remove from heat and drain off the liquid. Shell and
devein shrimp, wash in cold water, and drain well. Time preparation of shrimp
to enable them to be served hot.

STEP TWO: CREOLE SAUCE

2	Tbsp. cooking oil	1	cup tomato puree
1	medium onion, diced	1	cup tomatoes, chopped and
1	green pepper, diced		drained
2	stalks celery, diced	½	cup canned mushroom pieces
1	small clove garlic, chopped fine	1	tsp. salt
2	Tbsp. flour	¼	tsp. cayenne pepper
1	cup chicken stock, warmed	½	bay leaf

In a clean 3-quart saucepan over medium heat, warm cooking oil. Sauté onion, green pepper, and celery 5 minutes, adding garlic for the last minute. Add flour and stir well. Add hot chicken stock, tomato puree, tomato pieces, and mushrooms. Season with salt, cayenne pepper, and bay leaf. Cover and cook at the simmer 30 minutes. Remove bay leaf.

STEP THREE: THE SERVICE

Cook four ½-cup servings of boiled rice (see page 153). Divide in four molds (or small casseroles) to shape, if desired. For individual servings, uncover a mold of hot cooked rice in center of individual serving dishes. Arrange about 10 shrimp around the rice and pour one cup hot Creole sauce over the shrimp, leaving rice white. Garnish by placing sprig of parsley in center of the rice. Serve hot.

15

THE MISSOURI PACIFIC RAILROAD

BAKED FILLET OF FRESH FISH POURTAGAISE

BEFORE YOU BEGIN

You'll need: baking dish, 1-quart sauce-pan
Preheat oven to 350 degrees
Preparation time: 45 minutes
Yield: 6 servings

2 lbs. lake trout or white fish fillets
1 15-oz. can crushed tomatoes

salt and pepper to taste
juice of 1 lemon

Butter baking dish well. Place fillets in baking dish and pour crushed tomatoes over. Season to taste with salt and pepper and drizzle lemon juice over. Bake until done, about 20 minutes.

POURTAGAISE SAUCE

1 Tbsp. butter
1 small onion, chopped fine
¼ lb. mushrooms, chopped fine
½ cup claret wine

2 cups brown gravy
1 pimento, chopped
1 tomato, cut into small dice
  salt and fresh ground pepper
    to taste

In the saucepan over medium heat, melt butter and add onion and mushrooms. Cover tightly, reduce heat and cook slowly for 4 minutes. Then add claret and cook until wine is reduced by one-third, about 10 minutes. Add brown gravy, pimento, and diced tomato. Bring mixture to a simmering boil and continue to simmer until thickened, about 20 minutes. Season to taste, adding a bit more wine if necessary. Pour sauce over individual portions of baked fish and serve hot.

BLANC MANGE (ALMOND–MILK PUDDING)

1 qt. milk
½ lb. blanched almonds
4 oz. sugar

1 envelope unflavored gelatin
½ pint whipping cream

Soak gelatin in ¼ cup of the milk. Place almonds in mortar, and mash fine with sugar. In the 2-quart saucepan, bring remaining milk to simmer, add almond/sugar mix, and continue to simmer for 15 minutes. Add gelatin. Before mixture stiffens, fold in whipped cream and pour into mold(s) that have been rinsed with cold water. Chill to set before serving.

BEFORE YOU BEGIN

You'll need: 1-quart saucepan, mortar, 2-quart saucepan, strainer, large bowl, 8 individual or 1 large pudding mold(s)
Preparation time: 30 minutes (plus 1 hour to chill before serving)
Yield: 8 servings

CASSEROLE OF PRIME BEEF JARDINIERE

1 cup flour
½ Tbsp. salt
½ tsp. paprika
2 lbs. lean stew beef,
    cut in 1½ inch cubes
3 Tbsp. bacon drippings
2 Tbsp. butter
1 cup carrots, coarsely sliced
1 cup celery, coarsely sliced
1 large onion, chopped
2 bay leaves

4 whole allspice
2 Tbsp. flour
2–3 cups beef stock
½ cup tomato puree
½ cup claret wine
3 carrots, diced small
1 turnip, diced small
18 whole pearl onions, cooked
½ cup peas, cooked
½ cup lima beans, cooked
3 Tbsp. butter

BEFORE YOU BEGIN

You'll need: large skillet, 4-quart covered saucepan, strainer, 1-quart saucepan, 3-quart casserole
Preparation time: 3 hours
Yield: 6 servings

In a dish, stir flour, salt, and paprika together well. Roll meat in flour mixture. In a large skillet over medium-high heat, melt bacon drippings and cook beef cubes until well browned. Meanwhile, in the 4-quart covered saucepan over medium heat, melt 2 tablespoons of butter and braise carrots, celery, and onions until soft, about 10 minutes. Add the browned beef, bay leaves, allspice and 2 tablespoons flour. Cook for a few minutes until flour is lightly browned, then add beef stock sufficient to just cover the meat. Add tomato puree and wine, stir, and bring to a boil. Reduce heat, cover, and cook slowly, stirring occasionally, until meat is done, about 2 hours. When fork-tender, pick meat out with a fork and place in a casserole. Strain the gravy over the meat. Meanwhile, in the 1-quart saucepan over medium heat, melt 3 tablespoons of butter and sauté diced carrots and turnips, small onions, peas, and lima beans until tender and heated through, about 10 minutes. Scatter sautéed mixed vegetables on top of the meat casserole before serving.

COLD SLICED BREAST OF TURKEY ISABELLE

*You'll need: serving
    platter, small bowl
Preparation time:
    30 minutes (plus 1
    hour to chill sauce
    before serving)
Yield: 6 servings*

Colorful, tasty, and nutritious, this delightful summer dish became a year-round favorite of Missouri Pacific patrons.

1½ lbs. turkey breast, cooked	4 thin strips green pepper
1 head lettuce, finely shredded	2 Tbsp. mayonnaise
3 cups boiled rice, cold	12 slices tomato
1 Isabelle sauce recipe	6 dill pickles or 12 gherkins
18 fresh asparagus tips, cooked	12 each, green and ripe olives
4 thin strips pimento	2 hard-boiled eggs, chopped fine

Slice turkey breast thin. Place shredded lettuce evenly over a large cold platter. In the middle of the platter shape the cold boiled rice (see page 153) in an oblong form. Place sliced turkey breast on top of the rice and pour Isabelle sauce over the turkey. On each end of the platter place 9 asparagus tips with a band over the end of each portion made up of 2 thin strips each of pimento and green peppers. Top with a dash of mayonnaise over the tips. On each side of the platter place six slices of tomato flanked by the pickles, cut in fan shape, and olives. Sprinkle finely chopped hard-boiled egg over the whole dish before serving.

ISABELLE SAUCE

1 small onion, chopped fine	1 tsp. Worcestershire sauce
1 bunch watercress, chopped fine	6 drops Tabasco sauce
½ bunch parsley, chopped fine	3 oz. sherry wine
2 cups Thousand Island dressing	

Combine and chop the onion, watercress, and parsley together. In a small bowl, add this to the Thousand Island dressing. Add Worcestershire sauce, Tabasco sauce and sherry wine and stir well. Chill before using.

COLE SLAW

This tangy side dish can be adjusted to serve any size gathering. It goes well with a seafood main course, from those with a "bite," such as the Illinois Central's Shrimp Creole (p. 228), to milder fare, such as the Atlantic Coast Line's Fillet of Fish, Spanish style (p. 166), or the Missouri Pacific's own Fried Oysters with Remoulade Sauce (p. 234).

BEFORE YOU BEGIN

*You'll need: grater,
  small mixing bowl,
  large mixing bowl
Preparation time:
  20 minutes
Yield: 12 servings*

¼ cup white vinegar
2 cups mayonnaise
¼ cup onion, chopped fine
¼ cup green pepper, chopped fine

¼ cup red pepper, chopped fine
salt to taste
5 cups white cabbage, shredded

In small mixing bowl, combine vinegar and mayonnaise thoroughly (NOTE: portions here give a tangy flavor, so adjust vinegar to taste.) Add onions, green and red peppers, and salt. Mix thoroughly and set aside. In large bowl, shred cabbage. Add dressing to cabbage and mix thoroughly. Chill before serving.

CREAM OF FRESH SPINACH FLORENTINE

BEFORE YOU BEGIN

*You'll need: 3-quart
  saucepan
Preparation time:
  45 minutes
Yield: 8 servings*

12 oz. fresh spinach
3 Tbsp. butter
1 small onion, diced
2 stalks celery, diced

3 Tbsp. flour
2 qts. chicken stock, heated
salt and pepper to taste
1 cup bread croutons

Wash spinach thoroughly, drain, and set aside. In the saucepan over medium heat, melt butter. Add onion and celery, cover tightly, and cook slowly until vegetables are somewhat soft, about 5 minutes. Add flour, stirring constantly to blend well, and cook for another 3 minutes. Gradually add hot chicken stock, stirring constantly to blend well, with the flour. Bring all to a rolling boil and add spinach. Reduce heat and slow boil for 30 minutes. Season to taste and serve hot, sprinkled with bread croutons.

ESCALLOPS OF VEAL PIQUANTE

BEFORE YOU BEGIN

You'll need: meat cleaver, two large skillets
Preparation time: 45 minutes
Yield: 4 servings

1 lb. veal cutlets	2 Tbsp. flour
flour to coat	½ cup malt vinegar
3 Tbsp. butter	½ cup beef stock
2 Tbsp. onions, chopped fine	¼ tsp. salt
2 Tbsp. green peppers, chopped fine	⅛ tsp. pepper
2 Tbsp. dill pickles, chopped fine	pinch, dry mustard
2 Tbsp. capers, chopped fine	

In a large skillet over medium heat, melt 2 tablespoons butter and sauté onions, green peppers, dill pickles and capers until tender, about 4 minutes. Add flour to thicken, stirring constantly. Now add malt vinegar, stock, salt, pepper, and dry mustard. Stir to mix and heat through. Meanwhile, flatten veal cutlets to ⅛-inch thickness using cleaver. In a second large skillet over medium heat, melt 1 tablespoon of the butter. Roll veal in flour and fry to a light brown, about 2 minutes, turning once. Add veal to sauce and simmer for 15 minutes. Serve on a hot dish and garnish with chopped parsley.

―•― ✠ ―•―

FRIED OYSTERS WITH REMOULADE SAUCE

BEFORE YOU BEGIN

You'll need: deep fryer, small bowl
Preheat frying oil to hot
Preparation time: 30 minutes
Yield: 1 serving

6 oysters	1 egg, well beaten
flour to coat	¼ cup bread crumbs

Drain and bread oysters by dipping in flour, then in beaten egg, then in bread crumbs. Drop in preheated fryer until crisp and lightly browned. Remove and drain. To serve, place on a platter with Remoulade sauce along side, include a generous scoop of the Missouri Pacific's own cole slaw.

REMOULADE SAUCE

1 hard-boiled egg, chopped very fine	1 cup mayonnaise
2 Tbsp. parsley, chopped very fine	1 tsp. anchovy paste
1 Tbsp. capers, chopped very fine	

Mix all ingredients together well.

POACHED SLICE OF SALMON NORMANDIE

BEFORE YOU BEGIN

1½ lbs. salmon steaks
½ cup fish stock

½ cup dry white wine

*You'll need: baking
dish, buttered
waxed paper,
1-quart saucepan,
medium mixing
bowl*
*Preheat oven to 400
degrees*
*Preparation time:
1 hour*
Yield: 4 servings

Select salmon steaks cut into individual portions of about 6 ounces each. Butter baking dish well. Add salmon steaks and fish stock and pour white wine over. Cover with well-buttered waxed paper and place in oven until done, about 8–10 minutes. Serve on a platter covered with sauce Normandie. Retain ½ cup of liquid from baking dish.

SAUCE NORMANDIE

½ cup sliced mushrooms
½ Tbsp. butter
6 Tbsp. butter
6 poached oysters, cut in half
6 boiled shrimp, cut in half
3 Tbsp. flour
1 cup fish stock, hot
1 egg yolk, lightly beaten

2 Tbsp. heavy cream
1 tsp. Worcestershire sauce
juice of ½ lemon
¼ tsp. salt
⅛ tsp. white pepper
pinch, cayenne pepper
½ cup poaching liquid

Before starting, sauté mushrooms in ½ tablespoon butter, poach oysters, and boil shrimp. In a 1-quart saucepan over medium heat, make a light roux of the butter and flour. Add hot fish stock and simmer to reduce by one-third. Meanwhile, in a medium mixing bowl, stir together the beaten egg yolk, cream, Worcestershire sauce, lemon juice, salt, pepper, cayenne pepper, and poaching liquid. Pour hot cream sauce over ingredients in mixing bowl, stirring constantly. Return mixture to saucepan, add the poached oysters, boiled shrimp, and mushrooms, and heat through.

STUFFED CELERY RAINBOW

BEFORE YOU BEGIN

*You'll need: food
grinder, large mix-
ing bowl
Preparation time:
30 minutes (plus 1
hour to chill)
Yield: 12–24 servings*

12	stalks celery	1	oz. Roquefort cheese
6	ripe olives, pitted and diced fine	½	pint cottage cheese
¼	cup green peppers, chopped fine	1	Tbsp. olive oil
¼	cup pimentos, chopped fine	½	Tbsp. malt vinegar
6	green onions, chopped fine	¼	tsp. paprika
4	oz. yellow American cheese		pinch, salt

Separate celery stalks, remove leaves and white ends, wash clean, dry, and set aside. Pass ripe olives, green peppers, pimentos, and green onion through food grinder three times to make smooth. Pass American and Roquefort cheese through grinder, then add cottage cheese. Mix all ingredients together in a large bowl and add olive oil, malt vinegar, paprika, and salt. Whip all ingredients into a stiff, smooth, and creamy mixture. Place mixture in pastry bag and use to fill dry celery stalks. Chill to set, cut to desired lengths, and place over bed of lettuce to serve.

SUNFLOWER SALAD
WITH SUNSHINE DRESSING

BEFORE YOU BEGIN

*You'll need: medium
bowl, whisk
Preparation time:
15 minutes (allow 1
hour for dressing to
chill)
Yield: 1 serving*

¼	head lettuce	1	orange
½	English walnut meat, whole		Sunshine dressing

Shred or tear lettuce and place on salad dish. Place English walnut meat in center of lettuce bed. Peel and clean orange of membrane, then separate into sections. Arrange orange sections around walnut to resemble a sunflower. Serve Sunshine dressing on the side.

SUNSHINE DRESSING

1	cup mayonnaise	1	medium green pepper,
½	cup chili sauce		chopped fine
1	hard-boiled egg, chopped fine	1	pimento, chopped fine
1	tsp. chopped parsley	1	Tbsp. heavy cream
1	tsp. chopped chives		

In a bowl, combine first seven ingredients. Add cream, mix well together, and serve cold.

16

THE NEW YORK CENTRAL SYSTEM

BROCHETTE OF SHRIMP

BEFORE YOU BEGIN

You'll need: 2-quart saucepan, wire rack, shallow baking pan, 4 skewers, deep fryer, small mixing bowl, small skillet- Preheat oven to 400 degrees

Preheat deep fryer to hot

Preparation time: 45 minutes

Yield: 1 serving

12	shrimp (½ lb.)	2	eggs, beaten
4	strips bacon	1	cup fine fresh bread crumbs
¼	cup flour	1	slice white bread, toasted
⅛	tsp. salt	2	Tbsp. Maitre d'Hotel butter, melted
	pinch, pepper		

Cook, shell, and devein shrimp (see page 156). Lay bacon strips on a wire rack over a shallow baking pan and place in oven until cooked but not crisp, about 10 minutes. Meanwhile, in a bowl for dipping, mix flour, salt, and pepper. In a separate bowl, beat eggs well, until of a smooth lemon color. When shrimp have cooled, dip each in seasoned flour, then in beaten egg, then in bread crumbs. Skewer by wrapping shrimp in and around the bacon, allowing 1 strip of bacon and 3 shrimp for each skewer. Drop skewers into hot fat and fry until golden brown. Trim toast to diamond shape. Place skewers across toast and pour melted Maitre d'Hotel butter over each. Garnish with parsley and a lemon wedge.

MAITRE D'HOTEL BUTTER

½	lb. butter, room temperature		juice of 1 lemon
3	tsp. chopped parsley	½	tsp. Worcestershire sauce

Cream butter by beating. Add remaining ingredients as you continue beating. Mix well and chill. Use as directed.

BISQUE OF CRAB CARDINAL

This hearty bisque has a cardinal color and a predominant crab flavor.

1 lb. crabmeat	1 tsp. paprika
6 Tbsp. shortening	1 cup tomato juice, heated
½ medium onion, minced	5 cups fish stock or clam base, heated
1 stalk celery, minced	1 cup strained clam bouillon, heated
6 Tbsp. flour	salt to taste
⅛ tsp. white pepper	

Clean and pick over crabs to remove any tissue and bits of bone or shell. In the saucepan over medium heat, melt shortening and sauté onion and celery slowly until tender, but do not brown. Stirring constantly, add the flour and cook 3–5 minutes. Stir in pepper and paprika. Slowly add hot tomato juice, stirring until mixture thickens. Add hot stock, clam bouillon, and crabmeat and simmer 30 minutes. Strain and remove half the crabmeat for garniture. Return broth and remaining crabmeat to the pot and continue simmering 15 more minutes. Add retained crabmeat garniture, season with salt and additional pepper to taste. Add minced sauteed fresh mushrooms if so desired.

CALF'S LIVER EN CASSEROLE VENETIAN

You'll need: small
saucepan, small
skillet, 2 large skil-
lets
Preparation time:
1 hour
Yield: 6 servings

24 small pearl onions	¼ tsp. pepper
2 Tbsp. butter	flour to dust
1½ lbs. calf's liver, ¼-inch slices	2 Tbsp. bacon drippings
½ tsp. celery salt	1 qt. Venetian sauce

Place small onions in boiling water until tender, about 5 minutes. Drain, sauté in butter until brown, and keep warm for use later. Meanwhile, wash calf's liver in cold water, dry it thoroughly, and remove skin, veins, and clots. Cut liver into 2½-inch squares. Season with celery salt and pepper, dust lightly with flour, and sauté quickly in bacon drippings over medium heat. Brown on both sides but remove while rare. Place in Venetian sauce which is at the boiling point, and cook for 2 minutes. To serve, place in well-heated individual casserole and cover with a generous amount of sauce. Add 4 sautéed onions to each serving.

VENETIAN SAUCE

2 Tbsp. butter	6 large green olives, pitted
½ cup finely minced onion	1 qt. demi-glace
⅔ cup mushrooms, sliced	pinch, curry powder

In a large skillet over medium heat, melt butter and sauté minced onions and mushrooms until tender. Cut green olives into quarters. Meanwhile, in the 2-

quart saucepan season demi-glace (see page 154) with a pinch of curry powder and heat through. Add onions, mushrooms, and olives to demi-glace. Simmer gently until flavors are well blended, about 30 minutes.

EGGS BRETAGNE

8 shrimps, cooked
1 cup rich cream sauce, heated
2 eggs

1 slice toast, ½ inch thick
  green pepper, sliced thin

BEFORE YOU BEGIN

You'll need: egg-poaching pan, 1-quart saucepan, whisk
Preparation time: 30 minutes
Yield: 1 serving

Add shrimps to hot cream sauce and simmer until heated through. Meanwhile, poach eggs (see page 302). Pour warmed shrimp/cream sauce over toast placed in an individual serving dish. Place poached eggs on top. Top with slivers of green pepper.

RICH CREAM SAUCE

2 Tbsp. butter
2 Tbsp. flour
1 cup heavy cream, warmed

¼ tsp. salt
⅛ tsp. white pepper

In the saucepan over medium heat, make a roux of the butter and flour. Cook for 2–3 minutes. Gradually add hot cream, stirring constantly with a whisk to prevent lumps. Continue cooking until sauce thickens, about 3–5 minutes longer. Add seasonings. Sprinkle a dot of butter over top to prevent a crust from forming if sauce will not be used immediately.

PECAN AND ORANGE STICKS

2 cups flour
4 tsp. baking powder
¾ tsp. salt
2 cups milk
½ cup orange juice
1 tsp. grated orange rind

½ cup shortening
1 cup powdered sugar
3 egg yolks, well beaten
1 cup chopped pecans
3 egg whites, beaten stiff

BEFORE YOU BEGIN

You'll need: 3 small mixing bowls, large mixing bowl, sifter, large cookie pan
Preheat oven to 350 degrees
Preparation time: 1 hour
Yield: 24 sticks

Grease cookie pan lightly and set aside. Sift together the flour, baking powder, and salt. In another bowl combine milk, orange juice, and grated rind and retain for use. Cream shortening to soft, smooth texture. Gradually add sugar and continue creaming until fluffy. Beat while adding beaten egg yolks. Alternately add dry ingredients and milk/orange mixture, beating after each addition until smooth. Add nuts. Fold in beaten egg whites. Spread onto a greased cookie pan and bake for 30–40 minutes, until lightly browned. While still hot, cut in strips to serve.

LOBSTER NEWBURG NEW YORK CENTRAL

1 1-lb. lobster, boiled	½ cup sherry wine
½ cup butter	4 egg yolks
⅛ tsp. paprika	4 triangles toasted corn bread
1 cup heavy cream, warmed	

Split lobster, remove and dice meat, and set aside. Melt butter in the saucepan over medium heat. Add diced lobster meat. Sprinkle with paprika. When heated through, add hot cream and sherry wine and increase heat to medium-high. Stir until liquid just boils and remove from heat. Meanwhile, in a large mixing bowl, beat egg yolks until smooth and of a lemon color. Now, quickly and briskly stir hot cream sauce into the egg yolks with a whisk. Return to saucepan over low heat and continue stirring until mixture has the consistency of a cream sauce and is heated through. Do not boil once egg yolks have been added. Pour one serving into an individual casserole. Toast corn bread by placing a lightly buttered side 5 inches under a broiling element just long enough to brown lightly. Serve the bread triangles next to dish of Lobster Newburg.

PEPPER POT LOUISIANNE

4 Tbsp. butter	½ tsp. chili powder
1 cup celery, diced	½ tsp. red pepper
½ cup Spanish onion, diced	3 qts. chicken stock
½ cup leeks (in rings)	salt to taste
1 medium green pepper, diced	1 cup white meat of chicken,
1 clove garlic, cut fine	cut in julienne strips
½ cup yellow rice	

Melt butter in the saucepan over medium heat. Add diced vegetables and sauté slowly until tender, but not browned, about 5 minutes. Add garlic for the last minute. Meanwhile, wash rice thoroughly and drain. Add rice to sautéed vegetables, reduce heat to medium-low, cover, and slow-simmer for 15 minutes. Then add chili powder and red pepper, stirring to mix well. Add 1 quart of chicken stock and cook slowly until thoroughly done, about 15 more minutes. Add remaining chicken stock, season with salt, and bring to a boil. Allow to boil for 30 minutes. Just before serving, add julienne of chicken and heat through. Serve hot.

SCALLOPINES OF PORK TENDERLOIN
WITH RIESLING WINE SAUCE

BEFORE YOU BEGIN

You'll need: large skil-
let, small saucepan,
mallet or cleaver
Preparation time:
45 minutes
Yield: 6 servings

2 lbs. pork tenderloin	2 Tbsp. butter
6 slices of ham, each ⅛-inch thick	

Trim and remove tissues from pork tenderloin, cut in 1½-inch pieces, and flatten pieces to ⅛-inch thick slices with mallet or cleaver. Cut ham to same size pieces as tenderloin. In a large skillet over medium heat, melt butter and sauté both meats until cooked through but not browned, about 2–3 minutes, turning once. Arrange ham and pork slices alternately on a platter and pour Riesling wine sauce over all.

RIESLING WINE SAUCE

1 Tbsp. butter	1 cup veal stock, warmed
2 Tbsp. onion, finely chopped	¼ cup Riesling wine
2 Tbsp. cooked mushrooms, minced	

In small saucepan over medium heat, melt butter and sauté onions. Add mushrooms. Slowly add stock (chicken stock can substitute) and wine, stirring constantly. Reduce heat and simmer slowly for 30 minutes.

STUFFED PORK LOIN EN CASSEROLE

BEFORE YOU BEGIN

You'll need: skewers,
large roasting pan,
small skillet
Preheat oven to 400
degrees
Preparation time:
3 hours
Yield: 6 servings

This dinner is authentically accompanied by Potatoes Romanoff (see page 228), a grilled Spanish onion, and any fresh vegetable of the season.

3 lbs. boneless pork loin	1 lb. carrots, thick sliced
6 cups dressing	1 lb. celery, cut into 1-inch slices
1 tsp. grated orange rind	3 cups rich brown sauce
½ lb. onion, peeled, and quartered	4 Tbsp. butter, melted

Prepare the dressing of your choice (or see pages 221, 272, 303, and 321), adding grated orange rind, and set aside. Trim pork loin of surplus fat and tissue and split lengthwise through the center to make a pocket, taking care not to cut all the way through. Fill the pocket with dressing and skewer split tightly. Score the top of loin lightly with a knife and place in a roasting pan atop and among the vegetables. Butter the pork with the melted butter and place in oven until tender, about 1½ hours, basting and turning often. To serve, cut in 2-inch lengths and top with a rich brown sauce poured over (see page 156).

*You'll need: 2-quart
saucepan, strainer,
large pot
Preparation time:
3½ hours
Yield: 8 servings*

TERRINE OF RAGOUT À LA DEUTSCH

*This menu item is served in an individual casserole with steamed or boiled Parisienne
vegetables of the season and a little chopped parsley over all.*

3 lbs. sirloin beef	4 cups strong vegetable-seasoned
4 veal kidneys	beef stock
¼ cup shortening	2 green peppers, cut into 1-inch dice
salt and pepper to taste	3 medium onions, cut into 1-inch dice
2 Tbsp. flour	1 cup minced mushrooms

Cut beef in oblong blocks, 2½ inches long, 1 inch thick, and 1 inch wide. Skin
the kidneys, cut in sections, remove tissues and rinse in cold water. In a large pot
over medium-high heat, melt shortening and quickly sauté beef and kidneys all
around, seasoning with salt and pepper. When meats are browned, stir constantly
and add sufficient flour to absorb drippings. Slowly add hot stock, stirring constantly to avoid lumps. Bring to a boil, reduce heat, cover, and simmer until meat
is three-quarters cooked, about 1½ hours, adding more stock if needed. Add green
peppers and onions and cook until tender, about 10 minutes. Add mushrooms,
stirring them in thoroughly. Continue cooking, seasoning to taste, until meat is
tender, about 20 more minutes.

VEGETABLE-SEASONED BEEF STOCK

6 cups beef stock	1 stalk celery, sliced
1 carrot, sliced	1 small onion, sliced

In a 2-quart saucepan, bring beef stock, carrot, celery, and onion to a boil. Reduce heat and simmer until reduced to two-thirds of original quantity, about 1
hour. Strain before using as directed.

*You'll need: medium
mixing bowl, large
mixing bowl, pan-
cake griddle
Preparation time:
30 minutes
Yield: 16 6-inch pan-
cakes*

WHEAT CAKES

*Like so many details of the New York Central System's dining-car service, this recipe
differs from the run-of-the-mill in several ways.*

2 egg yolks	2 cups flour
2 cups milk	2 tsp. baking powder
3 Tbsp. maple syrup	5 Tbsp. shortening, melted
½ tsp. salt	

Whip egg yolks well, until frothy but not stiff. Continue whipping as you slowly add milk, then maple syrup. Sift salt, flour, and baking powder together and
add to mixture. Stir in shortening. When entire mixture is smooth, let stand a
few minutes before cooking. Do not turn cakes on griddle more than once, and
be sure griddle is not too hot.

17

THE NEW YORK, NEW HAVEN AND HARTFORD RAILROAD

APPLE, PEANUT BUTTER, AND CHEESE SALAD

BEFORE YOU BEGIN

You'll need: two small mixing bowls, covered container
Preparation time: 30 minutes
Yield: 4 servings

2 Red Delicious apples
   French dressing
2 3-oz. pkgs. cream cheese, softened
½ cup smooth peanut butter
¼ Tbsp. salt

Clean, polish, core, and slice large red apples in ½-inch thick crosswise slices. Sprinkle and rub slices lightly with French dressing to prevent discoloration. Blend cream cheese, peanut butter, and salt well and form into small balls. Place balls in center of apple slices. Serve with Bretton Woods dressing.

BRETTON WOODS DRESSING

1¼ tsp. salt
½ tsp. pepper
½ tsp. paprika
½ cup apple juice
¼ cup lemon juice
½ cup olive oil
2½ Tbsp. sugar

Mix all ingredients together well and chill. Beat hard with egg beater or whisk just before serving. You can substitute other fruit juices for the apple juice, in which case omit sugar if sweet canned fruit juices are used.

CARROTS IN MINT SAUCE

BEFORE YOU BEGIN

*You'll need: 2-quart
saucepan, small
mixing bowl
Preparation time:
30 minutes
Yield: 6 servings*

3 **cups carrots, diced**	1 **cup cold water**
6 **Tbsp. butter**	3 **Tbsp. mint leaves, shredded**
1 **Tbsp. cornstarch**	1 **tsp. lemon juice**
3 **Tbsp. granular sugar**	

Cook carrots in boiling water to cover until just tender, about 6 minutes, then drain and set aside. Melt butter in clean saucepan over medium heat. Meanwhile, in small bowl, blend cornstarch and sugar with cold water until dissolved. Add mint leaves and lemon juice and mix thoroughly. Stir this mixture into the melted butter. Add cooked carrots and stir. Continue cooking over medium heat until sauce is clear.

CHICKEN CADILLAC

BEFORE YOU BEGIN

*You'll need: scalloped
tartlet tins, 2-quart
saucepan, two small
saucepans
Preheat oven to 425
degrees
Preparation time:
1 hour
Yield: 8 servings*

1 **meal pie pastry recipe**	¾ **cup cooked ham,**
6 **Tbsp. butter**	**cut in small cubes**
6 **Tbsp. flour**	¾ **cup celery, diced**
1½ **cups chicken stock, hot**	½ **tsp. paprika**
1½ **cups milk, heated**	
3 **cups cooked chicken,**	
cut in small cubes	

STEP 1

Make pastry cases by rolling out meal pastry (see page 155) thin on a floured surface. Stamp out in 5-inch circles and shape over inverted scalloped tartlet tins. Take care not to let pastry catch under edge and bake on. Prick dough surface several times and bake 10–15 minutes, until lightly browned.

STEP 2

In the 2-quart saucepan over medium heat, make a roux of the butter and flour. Slowly add hot chicken stock and milk. Bring to a boil, stirring constantly, and boil for 2 minutes. Reduce heat and add chicken, ham, celery, and paprika. Stir to mix well and cook until heated through, about 5 minutes. Ladle mixture into the cooked pastry cases to serve.

CODFISH BALLS

2 cups fresh codfish
4 cups white potatoes, diced
2 Tbsp. butter

2 eggs, well beaten
¼ tsp. white pepper
salt to taste

BEFORE YOU BEGIN

*You'll need: 2-quart
saucepan, small
bowl, deep fryer
Preheat deep fryer to
hot
Preparation time:
45 minutes
Yield: 6 servings*

Wash the codfish thoroughly and break or cut into very small pieces. Place codfish pieces and potatoes in the saucepan and add water to cover. Bring to a boil and cook until potatoes are nearly done, about 20 minutes. Drain well, return to saucepan, and shake over heat until thoroughly dry. Add butter, well-beaten eggs, pepper, and salt. Beat thoroughly until mixture is very light. Drop by heaping tablespoonsful into deep fryer of hot fat and fry until golden brown. Serve hot, garnished with a sprig of parsley.

CREAMED SHRIMPS AND OYSTERS EN CASSEROLE

1 lb. shrimp
12 large oysters
2 Tbsp. butter
¼ lb. fresh mushrooms, peeled
½ green pepper, diced

1 cup cooked crabmeat
2 cups medium white sauce
½ cup chopped pimento
4 slices white bread, ⅜ inch thick
chopped parsley

BEFORE YOU BEGIN

*You'll need: 3-quart
saucepan, large skillet
Preparation time:
1 hour
Yield: 8 servings*

Clean and pick over crabmeat to remove any bits of shell. Wash shrimp in cold water, drop into 3-quart saucepan filled with boiling water to cover, and cook 6 minutes. Plunge into cold water to arrest cooking, shell and devein, and set aside. Meanwhile, shuck 12 large oysters and retain liquor. In large skillet over medium heat, heat oysters in their liquor for 8 minutes or until edges curl. Drain and set aside. In clean 3-quart saucepan over medium heat, melt butter and sauté mushrooms and diced pepper for 3 minutes. Add crabmeat, shrimp, and oysters. Add white sauce (see page 156, but cook roux only 5 minutes) to seafood. Add chopped pimento. Stir well and heat through. Meanwhile, toast bread, remove crusts, and cut diagonally. Dip toast tips in chopped parsley, place one toast triangle on individual plate, and ladle on seafood mixture to serve.

---◆━◈━◆---

CREAMED CRABMEAT *YANKEE CLIPPER*

BEFORE YOU BEGIN

*You'll need: large skil-
let
Preparation time:
30 minutes
Yield: 8 servings*

1 lb. fresh crabmeat
4 Tbsp. butter
½ lb. fresh mushrooms,
 cleaned and sliced
2 pimentos, diced

3 cups cream sauce
8 slices white bread,
 ⅜-inch thick
¼ cup chopped parsley

Clean and pick over crabs to remove any bits of shell. In a large skillet over medium heat, melt butter and sauté mushrooms until soft. Add crabmeat, pimentos, and cream sauce made with fish stock (see page 153). Continue cooking until heated through. Meanwhile, toast bread, remove crusts, and cut diagonally to form triangles. Dip toast tips in parsley. Place toast points in individual casseroles or serving dishes and cover with crabmeat mixture.

---◆━◈━◆---

LOBSTER THERMIDOR,
MERCHANTS LIMITED STYLE

BEFORE YOU BEGIN

*You'll need: 3-quart
saucepan, 1-quart
saucepan, small
skillet
Preheat oven to 350
degrees
Preparation time:
1 hour (starting
with cooked lobsters)
Yield: 4 servings*

More than one authority, from veterans of the New Haven's Dining Car Department to food critics for national magazines, claimed no one made lobster thermidor to compare with this specialty.

4 cold boiled New England lobsters
2 cups half-and-half
4 Tbsp. butter
2 tsp. chopped onion
2 tsp. chopped parsley
4 Tbsp. flour
2 tsp. English mustard

dash salt
pinch, cayenne
2 Tbsp. butter
½ lb. mushrooms, sliced
2 Tbsp. sherry
½ cup grated Parmesan cheese

Remove heads, claws, and legs from the bodies of the boiled lobsters and remove feelers from the tails without splitting the shells. Remove all meat and cut in dice, retaining shells for later use. In the 1-quart saucepan, heat half-and-half. In the 3-quart saucepan over medium heat, melt the 4 tablespoons of butter and sauté onion and parsley for 3 minutes. Blend in flour to make a roux. Gradually add hot half-and-half, stirring constantly, and increase heat to medium-high until mixture comes to the boil. Let boil 2 minutes. Stir in English mustard, salt, and cayenne. Add diced lobster meat, reduce heat, and simmer until heated through. Meanwhile, in a small skillet over medium heat, melt the 2 tablespoons of butter and sauté mushrooms for 3 minutes. Add sauteed mushrooms with butter to lobster mixture. Stir in sherry and simmer until heated through. To serve, fill empty lobster shells with mixture and sprinkle each with 1 tablespoon grated cheese. Place in oven long enough to brown cheese topping. Garnish with parsley before serving.

RHUBARB AND STRAWBERRY PIE

2 eggs, beaten
4 cups strawberries, halved
2 cups rhubarb, cut in ¾-inch pieces
2 cups sugar
¼ cup flour

pinch, salt
unbaked pie pastry for
    2-crust, 9-inch pie
8 thin slices American cheese

BEFORE YOU BEGIN

You'll need: 9-inch pie tin, large mixing bowl, small mixing bowl
Preheat oven to 425 degrees
Preparation time: 1 hour
Yield: 1 pie

Retain 1 teaspoon egg white before beating rest of eggs. Place the clean and cut strawberries and cut rhubarb in large mixing bowl. Add sugar, flour, beaten eggs, and salt and stir well to mix, taking care not to crush strawberries. Pour mixture into a pastry-lined 9-inch pie tin. Arrange lattice top made of ½-inch strips of pie pastry. Brush with egg wash made of 1 teaspoon each of retained egg white and water. Place in oven on bottom shelf for 10 minutes. Then, move to middle shelf, reduce heat to 350, and bake another 30 minutes or until fruit is tender and crust lightly browned. Cool 15 minutes to serve. Top each serving with a thin slice of American cheese.

SAVORY MUSHROOM DRESSING

Allow three quarters to one cup of stuffing for each pound of bird you intend to stuff.

3 Tbsp. butter
1½ cups mushrooms, chopped fine
3 cups stale bread crumbs
1½ tsp. salt
¼ tsp. pepper
    pinch, ground cayenne

pinch, ground nutmeg
1 Tbsp. chopped parsley
1 Tbsp. chopped onion
1 Tbsp. melted butter
¼ cup chicken stock

BEFORE YOU BEGIN

You'll need: pot sufficient for stuffing to be made, large bowl
Preparation time: 30 minutes
Yield: 4–5 cups

In a large skillet, melt butter over medium heat. Add mushrooms and sauté until tender. Add remaining ingredients. Mix well with a fork. Pack bird lightly with stuffing before closing. Bake extra stuffing in covered greased baking dish alongside bird during last 30–45 minutes of roasting.

SCALLOPS À LA NEWBURG

1 **lb. scallops**	1 **Tbsp. flour**
¼ **cup butter**	4 **egg yolks, slightly beaten**
1 **Tbsp. lemon juice**	1 **cup heavy cream**
2 **Tbsp. butter**	¼ **cup sherry wine**

Wipe scallops with a damp cloth and cook in the large skillet over medium heat, stirring occasionally, until they begin to shrivel. Remove from heat, drain thoroughly on clean paper towels, cut into halves, and set aside. In a clean large skillet over medium heat, melt the ¼ cup butter and cook halved scallops in it for 3 minutes. Stir in lemon juice and cook 1 minute longer. Meanwhile, in the 1-quart saucepan over medium heat, make a roux of the 2 tablespoons of butter and 1 tablespoon of flour. In a small bowl, beat egg yolks until of lemon a color. Slowly add warm cream, stirring constantly. Add egg yolk/cream mixture to roux, stirring constantly. Do not boil after adding egg yolks or sauce will "crack." Add scallops with butter they were sauteed in, add the sherry, and stir until smooth and heated through. Garnish with lobster coral or chopped parsley.

WASHINGTON FRUIT SALAD
MERCHANTS' LIMITED

BEFORE YOU BEGIN

*You'll need: two small
mixing bowls
Preparation time:
15 minutes (plus at
least 1 hour to chill
dressing)
Yield: 2 servings*

2 leaves romaine or other lettuce
1 orange, sectioned
1 grapefruit, sectioned
24 grapes, halved and seeded
2 Tbsp. walnuts, chopped

For each serving, place romaine or lettuce of your choice in salad bowl and arrange orange and grapefruit sections and grapes on top. Sprinkle each with 1 tablespoon of chopped walnuts. Serve with Washington salad dressing to suit.

WASHINGTON SALAD DRESSING

1 cup mayonnaise
2 tsp. chili sauce
2 Tbsp. whipped cream
juice of 1 lemon
1 Tbsp. fines herbes

Mix all ingredients well and allow to chill at least 1 hour before serving.

FINES HERBS

1 Tbsp. parsley, finely chopped
1 tsp. mint, finely chopped
½ tsp. marjoram, finely chopped
1 tsp. grated onion
1 leaf sage, crushed
½ tsp. ground cinnamon
¼ tsp. ground nutmeg

Mix well together before adding to the Washington dressing ingredients. You can use the remaining portion of fines herbs to make a sauce for fish or vegetables by first creaming ¾ cup of butter, then adding the herb mixture.

18

THE NORTHERN PACIFIC RAILWAY

CONFETTI SALAD
WITH "OUR OWN" FRENCH DRESSING

BEFORE YOU BEGIN

*You'll need: large
bowl, whisk, small
bowl, 1½-quart
sealed container
Preparation time:
30 minutes (plus 1
hour to chill before
serving)
Yield: 4 servings*

The salad dressing that accompanies this salad was in such demand that the Northern Pacific bottled it and sold it to dining-car patrons.

4 radishes	4 leaves iceberg lettuce
1 stalk celery	2 cups cottage cheese
1 small green pepper	French dressing
4 pineapple rings	

Julienne the radishes. Cut the celery and green pepper into 1-inch lengths and julienne. To assemble the salad, place a pineapple ring on a bowl-shaped crisp lettuce leaf. Place a ½-cup mound of cottage cheese in the center of the ring. Sprinkle celery, radish, and green pepper strips over the cottage cheese. Serve with French dressing on the side.

"OUR OWN" FRENCH DRESSING

2 medium eggs	4 cups salad oil
6 Tbsp. sugar	2½ Tbsp. salt
¼ cup catsup	1 cup tarragon vinegar
1 Tbsp. dry mustard	¼ cup lemon juice
2½ Tbsp. paprika	

In a large bowl, whip eggs with a whisk for several minutes until well beaten. In a small bowl, mix sugar, catsup, dry mustard, and paprika with a little of the salad oil. Add to the beaten eggs slowly, beating well constantly. Continue beating while slowly adding remaining salad oil. In order, slowly add salt, vinegar, and lemon juice, beating constantly. Refrigerate in tightly sealed container 1 hour before serving. Yield: 1½ quarts.

BAKED RABBIT PIE

One "approved" variation on this recipe called on the chef to cook small amounts of carrots and potatoes separately, then add them during the last five minutes of cooking. See page 154 to make pie pastry before beginning.

BEFORE YOU BEGIN

You'll need: large, heavy-bottomed saucepan
Preparation time: 1¼ hours
Yield: 1 9-inch pie

1 **large rabbit, cut in pieces**	¼ **cup dry white wine**
water to cover	⅛ **tsp. pepper**
3 **Tbsp. butter**	⅛ **tsp. salt**
¼ **cup chopped onions**	**dash ground nutmeg**
2 **parsley sprigs, chopped**	1 **Tbsp. lemon juice**
½ **cup chopped mushrooms**	1 **9-inch pie shell, baked**
4 **Tbsp. flour**	1 **7-inch pastry cover, baked**

In the saucepan, bring enough water to cover rabbit to a boil. Add rabbit pieces, return to a boil, lower heat, and simmer for 30 minutes. Drain rabbit, reserving 1 cup broth. Remove rabbit meat from bones and cut in small pieces. In same saucepan over medium heat, melt butter, add rabbit meat, and sauté for 5 minutes. Add onion, parsley, and mushrooms and saute 5 minutes longer. Stir in flour. Add wine, 1 cup reserved broth, pepper, salt, and nutmeg. Cook 30 minutes or until rabbit is tender. Stir in lemon juice and heat through. Pour into prepared pie shell and top with pastry cover. Makes one 9-inch pie.

HAWAIIAN POT ROAST

BEFORE YOU BEGIN

You'll need: large pot with cover, slotted spoon, warming platter
Preparation time: 3 hours
Yield: 8 servings

4 **lb. arm or blade cut of beef**	1 **medium onion, sliced**
2 **Tbsp. lard or drippings**	¾ **cup mushroom pieces**
¼ **cup soy sauce**	½ **cup sliced celery**
¾ **cup hot water**	1 **8-oz. can pineapple chunks**
¼ **tsp. pepper**	2 **Tbsp. flour**
¼ **tsp. ground ginger**	¼ **cup cold water**

In large pot, brown pot roast in lard or drippings. Pour off fat. Add soy sauce, hot water, pepper, ginger, and onion. Cover tightly and simmer over low heat approximately 2 hours. Add mushrooms, celery, and pineapple. Continue cooking for 20 more minutes. Celery should remain slightly crisp. Remove meat, vegetables, and pineapple to a platter and keep warm. Blend flour and cold water, then add to cooking liquid, stirring constantly. Cook until thickened, then stir vegetables and pineapple into thickened sauce. Serve beef sliced, with a portion of sauce poured over.

BOILED HALIBUT WITH SHRIMP SAUCE

BEFORE YOU BEGIN

You'll need: large
saucepan, medium
saucepan, 12-inch
square cheesecloth
and string
Preparation time:
30 minutes
Yield: 4 servings

2 lbs. halibut steaks	1 bay leaf
1 slice lemon	pinch, thyme
salt and pepper to taste	2 whole cloves
3 sprigs parsley	1 hard-boiled egg

Make bouquet garni (see page 153) of parsley, bay leaf, thyme, and clove and set aside. Place halibut steaks in large saucepan with water to cover. Add lemon, salt, pepper, and bouquet garni. Over medium heat, bring to simmer and cook gently for 8–10 minutes, until done. Place halibut steaks on dinner plate and pour shrimp sauce over each. Garnish with chopped white and yolk of the hard-boiled egg.

SHRIMP SAUCE

4 Tbsp. butter	1 egg yolk, beaten
4 Tbsp. flour	½ cup cooked shrimp, diced
2 cups milk, warmed	cayenne pepper to taste

In a medium saucepan over medium heat, make a roux of the butter and flour. Continue stirring as you add milk and egg yolk. When cream sauce is formed, add shrimp and season with cayenne pepper. Heat through before serving.

◆┈ ╳◈╳ ┈◆

HERB-BUTTERED BEETS

BEFORE YOU BEGIN

You'll need: 1-qt.
saucepan, small
saucepan, colander
Preparation time:
20 minutes
Yield: 6 servings

2 cups whole baby beets	1 tsp. finely chopped onion
1 Tbsp. butter	¼ tsp. ground thyme
1 tsp. parsley flakes	¼ tsp. dried tarragon, crushed

In a 1-qt. saucepan, place beets in water to cover and bring quickly to a boil. Reduce heat and simmer until tender, about 9 minutes. Meanwhile, in small saucepan, melt butter over medium heat. Add parsley, onion, thyme, and tarragon, mix well, and heat through. Drain beets, return to saucepan, and pour herb butter over them. Mix lightly and serve warm.

HONEY MAYONNAISE DRESSINGS FOR FRUIT

BEFORE YOU BEGIN

Two varieties of this light dressing graced the Northern Pacific's dining-car menus. Serve either version poured over or mixed well with fresh fruit and accompanied by the Union Pacific's Orange Tea Biscuits (see page 288)

You'll need: small mixing bowl
Preparation time: 10 minutes (plus 1 hour to chill before using)
Yield: 2½ or 1¾ cups, respectively

2 cups mayonnaise		2 Tbsp. orange juice
⅓ cup honey		1 Tbsp. grated orange rind
	or	
1⅓ cups mayonnaise		dash, paprika
½ cup honey		

In a small bowl, stir mayonnaise until smooth. Continue stirring as you add honey and mix well. Add remaining ingredient(s) and stir through. Place in refrigerator at least 1 hour before serving.

NORTHERN PACIFIC DARK FRUIT CAKE

BEFORE YOU BEGIN

The popularity of this Northern Pacific specialty item was marked by its extensive sales. In one representative year, 1949, the railroad sold 4,004 3-pound fruit cakes and 637 5-pound cakes, or more than 7½ tons of them, to train patrons. Famous across the country, the cakes could be ordered from the dining-car steward.

You'll need: large airtight storage container, four 9½" x 5¼" bread pans, heavy brown paper, large mixing bowl
Preheat oven to 300 degrees
Preparation time: 2½ hours
Yield: 4 loaves

2 lbs. seedless raisins	1 tsp. ground nutmeg
2 lbs. currants	1 tsp. ground cardamom
1 lb. mixed glazed fruits, sliced	12 eggs
1 lb. glazed whole cherries	1 Tbsp. lemon extract
1 lb. candied pineapple, diced	1 Tbsp. vanilla extract
2¼ cups granular sugar	1 Tbsp. sherry or port wine
2 cups butter	5 cups flour
½ tsp. salt	1 cup walnut halves or pieces
1 tsp. ground cinnamon	1 cup pecan halves
1 tsp. ground mace	1 cup whole almonds, blanched

Mix raisins, currants, mixed fruits, cherries, and pineapple the day before cooking and store in a cool place to blend flavors. Grease the four bread pans. Tightly line bottoms and sides of bread pans with strips of heavy brown paper. Grease the paper. Lightly cream sugar, butter, and salt. Add spices. Gradually stir eggs in to blend. Add extracts and wine and stir to mix. Then add flour, mixing lightly. Add fruits and nuts; combine well. Pour into prepared bread pans, filling them three-quarters full. Place in oven and bake approximately 1 hour and 45 minutes. Cool thoroughly before removing from pans. NOTE: Since oven temperatures vary, watch closely so as not to overbake.

PUGET SOUND CLAM CHOWDER

BEFORE YOU BEGIN

*You'll need: medium
skillet, 2-quart
saucepan or stew
pot, two small
saucepans, small
skillet
Preparation time:
45 minutes
Yield: 4 servings*

2	6½-oz. cans minced clams	6	Tbsp. flour
1	¼-inch cube salt pork, diced	1¼	cups boiling water
½	small onion, sliced thin	2	cups scalded milk
2	cups potatoes, peeled and	3	Tbsp. butter
	cut in ¾-inch dice	4	soda crackers
1½	tsp. salt		cold milk
⅛	tsp. pepper		

Drain clams, reserving liquor. In medium skillet over medium heat, fry salt pork until fat is rendered. Add onion and sauté until onion is tender, about 5 minutes. Strain off fat. Pour salt pork and onion into stew pot. Meanwhile, in small saucepan, parboil potatoes in water to cover for 5 minutes. Drain. Now, on top of salt pork and onion in stew pot, layer half of the potatoes and half of the salt and pepper and dredge with 2 tablespoons flour. Repeat with the other half of potatoes, salt, and pepper and 2 tablespoons flour. Add boiling water. Over medium heat, simmer for 10 minutes, watching to insure mixture doesn't burn. Stir in milk, clams, and 2 tablespoons butter. Cook 3 minutes, stirring occasionally. Meanwhile, soak crackers in just enough milk to moisten. Add crackers to chowder. In small saucepan, heat reserved clam liquor to boiling. In small skillet melt 1 tablespoon butter, then stir in 2 tablespoons flour. Slowly add hot clam liquor. Add thickened clam liquor to chowder just before serving. NOTE: Clam liquor is added last because it tends to cause the milk to separate.

RICE AND HAM GRIDDLE CAKES

BEFORE YOU BEGIN

*You'll need: medium
bowl, pancake grid-
dle
Preparation time:
30 minutes
Yield: 15 griddle cakes*

2	eggs, well beaten	1	cup flour
1	cup cooked rice	5	tsp. baking powder
2	cups milk	½	tsp. salt
3	Tbsp. butter, melted	1	cup cooked ham, diced

In medium bowl, beat eggs until frothy. Stir in cooked rice, milk, and melted butter and mix well. Sift together flour, baking powder, and salt and add to above mixture. Beat with a spoon until well blended. Stir in diced ham. Spoon batter onto a hot, greased griddle to form 4-inch cakes. Cook on one side until a number of bubbles appear. Turn once and cook to a golden brown. Serve hot with butter and syrup.

SWEET DOUGH

This small, rich roll makes a featured attraction in an assortment of hot rolls served for brunch (See pages 178, 221, and 305 for other roll recipes).

BEFORE YOU BEGIN

You'll need: small bowl, large bowl, wooden spoon, medium bowl, roller, two 9" x 13" baking pans
Preheat oven to 375 degrees
Preparation time: 3 hours
Yield: 30 3-inch rolls

3	pkgs. active dry yeast	1/16	tsp. ground mace
2	cups warm milk (heated to 100–110 degrees)	6	eggs
		½	tsp. vanilla extract
⅔	cup shortening	10½–11	cups flour, sifted
2¼	cups sugar, divided	4	Tbsp. butter, melted
1	Tbsp. salt	2	tsp. ground cinnamon

Combine yeast with milk and let stand. In large bowl, lightly cream shortening, 2 cups of sugar, salt, and mace. Add eggs, one at a time, creaming well after each addition. Slowly add yeast/milk mixture. Add vanilla. Beat in 3 cups flour. Add 3 more cups flour, one at a time, beating well with electric mixer after each addition. Using a wooden spoon, gradually work in remaining flour, mixing until dough is stiff enough to leave sides of bowl. Knead dough until smooth and elastic. Place in a greased bowl, turning to grease top. Cover with a damp cloth and let rise in a warm place until doubled, about 45 minutes. Punch down dough, divide it in half, and let it rest 10 minutes. Roll half of dough into a 12" x 16" rectangle. Brush with 2 tablespoons melted butter; sprinkle with 2 tablespoons sugar and 1 teaspoon cinnamon. Roll up from long side, jelly-roll fashion, and pinch seam to seal. Cut crosswise into 15 slices and place slices in the greased baking pan, cut side down. Prepare the other half of dough in the same manner. Cover both again and let rise until doubled, about 40 minutes. Place in oven for 20 minutes. While still warm, frost with icing made from confectioners' sugar.

CONFECTIONERS' FROSTING

16	oz. confectioners' sugar	1½	tsp. vanilla extract
6	Tbsp. butter, room temperature	⅛	tsp. salt
3-4	Tbsp. milk		

In a large bowl, beating continuously, mix ingredients in order until smooth. Add milk sufficient only to make frosting smooth enough to spread on the cooked rolls.

SPECIAL SAUCE FOR BAKED HAM

*You'll need: medium
saucepan, double
boiler (to reheat)
Preparation time:
20 minutes
Yield: 3 cups*

See pages 157, 219, and 268 for baked-ham recipes.

2 cups orange juice	juice of ½ fresh lemon
½ cup granular sugar	grated rind of 1 fresh orange
½ cup white raisins	2 Tbsp. cornstarch
2 oz. maraschino cherries, quartered	1 Tbsp. water
½ cup orange marmalade	

Dissolve cornstarch in water and set aside. Place the first seven ingredients in medium saucepan. Bring to a boil over medium heat, stirring occasionally. Remove from heat and stir in dissolved cornstarch. When ready to serve, reheat in double boiler. If too thick, thin with a little juice from pineapple or maraschino cherries.

THE SPECIALTY ITEM: THE GREAT BIG BAKED POTATO

The transcontinental railroads, often in competition with more than one other railroad for passengers to the major cities in their territory, employed among their promotional bag of tricks the specialty dish. There was the superb French toast on the Santa Fe, The Casserole and Salad Bowl on the Southern Pacific, the Creole dishes of the Illinois Central, chicken pie with a "secret" ingredient on the Great Northern, the prime-grade steaks on the Union Pacific, and any number of items "à la (insert sponsoring railroad name here)." Great care was taken to promote the item and its exclusive availability on the railroad in question. None of these specialties was more widely advertised, nor gained more fame, than the Northern Pacific's Great Big Baked Potato.

Early in the twentieth century, farmers in the Yakima Valley of the Columbia Basin in Washington astonished agriculturists around the country by producing gigantic potatoes that were more than a foot long and weighed from one to five pounds (potatoes found in grocery stores today are graded "medium" and weigh between five and ten ounces). Selling the beasts, labeled Washington No. 1 or Netted Gem Bakers, had proven a challenge because homemakers and chefs alike deemed them impossible to bake. When Hazen J. Titus of the

A promotional blotter originally showed The Big Baked Potato at its actual size of 9½ inches long.

(COURTESY OF GARY W. WIDELL)

Dining Car Department on the Northern Pacific Railway discovered them, they were being fed to pigs.

The Northern Pacific, whose mainline (not coincidentally) ran through the potato-producing valley, viewed the super spuds differently. Then in fierce competition with the Great Northern Railway and its special Chicken Pie for ridership, the railroad posted notices at all stations across its system

(COURTESY OF WILLIAM A. MCKENZIE AND THE MINNESOTA HISTORICAL SOCIETY)

offering top prices for the new potato. The potatoes were carefully inspected to insure no blemishes, bruises, knobs, or cuts were visible. A technique for baking the potato was perfected, the key being a standard weight of not more than two pounds, and on February 8, 1909, the item was introduced on the menu of the *North Coast Limited*, the railroad's premier train. Oversized replicas of the potato topped stations and commissary buildings along the right-of-way. Its popularity resulted

in the consumption of 265 tons of the so-called "Great Big Baked Potato" in Northern Pacific dining cars each year. The potato possessed a flavor argued to be superior to that of the Idaho russet, and when properly baked was snowy white, tender, and mealy. To duplicate this recipe, ask for Russet Burbank potatoes, generally available commercially today only in the western United States. The railroad's instructions for recreating this most famous specialty menu item are as follows:

NORTHERN PACIFIC
GREAT BIG BAKED POTATO

BEFORE YOU BEGIN:
You'll need: an ice pick
Preheat oven to 350 degrees
Preparation time: 1½–2 hours
Yield: 1 serving

With potato at room temperature, scrub it thoroughly, then pierce each end deeply with an ice pick. Place in oven and bake for 1½ hours (spring and summer) or 2 hours (fall and winter). In spring and summer, it is recommended you place a pan of water in the oven with the potato to compensate for the loss of natural moisture that occurs during storage in this warmer time of year. Give each potato an occasional quarter turn during baking. Remove potato from oven and gently roll to loosen the meaty part from the skin. Cut a crevice end to end on the top (flat side), spread open, fluff potato pulp with a fork, and serve steaming hot with a large pat of butter in the center.

(COURTESY OF CRAIG AND MARTY NEROS)

(COURTESY OF CRAIG AND MARTY NEROS)

19

THE PENNSYLVANIA RAILROAD

BAKED POTATO PENNSYLVANIA

BEFORE YOU BEGIN

*You'll need: medium
saucepan, potato
masher, baking dish
Preheat oven to 350
degrees
Preparation time:
45 minutes (after
all potatoes are
cooked and cooled)
Yield: 4 servings*

The railroad offered these variations on this recipe:

1. Mash baked potato pulp with salt, pepper, 2 tablespoons butter, a heaping teaspoon each of chopped parsley and chopped chives, and ⅓ cup light cream, then refill the shells, sprinkle with melted butter, and brown in the oven.
2. Substitute ⅔ cup shredded cheese for the chopped parsley and chives, and sprinkle the top with additional shredded cheese.
3. Mash the potato pulp with 4 tablespoons butter, 2 ounces Roquefort or Bleu cheese, 2 tablespoons hot light cream, and a dash of salt and paprika. Return mixture to shells and rebake until the tops brown.

2 **cups boiled new potatoes, mashed**	**salt and pepper to taste**
4 **Idaho baking potatoes**	**Garnish: bread crumbs,**
1½ **cups light cream**	**paprika, grated Parmesan,**
2 **oz. butter**	**melted butter**

Place 4 or 5 medium new potatoes in medium saucepan, cover with salted water, and bring to a boil. Cover and cook for 25 minutes. Drain and let stand to cool to room temperature. Meanwhile, bake Idaho potatoes well, about 1 hour in 350-degree oven. Cool baked potatoes and cut tops off lengthwise. Scoop out the potato pulp until shell is well hollowed out. Now remove skins from boiled new potatoes, place in medium saucepan, and mash thoroughly. Make mashed-in-cream filling by adding cream and butter to mashed boiled new potatoes and mixing well. Season to taste and, over medium heat, cook for about 10 minutes, until butter melts and mixture is bubbly. Place the hollowed-out potato shells in a baking dish and fill each with potato mixture. Sprinkle tops with a pinch of paprika, bread crumbs, grated cheese, and a few drops of melted butter. Bake until golden brown. Serve very hot.

CORN AND GREEN PEPPER SAUTÉ

2 cups corn
2 Tbsp. butter

1 cup green pepper, diced
salt to taste

BEFORE YOU BEGIN

You'll need: 1-quart
saucepan
Preparation time:
15 minutes (after
corn-on-the-cob is
cooked)
Yield: 6 servings

Cut kernels from ears of cooked corn, or use frozen or canned corn, well drained. In saucepan over medium heat, melt butter. Add corn and green pepper and sauté, stirring occasionally, until tender and heated through, approximately 5 minutes. Season with salt only.

CREAM OF CHICKEN SOUP ROQUEFORT

¼ lb. butter
1 white onion, sliced thin
2 outer stalks celery, sliced thin
½ cup flour

4 oz. Roquefort cheese
2 qts. chicken broth, seasoned
  to taste
1 cup heavy cream

BEFORE YOU BEGIN

You'll need: 3-quart,
2-quart, and small
saucepans; large
whisk
Preparation time:
45 minutes
Yield: 8 8-oz. servings

Melt butter in the 3-quart saucepan over medium heat. Sauté onion and celery, stirring occasionally, until tender but not browned, about 5 minutes. Add flour, stirring constantly, to make a roux. Reduce heat and allow to simmer for about 5 minutes. Crumble Roquefort cheese and stir into roux until melted. Meanwhile, bring chicken broth to a boil. Slowly add hot chicken broth to roux, stirring constantly with a whisk to avoid lumps. Let soup slow boil over low heat for 30 minutes. Meanwhile, heat cream just to boiling. Strain soup, return it to the saucepan, and bring back to slow boil. Slowly add hot cream, stirring constantly to mix thoroughly. Serve piping hot.

MELON MINT COCKTAIL

The New York, New Haven and Hartford Railroad's version of this light appetizer had you marinate the melon balls in the mint sauce at least one hour before serving. Either way wins raves.

½ cup sugar
½ cup water
1 Tbsp. mint leaves, chopped
  juice of 1 lemon, strained

juice of 1 orange, strained
1 large melon or 2 half melons
  of the season

BEFORE YOU BEGIN

You'll need: small
saucepan, strainer,
melon baller, small
bowl
Preparation time:
15 minutes (allow
1 hour for syrup to
chill)
Yield: 4 servings

In saucepan, stir sugar and water together, bring to a boil, and reduce heat to slow boil for 5 minutes. Place chopped mint in bowl. Pour boiling syrup over mint. Stir to mix, set aside to cool. Strain syrup and stir in lemon juice and orange juice. Place in refrigerator and chill through. Meanwhile, halve the melon(s), remove seeds, cut into balls, and chill. To serve, place 10 melon balls in dish, pour syrup over all, and garnish with fresh mint sprigs.

DEVILED SLICE OF ROAST BEEF
WITH MUSTARD SAUCE

BEFORE YOU BEGIN

*You'll need: broiling
rack, saucepan,
strainer
Preparation time:
30 minutes
Yield: 1 serving*

Instructions were to prepare this specialty to order only. It can be the centerpiece of a fast but elegant meal.

ROAST BEEF

¼-inch slice roast beef, cooked
salt and pepper to taste
½ Tbsp. butter, melted

½ Tbsp. English mustard
soft white bread crumbs to cover

Season one side of the roast beef with salt and pepper. Sprinkle with melted butter, then spread with mustard. Sprinkle lightly with bread crumbs. Broil 5 inches from heat source until warmed through and lightly browned, about 4 minutes. Serve on a dinner plate, set in mustard sauce, and garnished with well-washed sprig of fresh parsley.

MUSTARD SAUCE

1 small onion, chopped
⅛ tsp. fresh ground black pepper
1 Tbsp. white vinegar
⅓ cup brown gravy

1 Tbsp. English mustard
¼ tsp. seasoning salt
½ Tbsp. butter
¼ tsp. parsley, chopped

Place onion and black pepper in saucepan with vinegar. Cook over medium heat until vinegar evaporates, about 5 minutes. Add gravy, mustard, and seasoning salt and simmer for 15 minutes. Strain and add butter and chopped parsley. Return to saucepan and heat until butter is melted. The key to this sauce is that it be very well seasoned.

◆—◆▷◁◆—◆

GINGER MUFFINS

BEFORE YOU BEGIN

*You'll need: 15-por-
tion 2½-inch cup
muffin pan(s), mix-
ing bowl, sifter
Preheat oven to 400
degrees
Preparation time:
45 minutes
Yield: 15 muffins*

Excellent with tea, or a unique addition to your dinner bread basket.

2 cups flour
2 tsp. ginger
1 tsp .cinnamon
1 heaping tsp. baking soda
½ tsp. salt
½ cup butter, softened

½ cup powdered sugar
2 eggs
½ cup dark molasses
½ cup hot water (heated to
100–110 degrees)

Grease muffin cups well all around and set aside. Sift together first five (dry) ingredients and set aside. With butter at room temperature, cream it together with the powdered sugar in large mixing bowl. Continue beating butter/sugar as you add eggs one at a time, then add molasses. Add dry ingredients, and stir with fork to moisten. Add hot water. Stir until mixture is smooth. Spoon batter to fill muffin-pan cups to three-quarters full. Wipe clean of spills outside cups. Bake until well risen and a toothpick inserted in center comes out clean, approximately 20 minutes. Remove immediately to wire rack. Serve at once. If necessary to hold before serving, tip muffins slightly in cups to allow steam to escape.

PENNEPICURE PIE

You'll want to prepare sufficient pie-crust dough in a pie tin(s) before proceeding to make this light, flavorful dessert.

BEFORE YOU BEGIN

You'll need: large mixing bowl, small mixing bowl, small saucepan, electric beater, 9-inch pie tin
Preheat oven to 350 degrees
Preparation time: 2 hours (plus 1 hour to allow baked pie to cool)
Yield: 1 pie

3 egg yolks	dash, salt
4 Tbsp. granular sugar	1½ cups heavy cream, boiling
¼ tsp. ground cloves	½ cup seedless raisins, chopped very fine
¼ tsp. ground cinnamon	1 unbaked dessert pie crust (see page 154)
¼ tsp. ground nutmeg	

Separate eggs, place yolks in large mixing bowl, retain whites for meringue. Separately, mix well together the sugar, cloves, cinnamon, nutmeg, and salt. Add spices mixture to egg yolks and beat until smooth and stiff. Meanwhile, bring cream just to a boil. Then, continue beating egg and spices mixture while adding cream slowly. Continue beating while adding raisins. Pour mixture into pastry-lined pie tin. Bake until firm and of a nice color, about 75 minutes. Remove to wire rack and allow to cool.

MERINGUE

3 egg whites	4 Tbsp. powdered sugar

In small mixing bowl, beat egg whites until lightly whipped. Add sugar and continue beating until thoroughly mixed and formed peaks remain. Cover pie to edge of the crust with the mixture. Place on top shelf of 400-degree oven and bake until meringue is delicately colored, about 10 minutes. You may find it helpful to dip the blade of your cutting knife in boiling-hot water before each cut.

POTTED FLANK OF BEEF TRINIDAD

BEFORE YOU BEGIN

*You'll need: large skil-
let, strainer, small
saucepan
Preparation time:
1 hour
Yield: 4 servings*

¼ cup carrots, sliced	2 lbs. beef flank steak
¼ white onion, sliced	¼ cup flour
¼ cup celery, sliced	1½ cups water
4 Tbsp. bacon fat	½ cup canned tomatoes, diced
¼ tsp. salt	1 bay leaf
¼ tsp. pepper	4 whole allspice
¼ tsp. paprika	1 tsp. Angostura Bitters

Peel, wash, dry, and slice carrots, onions, and celery and set aside. In a large skillet, heat bacon fat hot to smoking. Meanwhile, combine salt, pepper, and paprika.
Coat all sides of meat with seasonings mixture. Place meat in hot fat and sear, turning occasionally, until well browned on all sides. Remove meat. Place vegetables in
hot fat and cook, stirring constantly, until well browned, about 5 minutes. Add
flour, stirring constantly, and reduce heat. Cook until entire mixture is well browned,
about 10 minutes. Add water, tomatoes, bay leaf, and allspice, increase heat to medium-high, and stir until mixture come to a boil. Return meat to pot, cover, reduce
heat, and cook at slow boil until meat is tender, about 30 minutes. Remove meat
to platter. Carefully strain sauce into small saucepan, add bitters, and return to a
boil and simmer 5 minutes. Serve hot by slicing beef thin and at a bias, placing on
serving dish, and pouring sauce over.

⊷ ⊶

SALAD BOWL
WITH PENNSYLVANIA DRESSING

*The food-service manual warned on-train chefs to be sure all salad ingredients were dry
before adding the railroad's tasty specialty dressing, or the dressing would not coat.*

BEFORE YOU BEGIN

*You'll need: salad mix-
ing bowl, medium
mixing bowl,
whisk, 1-pint
covered jar
Preparation time:
½ hour (chill dress-
ing 1 hour before
serving)
Yield: 1 individual
serving*

SALAD BOWL

¼ head crisp lettuce	3 radishes, sliced thin
1 large tomato, ripe	1 stalk celery, sliced thin
¼ cucumber	¾ oz. Roquefort cheese
2 scallions, both whites and greens,	Ry-Krisp
sliced thin	

Wash all vegetables well and pat or drain dry. Core the lettuce and separate leaves.
Cut tomato into 8 wedges. Peel cucumber, remove seeds, and slice thin. Place all
vegetables in a bowl. Break up the cheese and sprinkle over. Add three generous
tablespoonsful of Pennsylvania dressing and mix well. Place in salad bowl. Serve
with Ry-Krisp or similar crackers.

PENNSYLVANIA DRESSING

2 hard-boiled egg yolks
dash, tarragon vinegar
1 tsp. paprika
1 tsp. celery salt
1 heaping tsp. powdered sugar
1 green pepper, chopped medium fine
6 chives or small young onions,
chopped very fine

1 sprig parsley, chopped fine
2 hard-boiled egg whites,
chopped fine
juice of ½ lemon, strained
½ cup olive oil
1 cup mayonnaise

Mash egg yolks with enough tarragon vinegar to make a smooth paste. Add each ingredient in the order listed, mixing well before adding the next. Beat all with a whisk until blended through, about 1 minute. Pour into a glass jar and cover tightly. Chill at least 1 hour before serving. Makes 1 pint.

━━━ ⊫◈⊨ ━━━

STUFFED CELERY

This variation on a staple of the relish dish can also be served with bitters and almonds left out, but with a pinch of paprika added just before serving.

1 stalk celery
1½ oz. Roquefort or Bleu cheese
2 oz. butter, softened

½ tsp. Angostura Bitters
1½ Tbsp. unsalted almonds,
finely chopped

BEFORE YOU BEGIN

You'll need: small mixing bowl
Preparation time:
15 minutes; prepare at least 1 hour before serving
Yield: 2 servings

Wash the celery stalk well, trim ends, and separate into 6 pieces. Blend cheese, butter, and bitters together until smooth. Using a small butter knife, fill each piece of celery with a generous mound of the mixture and, while it is still soft, roll in almonds to coat. Place in the refrigerator until very cold, at least 1 hour.

VEAL CUTLETS IN PAPRIKA SAUCE

1 lb. veal cutlets **salt and pepper to taste**	**1 Tbsp. butter**

Season each side of cutlets with salt and pepper. Heat butter in cast-iron skillet to medium-hot. Fry cutlets until of light brown color and cooked through, turning once. Allow about 2 minutes to a side. Remove to a platter and keep warm until ready to serve.

PAPRIKA SAUCE

1 Tbsp. butter	**1½ tsp. paprika**
¼ cup raw ham, minced	**1½ cups cream sauce**
1 small onion, sliced thin	**½ cup heavy cream**
1 outside stalk celery, **minced fine**	**salt to taste**

In the saucepan, melt butter over medium heat. Sauté ham, onion, celery, and paprika until vegetables are tender, about 10 minutes. Add cream sauce (see page 153), stirring constantly to mix well. Reduce heat and simmer 20 minutes. Add cream and mix well. Add salt, stir, and strain. Serve hot over veal cutlets.

20

THE SOUTHERN PACIFIC LINES

APPLE PANCAKES

1 heaping tsp. sugar
1 cup milk
1 cup flour
2 eggs
1 Tbsp. butter, melted

2 mealy apples
salt to taste
shortening (optional)
powdered sugar

In the mixing bowl, dissolve sugar in milk. Add flour and whip until smooth. Add eggs and butter and beat well. Peel, core, halve, and slice apples thin. To prepare, place apples on a well-heated griddle or frying pan on which a small amount of shortening has been heated. Fry apples until they begin to soften, then cover thinly with batter and let bake until topside shows dry. Turn once. When nicely browned and done, dust with powdered sugar and serve.

BEFORE YOU BEGIN

You'll need: medium mixing bowl, whisk, pancake griddle
Preparation time: 30 minutes
Yield: 12 6-inch pancakes

AVOCADO COCKTAIL

1 medium-size avocado
2 Tbsp. catsup

2 Tbsp. French dressing
juice of ½ lemon

Cut avocado in half and gently remove the pit. Use a melon baller to scoop avocado from shell. Heap balls loosely into cocktail glasses. Mix catsup, French dressing, and lemon juice thoroughly. Cover each portion with one spoonful of this sauce and serve chilled.

BEFORE YOU BEGIN

You'll need: melon baller, cocktail glasses, small mixing bowl, medium mixing bowl
Preparation time: 15 minutes
Yield: 4 servings

FRENCH DRESSING

1 tsp. paprika
1 Tbsp. English mustard
1 tsp. salt
1 Tbsp. white pepper

¼ cup white vinegar
2 cups olive oil
2 Tbsp. cold water

In mixing bowl, combine spices (first four ingredients). Moisten through with a few drops of vinegar. Pour oil slowly into spices, stirring constantly. When mixture begins to thicken, trickle in remaining vinegar. Add cold water and mix thoroughly. Store unused portion in refrigerator.

BAKED POTATO SURPRISE, SOUTHERN PACIFIC STYLE

4 large baking potatoes	4 5-oz. filets mignons
1 egg yolk	12 fresh button mushrooms
6 Tbsp. butter	4 strips bacon
salt and pepper	2 Tbsp. Parmesan cheese
1 tsp. chopped parsley	watercress

Wash potatoes well, pierce by cutting ends, and bake until done, about 1 hour. Increase oven temperature to 400 degrees. Remove a strip of potato skin lengthwise from the part best suited as the top. Scoop out all potato, taking care not to break the skins. In the mixing bowl, mash potato pulp. To the mashed potato, add the egg yolk, 2 tablespoons of butter, salt, pepper, and the chopped parsley. In a small skillet over medium heat, melt 2 tablespoons butter. Dip filets in butter and place in a hot medium skillet only long enough to sear, about 30 seconds each side. Meanwhile, in a clean small skillet over medium heat, melt 1 tablespoon butter and sauté mushrooms. In another small skillet, fry the bacon strips crisp. To assemble, place a filet mignon in each hollowed potato shell. Garnish each with sauteed mushrooms and a strip of cooked bacon. Completely refill the shell with the mashed potato mixture, covering the shell opening completely. Sprinkle with grated Parmesan cheese, dot with sliver of butter, and bake until nicely browned. Serve garnished with watercress.

—+ ❧❦❧ +—

BAKED SUGAR-CURED HAM SOUTHERN PACIFIC

1 cup sugar	2 oz. whole cloves
1 4–6 lb. raw ham with bone, or allow 1 lb. raw weight per person	2 cups apple cider, boiled
	1 lb. brown sugar

In a pot large enough to hold the ingredients, dissolve 1 cup sugar with water to cover ham and soak overnight. About 5 hours before mealtime, discard water, wash ham thoroughly, and replace in fresh water to cover. Heat to a boil, reduce heat, and simmer for 20 minutes per each pound of ham. Remove from heat and leave ham to soak in broth for one more hour. Remove ham from broth, retaining 1 cup of broth, and plunge into cold water, then skin, leaving about ¼ inch of fat. Press whole cloves into fat, one inch apart. Place in roasting pan to hold, coat with cider, and sprinkle with brown sugar. Bake, basting occasionally with hot cider, and sprinkling with brown sugar, until nicely browned and done, about 1 hour. Retain drippings. Serve hot with the following sauce.

SAUCE

1 medium onion, sliced
1 young carrot, sliced
2 stalks celery, sliced
3 Tbsp. ham drippings
2 Tbsp. flour

1 cup ham broth
1 qt. tomatoes, chopped
 salt and pepper to taste
1 cup apple cider

In a 2-quart saucepan over medium heat, sauté onion, carrot, and celery in ham drippings. Add flour, stirring constantly to avoid lumps. Add ham broth and tomatoes. Bring to a boil, reduce heat, and simmer until cooked through. Season and pass through strainer or puree in blender. Meanwhile, in a small pan, bring cider to the boil. Add boiled cider to strained mixture and stir to mix before serving.

CALIFORNIA PEACH AND RICE FRITTERS

1 cup short-grain rice, well washed
2 cups milk, scalded
¼ cup sugar
2 Tbsp. butter
3 egg yolks

2 Tbsp. heavy cream, warmed
1 tsp. vanilla
1 large or 2 small cans peach
 halves, in heavy syrup

BREADING

2 Tbsp. flour
2 whole eggs, well beaten

1 cup fresh bread crumbs
 powdered sugar

BEFORE YOU BEGIN

*You'll need: double boiler, baking sheet or pan, deep fryer, several small mixing bowls, small saucepan
Preparation time: 1 hour
Yield: 8 servings*

Butter baking sheet all over and set aside. Combine rice, milk, sugar, and butter in double boiler and cook until rice is tender. Meanwhile, beat egg yolks to lemon color, then slowly beat in the hot cream. When rice is cooked, stir in egg yolks/cream mixture. Add vanilla and mix thoroughly. Spread mixture on the buttered baking pan to cool. Meanwhile, drain peaches and retain syrup. When rice mixture is cool enough to handle, mold enough rice onto each peach half to produce the shape of a whole peach. Dredge lightly in flour, dip in beaten egg, and roll in bread crumbs. Deep fry in hot oil until nicely browned. Meanwhile, in a small saucepan, heat peach syrup to a boil, reduce heat, and simmer until liquid thickens. Dust peach fritters with powdered sugar and serve set in peach syrup sauce.

CHICKEN GUMBO SOUTHERN PACIFIC

½ cup butter,
1½ lbs. boneless chicken meat, cut into 1-inch pieces
3 ozs. veal, cut small
2 ozs. raw, lean ham, cut small
½ cup onions, cut small
½ cup celery, sliced thin
½ cup bell peppers, cut small
½ cup okra, sliced

2 medium tomatoes, skinned and quartered
1 qt. water
½ cup shrimp
1 Tbsp. butter
1 tsp. salt
⅛ tsp. white pepper
pinch, thyme
pinch, gumbo filé
2 cups cooked rice

In the saucepan, melt the butter and braise meats. When tender, add onions, celery, and peppers, and continue cooking until soft. Add okra, tomatoes, and water. Bring to a boil, reduce heat, and boil slowly for 30 minutes. Meanwhile, in small skillet over medium heat, sauté shrimp in 1 tablespoon butter. Add shrimp to gumbo and continue to slow boil 10 minutes more. Add salt and seasonings to taste and stir well. To serve, mold ½ cup of boiled rice (see page 153) in the center of each soup plate and pour gumbo over.

——◆——

CURRIED CHICKEN COLOMBO WITH INDIAN CHUTNEY

1 2–3 lb. whole chicken, cut up
¼ lb. flounder fillet
3 oz. butter
½ cup onions, finely chopped
½ cup green pepper, diced
1 banana, peeled and sliced
2 slices pineapple, cut small
pinch garlic, minced

1 Tbsp. flour
1 Tbsp. Madras curry powder
½ cup Indian chutney
3 cups chicken broth
salt to taste
1 cup cooked rice

Wash and disjoint chicken, saving breasts and legs, or begin with same chicken parts. Place flounder fillet(s) on lightly greased baking sheet in oven to bake dry and crisp, about 25 minutes. Flake flounder and set aside. In the large saucepan over medium heat, melt butter. Add onions and green peppers, reduce heat, cover, and braise until cooked soft, 5 minutes. Add banana, pineapple, and garlic, stir, and let cook for another minute. Then, stirring constantly, sprinkle in flour and curry powder. Cook until lightly browned, then add chutney and chicken broth. Let simmer for 20 minutes, then pass through a strainer into a 3-quart saucepan and bring to a simmer. Meanwhile, salt the chicken parts, dredge lightly with flour, and fry in hot oil, turning occasionally, until nicely colored. Drain and put into curry sauce, cover, and let simmer for 20 minutes. Serve on a bed of rice, and garnish with flakes of dried flounder.

INDIAN CHUTNEY

3 medium-sized ripe tomatoes	¾ lb. brown sugar
1 cup seeded raisins, chopped	1 cup cider vinegar
1 cup green apples, chopped	2 oz. white mustard seeds
½ cup onion, minced	1 oz. preserved ginger
2 Tbsp. salt	pinch, cayenne pepper

Peel (see page 155) and quarter tomatoes. In the 2-quart saucepan, combine all ingredients well. Bring to a boil, reduce heat, and cook slowly, uncovered, for 3 hours. Store in airtight container in refrigerator.

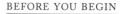

FILLET OF SOLE AS YOU LIKE IT

1 12–16 oz. sole fillet	2 fresh mushrooms, sliced
salt and pepper to taste	2 Tbsp. butter
juice of ½ lemon	1 Tbsp. flour
6 oysters	¾ cup heavy cream, warmed
6 shrimp	½ cup fresh bread crumbs

BEFORE YOU BEGIN

You'll need: baking dish, small skillet, small saucepan
Preheat oven to 375 degrees
Preparation time: 1 hour
Yield: 2 servings

Season sole fillet(s) with salt and pepper and sprinkle with lemon juice. Fold as needed and place in buttered, fire-proof baking dish. Arrange oysters and shrimp along sides. Meanwhile, in small skillet, sauté mushrooms in 1 tablespoon of the butter and add to the baking dish. In small saucepan, make a roux with the other tablespoon of butter and the flour, then slowly add cream and simmer until thickened. Pour cream sauce over sole. Sprinkle bread crumbs over all, dot with butter, and bake until nicely browned and bubbly, about 30 minutes.

GARDEN SALAD BOWL
WITH SOUTHERN PACIFIC DRESSING

Garden-fresh fruits and vegetables were always in their season somewhere along the right-of-way of the Southern Pacific's far-flung western system. That fact enabled chefs to delight dining-car patrons with a wide variety of tossed salads. This is one of the most popular.

SALAD

4 medium tomatoes	½ green pepper, cut in strips
2 medium heads lettuce	1 tsp. sugar
1 cucumber	pinch, salt
½ bunch radishes, sliced thin	⅓ cup Southern Pacific dressing

Peel tomatoes (see page 155). Cut each tomato into quarters and set aside to cool. Meanwhile, break lettuce into bite-sized pieces into a bowl. Pare the cucumber, score all sides lengthwise with the tines of a fork, and slice thin. In a large salad bowl, arrange a bed of lettuce. Top with tomato wedges, cucumber, radishes, and green pepper. Sprinkle sugar and salt over all. Pour on the dressing and toss lightly before serving.

SOUTHERN PACIFIC DRESSING

1 Tbsp. English mustard	½ cup currant jelly
1 level tsp. salt	2 cups mayonnaise
¼ cup white vinegar	1 cup catsup

Stir mustard and salt into the vinegar until dissolved. Add jelly and stir until smooth. Add mayonnaise and catsup and mix thoroughly. Store in an airtight container.

SPANISH BEANS

2 cups (1 lb.) kidney beans	½ cup onions, minced
¼ tsp. baking soda	2 cups tomatoes
½ Tbsp. salt	1 Tbsp. sugar
½ lb. bacon, chopped	⅛ tsp. cayenne pepper

Pick beans clean, place in the saucepan, cover generously with cold water, and add baking soda. Bring to a boil, reduce heat, and let simmer for 5 minutes. Drain, wash, and return to saucepan. Cover with new boiling water, and add salt. Return to a boil, reduce heat, and slow boil, uncovered, for 1½ hours, adding boiling water as needed to keep from drying out. Meanwhile, heat bacon in a large skillet, add onions, and fry until lightly browned. Add fried bacon, onions, tomatoes, sugar, and cayenne pepper to the beans. Continue to slow boil, covered, until done, about 1 hour more.

✦━━ ⊫◈⊨ ━━✦

THE CASSEROLE

This unusual item, along with the Garden Salad Bowl, were two specialties of the road served at table in large containers, accompanied by individual serving plates. Guests were invited to "dig in."

BEFORE YOU BEGIN

You'll need: 3-quart saucepan, 3-quart covered casserole, small saucepan, small skillet.
Preheat oven to 350 degrees
Preparation time: 1½ hours
Yield: 6 servings

¼ lb. butter
2½ lbs. lamb shoulder, skinned, boned and cut in 1¾-inch squares
  salt
  white pepper
1 medium onion, minced
2 stalks celery, sliced
1 heaping Tbsp. flour
1 pint broth, made of lamb bones
1 cup tomatoes, pureed

1 bunch young French carrots, shaped small
4 young turnips, quartered and shaped
12 pearl onions
12 small rounded potatoes, boiled in salted water
1 cup peas, boiled in plain water
  parsley, chopped

Melt butter in the saucepan over medium heat. Dredge lamb lightly with salt and white pepper and sauté in butter in batches, taking care not to brown. Return all lamb to saucepan. Add the minced onion and celery, stirring occasionally, and continue cooking until vegetables become soft. With the moisture disappearing, add flour to make a brown roux. When the roux has browned, add hot lamb broth and tomato puree. Stir to mix, and bring to a boil. Pour all into a casserole. Meanwhile, separately, in small amounts of butter, braise carrots and turnips, and brown the onions. Add all three to the casserole. Cover the casserole, place in oven, and bake until contents are done, about 40 minutes. Meanwhile, boil and peel the potatoes, then brown over medium heat in a small amount of butter. Boil and drain the peas. To serve, remove casserole lid, skim off surplus fat, and garnish with scattered potatoes, peas, and a sprinkle of chopped parsley.

PROMOTING SHIPPERS' WARES: APPLES ON THE GREAT NORTHERN

The dining-car department, in addition to its duties as a ridership booster, actively promoted the goods of the railroad's freight shippers to train passengers and others. When menus were planned, close attention was paid by the superintendent to the fruits and vegetables of the season, especially those grown in areas served by the railroad. Employees were urged to consume goods shipped on their lines' freight trains. The Milwaukee Road celebrated the daffodils decorating its dining-car tables. The Union Pacific food-service manual had twenty-eight recipes for potatoes. Publicity cam-

(COURTESY OF GREAT NORTHERN RAILWAY COMPANY RECORDS, MINNESOTA HISTORICAL SOCIETY)

spring, Texas berries were replaced by those of Louisiana in March, by Arkansas berries in April, and finally, by Missouri's own Ozark Aromas in May. Other commodities that the line hauled and served were Irish and sweet potatoes from Arkansas and Louisiana, radishes from Louisiana, grapefruit from the Rio Grande Valley, figs from Texas, seafoods from Louisiana, beef and pork from Missouri, and cantaloupes, honeydews, and watermelons from Colorado.

paigns staged by the producer's association were often the focus of railroad advertising, ticket-office window displays, and on-train activity.

Glenn F. Wallace, farm marketing agent for the Missouri Pacific Lines in the 1920s, wrote a monthly "Featuring Our Own Products" column for the *Missouri Pacific Lines Magazine*. In April 1926 he wrote, "The passenger department has been cooperating for some time by featuring on our dining cars and in our restaurants . . . those products grown along our lines." As a case in point, Wallace notes that the first strawberries, from the lower Rio Grande Valley, were noted on a card attached to train menus "so all who enjoyed them might know where they came from." Then, following the advancing

Wallace's column concluded, "There isn't any good reason why any of us should ever eat any fruits or vegetables from any other section when we can get better products from along our own lines."[1] Elsewhere, the railroad's employees were urged, when they purchased such things as fuel and lumber, to ask where it came from and on what railroad it was shipped. Whether this was a way of prospecting for new shippers, or of pressuring local merchants to support Missouri Pacific's shippers, is left for interpretation.

In 1938, the Union Pacific established a research and test kitchen to create new recipes for the railroad's dining cars, hotels, station restaurants, and the general public. When, in 1939 alone, the kitchen published eighty-three new recipes, with names like the

"Sun Valley Baked Apple," western shippers were made aware that their produce would receive the maximum benefit of this kitchen through the development of various recipes if they shipped UP. A press release pointed out, "Our experts are continually endeavoring to develop such recipes as will eventually increase the use of food stuffs in every state served by our railroad." The wives of Union Pacific men, too, were urged to cook and serve foods shipped by the railroad.

The management of the Missouri Pacific, among others, made it a point to purchase the prize-winning beef at farm shows throughout the territory it served. It was not uncommon for the railroad's president to show up at such events, checkbook in hand.

Nowhere was the close relationship between railroads and their shippers more evident than between the Great Northern Railway and the Wenatchee Valley apple growers in the state of Washington. Claiming to have "discovered" these large and flavorful apples, the railroad set about to promote them through special dishes served on the dining cars and with window displays in ticket offices throughout America. During National Apple Week, GN trains making stops in the Wenatchee Valley were boarded by representatives of the apple growers—often beauty queens—who distributed free apples to all the train's passengers. Praise for the apples went something like this blurb, taken from a booklet entitled "Great Northern Chef Secrets," also distributed during National Apple Week:

The charm of Great Northern baked apples is expressed in flavor and size, made possible only when grown in the famous Wenatchee Valley. Someone in the long-ago days gave to the apples we serve a name, "Rome Beauty," and a beauty it is. Think of a word that expresses bigness and you have a good description of our apple. In the language of the trade it is called a "48 to 56," meaning each box contains only 48 to 56 apples. Now recall the average size you buy in the stores, 100 to 125 to the box, and marvel on the size of our Rome Beauty. Visualize, just for a moment, this delightful gift of nature, baked to a golden brown crisp confection, served with pure rich cream, and thank a fate that brings Rome Beauty to you as delivered by Great Northern dining cars. Here's how to bake these apple treats:

BAKED WENATCHEE APPLE

BEFORE YOU BEGIN
You'll need: baking dish to hold six apples, small saucepan
Preheat oven to 350 degrees
Preparation time: 1½ hours
Yield: 6 servings

BAKED APPLE

6 Super size (48–52) Rome Beauty apples	1 Tbsp. butter water to moisten
2 cups sugar	

Core the apples thoroughly and pare each around one-third down from the top. Retain cores and parings for sauce. Place the apples upright in a baking pan and fill the core of each with ¼ cup of sugar. Dot each with a pat of butter. Sprinkle the remaining ½ cup of sugar around the apples and add just enough water to moisten the sugar. Bake for 1 hour. After syrup begins to form in baking pan, baste apples frequently, at least six times. Remove from oven. Cool 15 minutes before serving. Serve each apple with plenty of thick sauce.

SAUCE

In small saucepan, place cores and peels. Cover with water and add 2 tablespoons of sugar, stirring until sugar is dissolved. Over medium-high heat, simmer until mixture is reduced to half and apple parts turn mushy, stirring occasionally to break up apple parts. When mixture has thickened, strain, and pour over baked apple.

WENATCHEE APPLE CAKE

BEFORE YOU BEGIN
You'll need: 9" x 13" baking dish, medium
    mixing bowl, small saucepan
Preheat oven to 450 degrees
Preparation time: 1½ hours
Yield: 12 servings

1 lb. butter, room temperature	4 Tbsp. powdered sugar
1 lb. flour	3 eggs, slightly beaten
1 cup milk, cold	¼ lb. sugar
12 cups Rome Beauty apples	2 cups milk, scalded
1 Tbsp. ground cinnamon	

Make a dough of the butter, flour, and milk (see page 154 for directions). Roll dough thin and use to line baking dish. Core, peel and slice fresh apples and place in the dish. Mix cinnamon and powdered sugar and sprinkle evenly over the apples. Place in oven for 15 minutes, then reduce heat to 350 degrees and continue baking until nearly done, about 30 minutes. Meanwhile, to make a custard, beat eggs slightly, then add sugar and slowly stir in the scalded milk. Mix well. Pour custard over nearly done apples and return to oven. Continue to bake until custard sets, about 30 minutes.

APPLE PIE

Chefs were advised that fine-quality apples should not be boiled before making this pie, but coarse apples should.

BEFORE YOU BEGIN
You'll need: 1 9-inch pie pan
Preheat oven to 450 degrees

Preparation time: 1½ hours
Yield: 1 pie

6 large Rome Beauty apples	1 tsp. ground cinnamon
1½ cups sugar	dessert pie crust for 2-crust pie
juice of 1 lemon	

Line pie pan with pie pastry (see page 154). Slice apples thin, mix gently with sugar, and scatter into pie pan. Drizzle lemon juice over apples, then dust with cinnamon. Cover with pastry top and make cuts to allow steam to escape while baking. Place in oven and bake for 15 minutes, then reduce heat to 350 degrees and bake 45 minutes longer.

APPLE PAN DOWDY

BEFORE YOU BEGIN
You'll need: large mixing bowl, 8" x 8" baking
    pan, medium mixing bowl, small mixing
    bowl
Preheat oven to 400 degrees
Preparation time: 45 minutes
Yield: 9 servings

8 cups Rome Beauty apples, cored and sliced	1 tsp. nutmeg
1 cup sugar	2 cups Bisquick®
2½ Tbsp. molasses	½ cup milk
1 tsp. ground cinnamon	1 pint whipping cream

In a large bowl, gently combine apple slices, sugar, and molasses. Add spices and mix well. Place mixture in bake pan and pat flat. Cover with foil and bake for 15 minutes or until apples are tender. Meanwhile, combine Bisquick® and milk to form a dough. Roll dough to size to cover apples. Seal to edges and make slits in top for steam to escape. Return to oven for about 20 minutes until crust is golden brown. To serve, cut in squares. Place crust in serving dish and top with apples. Add a dollop of whipped cream.

21

THE SOUTHERN RAILWAY SYSTEM

BUTTERMILK BISCUITS

BEFORE YOU BEGIN

You'll need: large mix-ing bowl, small saucepan, small mixing bowl, pastry cutter, 2-inch or 3-inch biscuit cutter, 2 large cookie sheets, 2 towels, fork, small skillet, pastry brush
Preheat oven to 400 degrees
Preparation time: 1 hour
Yield: 24 biscuits

These biscuits were popular alone or as an accompaniment to many railroad dishes. The Southern's food-service manual instructed its dining-car personnel to avoid handling these delicacies unnecessarily.

4 cups sifted all-purpose flour	½ cup warm water
2 tsp. baking powder	2 Tbsp. sugar
1 tsp. salt	⅓ cup shortening
1 cup buttermilk	2 Tbsp. melted butter
1 pkg. active dry yeast	

Sift flour 4 times before measuring. Then, sift flour, baking powder, and salt into large bowl. Slowly heat buttermilk in small saucepan. When bubbles form around edge, remove from heat and cool to lukewarm. Grease cookie sheets and set aside. In small bowl, sprinkle yeast over warm (100–110 degrees) water and allow to set 5 minutes. Add sugar and stir until completely dissolved, then stir in warm but-termilk. Using pastry blender, cut shortening into sifted flour mixture until coarse. Make a depression in center of flour and pour all liquid into it at once. Stir with fork to mix until coarse and dampened through. Place dough on light-ly floured surface, knead gently (fold dough toward you and flatten with heel of hand). Turn dough one quarter and repeat, kneading until the dough is smooth, about 5 minutes. With lightly floured rolling pin, roll dough out to ½-inch thick-ness. Flour biscuit cutter and press firmly to cut biscuits through without twist-ing. Reroll remaining dough and repeat until all dough is cut. Place biscuits 1 inch apart on greased cookie sheets. Puncture tops lightly with a fork, cover loose-ly with a towel, and let rise in warm (90 degrees) draft-free place until they dou-ble in size, about ½ hour. Before baking, brush tops with melted butter. Place biscuits in oven and bake 12–15 minutes, until golden brown. Serve while still warm.

BAKED FISH IN CREOLE SAUCE

The Superintendent's instructions to dining-car personnel were simple: "Use best fish market affords for baking."

4 **6-oz. fish fillets**	**paprika to taste**
cooking oil to coat	2 **cups Creole sauce**

BEFORE YOU BEGIN

You'll need: baking pan, 3-quart saucepan
Preheat oven to 350 degrees
Preparation time: 1 hour
Yield: 4 servings

Rub fillets all over with cooking oil and place in baking pan. Dust with paprika to taste and place in oven. Bake until done, about 10 minutes. To serve, pour Creole sauce generously over fillets and garnish with parsley and ⅛ lemon wedge.

CREOLE SAUCE

4 **Tbsp. butter**	1 **cup mushrooms, sliced**
3 **medium onions, chopped coarse**	1 **whole clove**
3 **green peppers, cut into**	1 **cup small green peas**
1-inch julienne strips	1 **cup pimentos, cut into**
2 **garlic cloves, diced**	**1-inch slices**
3 **cups peeled whole tomatoes, diced**	

In the saucepan over medium heat, melt butter and sauté onions and green peppers about 5 minutes. Add diced garlic during last minute of sautéing. Add tomatoes, mushrooms, and clove, bring to a boil, then reduce heat and simmer about 30 minutes. Add peas and pimentos and allow to simmer until tender, about 10 minutes more.

CHICKEN SALAD SANDWICH

1 **boiling chicken, 4½–6 lb.,**	¼ **cup mayonnaise**
cooked and diced	6 **leaves of lettuce**
2 **cups celery, diced**	6 **dill slices**
⅔ **cup mayonnaise**	**prepared mustard to taste**
18 **slices white or whole wheat**	
bread, to taste	

BEFORE YOU BEGIN

You'll need: large mixing bowl, fancy toothpicks
Preparation time: 30 minutes
Yield: 6 servings

Pick white and dark meat off boiled chicken (approximately 4–5 cups of chicken). Chop chicken, add celery, and combine with just enough mayonnaise to hold ingredients together. Each sandwich consists of 3 layers of bread, as desired. Place mayonnaise and lettuce between 2 slices of bread. Place generous portion of chicken salad between second and third slices of bread. Cut sandwich diagonally and serve on lettuce leaf on large plate. Garnish sandwich by placing a slice of dill pickle on top of sandwich and a slice of tomato in front of sandwich in center of the plate facing the guest. Poke toothpick through each section of sandwich to hold together. Serve with prepared mustard on side in original container.

GRILLED HAM STEAK
WITH PINEAPPLE FRITTERS

1 can sliced pineapple in own juice   4 ham slices, ¼ inch thick

Drain pineapple slices, retaining juice. Coat individual ¼-inch thick ham slices liberally with pineapple juice. Place ham slices 5 inches from grill element and grill 3–5 minutes. Turn and coat uncooked side with remaining pineapple juice and return under broiler for another 3–5 minutes.

PINEAPPLE FRITTERS

1 cup flour	**1 egg**
1 tsp. baking powder	**½ cup milk**
¼ tsp. salt	**1 tsp. melted butter**
1 tsp. powdered sugar	**8 slices pineapple**

Sift dry ingredients together in a mixing bowl. Break egg into the center. Add some milk and stir gradually. Continue adding milk only until a fairly thick batter is obtained. Beat well until all lumps have been removed. Stir in the melted butter. Dry pineapple and dip into batter until well coated. Fry in deep, hot grease until browned, about 5 minutes. Drain fritters on a clean paper towel. Serve ham on warm plate with pineapple fritters to the side. Garnish with parsley.

✦ ━◈≳ ✦

OYSTERS IN CREAM STEW

6 oysters in liquor   1 cup heavy cream, hot

In a small saucepan over medium heat, stew oysters in their own juice until they curl, about 8 minutes. Meanwhile, in another small saucepan, heat cream, taking care not to boil. Pour stewed oysters and liquor in hot cream and heat through, but do not let come to a boil. Serve with crackers.

PECAN PIE

¼ cup lightly toasted white bread
    crumbs, crushed fine
¼ cup lightly toasted whole wheat
    bread crumbs, crushed fine
¼ cup butter, room temperature
½ cup sugar
¼ tsp. salt

3 eggs, lightly beaten
2 cups dark Karo syrup
½ tsp. vanilla
1 cup pecan halves
    unbaked 9-inch dessert
      crust pie

BEFORE YOU BEGIN

*You'll need: cookie
sheet, large mixing
bowl, electric beater,
9-inch pie pan
Preheat oven to 225
degrees, increase to
450 degrees after
toasting bread
Preparation time:
1½ hours
Yield: 1 pie*

To make crumbs, remove crust from 2 or 3 slices each of white and whole wheat bread and place in 225-degree oven to dry out thoroughly. Turn occasionally until crisp but not browned. Roll toasted bread fine with rolling pin. Cream butter, then add sugar, salt, and bread crumbs and mix well. Continue beating and slowly add eggs. Then add syrup. Add vanilla last. Pour in unbaked 9-inch pie shell (see page 154) and sprinkle pecan halves evenly over the pie. Place in 450-degree oven for 10 minutes, reduce heat to 350 degrees, and bake for approximately 30 minutes more, or until knife inserted in center comes out clean. Allow to cool slightly before serving.

PRINCESSE SALAD AND VINAIGRETTE SAUCE

The key to success with this salad is to be sure all ingredients are well chilled before assembling.

¼ head lettuce, shredded
1 thick slice tomato
1 6-inch asparagus spear

1 thin strip pimento
1 Tbsp. vinaigrette sauce

BEFORE YOU BEGIN

*You'll need: small bowl
Preparation time:
10 minutes (plus 1
hour to chill ingre-
dients)
Yield: 1 serving*

On individual serving plate, make a bed of shredded lettuce. Top with tomato slice, then asparagus spear, then strip of pimento across the asparagus. Pour vinaigrette sauce over all.

VINAIGRETTE SAUCE

1 onion, chopped fine
1 dill pickle, chopped fine
1 Tbsp. parsley, chopped fine
1 hard-boiled egg white,
    chopped fine

1 hard-boiled egg yolk,
    chopped fine
1½ cups French dressing

Mix all ingredients together and chill well before serving.

SOUTHERN CORN CAKES
WITH SYRUP OR HONEY

2	cups white corn meal	
½	cup white flour	
2	Tbsp. sugar	
1	tsp. salt	

2	tsp. baking powder
2	eggs
1¼	cups milk
	maple syrup or honey

Grease muffin cups all around and set aside. Sift dry ingredients together. Add eggs and milk and beat until a smooth, thin batter forms. Fill greased muffin cups to two-thirds full, taking care not to spill mixture outside cups. Place in oven and bake until light golden brown (a toothpick inserted in the center comes out dry), about 20 minutes. Tip muffins in cups to allow steam to escape. Serve hot on a warmed serving plate with butter and syrup or honey on side.

FRESH STEWED CORN

6	ears fresh corn
1	cup water
1	cup milk

2	Tbsp. bacon drippings
¼	tsp. salt to taste
⅛	tsp. white pepper to taste

Into the saucepan, cut corn from cob using a very sharp knife, taking care to cut off only to about half the depth of the kernels. After cutting all around an ear, use the back of the knife to scrape out remaining juice and pulp, scraping up only, not back and forth. Stir in water and bring to a boil. Cover, reduce heat, and simmer gently for 10 minutes or until tender. Add milk and bacon drippings and simmer 10 minutes longer, until heated through. Add salt and pepper, stir, and serve hot.

SWEET POTATOES AND APPLES

1 lb. sweet potatoes
½ cup butter
1 cup light brown sugar
½ cup water
juice of 1 lemon
1 lb. tart apples

Place sweet potatoes in their skin in large saucepan with water to cover, bring to a boil, and cook until tender, about 25 minutes. Meanwhile, in small saucepan, melt butter over medium heat, add sugar, water, and lemon juice. Bring to a boil, reduce heat, and simmer for 5 minutes. Peel and cut potatoes in half lengthwise. Peel, core, and slice apples thin. Place potato halves and apple slices in baking dish. Pour syrup over all and place in oven until apples are tender, about 30 minutes. Baste with syrup from time to time. Serve hot. Pour syrup left in pan over potatoes and apples when served.

BEFORE YOU BEGIN

You'll need: 3-quart saucepan, 1-quart saucepan, 2-quart baking dish
Preheat oven to 350 degrees
Preparation time: 1¼ hour
Yield: 6 servings

VEGETABLE SOUP

Lest it be thought recipes were cast in stone once distributed to the steward or chef, this recipe reminds: "If fresh peas, string beans, or lima beans, are on car, add some to soup."

1 Tbsp. bacon drippings
1 onion, sliced
1 carrot, sliced
2 cups white turnips, cut into ½-inch dice
2 outside stalks celery, sliced
3 qts. beef, veal, or chicken stock
1 cup diced tomato
salt and pepper to taste
½ Tbsp. chopped parsley

In the large pot over medium heat, melt bacon drippings. Add vegetables and sauté until heated through. Add stock and tomatoes. Bring to a boil, reduce heat, and slow boil until vegetables are done and soup mixture is reduced by one third, about 1 hour. Season to taste, then add chopped parsley. Serve with crackers.

BEFORE YOU BEGIN

You'll need: 8-quart pot
Preparation time: 1½ hours
Yield: 8 servings

22

THE UNION PACIFIC RAILROAD

BARBECUED LAMB SHANKS

BEFORE YOU BEGIN

You'll need: roasting pan, 3-quart saucepan, coarse sieve
Preheat oven to 350 degrees
Preparation time: 2 hours
Yield: 8 servings

3½ lbs. lamb shank
½ cup flour
1 tsp. salt
½ tsp. pepper

1½ tsp. Accent
1 qt. beef stock
Union Pacific barbecue sauce

Remove a little fat from lamb and place in roasting pan to heat in preheated oven. Mix flour, salt, pepper, and Accent to make a coating. Roll the lamb shank in coating and place in roasting pan with hot fat. Brown well in oven. Add stock to a depth of about 3 inches, cover pan, and return to oven to bake for about 1½ hours. Near the end of the cooking period, when the lamb shanks are practically fork-tender and pan stock is well reduced, cover with Union Pacific barbecue sauce and continue baking, basting frequently until the shanks are glazed. Serve with remaining sauce over the meat.

UNION PACIFIC BARBECUE SAUCE

1 28-oz. can crushed tomatoes
4 cups beef consommé
1 28-oz. can tomato puree
4 Tbsp. sugar
4 Tbsp. Worcestershire sauce
4 tsp. chili powder
   juice of 4 lemons
½ cup wine vinegar
½ tsp. cayenne

4 tsp. black pepper
2 large onions, chopped
1 clove garlic, chopped
2 bay leaves
½ tsp. Tabasco sauce
½ lb. butter
4 tsp. dry mustard
4 Tbsp. Accent
4 tsp. salt

In a saucepan, combine all ingredients. Bring to a boil, cover, reduce heat to low, and simmer for 1 hour. Strain through a coarse sieve before using. Refrigerate for no more than one week.

APRICOT PIE

2 lbs. fresh apricots
1 qt. water
¾ cup cornstarch

4 cups sugar
½ Tbsp. salt
dessert pie crust for 2-crust pie

BEFORE YOU BEGIN

*You'll need: large
bowl, small bowl,
2-quart saucepan,
9-inch pie tin*
*Preheat oven to 425
degrees*
*Preparation time:
3 hours*
Yield: 1 pie

Do not peel apricots if they are nicely ripened, as the skins will soften during baking and add to the flavor of the pie. Over a large bowl, wash and carefully slice fresh apricots, retaining any juice formed. Strain retained juice into a small bowl and return apricot slices to large bowl. Dissolve cornstarch in retained cold apricot juice with fingers and let stand 5 minutes. In saucepan, bring water to a boil. Slowly stir cornstarch/apricot juice mixture into boiling water. Stir in sugar and salt until both dissolve. Return to a boil, remove from heat, and pour over the sliced fruit. Mix the two together lightly and let stand until cool. Make a 2-pie crust (see page 154). Line a 9-inch pie tin with pastry. Pour cooled apricot mixture into pastry-lined pie tin. Make a lattice of the top crust. Place in oven and bake for 1 hour, until crust is golden brown.

BARBECUED CRAB

1 lb. crabmeat
¼ clove garlic, minced

dash, salt
1½ cup sauce

BEFORE YOU BEGIN

*You'll need: small
saucepan, small
bowl, individual
small covered casse-
role(s)*
*Preheat oven to 350
degrees*
*Preparation time:
45 minutes*
Yield: 4 servings

Clean and pick over crabmeat to remove any bits of shell or bone. Heat the crabmeat and neatly arrange meat in single small casserole. In a small bowl, make a fresh garlic salt by smashing together the minced garlic and salt, and sprinkle directly over crab. Pour boiling hot sauce over crab. Cover and set in oven to become steaming hot, about 20–30 minutes. To serve, pour hot barbecue sauce from the casserole in which crab was steamed into a separate sauce boat and place alongside individual servings of crabmeat.

SAUCE

1 cup soy sauce
1 cup clear (chicken) consommé
2 cups beef bouillon, made
   of extract of beef

½ tsp. Worcestershire sauce
2 drops Tabasco sauce

In a medium mixing bowl, combine soy sauce, consommé (see page 153), beef bouillon, Worcestershire sauce, and Tabasco sauce. Stir to mix well. Flavor should not be too sharp.

FRINCANDEAU OF VEAL

BEFORE YOU BEGIN

*You'll need: 3-quart saucepan, slotted spoon, holding dish, small saucepan, medium bowl
Preparation time: 1¼ hour
Yield: 8 servings*

2½ lbs. veal for stew, 1 inch cubes	½ cup light cream
3 Tbsp. butter	¼ tsp. celery salt
3-4 Tbsp. flour	¼ tsp. garlic salt
1½ cups veal stock, heated	¼ tsp. white pepper
¼ lemon	4 Tbsp. fresh chopped parsley
4 egg yolks	

Melt butter in the 3-quart saucepan over medium-high heat. In two batches, brown veal cubes in butter until slightly brown all over and remove cubes to a holding dish with a slotted spoon. Meanwhile, heat but do not boil veal stock in a small saucepan. Reduce heat under butter and veal drippings to medium and stir in enough flour to make a rather heavy roux and cook for 3 minutes. Add lemon, return browned veal cubes, cover, reduce heat to low, and simmer until meat is tender but firm, about 45 minutes. Remove from heat. Meanwhile, in a bowl, beat egg yolks and cream. Season with celery salt, salt, and white pepper. Stir a small amount of the heated sauce from cooking veal into the egg/cream mixture. Now, stirring constantly, slowly add egg/cream mixture to cooking veal and heat through but do not boil. Remove the lemon and sprinkle with chopped parsley. Serve with mashed or boiled potatoes.

FRUIT SALAD DRESSING

BEFORE YOU BEGIN

*You'll need: medium mixing bowl, electric beater, airtight container
Preparation time: 15 minutes
Yield: 1 pint*

This dressing, intended for an assortment of fresh fruit, goes just as well on a cold vegetable salad.

1 clove garlic	2 Tbsp. white vinegar
½ Tbs. sugar	1 egg
½ tsp. salt	⅓ cup olive oil
½ tsp. paprika	½ cup salad oil
¼ tsp. dry mustard	¼ cup chili sauce
juice of 1 lemon, strained	

Slice a garlic clove in half and rub the lower half of the bowl with both halves. Place the sugar, salt, paprika, and dry mustard in the bowl and mix thoroughly, stirring around the bowl to absorb garlic flavor. Add the lemon juice, vinegar, and egg and beat vigorously with a whisk or beater until well blended. Continue beating as you slowly add the olive oil and salad oil, alternating a little of each at a time, and blend well together, beating about 15 minutes. Add chili sauce and whip until thoroughly mixed. Place in container and chill until ready to serve.

HOT CHILI ROQUEFORT CANAPÉS

1½ oz. Roquefort cheese, softened
4 oz. cream cheese, softened
1 Tbsp. catsup
1¾ tsp. chili powder
¼ tsp. paprika
1/16 tsp. garlic powder
slices of bread
paprika to garnish

BEFORE YOU BEGIN

You'll need: small bowl, baking sheet
Preheat oven to broil
Preparation time: 30 minutes
Yield: 4 servings

Crumble Roquefort cheese and blend with cream cheese. Add catsup and spices and mix well. Trim crust from bread and toast on both sides. Spread with cheese mixture and cut each piece in 3 strips crosswise. Place on baking sheet and broil 5 inches from heat source until browned and bubbly. Sprinkle paprika lightly over top to finish.

MACARONI AND CHEESE WITH OLIVES

20 oz. macaroni
6 Tbsp. butter
6 Tbsp. flour
1 qt. hot milk
1 Tbsp. prepared mustard
½ Tbsp. Worcestershire sauce
1 tsp. salt
½ tsp. white pepper
1 cup stuffed olives
10 oz. American cheese, shredded
1 cup buttered soft bread crumbs

BEFORE YOU BEGIN

You'll need: 6-quart saucepan, 2-quart saucepan, whisk, 9" x 13" baking dish
Preheat oven to 375 degrees
Preparation time: 1 hour
Yield: 12 servings

Grease baking dish and set aside. Cook macaroni in 4 quarts boiling salted water until tender, about 13 minutes. Drain well and return to saucepan. Meanwhile, in the 2-quart saucepan over medium heat, prepare a cream sauce by melting butter and whisking in flour and hot milk. Add mustard, Worcestershire sauce, salt, pepper, and olives. Slowly stir in cheese and continue to stir until the cheese is melted. Stir into cooked macaroni. Pour into greased baking dish and sprinkle buttered soft bread crumbs over all. Place in oven and bake until bubbly and browned, about 20 minutes.

ORANGE TEA BISCUITS

BEFORE YOU BEGIN

*You'll need: large
bowl, pastry
blender, baking
sheet, small bowl
Preheat oven to 400
degrees
Preparation time:
45 minutes
Yield: 14 2-inch bis-
cuits*

2 cups flour
½ tsp. salt
3 tsp. baking powder
2 Tbsp. finely grated rind
   of orange

¼ cup lard, soft
¾ cup milk, very cold
1 Tbsp. butter, melted
1 Tbsp. sugar
1 Tbsp. grated orange rind

Grease baking sheet and set aside. Sift together the flour, salt, and baking powder. Add 2 tablespoons orange rind and mix thoroughly. Using pastry blender, cut in lard until thoroughly blended and flaky. Add milk, using a spoon, so dough is not made too stiff from excessive handling while mixing. Roll out to ½-inch thickness and cut with a 2-inch biscuit cutter. In a small bowl, mix 1 tablespoon each of grated orange rind and sugar. Brush tops of biscuits with melted butter, then sprinkle with orange rind/sugar mixture. Bake for 20–30 minutes and serve piping hot.

PICKLED SHRIMP WITH ONIONS

BEFORE YOU BEGIN

*You'll need: large
saucepan, large
bowl, colander, cov-
ered 1-quart con-
tainer, small bowl,
whisk
Preparation time:
30 minutes (plus 24
hours to marinate
shrimp)
Yield: 6 servings*

1½ lbs. shrimp, smallest type
¼ cup celery tops
3 Tbsp. mixed pickling spice
½ tsp. salt
½ cup sliced onion
2 bay leaves

½ cup salad oil
½ cup white vinegar
1 Tbsp. capers and juice
1 tsp. celery seeds
3 drops Tabasco sauce
1 tsp. salt

Shell and devein shrimp. Bring 3 quarts water, with celery tops, pickling spices, and salt added, to a boil. Allow to boil 15 minutes, then add shrimp, cover, and cook at a boil 6 minutes. Drain shrimp and plunge into ice water to arrest cooking. Drain shrimp well again. In a covered container, alternate shrimp and onions. Add bay leaves. In a small bowl, whisk together the remaining ingredients and pour over layered shrimp and onion. Chill at least 24 hours. Shrimp pickled in this manner will keep about 1 week in the refrigerator.

POACHED EGGS, SPANISH STYLE
WITH RISOTTO

BEFORE YOU BEGIN

You'll need: egg-poaching pan, medium skillet, 2-quart saucepan, 6-quart stock pot
Preparation time: 2 hours (Spanish sauce can be prepared ahead)
Yield: 1 serving

2 medium eggs, poached
½ cup risotto
¼ cup Spanish sauce

2 dashes paprika
1 slice bread, toasted

Poach eggs (see page 302). On an individual serving plate, arrange two ¼ cup mounds of risotto. Place a poached egg on each mound. Add Spanish sauce on one side of eggs and place toast triangles, crust removed, on the other side. Add a dash of paprika on each egg and garnish with parsley.

RISOTTO

¼ cup finely diced bacon
4 Tbsp. butter
¼ cup finely minced onions
¼ cup finely minced green pepper
¼ cup finely minced celery

¼ cup breast of chicken, diced
¼ cup grated American cheese
3 cups steamed rice
½ cup tomato, diced and drained

In a skillet over medium heat, sauté the bacon moderately crisp. Add butter and allow to melt before adding onions, green pepper, celery, chicken, and cheese. In the 2-quart saucepan, add mixture to 3 cups of boiled rice (see page 153). Add tomatoes. Stir well to mix, reduce heat to low, and simmer for 30 minutes.

SPANISH SAUCE

2 cups onion
1 cup celery
1 cup green peppers
1 garlic clove, minced
¼ cup cooking oil
1 cup bacon or ham
   cut into ¼-inch dice
2–3 Tbsp. flour
2 Tbsp. paprika
8 cups crushed tomatoes
8 cups rich stock

⅛ tsp. celery salt
⅛ tsp. salt
⅛ tsp. white pepper
   dash, cayenne pepper
1 tsp. sugar
2 Tbsp. Worcestershire sauce
1 cup mushroom pieces,
   cooked, drained
¼ cup pimento, diced
½ cup green peas, cooked

Cut onions, celery, and slice and cut green peppers into 1-inch lengths and sliver. In a 6-quart stock pot over medium heat, heat oil and sauté meat, onions, celery, and green peppers until soft, about 5 minutes, adding minced garlic during last minute. Then add enough flour to absorb the grease and make a roux. Cook for 5 more minutes, stirring well and adding paprika. Add tomatoes and stock. Season with celery salt, salt, white pepper, cayenne pepper, sugar, and Worcestershire sauce. Add mushrooms, pimento, and green peas. Reduce heat and simmer for 1 hour.

WALNUT CHICKEN, HONG KONG STYLE

BEFORE YOU BEGIN

*You'll need: two medium bowls, one small bowl, large covered skillet, slotted spoon, small saucepan
Preparation time:
1 hour
Yield: 6 servings*

1½ boneless chicken breasts
1 tsp. salt
2 Tbsp. sugar
3 Tbsp. sherry wine
1 Tbsp. soy sauce
3 Tbsp. cornstarch
⅓ cup salad oil
1 cup blanched walnuts

1 egg, beaten
1 tsp. powdered ginger
2 cloves garlic, minced
¾ cup boiling water
1 tsp. Accent
1 cup canned bamboo shoots, sliced thin

Cut the uncooked chicken into 1-inch strips as for stir-fry. Combine salt, 1 teaspoon sugar, sherry, and soy sauce in a medium bowl. Place chicken in this mixture, stir to thoroughly coat with mixture, and let marinate for 15 minutes. Remove chicken to a separate dish, reserving half of the marinade. Sprinkle cornstarch over chicken strips and mix to coat well. Meanwhile, heat oil in skillet over medium-high heat until it bubbles. Add the walnuts and sauté until they are brown, taking great care not to burn. Using a slotted spoon, remove walnuts and set aside. Dip each piece of chicken in beaten egg. To oil remaining in skillet, stir in the ginger, garlic and chicken and brown well. Slowly add the boiling water, Accent, remaining sugar and retained marinade. Stir to mix, cover and cook over low heat for 10 minutes or until chicken is tender, stirring occasionally. In a separate saucepan, cook bamboo shoots in their own liquid for 10 minutes, then drain well. Add walnuts and bamboo shoots to chicken. Cook at medium heat for five minutes. Serve hot with boiled rice (see page 153).

23

THE WESTERN PACIFIC RAILROAD

HOT CHICKEN TIMBALE
WITH CHEESE SAUCE

1 6-lb. boiling hen, cooked
1 qt. milk, warmed
4 oz. butter, melted
4½ cups bread crumbs

12 eggs
2 Tbsp. chopped parsley
   salt and white pepper to taste
   cheese sauce

BEFORE YOU BEGIN

*You'll need: 2 large
  mixing bowls, 9" x
  13" baking pan,
  10" x 15" (or larger)
  baking pan,
  2-quart saucepan,
  grater*
*Preheat oven to 350
  degrees*
*Preparation time:
  1 hour*
Yield: 12 servings

Butter the 9" x 13" baking pan well and set aside. Remove two pounds of white and dark meat from chicken carcass, dice small, and set aside. In a large mixing bowl, stir warmed milk into melted butter, add bread crumbs, and let stand for 5 minutes. Meanwhile, beat eggs well until of a light lemon color and add chopped parsley. Add diced chicken to beaten eggs, season to taste, and blend together. Then combine with soaked bread crumbs and pour into the buttered baking pan. Place the pan inside a larger pan containing water and bake until firm, about 30–40 minutes. To serve, cut in 3" x 4" squares and serve in individual serving dish with cheese sauce over. Serve piping hot.

CHEESE SAUCE

4 Tbsp. butter
4 Tbsp. flour
3 cups milk, warmed
1 tsp. salt
½ tsp. white pepper

1½ cups Longhorn cheese, grated
¼ tsp. paprika
¼ tsp. dry mustard
1 Tbsp. hot water
1 Tbsp. chopped parsley

In the saucepan over medium heat, make a light roux of butter and flour. Stirring constantly, slowly add hot milk, salt, and pepper, being careful not to brown the roux. Add grated Longhorn cheese and stir until cheese is melted and well blended with sauce. Add paprika and dry mustard which has been creamed in hot water. Season further to taste and use as directed. Garnish with finely chopped parsley.

ARABIAN PEACH SALAD

BEFORE YOU BEGIN

*You'll need: 3 small
plates to roll date
bars in coatings,
grater
Preparation time:
30 minutes
Yield: 4 servings*

2 cups black dates, chopped
   French dressing
⅓ cup pistachio nuts,
   finely chopped
⅓ cup Swiss cheese, grated fine

1 fresh peach
4 romaine leaves
8 pimento strips
4 watercress rosettes

Mold chopped black dates into bars ½-inch square by 1½ inches long. Dip or gently roll bars in French dressing to coat, then roll in finely chopped pistachio nuts and grated Swiss cheese. To serve, peel and cut peach in half, remove the pit, and cut in ¼-slices. Place 1 leaf of romaine on the individual serving plate. Using 3 slices of peaches and 2 bars of dates, alternate peach and date bar, across romaine. Pour a small portion of French dressing over the salad and garnish with a cross of pimento and rosette of watercress.

COCKTAIL SAUCE RAVIGOTE

BEFORE YOU BEGIN

*You'll need: large mix-
ing bowl
Preparation time:
45 minutes (plus 1
hour to chill before
using)
Yield: 1 quart*

3 egg yolks
1 tsp. dry mustard
1 tsp. paprika
½ tsp. salt
½ tsp. sugar
2 cups oil
¼ cup white vinegar
1 cup chili sauce

1 oz. anchovy paste
1 bunch green onions, chopped fine
2 pimentos, chopped fine
2 gherkins, chopped fine
1 Tbsp. parsley, chopped fine
½ cup celery, chopped fine
   salt and pepper to taste

All ingredients must be thoroughly chilled before starting. In the large mixing bowl, combine egg yolks, dry mustard, paprika, salt, and sugar, and beat well. Slowly add oil, beating constantly, until sauce begins to thicken. Then alternately add vinegar and remaining oil, beating constantly. It is finished when it has the consistency of mayonnaise, after about 30 minutes. Add chili sauce and anchovy paste and blend well. Add green onions, pimento, gherkins, parsley, and celery. Season to taste. Serve cold.

CREAMED TUNA FISH
WITH FRIED NOODLES AU GRATIN

½ cup chinese fried noodles
1 6½-oz. can tuna fish, drained
1 cup cream sauce
⅛ tsp. salt
   dash, white pepper

¼ cup bread crumbs
2 Tbsp. Parmesan cheese, grated
½ Tbsp. butter, melted
   dash, paprika

BEFORE YOU BEGIN

You'll need: 2 individual au gratin dishes, 1-quart saucepan
Preheat oven to 375 degrees
Preparation time: 45 minutes
Yield: 2 servings

Butter au gratin dishes all around and arrange fried noodles within. Break drained tuna fish into medium-size flakes. In the saucepan over medium heat, combine flaked tuna, cream sauce, salt, and white pepper and heat through. Pour creamed mixture over noodles, filling the au gratin dish well. Sprinkle bread crumbs over, top with Parmesan cheese, dot with butter, and sprinkle lightly with paprika. Place on top shelf of oven and bake until golden brown and bubbly, about 20 minutes.

DEVILED HAM CANAPÉ

The diamond-shaped green-pepper garnish duplicated the Western Pacific's herald.

1 cup boiled ham, diced fine
½ cup sweet gherkins, diced fine
¼ cup green peppers, diced fine
¼ cup pimento, diced fine
1 Tbsp. Worcestershire sauce
½ tsp. dry mustard
   juice of 1 lemon

¼ cup butter, softened
24 canapé wafers
½ cup butter, softened
   a few drops green food coloring
24 diamond-shaped pieces
   green pepper

BEFORE YOU BEGIN

You'll need: medium bowl, pastry bag
Preparation time: 30 minutes (plus 1 hour to chill before serving)
Yield: 6 servings

In a medium bowl, combine boiled ham, gherkins, green peppers, pimento, Worcestershire sauce, dry mustard, and lemon juice. Add just enough softened butter to bind and work all into a smooth paste. Spread the paste on canapé wafers (or on 6 slices thin buttered toast trimmed of crust and cut into quarters). Garnish the center of each canapé with a diamond-shaped piece of green pepper. Combine ½ cup softened butter and sufficient green food coloring to make green butter. Use a pastry tube to make a very thin border around each canapé with the green butter. Canapé must be kept cool until served.

✦ ❖ ✦

FRESH STRING BEANS SAUTÉ

2 lbs. fresh string beans	**salt and pepper to taste**
4 oz. butter	**pinch, sugar**

Remove strings from beans and cut in 1-inch lengths. Wash them well and let stand for a few minutes in cold water to which a little salt has been added. Meanwhile, in a large saucepan, bring sufficient water to cover beans to a boil. Drain beans and plunge them into the boiling water for 1 minute. Remove and drain the beans immediately and plunge them into a large bowl containing water and ice to cover. Cool, about 5 minutes. Drain and dry beans and set aside. Meanwhile, in a large skillet over medium heat, melt butter but do not allow to brown. Add salt and pepper to taste and a pinch of sugar. Add blanched beans and stir constantly until heated through, about 5 minutes. Serve piping hot.

✦ ❖ ✦

GRILLED SUGAR-CURED HAM STEAK
WITH YORKSHIRE SAUCE

For each serving, use one ¼-inch-thick, 6-ounce slice of sugar-cured ham (see page 268). Place ham slice(s) 5 inches from grill element and grill 10 minutes, turning twice.

YORKSHIRE SAUCE

1 oz. grated orange peel	**½ cup orange juice**
1 qt. Espagnole sauce	**⅓ cup currant jelly**
½ cup port wine	**salt and pepper to taste**

In a small saucepan, boil grated orange peel in water for 5 minutes, drain thoroughly, and discard the water. In the 2-quart saucepan over medium heat, combine Espagnole sauce (page 154), port wine, and orange juice. Work the currant jelly in thoroughly with a whisk. Last, add the boiled grated orange peel. Season to taste and simmer 30 minutes. Serve sauce under ham steak and garnish with sprig of parsley.

SOUTHERN ROAST BEEF HASH

2 lbs. roast beef
2 Tbsp. butter
1 cup onions, diced coarse
½ large green pepper, diced
1 tsp. salt
½ tsp. pepper
1 cup beef stock, heated

1 cup white potatoes, diced
1 15-oz. can diced tomato
¼ clove garlic, minced
pinch, poultry seasoning
2 Tbsp. butter
2 Tbsp. flour

BEFORE YOU BEGIN

You'll need: large skillet, small skillet, small saucepan
Preparation time: 1 hour
Yield: 8 servings

Trim brown crust from cold roast beef, remove bone, and cut in ½-inch cubes. Melt butter in a large skillet over medium heat. Add roast beef cubes, onions, green pepper, and a dash of the salt and pepper. Cover, reduce heat, and slowly sauté until vegetables are almost browned, about 15 minutes. Add a little beef stock from time to time during the cooking to prevent meat from burning, and turn ingredients several times during cooking. Add diced potatoes, cover, and continue slow cooking until potatoes are almost browned. Add tomatoes, minced garlic, poultry seasoning, and remaining salt and pepper. In a small skillet over medium heat, make a dark roux of butter and flour. Heat and add remaining beef stock to roux, stirring constantly. Add thickened stock to other ingredients, stir well, and let simmer for about 25 minutes. Serve piping hot en casserole.

STUFFED CELERY

18 4-inch lengths center stalk celery
6 Tbsp. Roquefort cheese
juice of ½ lemon
1 tsp. Worcestershire sauce

6 Tbsp. cream cheese
1 Tbsp. whipped cream
paprika

BEFORE YOU BEGIN

You'll need: small mixing bowl, fine sieve, pastry bag
Preparation time: 20 minutes (plus 1 hour to chill before serving)
Yield: 6 servings

Wash and dry celery, cut in 4-inch lengths, and trim large ends to a point. In a small bowl, moisten the Roquefort cheese with lemon juice and crumble into small pieces. Add Worcestershire sauce, mix thoroughly, and force through fine sieve. Add the cream cheese and whipped cream and mix into a soft paste. Place in a pastry bag and fill each stalk of celery with the mixture forced through the pastry bag. Sprinkle with paprika and refrigerate before serving.

STUFFED DEVILED EGGS

BEFORE YOU BEGIN

You'll need: medium bowl, pastry bag
Preparation time: 30 minutes
Yield: 4 servings

4	hard-boiled eggs	1	Tbsp. mayonnaise
½	tsp. dry mustard		salt and white pepper to taste
1	tsp. lemon juice		parsley, finely chopped
1½	Tbsp. butter, melted		paprika

Cut eggs in half lengthwise and carefully remove the yolk. In a medium bowl, use a spoon to pound the yolks into a paste. Add dry mustard, lemon juice, melted butter, mayonnaise, salt, and white pepper. Work the yolk mixture into a smooth paste. Place in a pastry tube and refill the whites of the eggs, making a rosette in each. Sprinkle with parsley and paprika. To serve, place neatly on plate or platter. Eggs must be kept cool.

━━◄◆➤━━

WESTERN PACIFIC RICE CREAM PIE

BEFORE YOU BEGIN

You'll need: two 8- or 9-inch pie tins, electric mixer, large mixing bowl
Preheat oven to 425 degrees
Preparation time: 2½ hours (using baked pie crusts)
Yield: 2 pies

1¼	cups rice, uncooked		pinch, salt
4	cups whole milk	⅛	tsp. lemon extract
1¼	Tbsp. cornstarch	⅛	tsp. mace
5	eggs	1	Tbsp. butter, melted
1¼	cups sugar	1	pint whipping cream

Prepare dessert pie crust for 2 single-crust pies (see page 154). Place pie pastry in pie tins and prick bottom and sides frequently with a fork to prevent puffing during baking. Place pie pastry in oven until lightly browned, about 15 minutes. Set aside to cool before using. Now, in a small saucepan, steam rice with 2 cups of milk until rice is soft and milk is absorbed. Meanwhile, dissolve cornstarch in 2 tablespoons cold water. Prepare custard by beating eggs, sugar, and salt in a large mixing bowl at low speed until lemon colored. Slowly add the remaining 2 cups of milk, lemon extract, mace, dissolved cornstarch, and butter. When well mixed, stir in cooked rice with a whip. When custard has thickened, pour into baked pie crusts two-thirds full and refrigerate until set before serving. Serve topped with a dollop of whipped cream.

24

THE FRED HARVEY COMPANY

BRANDY FLIP PIE

At Chicago's Union Station, Chef Adolphe Achenback offered guests this sophisticated variation on a popular dessert. You'll need a cooled baked dessert pie crust (see page 154) to start.

BEFORE YOU BEGIN

*You'll need: small bowl, small mixing bowl, small saucepan, large mixing bowl, double boiler, 9-inch pie pan, potato peeler
Preparation time: 1 hour
Yield: 1 pie*

1 **Tbsp. unflavored gelatin**	1 **Tbsp. sugar**
¼ **cup cold water**	½ **tsp. nutmeg**
4 **egg yolks, lightly beaten**	4 **Tbsp. brandy**
½ **cup sugar**	1 **baked 9-inch pastry shell**
½ **cup milk, scalded**	1 **pint whipped cream, whipped**
4 **egg whites**	**bitter or semi-sweet chocolate**

In small bowl, pour gelatin over cold water and let stand 5 minutes to soften. In double boiler over slow-boiling water, combine egg yolks, ½ cup sugar, and scalded milk. Cook until mixture coats spoon, then remove from heat. Add softened gelatin and stir until dissolved. Chill in refrigerator until mixture is slightly thickened. Meanwhile, beat egg whites stiff with 1 tablespoon sugar, nutmeg, and brandy. In a large mixing bowl, gently fold egg-white mixture into chilled mixture and pour into cooled, baked pie shell. Return to refrigerator and chill until firm. Before serving, top with whipped cream and garnish with chocolate curls. Shave chocolate curls from slightly warmed bitter or semi-sweet chocolate, using the blade of a potato peeler.

---+ ⊨◊⊨ +---

CAULIFLOWER GREENS RESTELLI

BEFORE YOU BEGIN

You'll need: 2-quart saucepan, 1-quart saucepan, colander
Preparation time: 30 minutes
Yield: 4-6 servings

The Harvey-operated restaurant in St. Louis's Union Station first opened in the early 1890s. With few hotels in St. Louis then, the Harvey dining room catered the city's top social and civic affairs. During World War II, more than 1.5 million members of the armed forces ate in the room. Another dining room was reserved in the early days of the station for the thousands of immigrants passing through St. Louis en route to the frontier. Sous Chef Victor Restelli created this memorable dish for patrons of the "upstairs" dining room.

2	tsp. olive oil	½	garlic clove, minced
1	Tbsp. chopped onion	1	1¼-lb. head cauliflower
3	strips bacon, diced		salt to taste
½	cup tomatoes, chopped	¼	cup grated Parmesan cheese
½	cup tomato puree		

In the 2-quart saucepan over medium heat, sauté onion and bacon in olive oil until tender. Do not brown. Add chopped tomatoes, tomato puree, and garlic. Bring to near boil, reduce heat, and simmer until reduced to half, about 20 minutes. Meanwhile, wash cauliflower and separate into small flowerets. Chop good leaves and stems fine. Place cauliflower in the 1-quart saucepan with water to cover, add salt, and bring to a boil. Cook 5 minutes, drain well and add to thickened tomato sauce. Stir to mix well and serve hot, sprinkled with grated Parmesan.

---+ ⊨◊⊨ +---

CHICKEN MACIEL

BEFORE YOU BEGIN

You'll need: large skillet, 2-quart saucepan, 2-quart casserole, grater
Preheat oven to broil (or 400 degrees, if casserole is glass)
Preparation time: 45 minutes
Yield: 8 servings

A favorite from the Westport Room in Kansas City, this dish was created by Chef Joseph Amherd. A fifteen-year veteran with Fred Harvey, Amherd had many fans, including President Truman's daughter Margaret, silent-film star Corrine Griffith, Washington Redskins owner Preston Marshall, and Kansas City Club manager H. J. Fawcett.

1	lb. chicken breast meat, cooked	2	cups boiled rice
¼	lb. butter	1	qt. cream sauce
2	tsp. curry powder		salt and pepper to taste
¼	cup sherry wine	¾	cup grated Swiss cheese

Dice chicken into 1-inch squares. In large skillet over medium heat, melt butter and stir in curry powder and sherry. Add chicken to this mixture and sauté 5 minutes. Meanwhile, cook rice (see page 153). Using a 2-quart saucepan, heat cream sauce (see page 153). Carefully blend chicken and cooked rice into hot cream sauce. Stir carefully until well mixed. Place in casserole, top with grated Swiss cheese, and place under broiler until browned, about 4 minutes, or bake in glass dish at 400 degrees until browned and bubbly, about 10 minutes.

CREAM OF WISCONSIN CHEESE SOUP

BEFORE YOU BEGIN

You'll need: 2-quart saucepan, small skillet, baking sheet
Preheat oven to warm
Preparation time: ½ hour
Yield: 6 servings

This regional specialty, from Chef Stanley Hamilton's St. Louis Union Station restaurant, was a favorite of President Harry S. Truman, a frequent guest.

12 saltine crackers	3 Tbsp. all-purpose flour
1 qt. beef broth	1 Tbsp. Worcestershire sauce
3 cups grated sharp Cheddar cheese	1 cup light cream
3 Tbsp. butter	¼ tsp. white pepper

Place saltines in oven to warm. In the saucepan heat two cups of broth over medium heat. Add cheese, stirring constantly as it melts. Add remaining broth and simmer until smooth. Meanwhile, in small skillet over medium heat, make a roux with butter and flour. When smooth, add to first mixture. Continue stirring as you slowly add cream, Worcestershire sauce, and pepper. Stir constantly at simmer for 15 minutes. Serve with toasted crackers.

FRENCH APPLE PIE WITH NUTMEG SAUCE

BEFORE YOU BEGIN

You'll need: 3-quart saucepan, 9-inch pie tin, small mixing bowl, small saucepan
Preheat oven to 425 degrees
Preparation time: 1 hour
Yield: 1 pie

From Head Baker Henry C. Ibsch in Los Angeles' Union Station, this specialty comes from the days when fresh fruits were not available except during regional growing seasons.

8 cups tart apples	½ cup all-purpose flour
½ cup water	½ cup sugar
1½ cups sugar	⅓ cup butter, room temperature
1 recipe dessert pie crust	a few drops vanilla
1 cup graham cracker crumbs	

Pare and slice apples and place in the saucepan with water to cover. Bring to a boil and cook until tender, about 5 minutes. Add sugar, mixing gently to avoid damaging apples. Using slotted spoon, arrange apples in pie tin lined with pastry. In a small bowl, stir to mix graham cracker crumbs, flour, and sugar. Add butter and vanilla and stir thoroughly with a fork until mixture has a coarse, crumbly texture. Sprinkle the graham cracker topping evenly over apples. Place in oven for 10 minutes, then reduce temperature to 350 degrees and bake for 30 minutes, or until pastry turns light brown. Serve topped with nutmeg sauce.

NUTMEG SAUCE

1 egg yolk	1 cup milk
½ cup sugar	1 tsp. nutmeg

In small saucepan, beat the egg yolk, sugar, and milk together well. Heat to just boiling and remove from heat immediately. Add nutmeg and stir thoroughly.

HOT STRAWBERRY SUNDAE

Chef Joe Maciel was served a sundae made with hot maple syrup and strawberries at the 1934 Chicago World's Fair. Patrons enjoyed his adaptation in the Westport Room of Kansas City's Union Station.

1	**pint strawberries, cut in half**	4 **Tbsp. lemon juice**
4	**Tbsp. Jamaica (dark) rum**	**rind of 1 orange, cut in strips**
¾	**cup strained honey**	1 **qt. vanilla ice cream**

Marinate strawberries in rum one hour. In a small saucepan, slowly bring honey, lemon juice, and orange rind to a boil. Remove the orange rind. Combine strawberry/rum mixture with flavored honey, remove from heat, and serve immediately over vanilla ice cream.

━━◆━◆━━◆━━

LA FONDA PUDDING

New Mexicans who had a sweet tooth could find this favorite dessert at the La Fonda in Santa Fe. It is the invention of Chef Allgaier, based on his background in Continental and American cooking, and it drew raves from locals and travelers alike.

1	**cup finely crushed graham crackers (12)**	½ **tsp. vanilla extract**
3	**egg yolks, well beaten**	1 **tsp. baking powder**
1	**cup sugar**	3 **egg whites, stiffly beaten**
⅛	**tsp. salt**	1 **pint heavy cream, whipped**
½	**cup chopped walnuts**	½ **cup walnuts, chopped**

Crush graham crackers fine using a rolling pin and set aside for later use. Butter bottom and sides of baking pan and set aside. Separate egg yolks from whites. In medium mixing bowl, beat egg yolks until thickened and of a lemon color. Continue beating constantly as you gradually add the sugar. Into the yolk/sugar mixture, fold the graham cracker crumbs, salt, chopped nuts, vanilla, and baking powder. Beat egg whites until light peaks form, then fold into mixture. Pour mixture into baking pan and bake for 45 minutes, until inserted knife blade comes out clean. Remove baking pan to wire rack and let cool for 10 minutes. Remove from pan and cut into 2-inch squares. Serve topped with whipped cream and a sprinkle of chopped walnuts.

PLANTATION BEEF STEW
ON HOT BUTTERMILK BISCUITS

BEFORE YOU BEGIN

*You'll need: 3-quart
saucepan
Preparation time:
3½ hours
Yield: 6 servings*

Many of the foods served to passengers had their origin in the chef's personal history. This stew, which originated long before the Civil War, was passed along to chef John Darden of Fred Harvey's Union Station Restaurant in St. Louis by his grandmother. As a small boy in Auburn, Kentucky, he watched her make it for her family of twenty-five children.

1½ lbs. beef in 1½-inch cubes	1 clove garlic, minced
1 qt. hot water	¼ tsp. fresh ground
2 cups diced potatoes	black pepper
½ cup diced onion	1½ tsp. salt
6 green onions, chopped	6 3-inch biscuits

Place meat and hot water in saucepan, cover, and bring just to a boil. Reduce heat and simmer for 1½ hours. Add 1 cup of diced potatoes, cover, and continue cooking 30–60 minutes, until the potatoes are mushy. Add remaining 1 cup potatoes, onions, and seasonings. Cook until vegetables are tender, about 20–25 minutes. To serve, split a hot buttermilk biscuit (see page 278) and ladle stew over bottom half. Replace top and add stew to suit. You can substitute chicken, veal, pork, or ham for beef to make this stew.

POACHED EGGS À LA REINE, HARLEQUIN

BEFORE YOU BEGIN

You'll need: 1-quart saucepan, 2-quart saucepan or egg poacher, small cup(s), slotted spoon
Preparation time: ½ hour
Yield: 4 servings

This creation of Chef Wolfgang Pschorr was a regular feature at the famous Sunday English breakfast served in the Harlequin Room of the Palmolive Building in Chicago, part of the city's then-new "Magnificent Mile."

4 **Tbsp. butter**	**salt and pepper to taste**
1 **cup mushrooms, finely chopped**	4 **eggs, poached**
1 **Tbsp. shallots, chopped**	4 **slices toast, trimmed round**
3 **Tbsp. flour**	16 **asparagus spears, cooked,**
1¼ **cups light cream, hot**	**warm or cold**
1 **cup chicken breast meat,**	4 **sprigs parsley**
cooked, chopped fine	**pimento strips**
¼ **cup sherry wine**	2 **pitted black olives**

In the 1-quart saucepan over medium heat, melt butter and sauté mushrooms until nearly tender. Add shallots and cook 2–3 minutes longer. Stirring constantly, blend in the flour, then the hot cream, and simmer slowly until smooth and thickened, about 5 minutes. Add chicken, sherry, and seasonings and heat through. Remove from heat. Meanwhile, poach eggs and place on pieces of round toast. Cover each with the chicken/mushroom mixture. Serve garnished with hot or cold asparagus on the side and a sprig of parsley, a strip of pimento, and half a pitted black olive on each egg.

POACHED EGGS

4 **eggs**	**dash, pepper**
1 **qt. water**	1 **Tbsp. white vinegar**
1 **tsp. salt**	

In the 2-quart saucepan, bring water to just below boiling point. Add salt, pepper, and vinegar, and stir. Add eggs one at a time by first breaking each into a cup, then slipping it carefully into simmering water. Swirl water around each egg to make it sink in whirlpool. Cook eggs just below boiling point until white is firm and yolk is covered by film, about 5 minutes. Remove with slotted spoon and drain before using.

RISOTTO PIEMONTAISE

BEFORE YOU BEGIN

You'll need: two 1-quart saucepans
Preparation time:
  35 minutes
Yield: 4 servings

Fred Harvey restaurants served passengers at station stopovers across the entire Santa Fe route. For those who dined before, between, or after trains arrived at or departed Los Angeles's Union Station, Fred Harvey Chef Louis Sognos created this risotto.

4 Tbsp. butter	2½ cups chicken broth
1 small onion, chopped fine	salt to taste
1 cup rice	¼ cup grated Parmesan cheese

In one of the saucepans over medium heat, melt butter and sauté onion until lightly browned. Stirring constantly, add uncooked rice and continue to heat until rice is slightly browned, about 10 minutes. Meanwhile, in another 1-quart saucepan, heat chicken broth to boiling and add salt to taste. When rice is browned, add boiling chicken broth, then cover. Reduce heat to low and simmer until rice is tender and excess liquid has evaporated, 18 to 20 minutes. Either mix the grated Parmesan cheese into the rice before serving or top each serving with the cheese. Serve hot.

ROMAN DRESSING

BEFORE YOU BEGIN

You'll need: 2 small
  mixing bowls, electric beater, airtight
  storage bottle
Preparation time:
  15 minutes
Yield: 1⅔ cups

The piquant flavor of this dressing, created by Chef Stanley Hamilton, enhanced tossed or combination salads in St. Louis's Union Station restaurant.

2½ cloves garlic, chopped	juice of 1 lemon
1½ tsp. salt	⅓ cup Parmesan cheese, grated
1 egg, well beaten	2 tsp. fresh ground black pepper
1 cup salad oil	¾ Tbsp. Worcestershire sauce

In small bowl, crush garlic with salt, set aside. Using electric beater, beat egg well, then begin adding oil slowly. As mixture thickens, alternate adding lemon juice and oil in small amounts, beating constantly. Add cheese, pepper, and Worcestershire sauce. Add fresh garlic salt/mixture. Chill to serve, stored in airtight bottle.

25

THE PULLMAN COMPANY

ASPARAGUS VINAIGRETTE

BEFORE YOU BEGIN

You'll need: medium mixing bowl, 1-quart covered container
Preparation time: 15 minutes (plus 1 hour to chill dressing)
Yield: 1 serving

6 stalks asparagus, cooked and chilled	1 leaf lettuce
	2 Tbsp. vinaigrette dressing

Arrange asparagus on a lettuce leaf. Pour vinaigrette dressing over.

VINAIGRETTE DRESSING

½ cup red wine vinegar	2 Tbsp. parsley, chopped fine
1 cup olive oil	½ tsp. salt
½ cup onions, chopped fine	¼ tsp. fresh ground black pepper
¼ cup capers, chopped fine	pinch, granular sugar
2 Tbsp. chives, chopped fine	pinch, dry mustard

In a medium bowl, stir first six ingredients together in order. Add salt, pepper, sugar, and dry mustard. Mix well. Refrigerate in covered container.

CHILLED SALMON PLATE

BEFORE YOU BEGIN

You'll need: individual serving plate
Preparation time: 10 minutes
Yield: 1 serving

1 6½–7 oz. can salmon	wedge of ¼ lemon
2-3 head-lettuce leaves	½ tsp. capers
2 gherkins	1 Tbsp. mayonnaise

Use only thoroughly chilled salmon which has been drained of packing juices. To serve, cover a chilled serving plate with two or three lettuce leaves. Empty salmon into center of the plate and flake lightly. Garnish with lemon and gherkins cut to fan shape along side. Sprinkle capers on top of salmon. Place ½ cup cole slaw with peppers (see page 306) on lettuce leaf to one side. On the other side, add ½ cup potato salad (see page 171) on which has been sprinkled a little finely chopped parsley or chives. Place mayonnaise separately on lettuce.

CINNAMON BUNS

Chef J. E. Burse, "the Scotch Minstrel," despite being partial to stews and pies, was nonetheless celebrated most for his cinnamon buns. He shared the recipe with Pullman employees in the April 1924 issue of The Pullman News.

8 cups flour	1¼ cup raisins
1 cake yeast	¼ tsp. cinnamon
1 qt. milk	1 Tbsp. ginger
1 egg	¼ tsp. nutmeg
1 cup dark molasses	½ cup brown sugar
½ cup butter, room temperature	

BEFORE YOU BEGIN

You'll need: 2 large bowls, 2-quart saucepan, electric beater, liquid thermometer, spatula, medium mixing bowl, 1 large or 2 small round baking pans
Preheat oven to 350 degrees
Preparation time: 2½ hours
Yield: 18 buns

STEP 1

Grease one large bowl and set aside. In another large bowl, combine yeast with 2 cups flour. Meanwhile, in the saucepan, slowly heat milk to 120 degrees. Using an electric beater set at low speed, gradually beat warmed milk into flour/yeast mixture. Increase speed of beater to medium and beat 2 minutes more, scraping side of bowl with spatula from time to time. Add egg, molasses, and 2 cups more flour and continue to beat 2 minutes more, again cleaning the sides of the bowl with a spatula. Now, using a spoon, stir in enough additional flour, 4–4½ cups, to make a soft dough. On a lightly floured surface, knead dough to smooth elasticity, about 10 minutes. Shape dough into a ball and place in the large greased bowl, turning once to grease top. Cover and let rise in a warm place until doubled in size, about 1 hour.

STEP 2

Grease baking pan(s) and set aside. In a medium bowl, combine butter, raisins, cinnamon, ginger, nutmeg, and brown sugar. Punch down the risen dough and roll out into an 18" x 12" rectangle. Spread butter/spices mixture evenly over the entire surface. Roll up along the 18-inch side of the rectangle and pinch seam to seal. With seam side down, use a sharp knife to cut in slices about 1 inch thick. Arrange rolls, cut side down, in greased baking pan(s), cover, and let rise in a warm place until doubled in size, about 45 minutes. Bake until lightly browned, about 25 minutes. Cool slightly on a wire rack before separating and serving.

COLE SLAW WITH PEPPERS

BEFORE YOU BEGIN

*You'll need: small bowl, wire whisk, large bowl, shredder/grater
Preparation time: 30 minutes (plus 1 hour to chill cole slaw)
Yield: 8 servings*

Pullman-car attendants were encouraged to add different fruits and vegetables, such as carrots, onions, apples, pineapple, or pimentos, to the cole slaw, as the season and circumstance dictated.

½ cup mayonnaise	1 medium head cabbage
1 Tbsp. white vinegar	1 green pepper, ¼-inch diced
½ tsp. sugar	parsley or chives, finely chopped
¼ tsp. salt	8 head lettuce leaves
⅛ tsp. pepper	

In a small bowl, make dressing by combining mayonnaise, vinegar, sugar, salt, and pepper. Mix, using wire whisk, until well blended. Shred fine a cabbage that is very crisp. In bowl sufficient to hold all, toss cabbage, diced green pepper, and dressing. Cover and chill thoroughly before serving. French dressing or ½ cup mayonnaise seasoned with one tablespoon of Maggi seasoning can substitute for dressing. Serve on a crisp lettuce leaf and sprinkle with a little finely chopped parsley or chives.

＋＊≡◆≡＊＋

CRAB GUMBO, SOUTHERN STYLE

BEFORE YOU BEGIN

*You'll need: 3-quart covered saucepan, large skillet, 2-quart saucepan
Preparation time: 2 hours
Yield: 8 servings*

Edward Gauffney, worked for the Pullman Company, for more than forty years, beginning in 1884: first as a car cleaner, then as a porter, then up through the culinary department to chef. Guests enjoying his specialties included President Harding, Marshal Foch, General Pershing, Lillian Russell, Emma Calve, Anna Held, and Nellie Melba.

4 medium-size crabs	4 cups fresh okra, sliced
½ lb. ham, diced	1½ qts. fish stock
¼ cup bacon drippings	½ tsp. salt
2 medium onions, chopped fine	¼ tsp. black pepper
1 large green pepper, diced	⅛ tsp. paprika
1 clove garlic, minced	1 cup boiled rice
6 tomatoes, peeled and diced	

Clean and pick the crabs thoroughly by pulling the backs off and removing bits of bone and shell. Break each in four parts. Wash well in cold water, lay on clean towel to dry. Meanwhile, in the 3-quart covered saucepan over medium heat, melt bacon drippings and add ham. Cover, reduce heat, and braise ham until lightly browned, about 8 minutes. Add onions, green peppers, garlic, tomatoes, and finally the okra. Heat stock just to boil and stir into the mixture. Add the crabs, salt, pepper, and paprika, and let simmer for 1½ hours. Meanwhile, cook rice (see page 153). To serve, place a heaping tablespoon of rice in center of plate, pour gumbo all around, and place a piece of crab on each side of the rice.

GRILLED DOUBLE LAMB CHOP HOT PLATE

This was reported to be the most popular item served in Pullman's cafe cars.

2	¾-inch lamb chops	1	slice white bread, toasted
	salt		iceberg lettuce leaf
2	slices bacon	1	tomato slice, ½-inch thick

BEFORE YOU BEGIN

You'll need: serving plate, chop holders
Preheat oven to broil
Preparation time: 30 minutes
Yield: 1 serving

Leave sufficient fat on lamb chops to grill well. Season lamb chops with a little salt and place on grill dry, 5 inches from heating element. Broil on both sides until chop is medium or well done. Broil bacon until crisp. To serve, place toast in center of serving plate and top with chops. Add chop holders to bones. Place bacon on top of chop. To one side of chops, place ½ cup of hash browned potatoes (see below) and ½ cup serving of peas in butter (see page 309), both to be served very hot. Place tomato slice on crisp lettuce leaf along the other side of the chops. Garnish with a little crisp parsley or watercress.

HASHED BROWNED POTATOES

8	new potatoes	salt and pepper to taste
4	Tbsp. butter	

BEFORE YOU BEGIN

You'll need: 2-quart saucepan, large skillet
Preparation time: 30 minutes
Yield: 8 servings

Place potatoes in the saucepan with salted water to cover. Bring to a boil, reduce heat, and slow boil until just tender, about 20 minutes. Drain and chill potatoes. Peel chilled potatoes and cut to ¼-inch dice. In large skillet over medium-high heat, melt butter. Place diced potatoes in the skillet and season with salt and pepper. Brown, turning occasionally, until potatoes have a golden brown color over all.

ILLINOIS SANDWICH

You'll need: small bowl
Preparation time:
*   5 minutes*
Yield: 1 serving

2   slices rye bread, ⅜-inch thick
    butter to suit
2   lettuce leaves
    ¼-inch slices cold brisket of
    corned beef to taste

1   slice smoked liver sausage,
    ¼-inch thick
2   Tbsp. mayonnaise
2   drops, Gravy Master seasoning

Toast slices of rye bread light brown. Butter lightly. Place crisp lettuce leaf on each slice. Cover one piece of toast with number of slices of cold boiled brisket of corned beef desired. Cover the other piece with smoked liver sausage from which the casing/skin has been removed. Serve with potato salad (see page 171), a generous slice of tomato, and mayonnaise into which a few drops of Gravy Master seasoning has been stirred.

━━━ ❧❖❧ ━━━

OLD-FASHIONED SOUTHERN-STYLE
STRAWBERRY SHORTCAKE

You'll need: sifter,
*   large bowl, pastry*
*   blender, 3-inch bis-*
*   cuit cutter, baking*
*   sheet, small bowl,*
*   small deep bowl*
*   (chilled)*
Preheat oven to 350
*   degrees*
Preparation time:
*   1½ hours*
Yield: 8 servings

5   cups flour
1   tsp. sugar
½   Tbsp. salt
1   Tbsp. baking powder
⅔   cup butter, room temperature
⅔   cup lard, room temperature

4–6 Tbsp. milk
1   pint whipping cream, ice cold
2   Tbsp. sugar
    dash vanilla
2   qts. strawberries
    butter at room temperature

Sift flour four times. Add sugar, salt, and baking powder and sift once more. Using a pastry blender, work the lard and butter into the dry ingredients until of a course mealy texture. Add just enough milk, one tablespoonful at a time, to make a soft dough that is not sticky. On a lightly floured surface, knead smooth. Using a lightly floured rolling pin, roll dough out until ½ inch thick. Cut out 8 biscuits, place on a cookie sheet, and bake until a golden brown, about 20 minutes. While hot, open biscuits, butter well, and close. While biscuits cool, pour the ice-cold whipping cream into thoroughly chilled deep bowl. Whip it until stiff, adding sugar and vanilla to cream after it begins to stiffen, then place in refrigerator to chill. Meanwhile, crush the well-washed berries, retaining 8 large berries for decoration. To serve, put 2 generous tablespoons of berries on the bottom half of each biscuit and top off with 1 tablespoon of whipped cream. Then, top with other half of biscuit, another generous layer of berries, and two tablespoons of whipped cream. Garnish with 1 whole berry in the center of each biscuit top.

PEAS IN BUTTER

¾ cup small peas (canned or frozen), cooked and drained
1 Tbsp. butter

salt to taste
pinch granular sugar

BEFORE YOU BEGIN

You'll need: small saucepan
Preparation time: 10 minutes
Yield: 1 serving

Melt butter in small saucepan over low heat. Add peas and heat through. Add salt and sugar, stir to mix, and serve hot.

SAUTÉ OF CHICKEN À LA MARENGO

Napoleon's cook at the battle at Marengo, the story goes, could find nothing to prepare for the victor's dinner but a chicken, some oil, wine, and mushrooms. No wonder dining-car chefs like Henry Baldwin, a twenty-six-year veteran of the Pullman company, could relate to him. Both were on the move, working in limited space with simple supplies, yet expected, on short notice to produce delicacies guests would boast about later.

BEFORE YOU BEGIN

You'll need: large skillet, small skillet
Preparation time: 1½ hours
Yield: 4 servings

1 3–4 lb. frying chicken
1 cup water
2 Tbsp. olive oil
   dash red pepper
   salt to taste

1 Tbsp. flour
1 Tbsp. butter
½ cup mushrooms, sliced
1 cup sherry wine
1 small can pimentos, chopped

Wash, dry and quarter or otherwise cut the chicken as desired for sauté. In a large skillet over medium heat, combine water, olive oil, a dash of red pepper, salt, and flour. Add chicken pieces. Bring just to boil, reduce heat, cover, and simmer for 1 hour. Meanwhile, in small skillet over medium heat, melt butter and sauté mushrooms. Stir mushrooms, sherry, and pimentos into large skillet. Cover and cook for 15 minutes more. Serve hot on toast.

THE KAIBAB SQUIRREL

Lives only on the north rim of the Grand Canyon.

When it snows, he hides his dark coat under his white tail.

UNION PACIFIC

CHILDREN'S MENU

Menu Served only to Little Girls and Boys

LUNCHEON

30c
Cup of Soup or
Chicken Broth
Mashed Potatoes
With Gravy
Milk or Cocoa

45c
Creamed Chicken in
Mashed Potato Nest
or
Hot Vegetable Plate
with
Mashed Potatoes
Ice Cream
Milk

55c
Cup of Soup or
Chicken Broth
One Broiled Lamb Chop
Mashed Potatoes
Vegetable
Bread and Butter
Ice Cream, Cup Custard
or
Fruit or Jam
Milk or Cocoa

DINNER

35c
Bowl of Bread and Milk
or
Raisin Bread with
Jam
Milk or Cocoa

55c
Cup of Soup
Small Tender Steak
Two Fresh Vegetables
Toast
Jam or Fruit
Milk or Cocoa

A LA CARTE

Grapefruit or Orange Juice	.10	Baby Soup, Cup 10
Pureed Prunes or Apricots	.15	Peanut Butter and Jelly Sandwich 10
Apple Sauce	.10	Chicken Salad Sandwich 20
Sliced Orange	.15	Potatoes 10
Bartlett Pear	.15	Ice Cream 10
Cereals	.15	Chocolate Sundae 10
One Egg, as Desired	.10	

Cup Custard or Fruit
Jello with Cream 10

SPECIAL VEGETABLES
Pureed Spinach 15
Puree of Carrots 15
Puree of Peas 15
Strained Tomatoes 15

The Union Pacific's Kaibab Squirrel menu entertained, informed and offered foods of interest to the child. (COURTESY OF THE UNION PACIFIC MUSEUM)

Fresh Bread

The Chef's an earnest, busy man,
As we will try to show
He needs fresh bread for every meal,
That's why he kneads the dough

He raises it, he bakes it,
He serves it to you hot,
So, tho he makes fresh bread in loaves,
Fresh loafer he is not

Attending to children, that "next generation of ridership," was a specialty of the dining car crew. (COURTESY OF GREAT NORTHERN RAILWAY COMPANY RECORDS, MINNESOTA HISTORICAL SOCIETY)

(COURTESY OF CRAIG AND MARTY NEROS)

FOR THE CHILDREN

When children rode the train, special efforts were made to add to their dining pleasure. It might begin with the steward, cookie jar in hand, passing through the train handing out complimentary between-meal snacks. When he seated children in the dining car, he might hand each one a peppermint stick. The colorful children's menu, sometimes with a happy story or interesting facts included, often named the meals to enhance the fantasy children experienced when traveling by train. So chicken soup, a broiled lamb chop, mashed potatoes, carrot sticks, and ice cream became the "Engineer's Special Dinner." Children's mealtime favorites included spaghetti, a broiled hamburger with French fried potatoes, and French toast. A child could also receive a reduced portion from the adult menu for half price. Every effort was made to insure that all children ate and enjoyed their meals, and that memories of the experience lingered with them. They were, after all, the next generation of ridership.

These easy-to-prepare favorites can introduce a child to cooking and to the history of riding on a train. First, this recipe from the St. Louis Southwestern Railway Lines, nicknamed the Cotton Belt Route:

(PRINTED BY PERMISSION OF THE NORMAN ROCKWELL FAMILY TRUST, COPYRIGHT © 1946, THE NORMAN ROCKWELL FAMILY TRUST)

HOT COCOA

This recipe can be increased arithmetically to accommodate any number of children. Prepared in this manner, the Dining Car Department superintendent declared, a rich hot cocoa that had not turned "black."

1½ Tbsp. cocoa	condensed milk
2½ Tbsp. sugar	2 cups cold milk

In a small bowl, stir cocoa and sugar together until well mixed. Add only enough condensed

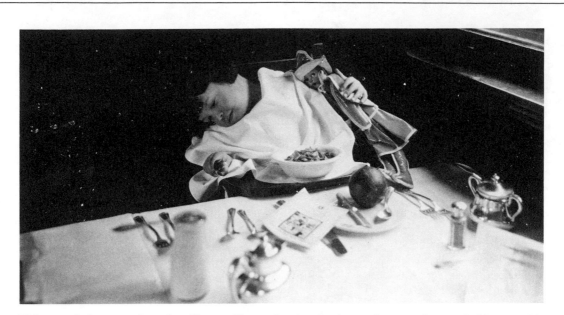

This young lady may not have found her meal interesting, but she gives testimony to the smooth ride one could expect on the Great Northern's Empire Builder. (COURTESY OF GREAT NORTHERN RAILWAY COMPANY RECORDS, MINNESOTA HISTORICAL SOCIETY

milk to make a smooth paste. Add 1 cup of cold milk, stirring thoroughly. Add the second cup of cold milk and stir again. Pour into a saucepan and place over medium-high heat. Bring just to a boil, stirring occasionally. Reduce heat and simmer for 2–3 minutes. Pour into a mug with 2 large marshmallows floating on top and serve hot.

A traditional favorite from the Western Pacific Railroad:

CINNAMON TOAST

2 Tbsp. powdered sugar	4 slices toasting
2 Tbsp. butter, softened	bread
½ Tbsp. ground	1 Tbsp. butter,
cinnamon	at room
	temperature

Preheat oven to 350 degrees. In a small bowl, use a fork to blend sugar and 2 tablespoons of butter together well. Blend in the cinnamon.

Toast bread and spread lightly and equally with 1 tablespoon of butter. Spread 1 tablespoon of mixture evenly on each piece of toast and place in the oven for 5–7 minutes.

And from the deep South, this special treat from the Illinois Central Railroad:

ORANGE PRALINE TOAST

1 cup brown sugar	½ cup chopped pecans
¼ cup fresh orange	8 slices toasting bread
juice, strained	2 Tbsp. butter, room
1 Tbsp. grated orange	temperature
rind	

Preheat oven to 400 degrees. In a small bowl, combine well the brown sugar, orange juice, orange rind, and chopped pecans. Toast the bread slices, then butter lightly. Spread one tablespoon of the praline mixture on each piece of toast. Place toast on an ungreased baking sheet and put in oven until sugar melts.

26

MISCELLANEOUS RAILROADS

THE ALASKA RAILROAD

SOURDOUGH PANCAKES

BEFORE YOU BEGIN

STEP 1: SOURDOUGH STARTER

½ tsp. dry yeast
2 cups warm water
  (heated to 100–140 degrees)

2 cups flour
1 tsp. salt
3 Tbsp. sugar

You'll need: 4-quart container with loose-fitting lid, small bowl, large mixing bowl, pancake griddle
Preparation time: 2–4 days
Yield: 6 servings

In a small bowl, dissolve the dry yeast in the water. In the 4-quart container, stir together the flour, salt, and sugar. Add yeast/water mixture and continue stirring until a smooth thin paste forms. Cover loosely and set in a warm place for 2–3 days to sour, stirring mixture several times a day.

STEP 2: BATTER

sourdough starter
2 cups flour
1 Tbsp. sugar

½ tsp. salt
2 cups water (approximately)

The night before making pancakes, stir flour, sugar, salt, and water into starter to form a thick paste. Return lid and let sit overnight. The mixture will thin down. In the morning pour enough dough for pancakes into a bowl, leaving at least one cup of sourdough starter in the pot. Return lid to starter container and refrigerate until needed for a new batch of batter. *(Continued on next page.)*

2 level Tbsp. sugar	1 egg, lightly beaten (optional)
1 tsp. salt	1 tsp. baking soda
3 Tbsp. bacon drippings, melted	1 Tbsp. water

To use the sourdough batter, add sugar, salt, bacon drippings, and egg if desired. Mix well. If the dough seems too thick, add a little more water. Meanwhile, dissolve baking soda in water. Fold soda mixture gently into the batter. Do not stir after adding soda mixture. Bake on a hot greased griddle. NOTE: Tough pancakes call for less sugar next time.

THE BALTIMORE & OHIO RAILROAD

BAKED STRING BEANS WITH MUSHROOMS

BEFORE YOU BEGIN

You'll need: 2-quart saucepan, colander, 12-inch skillet, small saucepan, 2-quart baking dish
Preheat oven to 375 degrees
Preparation time: 45 minutes
Yield: 6 servings

All railroad workers carried tools. The chef's tool kit consisted of his knives. He carried them in their own canvas satchel, kept them sharp, and took them with him from assignment to assignment. And it takes a sharp knife to safely sliver green beans on board a train moving at more than eighty miles an hour for this specialty side dish of the B & O.

½ lb. string beans, slivered	1 cup milk, warmed
1 Tbsp. butter	2 oz. buttered bread crumbs
½ lb. mushrooms, peeled and sliced	salt to taste
½ Tbsp. flour	

In saucepan, bring to a boil sufficient water (salted if you desire) to cover the beans. Place beans in boiling water, return to a boil, and cook until tender, about 6 minutes. Drain well in colander. In the large skillet over medium heat, melt butter and sauté mushrooms until soft. Add flour to make a roux, stirring constantly to avoid lumps. Continue stirring as you slowly add milk. Cook until thickened, stirring occasionally. Add beans and mix well. Pour mixture into baking dish, sprinkle bread crumbs on top, and bake until bread crumbs are browned and all is heated through, about 20 minutes.

CRAB IMPERIAL À LA GRADY

BEFORE YOU BEGIN

You'll need: small skillet, medium mixing bowl, three crab shells or individual baking dishes
Preheat oven to 325 degrees
Preparation time: 1 hour
Yield: 3 servings

In 1959, then–Mayor Harold Grady of Baltimore participated in a Fourth of July ceremony where B & O passenger trains departed Baltimore flying new forty-nine-star American flags. On July 9, a novel salute from the railroad to Pat Grady, the mayor's wife, included featuring her picture on the Capitol Limited's *dinner menu and offering this favorite recipe of hers as an entree.*

1 Tbsp. butter	1 heaping Tbsp. mayonnaise
1 Tbsp. chopped green pepper	2 Tbsp. heavy cream
1 Tbsp. chopped celery	dash, dry mustard
1 egg, well beaten	salt and white pepper to taste
1 lb. backfin crabmeat	

In small skillet over medium heat, melt butter and sauté green pepper and celery until just tender. In mixing bowl, beat egg. Clean and pick over crabmeat to remove any bits of shell. Add sauteed vegetables and remaining ingredients, stirring thoroughly to mix well. Place mixture in three crab shells or small baking dishes and bake in oven for 30–35 minutes, until brown.

GOURMET SAUCE

BEFORE YOU BEGIN

You'll need: 1-quart saucepan
Preparation time: 15 minutes
Yield: 2 cups

The Baltimore & Ohio used this specialty sauce on baked ham, baked spareribs, and barbecued dishes. It can also dress up leftover beef, pork, or ham, and is delicious on meat loaf.

3 Tbsp. butter	⅛ tsp. salt
⅓ cup minced onion	⅓ cup lemon juice
1 cup catsup	½ cup water
2 Tbsp. brown sugar	2 Tbsp. Worcestershire sauce
2 tsp. prepared mustard	

Melt butter in saucepan over medium heat and sauté the onions until they are tender but not brown, about 5 minutes. Stir in all other ingredients and mix well. Increase heat and bring just to a boil. Reduce heat, cover, and let simmer for 10 minutes.

CORN BREAD PIE

BEFORE YOU BEGIN

*You'll need: large
skillet, 2-quart
casserole, medium
mixing bowl
Preheat oven to 350
degrees
Preparation time:
1 hour
Yield: 8 servings*

The Baltimore & Ohio claimed that passengers would continue past their station stops in order to have a second helping of this specialty corn creation. It was one of the most popular items with both men and women.

1 lb. ground beef	¾ tsp. black pepper
1 large onion, chopped	1 Tbsp. chili powder
1 can tomato soup, condensed	½ cup green peppers, diced
2 cups water	1 cup whole-kernel corn (fresh,
1 tsp. salt	frozen, or canned), drained

Combine beef and onion in the large skillet and brown over medium heat. Add soup, water, seasonings, green pepper, and corn, stirring to mix well. Simmer for 15 minutes. Grease the casserole and fill no more than three-quarters full with meat mixture to leave room for the corn bread topping.

CORN BREAD TOPPING

¾ cup cornmeal	1½ tsp. baking powder
1 Tbsp. sugar	1 egg, beaten
1 Tbsp. flour	½ cup milk
½ tsp. salt	1 Tbsp. fat, melted

Sift the first 5 (dry) ingredients together. Add beaten egg and milk. Stir lightly and fold in melted fat. Pour corn bread topping over the meat mixture and bake for 18–20 minutes. The topping disappears into the meat mixture, only to rise during baking to form a flavorful layer of corn bread.

+ ═◆═ +

MARYLAND CRAB CAKES

BEFORE YOU BEGIN

*You'll need: mixing
bowl, large skillet
Preparation time:
45 minutes
Yield: 3 servings*

The discovery of these two recipes provides the opportunity to compare an on-train chef's personalization of an original recipe found in the B & O's Dining Car Department food service manual. Here are Chef George Fulton's adaptation and the Baltimore & Ohio's standard recipe for a popular regional specialty.

FULTON'S OWN MARYLAND CRAB CAKES

1 lb. crabmeat	few sprigs parsley, chopped
2 slices bread	few drops Tabasco sauce
1 egg	few drops Worcestershire sauce
1 Tbsp. mayonnaise	salt and white pepper to taste
1 tsp. dry mustard	

Clean and pick over crabs to remove any bits of shell. Trim bread of crust, and dice bread into small pieces. In a bowl, combine egg, mayonnaise, mustard, parsley, Tabasco sauce, Worcestershire sauce, salt, white pepper, and diced bread. Using hands or a fork, mix until ingredients form a paste. Fold crabmeat into mixture. Shape mixture into 6 or 7 individual cakes. In a large skillet over high heat, fry cakes in hot cooking oil about 5 minutes until browned, turning once.

B & O'S MARYLAND CRAB CAKES

1 slice white bread	1 tsp. white pepper
1 lb. crabmeat	1 Tbsp. mayonnaise
1 level Tbsp. dry mustard	1 egg, well beaten
¾ Tbsp. salt	

This recipe called for soaking the bread in water, squeezing it dry, and breaking it into small pieces. From that point, instructions were identical. The railroad did warn personnel to be careful not to break up the larger lumps of crabmeat, especially when forming the individual cakes.

OYSTER PIE

The Baltimore & Ohio operated in territory known for the finest oysters in the world. This renown led to a number of specialty dishes featuring oysters, and dining-car personnel were reminded to uphold the tradition by preparing the oysters with utmost care. To complete this main course, you'll need a thin flaky meal dish pie crust (see page 155).

¼ cup butter	2 potatoes, diced
½ cup flour	1 Tbsp. chopped parsley
½ cup milk	4 Tbsp. grated onion
½ cup oyster liquor	2 tsp. green pepper, finely chopped
1 pint oysters	dash, Tabasco sauce
4 carrots, diced	salt and pepper to taste

BEFORE YOU BEGIN

You'll need: large saucepan, small saucepan, oven-proof casserole
Preheat oven to 375 degrees
Preparation time: 45 minutes
Yield: 4 servings

In a large saucepan over medium heat, make a roux of the butter and flour. Add milk and oyster liquor, stirring until a fairly thick cream sauce forms. Put oysters in the sauce and cook over very low heat until the oyster edges begin to curl. Meanwhile, boil carrots and potatoes until tender, about 10 minutes. Drain and add them to the sauce. Add parsley, onion, green pepper, Tabasco sauce, salt and pepper. Stir to mix well and heat through. Put this filling in a deep casserole. Top with pie crust and place in oven for about 20 minutes, until crust is brown and filling bubbly.

✦—✦ ✕◈✕ ✦—✦

PORK CHOPS NORMANDY

BEFORE YOU BEGIN

*You'll need: baking
dish, meat ther-
mometer*
*Preheat Oven to 350
degrees*
*Preparation Time:
1 hour 45 minutes*
Yield: 3 servings

*The delicious flavor of this popular specialty, imparted by the apples, cider, and spices,
set it apart from the average pork chop dinner. The pork chops should be lean and from
the rib end. The Baltimore & Ohio's on-train chefs were known to substitute brown
sugar and a dot of butter on each pork chop for the ground clove, cinnamon, and nutmeg. Serve with the Southern's Sweet Potatoes and Apples (see page 283) and the Chesapeake & Ohio's French-Style Peas (page 196).*

3 pork chops, each 1¾-inches thick	ground clove to suit
salt and pepper to taste	ground cinnamon to suit
2 cups apple cider	ground nutmeg to suit
1 tart cooking apple, sliced thin	1 Bay leaf

Grease a baking dish of appropriate size. Place pork chops in baking dish. Season with salt and pepper. Pour cider over chops until it is level with their tops.
Arrange apple slices on the chops. Sprinkle apple slices with clove, cinnamon,
and nutmeg. Put a Bay leaf in the cider. Bake about 1½ hours, until lightly
browned on top and internal temperature reaches 170 degrees.

✦—✦ ✕◈✕ ✦—✦

SHIRRED SLICED TURKEY
WITH ASPARAGUS SUPREME

BEFORE YOU BEGIN

*You'll need: 3-quart
saucepan, medium
skillet, 2-quart
saucepan*
*Preheat oven to 300
degrees*
*Preparation time:
30 minutes*
Yield: 1 serving

¼ lb. turkey breast meat, cooked and sliced	4 asparagus spears, cooked
	½ cup Sauce Supreme

In a buttered shirred egg dish, place asparagus spears. Place slices of white and
dark turkey meat atop the asparagus. Pour Sauce Supreme over and place in warm
oven until ready to serve.

SAUCE SUPREME

¼ lb. butter, melted	1 Tbsp. butter
½ cup flour	4 oz. sherry wine
¼ lb. sliced mushrooms	1½–2 qts. milk

In the 3-quart saucepan over medium heat, make a light roux of the ¼ pound
butter and flour. Meanwhile, in a medium skillet over medium heat, melt the 1
tablespoon butter and sauté mushrooms until tender. Add sherry and simmer until sherry reduces by one half. Place this mixture to the side while you bring milk
to boil in the 2-quart saucepan. Add hot milk to the roux gradually, stirring constantly until mixture thickens. Let simmer for about 5 minutes, then strain
through a fine sieve and add mushrooms and sherry wine mixture. Stir until mixed
well.

THE BOSTON AND MAINE RAILROAD

BOSTON AND MAINE
NEW ENGLAND CLAM CHOWDER

2 qts. clams
¼ lb. fat salt pork, diced very fine
1 large onion, chopped fine
½ cup flour

2 qts. scalded milk
2 cups russet potatoes,
   cooked and diced
salt and pepper to taste

BEFORE YOU BEGIN

*You'll need: 6-quart
  saucepan, large
  skillet, strainer,
  3-quart saucepan
Preparation time:
  1 hour
Yield: 8 servings*

Clean and pick over clams to remove any bits of shell. Chop hard parts of clams fine and soft parts coarse. Place clams in the 6-quart saucepan with water to cover. Bring to a boil, reduce heat, and cook about 15 minutes. Strain off and save 1 cup of the juice. Meanwhile, fry salt pork in large skillet over medium heat. Then add onion and sauté until soft but not browned, about 5 minutes more. Strain fat into clean 6-quart saucepan, retaining salt pork and onions. Make a roux of fat and flour, stirring constantly until smooth. Meanwhile, in a 3-quart saucepan, bring milk to scald. Slowly add scalded milk to the roux, stirring constantly until mixture thickens. Increase heat to medium-high and bring to a boil for 2 minutes, stirring constantly to prevent burning. Add chopped clams, juice, pork, onion, and potatoes. Season with salt and pepper to taste and simmer until heated through.

THE CENTRAL OF GEORGIA RAILWAY

BEFORE YOU BEGIN

*You'll need: large
saucepan, small
saucepan, baking
dish
Preheat oven to 375
degrees
Preparation time:
1 hour
Yield: 4 servings*

HONEYED SWEET POTATOES, CENTRAL OF GEORGIA STYLE

4 sweet potatoes, boiled	¼ cup honey
¼ cup butter	¼ cup water
¼ cup sugar	

In water to cover, boil the potatoes until cooked through, approximately 25 minutes. Peel cooked potatoes and cut in half lengthwise. Arrange potato halves in a single layer in a baking dish. Meanwhile, in the small saucepan, heat butter, sugar, honey, and water to a boil. Reduce heat and simmer until a thin syrup forms, about 10 minutes. Pour syrup over potatoes. Bake uncovered until most of the syrup has been absorbed, about 30 minutes. Baste potatoes with syrup occasionally during baking.

THE CHICAGO, INDIANAPOLIS AND LOUISVILLE RAILWAY

BEFORE YOU BEGIN

*You'll need: 8-quart
roasting pan, meat
thermometer, small
saucepan, small
skillet
Preheat oven to 325
degrees, then to broil
Preparation time:
15 minutes (to cook
and cool roast, add 5
hours)
Yield: 12 servings*

HOOSIER GRILLED ROAST BEEF, MONON STYLE

1 5-lb. standing rib roast of beef	2 stalks celery, sliced
salt and pepper to taste	⅓ cup water
2 medium carrots, sliced	¼ lb. butter
2 medium onions, chopped coarse	

Sprinkle roast with salt and pepper and insert meat thermometer into thickest part, making sure it is to the center of the roast and not resting on bone or fat. Place in the 8-quart roasting pan and add carrots, onions, and celery around the roast. Place in oven and roast rare, to an internal temperature of 140 degrees, about 2¼ hours. Remove to cool. Strain and save juice from roast. Refrigerate roast to chill thoroughly. To finish, remove and discard fat from juices. Place juices in a small saucepan over medium-high heat. Add water and heat to simmering, stirring and mashing browned bits until dissolved. Keep juice warm. Meanwhile, melt butter in small skillet. Slice beef to desired thickness, season to taste, and drizzle butter over. Place under hot broiler to brown quickly on each side. Serve covered with hot meat juice.

ROQUEFORT DRESSING À LA EARL

Two tests were applied to this dressing: one, that the mayonnaise taste was eliminated (achieved by the addition of sugar); the other, that enough Worcestershire sauce was added to give it the proper zest. Preparation therefore calls for frequent tasting to insure the dressing achieves its goal: a full Roquefort flavor and "bite."

½ lb. Bleu cheese, at room temperature	½ cup French dressing
1½ cups mayonnaise	sugar
2 cloves garlic, chopped fine	Worcestershire sauce
juice of 1 small lemon	Roquefort cheese, crumbled

Using a fork, slowly work softened cheese into the mayonnaise. Then, separately, add garlic, lemon juice, and French dressing, blending each well into the mixture. Place in a sealed container and let stand overnight. Add sugar as necessary to remove the taste of the mayonnaise, taking care that only enough sugar is used to kill the mayonnaise taste. Do not sweeten the dressing. Add Worcestershire sauce until desired "bite" is achieved. Just before serving, sprinkle crumbled Roquefort on top of dressing after it is on the salad.

BEFORE YOU BEGIN

You'll need: small mixing bowl, sealed storage container
Preparation time: 15 minutes (plus time allowing dressing to stand overnight)
Yield: 1 quart

MONON ROUTE

SOUR-CREAM SALAD DRESSING

2 tsp. salt	2 Tbsp. lemon juice
2 Tbsp. sugar	4 Tbsp. white vinegar
¼ tsp. cayenne pepper	2 cups sour cream

In small bowl, combine dry ingredients well. Add liquids one at a time, mixing each thoroughly. Refrigerate before serving.

BEFORE YOU BEGIN

You'll need: small bowl, airtight container
Preparation time: 15 minutes (plus 1 hour to chill before use)
Yield: 3 cups

THE CHICAGO & NORTH WESTERN RAILWAY SYSTEM

CHICKEN MOUSSE

BEFORE YOU BEGIN

*You'll need: two small bowls, 2-quart saucepan, 2-quart mold, 12-inch cheesecloth square
Preparation time: 6 hours
Yield: 6 servings*

1 oz. unflavored gelatin
1 cup cold water
5 cups chicken broth highly seasoned
2 egg whites, beaten stiff
juice of 1 lemon
1 pint heavy cream

pinch, cayenne pepper
pinch, paprika
salt to taste
3 cups cooked white and dark chicken, diced fine
18–24 asparagus tips
1 large ripe avocado

Place mold in freezer. Bring 5 cups chicken broth to a boil, reduce heat and simmer until reduced to 3 cups. Soak gelatin in cold water 5 minutes. In the saucepan over low heat, dissolve gelatin mixture in hot chicken broth. Add beaten egg whites and lemon juice. Increase heat to medium and stir occasionally until a curdlike mass forms and broth just reaches the boiling point. Set aside for a few minutes, then strain through a cheesecloth. When liquid has cooled, but is still a liquid, pour sufficient quantity into chilled mold and swirl to let it run about entire mold and congeal into a thin coat. Place in refrigerator to set firm. Meanwhile, beat whipping cream until firm. To remaining cooled broth mixture; add cayenne pepper, paprika, salt, and chicken. Stir to mix, then pour into mold. Return mold to refrigerator and chill thoroughly. To serve, briefly dip mold into hot water, then turn out quickly. Slice and serve accompanied by 3–4 asparagus tips and slices of avocado.

HAWAIIAN SALAD

BEFORE YOU BEGIN

*You'll need: small mixing bowl
Preparation time: 15 minutes
Yield: 2 servings*

1 cup pineapple, shredded
sugar to taste
⅓ cup grated coconut

2 Tbsp. mayonnaise
1 Tbsp. peanuts, chopped fine

Cut up, shred, and drain fresh pineapple well. Add sugar to sweeten slightly. NOTE: If canned pineapple is used, omit sugar. Add coconut and mayonnaise and mix thoroughly. Serve on crisp lettuce leaves topped with peanuts.

SALAMAGUNDY SALAD

BEFORE YOU BEGIN

You'll need: small mixing bowl, covered container, large mixing bowl
Preparation time: 30 minutes (plus one hour for dressing to chill)
Yield: 8 servings

2 cups cooked ham, diced
½ cup potatoes, cooked and diced
½ cup carrots, cooked and diced
½ cup fresh peas, cooked
½ cup string beans, cooked
½ cup dressing

½ cup sweet pickles, chopped
2 hard-boiled eggs, chopped fine
1 cup mayonnaise
24 beet slices, cooked

Place ham and the vegetables in a bowl with the dressing and let stand for 20 minutes. Then add pickle, eggs, and mayonnaise and mix well together, taking care not to mash the vegetables. Arrange on crisp lettuce leaves and decorate with beets cut to a diamond shape.

DRESSING

¼ cup salad oil
¼ cup white vinegar
     salt and pepper to taste

pinch, dry mustard
1 medium onion, minced

Combine all ingredients well, cover, and chill before using.

STUFFED PRUNE SALAD

BEFORE YOU BEGIN

You'll need: small mixing bowl
Preparation time: 30 minutes
Yield: 6 servings

24 prunes, cooked
1 3-oz. pkg. cream cheese
½ cup cottage cheese
1 cup chopped walnuts

½ tsp. salt
½ cup mayonnaise
½ tsp. lemon juice, strained

When prunes have cooled, make one incision with a very sharp knife and lift out the stone. In a small bowl, combine cream cheese, cottage cheese, chopped walnuts, and salt. Moisten mayonnaise with lemon juice and add to filling mix. Stir to mix thoroughly. Fill prunes with the mixture. Serve on a bed of lettuce with a dollop of mayonnaise on the side.

THE CHICAGO, ROCK ISLAND
& PACIFIC RAILWAY

APPLE FRITTERS IN RED WINE SAUCE

BEFORE YOU BEGIN

You'll need: large mix-
ing bowl, large skil-
let, 2-quart
saucepan
Preparation time:
45 minutes
Yield: 6 servings

3 **Granny Smith apples**   **wheat cake batter**
   flour to coat

Peel and core apples and cut in ½-inch slices. Draw both sides through flour and dip in wheat cake batter. Fry in large skillet in shallow hot grease until golden brown. Remove to drain on a warming platter until ready to serve. Serve three apple fritters with a generous portion of wine sauce ladled onto each serving.

WHEAT CAKE BATTER

2 **eggs, lightly beaten**   4 **cups flour**
1 **Tbsp. sugar**   1 **Tbsp. baking powder**
½ **Tbsp. salt**   1 **Tbsp. butter, melted**
2 **cups milk**

In a large bowl, beat eggs until of light lemon color. Continue beating and add sugar and salt and continue beating until of uniform color. Slowly add milk, then flour, baking powder, and butter. Mix thoroughly until smooth.

RED WINE SAUCE

2 **cups Burgundy or claret wine**   1 **whole clove**
2 **cups water**   3 **inches lemon peel**
1 **cup sugar**   1 **oz. arrowroot powder**
½ **stick whole cinnamon**   ¼ **cup cold water**

Combine first six ingredients in the 2-quart saucepan and bring to a boil. Meanwhile, use fingers to dissolve arrowroot powder in water and set aside. Stir arrowroot mixture into wine sauce, reduce heat, and simmer 30 minutes. Strain before serving.

BONELESS BREAST OF CHICKEN, HAWAIIAN STYLE

BEFORE YOU BEGIN

You'll need: small bowl, large skillet, sieve
Preheat oven to Warm
Preparation time: 30 minutes
Yield: 1 serving

The Rock Island Line connected Chicago with Denver, Minneapolis, St. Louis, Kansas City, Houston, Little Rock, and Oklahoma City. It achieved early notice when it built the first railroad bridge across the Mississippi River (in 1856). It shocked other western railroads by being the first to add dining cars to its first-class trains. And it nearly traumatized its competitors when it proposed giving away the meals served in those cars. The railroad's crack passenger trains, The Rockets, *carried enough food in the dining car for a round trip.*

8 oz. boneless breast of chicken	1 thin slice baked ham
salt and pepper to taste	1 pineapple ring
flour to coat	1 slice white bread toast, crust
2 Tbsp. butter	removed, cut diagonally

Season chicken with salt and pepper, then dredge in flour to coat. In a large skillet over medium-high heat, melt butter and sauté chicken, turning occasionally, until golden brown, about 10 minutes. Remove from frying pan, leaving drippings. In drippings, fry ham slice until heated through. Remove from pan, again leaving drippings. Sauté pineapple slice in drippings until warmed. Remove from pan and save remaining drippings for sauce. Assemble by placing toast on plate, and topping with ham slice, pineapple slice, then chicken breast. Keep assembled serving warm while sauce is prepared.

SAUCE

drippings	dash, sherry wine
2 Tbsp. butter	2 Tbsp. heavy cream
2 Tbsp. sliced mushrooms	

Over medium heat, add butter to the retained drippings and allow to melt. Add mushrooms, sherry, and cream. Slowly bring to a boil and remove from heat. If you so desire, remove mushrooms, strain sauce through fine sieve, then return mushrooms. Pour sauce over assembled serving.

CHESAPEAKE BAY OYSTER PEPPER POT

BEFORE YOU BEGIN

You'll need: small saucepan, large saucepan, 12-inch square cheesecloth, string
Preparation time: 1 hour
Yield: 8 servings

½ **pint oysters in juice**
2 **Tbsp. butter**
1 **small onion, finely chopped**
½ **tsp. black pepper, fresh ground**
¼ **cup salt pork, chopped fine**
½ **stalk celery, diced**
½ **stalk leeks, diced**
1 **green pepper, diced**

2 **qts. beef stock**
   retained oyster juice
2 **cups raw potatoes, diced**
1 **tomato, peeled and diced**
¼ **cup rice, uncooked**
   bouquet garni
¼ **cup parsley, chopped fine**

In a small saucepan over medium-high heat, warm oyster juice to hot. Blanch oysters in the juice until edges curl. Remove and set aside to cool, retaining the oyster juice. In large saucepan over medium heat, melt butter and sauté onion and salt pork until tender but not browned. Add celery, black pepper, leeks, and green pepper. Add beef stock and oyster juice. Remove the muscle and beard from oysters, then cut each oyster into 4 pieces and add to soup. Bring to a boil for 5 minutes, then add potatoes, tomato, rice, bouquet garni, and parsley. Reduce heat and simmer until the potatoes are done, about 20 minutes. Remove the bouquet garni promptly or soup will turn bitter. Serve sprinkled with finely chopped parsley.

BOUQUET GARNI

   small piece celery
   small piece leek
2 **sprigs parsley**
   bay leaf

1 **whole clove**
   sprig of thyme
   small garlic clove

Enclose all ingredients in cheesecloth and secure tight with string.

FRESH ASPARAGUS DELMONICO

BEFORE YOU BEGIN

You'll need: 2-quart saucepan, 1½-quart casserole, 3-quart saucepan, Chinese strainer
Preheat oven to 350 degrees
Preparation time: 1 hour
Yield: 8 servings

2 **lbs. fresh asparagus**
   cream sauce

1 **cup white bread crumbs**
2 **Tbsp. butter, melted**

Cut first 6 inches of asparagus spears into 1½-inch pieces. Place in the 2-quart saucepan and add salted water to cover. Boil until tender, about 5 minutes, and drain well. Place asparagus in baking casserole, pour cream sauce to cover over, sprinkle with bread crumbs, and top with melted butter. Bake until brown.

CREAM SAUCE

¼ cup butter
¼ cup flour

1 qt. milk, boiling
salt and pepper to taste

In the 3-quart saucepan over medium heat, make a roux of butter and flour and cook for 5 minutes. Meanwhile, bring milk to the boil. Stir milk into roux with whisk, stirring constantly to keep sauce free of lumps. When the mixture has the consistency of rich cream, strain through Chinese strainer. Stir in salt and pepper and use as directed. Refrigerate remaining cream sauce for other uses for 3–5 days.

ROULADE OF PRIME BEEF, FERMIERE

8 slices beef flank steak
¼ cup celery, chopped fine
2 Tbsp. chopped parsley
½ cup green onions, chopped fine
¼ cup dill pickle, diced

4 strips bacon, diced
salt and pepper
3 Tbsp. bacon drippings
1½ cups boiling water

BEFORE YOU BEGIN

You'll need: covered roasting pan, string, small skillet
Preheat oven to 325 degrees
Preparation time: 2–2½ hours
Yield: 4 servings

Use beef flank steak from loin end, individually sliced to ¼-inch thickness by 4 inches square. Combine celery, parsley, green onion, dill pickle and bacon. Season nicely to taste with salt and pepper. Divide mixture evenly and place in center of beef slices. Roll and tie beef slices with string. In a roasting pan over high heat, melt bacon drippings and brown rolled beef all over. Add boiling water to fat, cover tightly and put into oven to cook until tender, about 1½–2 hours, basting frequently. Serve two rolls per portion, covering generously with rich brown gravy, accompanied by baked onions and rice (see page 153).

RICH BROWN GRAVY

2 Tbsp. butter
2 Tbsp. green pepper, diced fine
¼ cup onion, diced fine
¼ cup pan stock
¼ cup flour

1¾ cups pan stock or beef stock
salt and pepper to taste
1 pimento, chopped fine
1 small can of button mushrooms

In a small skillet over medium heat, sauté green pepper and onion in butter until tender but not browned. Meanwhile, skim excess fat from pan stock and remove stock from roasting pan. Start with ¼ cup of pan stock in roasting pan over low heat. Slowly stir in flour and brown, taking care not to burn. Gradually stir in 2 cups pan stock (bring to measure with canned beef stock). Increase heat and continue stirring until thickened. Simmer 5 minutes, then season. Strain. Add sauteed green pepper and onion mixture. Add chopped pimento and button mushrooms. Simmer until heated through.

---◆---

STUFFED TOMATO BRETONNE

BEFORE YOU BEGIN

You'll need: small mix-
ing bowl
Preparation time:
½ hour
Yield: 8 servings

8 medium tomatoes	½ cup chicory, chopped fine
½ cup head lettuce, finely chopped	1 recipe, dressing
½ cup romaine, chopped fine	2 hard-boiled eggs, quartered
½ cup escarole, chopped fine	8 each, ripe and green olives

Peel tomatoes (see page 155). Carefully remove tops and scoop out center of tomatoes, retaining tomato pulp. Dice pulp and combine with chopped greens. Add dressing and mix thoroughly. Stuff tomatoes generously with mixture. Place each on a lettuce leaf and garnish with egg wedge and olives.

DRESSING

¼ cup tarragon vinegar	½ tsp. dry mustard
½ tsp. sugar	1 tsp. chopped capers
1 tsp. freshly grated horseradish	

Combine all ingredients and mix well.

THE DELAWARE & HUDSON RAILROAD

LAKE CHAMPLAIN ICE FISH, D&H STYLE

8–12 ice fish
1 recipe egg batter
1 cup flour
1 cup cornmeal

cooking oil as needed
4 small lemons
4 sprigs parsley

Use ice fish that are split and cleaned, allowing 2 large or 3 small fish to a portion. Prepare the egg batter using a deep mixing bowl. In a shallow dish suitable for dipping fish before frying, stir flour and cornmeal together. Meanwhile, preheat ⅛-inch cooking oil in skillet over medium-high setting. Dip fish in egg batter, then roll each in a mixture of flour and cornmeal. Place coated fish on wire rack to dry for several minutes. Sauté fish in heated oil until slightly browned, 4–5 minutes to a side, turning once. Remove fried fish to warming platter and place in warmed oven until all fish are fried. Garnish each serving with a quartered lemon and a sprig of parsley and serve.

EGG BATTER

1¾ cups flour
2 tsp. baking powder
pinch, salt
pinch, pepper

pinch, paprika
3 Tbsp. peanut oil
1 cup water, lukewarm
2 egg whites

Sift flour. Add baking powder, salt, pepper, and paprika and stir to mix thoroughly. Add peanut oil and water and mix to form batter. Place in refrigerator for 1 hour. Just before using, beat egg whites until stiff and fold them into batter mixture.

BEFORE YOU BEGIN

You'll need: sifter, large mixing bowl, shallow plate, wire rack, large skillet, warming platter
Preheat oven to Warm
Preparation time: 30 minutes
Yield: 4 servings

THE DELAWARE, LACKAWANNA & WESTERN RAILROAD

BEEFSTEAK PIE WITH MUSHROOMS

BEFORE YOU BEGIN

*You'll need: large skillet, 3-quart covered saucepan, small skillet, strainer, small covered skillet, small saucepan, 6 individual casseroles
Preheat oven to 400 degrees
Preparation time: 2½ hours
Yield: 6 servings*

3 Tbsp. bacon drippings	2 cups beef stock, or enough to cover
¾ lb. beef, cut into 1-inch cubes	¾ lb. salt pork
salt and pepper to taste	cut into 1-inch cubes
1 Tbsp. butter	¼ cup water
½ cup chopped onion	18 small onions
½ cup carrots, sliced	1 Tbsp. butter
½ cup celery, sliced	18 mushroom caps
1 bay leaf	1 meal pie dish crust recipe
pinch, thyme	18 cooked potato balls
2 Tbsp. flour	¼ cup chopped parsley
1 cup tomatoes, diced	1 egg, well beaten

In the large skillet over high heat, melt bacon drippings. Season beef cubes with salt and pepper, and sauté in hot bacon drippings until browned all over. Remove from skillet and place in the 3-quart saucepan. In the small skillet over medium-low heat, melt butter and sauté onions, carrots, and celery until tender but not browned, about 10 minutes. Add sauteed vegetables to beef. Add one bay leaf and a pinch of thyme. Dust lightly with flour. Mix well. Add tomatoes and enough beef stock to cover. Heat to near boil, reduce heat, cover, and simmer until meat is tender, about 1 hour. Then remove meat and strain gravy. Meanwhile, in small skillet over medium-high heat, put salt pork cubes in water. Cover and simmer until done, about 10 minutes. Peel small onions and boil them in water to cover until tender, about 10 minutes. In the small saucepan over medium heat, melt 1 tablespoon butter and sauté mushroom caps until tender, about 5 minutes. Prepare one meal-pastry dough recipe (see page 155). To assemble in individual casseroles, place 4 cubes of beef, 3 small onions, 4 salt pork cubes, 3 potato balls, and 3 sauteed mushroom caps for each serving. Cover all with gravy and a little chopped parsley. Roll out pie pastry to ⅛-inch thickness, trim to size, and cover casseroles. Cut hole in pastry to allow steam to escape and brush with well-beaten egg. Bake until crust browns, about 45 minutes.

THE DENVER & RIO GRANDE
WESTERN RAILROAD

BOILED BLACK-EYED PEAS

2¾ qts. ham stock
1 large carrot
2 outside stalks celery
1 bay leaf
1 cup bacon, diced
½ tsp. Tabasco sauce
1 Tbsp. Worcestershire sauce
1 lb. black-eyed peas, washed
   thoroughly

BEFORE YOU BEGIN

*You'll need: 3-quart
   saucepan
Preparation time:
   3½ hours
Yield: 8 servings*

In 3-quart saucepan, bring the 2¾ quarts ham stock to a boil, reduce heat, and simmer until reduced to 2 quarts. Combine remaining ingredients in saucepan and return to a boil. Reduce heat and slow boil for approximately 2 hours, until beans are tender. Remove carrot and celery. Serve hot with chopped parsley sprinkled on top.

ISLANDER SHRIMP LUAU

1½ lbs. uncooked large or jumbo shrimp
¼ cup lemon juice
½ tsp. salt
1 tsp. curry powder
⅛ tsp. ginger
3½ oz. shredded coconut, unsweetened
1 cup flour
⅔ cup milk
1 tsp. baking powder
¼ cup shrimp marinade
   flour to coat

BEFORE YOU BEGIN

*You'll need: medium
   covered bowl, cookie
   sheet, small mixing
   bowl, deep fryer,
   small saucepan,
   medium bowl,
   strainer
Preheat oven to 300
   degrees, deep fryer
   to hot
Preparation time:
   1 hour (plus 4–6
   hours for shrimp to
   marinate)
Yield: 4 servings*

Carefully remove shell from shrimp, leaving tail. Devein and thoroughly rinse the shrimp. Make marinade by mixing lemon juice, salt, curry powder, and ginger. Pour marinade over shrimp, cover, and refrigerate 4–6 hours, stirring occasionally. Retain ¼ cup marinade for batter. Spread coconut on a cookie sheet and bake for 5–15 minutes or until dry. Make a batter by mixing flour, milk, and baking powder with a fork and stirring in the ¼ cup marinade. Draw shrimp through flour, dip in the batter, and then in coconut. Deep fry in hot fat (heated to 380 degrees) until golden brown, 3–5 minutes depending on size of shrimp. To serve, place mold of boiled rice (see page 153) in center of serving plate. Arrange 4 shrimp around rice, and garnish with wedge of lemon and sprig of parsley on opposite sides. Pour curry sauce over rice and shrimp or serve in a side dish.

CURRY SAUCE

4 Tbsp. butter	1 tsp. salt
1 small onion, chopped	½ tsp. curry powder
1 oz. raw ham, chopped fine	½ tsp. flour
½ stalk celery, chopped	1 cup chicken stock, heated
½ green pepper, chopped	1 egg yolk
sprig of thyme	2 Tbsp. cream
5 whole black peppers	

In a 1-quart saucepan over medium heat, melt butter and sauté onion, ham, celery, green pepper, thyme, and black pepper for 5 minutes, taking care not to brown ingredients. Stir in salt and curry powder. Add flour, stirring constantly to avoid lumps. Add hot chicken stock and stir well. Cook at a simmer for 20 minutes, stirring occasionally to prevent burning. Meanwhile, in a large bowl, beat egg yolk in cream. Gradually stir sauce into the yolk/cream mixture. Strain back into a clean 1-quart saucepan and keep warm until used. Do not boil.

OLD FASHIONED NAVY BEAN SOUP, RIO GRANDE STYLE

BEFORE YOU BEGIN

You'll need: 2 large saucepans or pots
Preparation time: 1½ hours (plus overnight to soak beans)
Yield: 30 servings

3 cups navy beans	4 Tbsp. flour
cold water to cover	4 quarts beef stock
2 medium onions, minced	3 large tomatoes, peeled and diced
2 medium carrots, diced	salt and pepper to taste
¼ cup bacon drippings	

In large saucepan or pot, cover beans generously with cold water and soak overnight. Bring beans and water in which they have been soaked to a boil, reduce heat, and continue cooking. Meanwhile, peel (see page 155) and chop tomatoes and heat through. In large covered saucepan over medium heat, melt bacon drippings and braise onions and carrots until tender. Stirring constantly, add flour to absorb bacon drippings. Add beef stock and tomatoes and heat through. Combine the above ingredients with the simmering beans and cook until beans are tender. Serve very hot. Ham bone or bacon rind may be added for flavor.

SILVER SALMON STEAK BAKED
WITH SOUR CREAM

BEFORE YOU BEGIN

*You'll need: shallow
metal baking pan
Preheat oven to Broil,
then 350 degrees
Preparation time:
30 minutes
Yield: 1 serving*

8 oz. silver salmon steak
salt and pepper to taste
¼ cup sour cream

1 thin slice of lemon
parsley, fresh chopped
2 Tbsp. water

Grease a shallow metal baking pan. Season salmon steak with salt and pepper.
Place in baking pan and cover with sour cream. Place a slice of lemon in center
of the steak, sprinkle with parsley, and place in broiler with top surface at least 5
inches from the heat source. Broil to light brown, about 5–7 minutes. Remove
from broiler and adjust oven to 350 degrees. Add water to fish dish and bake in
oven until cooked through, about 10 minutes. Garnish with sprig of parsley and
lemon wedge.

SPINACH, GERMAN STYLE

BEFORE YOU BEGIN

*You'll need: medium
saucepan, small
skillet
Preparation time:
1 hour
Yield: 8 servings*

4 cups cooked spinach
¼ lb. bacon, diced
½ cup onion, chopped fine

¼ cup red wine vinegar
salt and white pepper to taste
2 hard-boiled eggs, sliced

Cook spinach in boiling salted water to cover until tender, drain well, chop fine,
and return to saucepan. Meanwhile, in skillet, sauté bacon over medium heat until drippings are rendered but not crisp. Add onions and sauté until tender but
not browned, about 5 minutes. Combine bacon with drippings, sauteed onions,
and vinegar with cooked spinach. Add salt and white pepper and stir to mix thoroughly. Bring to a boil and remove from heat. Garnish each serving with two
slices of hard-boiled egg.

THE DOMINION ATLANTIC RAILWAY

CREAMED DIGBY SCALLOPS ON TOAST

BEFORE YOU BEGIN

*You'll need: 2 1-quart
  saucepans
Preparation time:
  30 minutes
Yield: 4 servings*

1 lb. Digby or bay scallops
2 Tbsp. butter
½ cup flour
2 cups milk, warmed

salt and white pepper to taste
4 slices white bread
chopped parsley
paprika

Bring lightly salted water sufficient to barely cover scallops to a boil. Add scallops and cook until firm and white, about 4 minutes. Drain scallops and retain liquor. Meanwhile, in one of the saucepans over medium heat, make a roux of the butter and flour. Add warm milk, stirring constantly. Thin to taste with liquor from scallops. Season and let stand to thicken. To serve, toast bread and remove crusts. Place scallops atop toast, pour cream sauce over, and sprinkle each serving with chopped parsley and dash of paprika.

THE ERIE RAILROAD

BAKED INDIAN PUDDING

BEFORE YOU BEGIN

You'll need: double boiler, small mixing bowl, small bowl, baking dish, 1-quart saucepan
Preheat oven to 275 degrees
Preparation time: 3½ hours
Yield: 8 servings

3 cups scalded milk
½ cup yellow cornmeal
5 eggs, well beaten
   pinch, baking soda
½ cup dark molasses
½ cup seedless raisins
1 tsp. grated lemon rind

½ tsp. ginger
1 tsp. cinnamon
4 Tbsp. butter
1 tsp. salt
¼ cup sugar
1 cup cold milk

In double boiler, bring milk to the scald. Add cornmeal, stirring constantly until mixture thickens, about 10 minutes. Remove from heat to cool partially. Meanwhile, beat eggs until of lemon color, and stir baking soda into molasses. Now, into partially cooled cornmeal, stir raisins, grated lemon rind, ginger, cinnamon, butter, molasses/baking soda mixture, salt, sugar, and beaten eggs. Pour mixture into greased baking dish. Stir in one cup of cold milk. Bake until cooked through, about 3 hours. Serve hot with fruit sauce.

FRUIT SAUCE

1 small can pineapple tidbits
1 orange
1 apple

juice of 1 lemon
1 cup sugar
1½ cups water

Drain juice from pineapple into a saucepan. Peel orange, remove membrane, and cut sections into 3 pieces each. Core, peel, and dice the apple into ¼-inch pieces. Stir water, sugar, and lemon juice into pineapple juice and bring to a boil. Add fruit to boiling syrup, reduce heat, and simmer for 10 minutes, until thickened.

THE FLORIDA EAST COAST RAILWAY

FLORIDA EAST COAST SALAD

BEFORE YOU BEGIN

*You'll need: salad serv-
ing plates
Preparation time:
15 minutes
Yield: 2 servings*

2 lettuce leaves
1 cup cottage cheese
2 maraschino cherries
1 large grapefruit
1 large orange

4 slices pineapple
6 green pepper rings
French dressing to suit
6 Saltines

Place a lettuce leaf on each salad plate. Center a ½-cup mound of cottage cheese atop it. Top with maraschino cherry. Peel grapefruit, remove membrane, section, and cut in ½-inch pieces. Peel orange, remove membrane, and cut into ¼-inch slices. Cut pineapple slices and orange slices in half. Around the cottage cheese, alternately arrange equal portions of grapefruit pieces, pineapple slices, and orange slices, then grapefruit pieces, and so on. Cut green pepper in thin rings and use as garnish atop fruit. Top with French dressing (see page 267) and serve with crispy Saltines on the side.

THE GULF, MOBILE & OHIO RAILROAD

GM&O SPECIAL SANDWICH

BEFORE YOU BEGIN

*You'll need: individual
serving plate
Preparation time:
10 minutes
Yield: 1 serving*

1 slice white bread, toasted
1 slice Swiss cheese
slice iceberg lettuce, 1-inch thick
¼ lb. white chicken meat,
cooked, and sliced
¼ cup Thousand Island dressing

2 slices bacon, cooked
1 thick slice, tomato
1 slice hard-boiled egg
1 tsp. black caviar
3 black olives
3 dill pickle chips

Place the piece of toast on serving plate. Top, in order, with slice of Swiss cheese, slice of lettuce, and sliced chicken. Pour Thousand Island dressing (see page 187) over all. Top dressing with bacon. Add slice of tomato, and top with slice of hard-boiled egg and black caviar. Garnish with black olives and dill pickle chips.

CURRY OF FRESH SHRIMP

BEFORE YOU BEGIN

64 jumbo shrimp
1 qt. shrimp water
1 tsp. Worcestershire sauce
¼ tsp. Tabasco sauce
   salt and pepper to taste
3 tsp. curry powder
⅓ tsp. ground ginger

½ cup butter
1 cup chopped onions
1½ cups chopped celery
¼ cup flour
2 egg yolks, beaten
2 cups milk, heated

You'll need: 3-quart saucepan, 1½-quart saucepan, small bowl, 1-quart saucepan
Preparation time: 1 hour
Yield: 8 servings

Shell and devein fresh shrimp before cooking. In the 3-quart saucepan, bring sufficient salted water to cover shrimp to a boil. Plunge shrimp in boiling water, cover, and cook 6 minutes. Drain shrimp, retaining 1 quart of water, and rinse in cold water to halt cooking. In the 1½-quart saucepan, combine shrimp water, Worcestershire sauce, Tabasco sauce, salt, pepper, curry powder, and ginger. Bring to a boil, reduce heat, and simmer slowly for 10 minutes. Meanwhile, in large skillet or pot over medium heat, melt butter and sauté onions and celery until tender. Add flour, stirring constantly, and simmer for 4 minutes. Very slowly, add hot liquid, stirring constantly to avoid lumps. Slowly blend heated milk into beaten egg yolks. Add egg/milk mixture to first mixture, stirring constantly. Heat through but do not boil after adding egg. To serve, place a bed of fluffy rice (see page 153) in center of plate, top with 8 jumbo shrimp, and pour curry sauce over all.

BLUEBERRY MUFFINS

BEFORE YOU BEGIN

You'll need: strainer, two 2½-inch cup muffin pans, electric beater, large mixing bowl, small bowl
Preheat oven to 375 degrees
Preparation time: 1 hour
Yield: 24 muffins

2 cups fresh blueberries	½ cup shortening
4 cups flour	½ cup sugar
4 tsp. baking powder	2 eggs well beaten
¾ tsp. salt	2 cups milk

Wash and set aside blueberries to drain well. Lightly grease muffin cups and set aside. Sift flour, baking powder, and salt together and set aside. Cream shortening and sugar. Add well-beaten eggs. Alternately add sifted ingredients and milk. Fold in drained blueberries. Spoon mixture evenly into greased muffin cups, cleaning any spills from muffin pan. Bake 20–25 minutes, until well risen, golden, and a toothpick inserted in the center comes out clean. Remove hot muffins to wire rack or tilt in cups to allow steam to escape.

THE KANSAS CITY SOUTHERN RAILWAY COMPANY

SPOON BREAD

BEFORE YOU BEGIN

You'll need: double boiler, 9" x 13" baking dish, small bowl, medium mixing bowl, large mixing bowl
Preheat oven to 350 degrees
Preparation time: 1¼ hours
Yield: 8 servings

2 cups water	2 Tbsp. sugar
1 cup grits	1 cup milk
⅓ lb. butter	3 egg yolks, well beaten
1 tsp. salt	3 egg whites, beaten stiff

Grease baking dish all around and set aside. In double boiler over boiling water, heat 2 cups water and stir in grits. Reduce heat to medium-high and allow to cook about 10 minutes, until thickened. Add butter, salt, sugar, milk, and well-beaten egg yolks, and stir to mix thoroughly. Pour into large mixing bowl and fold in egg whites beaten stiff but not dry. Pour mixture into the baking dish and place in oven until golden brown and a knife inserted comes out clean, about 50 minutes. Serve warm from baking dish.

THE LEHIGH VALLEY RAILROAD

LEHIGH VALLEY BAKED APPLE DISH

4 cups of granular sugar   3 maraschino cherries
6 large Rome Beauty apples

BEFORE YOU BEGIN

You'll need: baking
pan, apple corer
Preheat oven to 350
degrees
Preparation time:
1½ hours
Yield: 6 servings

Spread 4 cups of granular sugar in bottom of baking pan. Core apples and cut ¼-inch from top of each apple so that the top of apple can set upside-down on bottom of the pan on the sugar. Place apples in this position. Sprinkle water lightly along the edge of the baking pan to keep sugar from burning. Place baking dish in a 300-degree oven and bake until apples are fork-tender, about 1 hour. Baste occasionally as sugar forms syrup to coat each apple with a glaze. After apples become thoroughly glazed, turn them over and place half a maraschino cherry in center of each. Continue to baste until cooked through, about 15 minutes more. Serve hot.

THE LOUISVILLE & NASHVILLE
RAILROAD

+—— ⊱⊙⊰ ——+

BROILED SPRING CHICKEN ON TOAST,
BARBECUE STYLE

BEFORE YOU BEGIN

*You'll need: 1-quart
saucepan, covered
baking dish
Preheat oven to 350
degrees
Preparation time:
1¼ hours
Yield: 4 servings*

*Bill Rolling, for more than-twenty four years the chef on the L & N's Pan American,
preferred a plump broiled chicken to accompany his specialty sauce. This dish so impressed New York's Governor Al Smith when he was traveling in the early 1920s that,
while campaigning for president in 1928, he sought out the L & N for the Nashville-
to-Louisville leg of a whirlwind campaign trip just to have another serving of Chef
Rolling's creation. Never mind that the "Happy Warrior" had to have it for breakfast.*

2	oz. butter		pinch, nutmeg
1	tsp. dry mustard	¼	Tbsp. cayenne pepper
1	tsp. flour		salt to taste
2	Tbsp. white vinegar	2½	oz. tomato juice
2	Tbsp. honey	1	lb. boneless chicken breasts
	juice from 1 lemon	4	slices toasting bread
2	Tbsp. tomato catsup		(see page 173)

Melt butter in the saucepan over medium heat. Add mustard, flour, white vinegar, honey, lemon juice, catsup, nutmeg, cayenne pepper, salt, and tomato juice.
As each ingredient is added, continue stirring so sauce remains smooth and will
not stick to pan. Simmer until heated through, about 5 minutes. Meanwhile,
arrange chicken breasts in the baking dish. Pour sauce over, cover, and place in
oven. Allow to simmer for 30 minutes, remove cover, and simmer additional 30
minutes. To serve, prepare one slice of toasted bread (see page 173) for each portion. Place chicken portions on the toast and pour barbecue sauce over all.

+—— ⊱⊙⊰ ——+

CREAM OF CHICKEN SOUP WITH LEEKS

BEFORE YOU BEGIN

*You'll need: 2-quart
saucepan, sieve,
3-quart saucepan
Preparation time:
1 hour
Yield: 8 servings*

3	cups chicken stock	2	Tbsp. butter or chicken fat
12	leeks, whites only, quartered	2	Tbsp. flour
½	cup celery, diced	2	cups light cream, warm
3	Tbsp. white rice, uncooked	¼	tsp. white pepper
1½	cups cooked chicken, minced	2	Tbsp. chopped parsley
½	tsp. salt		

In the 2-quart saucepan over medium heat, warm chicken stock. Add whites of the leeks, celery, and rice and simmer until soft, about 10 minutes. Drain, returning stock to saucepan. Rub vegetables and rice through a sieve or place in blender to puree, then stir back into stock. Add cooked minced chicken and add salt. In the 3-quart saucepan over medium heat, make a roux of the butter and flour. Slowly stir in the warm cream. Add chicken stock mixture, stirring constantly, and continue stirring until thickened and heated through. Sprinkle with chopped parsley and serve hot.

✦ ⟪✦⟫ ✦

FRESH SHRIMP GUMBO, NEW ORLEANS STYLE

BEFORE YOU BEGIN

*You'll need: 8-quart stock pot, two 3-quart saucepans
Preparation time: 2 hours
Yield: 24 servings*

Warnings accompanied this recipe: Never boil the gumbo with the rice. Never add the filé while the gumbo is on the fire, as boiling after the filé is added will make the gumbo stringy and unfit for use. If reheating is necessary, place the gumbo in a heat-resistant jar and heat in double boiler. Do not reheat directly over a fire.

¾ cup cooking oil	¾ cup flour
3 onions, chopped fine	6 qts. strained shrimp stock, heated
2 green peppers, diced	2 qts. chicken stock, heated
3 sprigs parsley, chopped fine	1 tsp. salt
2 bay leaves	½ tsp. cayenne pepper
¼ lb. raw ham, diced	1 qt. small oysters, chopped
½ tsp. thyme	2 lbs. lake shrimp, cooked
¼ cup paprika	4 tsp. filé
2 cups tomatoes, peeled and diced	1 cup cooked rice (see page 153)
1 lb. okra, sliced	

In the stock pot over medium heat, warm cooking oil and sauté onions, green peppers, parsley, bay leaves, ham, thyme, and paprika until tender, about 5 minutes. Add tomatoes and okra and let cook for a few minutes, taking care not to burn. Add flour to make roux and continue simmering for 5 minutes to brown but not burn. Add hot shrimp stock, hot chicken stock, salt, and cayenne pepper. Bring mixture to a boil, reduce heat, and slow boil for 1 hour 30 minutes. Add the cooked shrimp and chopped oysters to gumbo 10 minutes before removing from stove. After removing from stove, add filé. Do not permit to boil after adding this ingredient. To serve, put a teaspoon of boiled rice in serving cup and pour gumbo over the rice.

SHRIMP COCKTAIL SAUCE

juice of ½ lemon, strained
1 Tbsp. vinegar
1 tsp. anchovy paste
1 cup mayonnaise

1 cup chili sauce
4 drops Tabasco sauce
salt to taste

In a small bowl, combine the vinegar and lemon juice. Slowly add anchovy paste, stirring to dissolve until smooth. Add remaining ingredients and stir well. Test before adding salt, as the anchovy paste may be salty enough. Place in sealed container and chill at least one hour before serving.

Dining-car departments were responsible both for feeding passengers and any others who came in contact with the railroad. These "others" included local patrons of their station restaurants, work gangs and wrecking and train crews at their work sites or layover points, tourists staying in parks operated by the larger railroads, and, during wartime, troops on trains of all railroads interchanging where a commissary was located. The St. Louis Southwestern Railway (Cotton Belt Route), a regional carrier connecting St. Louis with Memphis, Little Rock, and Dallas–Ft. Worth, in December 1945 carried out such duties from a commissary in Texarkana, Texas, with four dining cars, three emergency dining cars for special troop movements, two club cars, eight boarding camps with from thirty to one hundred men at each, and three eating houses (one each in East St. Louis, Illinois; Pine Bluff, Arkansas; and Hodge–Ft. Worth, Texas). These less spectacular aspects of dining-car department work often made up the larger portion of the department's activity. In 1944, a year of heavier-than-normal use of the system for wartime travel, the Cotton Belt nonetheless served only 175,345 meals in its dining cars, compared with 281,629 in boarding camps and 418,898 in eating houses.[1] Larger railroads had correspondingly larger operations and responsibilities.

S. E. Altman, an early crew cook on the payroll of the Union Pacific from February 9 to May 13, 1869, recorded his experience working for one such extra gang, the crew building the transcontinental railroad. Many of his days resembled February 24, 1869: "Arose pretty early this morning. Got breakfast in a hurry. Cleaned up after breakfast, made three beds,

swept out both tents, cleaned the table and all the benches, made some splendid sweet-cakes, got supper and cleaned up, cut some wood." Two days later, a cold wind kept his dough from rising, so he turned to baking pies. With the pride of many who cooked for the railroads, on March 5 he asserted, "I baked eight loaves of the best bread that has ever been this side of the Missouri River." Altman fed some crew members in the dining tent, which held three tables and seated twelve, but for others he had to pack up their meals and send them forward. His menu consisted of fish, beef, and game; breads, biscuits and pies; stewed apples, peaches, and blackberries, and coffee and tea. He complained of the water ("not of the best"), the lack of rest ("there was none for the cook"), and Indians ("they came around thick as hops today and spend their time in gab"). One of his rewards came on May 10, 1869, when he "drove a spike on the last rail of each railroad" as the Central Pacific and Union Pacific joined at Promontory Summit, Utah. Just seven days later he was back in Omaha, out of work.[2]

Under less extraordinary circumstances, the so-called "extra gangs" were hired to do construction, repair track, or clean up wrecks. In January 1917, the Milwaukee Road had sixteen such gangs, ranging in size "from fifty to several hundred men," scattered over its lines east of the Missouri River. One description of the extra gang said "many of them are interesting, cultured men, who have broken from their moorings and they work wherever the grub is good."[3] A well-stocked and managed camp-food service was therefore required if the railroad were to get good laborers who stayed on the job.

Often hundreds of miles from home, these

Mrs. Clark cooks for the crew.

Feeding the B & B gang.

men lived in bunk cars accompanied by a kitchen/commissary car and a dining car. A Milwaukee Road commissary car, restocked by passing trains, carried ninety-three separate eatables, including fresh and corned meats, sausages and fish, canned goods, and vegetables. As with Mr. Altman, the cook's major duty was baking: "The schedule is to bake daily, except Sunday. To do this, they use half a barrel of flour a day [to make] one hundred [four-pound] loaves" of bread. Cooking was done in a car which had outlived its usefulness as a revenue-producing freight carrier and thus was converted to a kitchen car. At mealtime, "in the interior of the car two long tables were set in the center. Their covering was neat, white oilcloth, a row of benches on either side was where we sat. From the roof of the car an oil lamp hung and shed its rays of soft light over the features of the rugged men. White-aproned waiters moved quickly around the table with big platters of steak, boiled beef, and steaming dishes of potatoes and macaroni. There was bread and hot biscuits, butter, pie, cake, and tea."[4]

For train crews, if suitable boarding facilities along the route were operated by local owners, the railroads contracted with them to put up their personnel. If not, the railroads built hotels and boarding houses when track was being laid. Intended for workmen and officials, they came to be commonly used by travelers as well. At the Union Pacific's restaurant in Green River, Wyoming, train crews ate at its forty-four-stool lunch counter and in the dining room. "Over these lunch counters and dining room tables" at the Milwaukee Railway Hotel and Passenger Station in Madison, Wisconsin, "officers and employees alike broke bread and held many interesting confabs."[5] Coach passengers and an occasional Pullman guest would also take the opportunity, while their train was being serviced, to have a meal.

This stew, a favorite of train crews on the Elgin, Joliet, and Eastern Railway, testifies to the simplicity of dishes prepared at boarding camps. Another favorite, Great Northern's Reindeer Mulligan, Hunter Style (see page 222), eventually made it onto the passenger-train menu.

OUTER BELT BISQUE

BEFORE YOU BEGIN
You'll need: large skillet, 2-quart saucepan, 2-quart casserole
Preheat oven to 375 degrees
Preparation time: 45 minutes
Yield: 8 servings

2 lbs. round steak, ground	1 10½-oz. can water
3 large onions, chopped coarse	1 16-oz. package egg noodles
2 10-½ oz cans tomato soup	salt and pepper to taste

Cook noodles according to package directions and drain. Meanwhile, brown meat and onion together. Add cooked noodles, tomato soup, and water. Season to taste, mix thoroughly, and heat through. Pour into casserole and place in oven for 30 minutes.

THE MISSOURI-KANSAS-TEXAS LINES

✦ ✦ ✦ ✦

KATY KORNETTES

BEFORE YOU BEGIN

You'll need: 1-quart saucepan, large mixing bowl, pastry bag (optional), 2 large cookie sheets Preheat oven to 400 degrees Preparation time: 1 hour Yield: 48 cakes

1 qt. boiling canned sweet milk
1 lb. white cornmeal
4 oz. butter, softened

1 Tbsp. sugar
1 tsp. salt

Lightly grease 2 large cookie sheets and set aside. Bring milk to a boil and pour into mixing bowl. Stirring constantly, add white cornmeal, butter, sugar, and salt and mix well. Let stand for 5 minutes. Using a pastry bag or tablespoon, drop silver-dollar-sized quantities onto cookie sheet. Cool at room temperature for 15 minutes, then place in oven for about 20 minutes, until cooked through.

✦ ✦ ✦ ✦

KATY SPECIAL ONION SOUP

BEFORE YOU BEGIN

You'll need: large skillet, 6-quart pot Preparation time: 45 minutes Yield: 8 servings

This dish originated with T. T. Turner, then superintendent of Missouri-Kansas-Texas dining service, to popularize Texas onions. When it was first introduced, stewards reported no great demand. Eventually, however, demand grew, and the railroad reported nine out of ten regular M-K-T passengers asking for this specialty in particular. Because the soup's taste can vary according to the skill of the cook, Superintendent Turner recommended following the recipe's directions carefully, using only good firm Texas onions. As confidence with the soup grows, he recommends experimenting with pinches and dashes of the ingredients to suit individual tastes. Other versions of the recipe, for example, have a half-cup of flour added to the onions-in-butter sauté, or salt and pepper added to taste. "If you have that certain something that is a natural attribute only of a master chef," Turner noted, "you'll be able turn out our Katy onion soup."

6 large onions, ⅛-inch diced
4 oz. butter
4 qts. rich chicken stock
4 sprigs parsley
1 clove garlic

2 bay leaves
¼ cup Worcestershire sauce
soup croutons
Parmesan cheese, fresh grated

Slice onions ⅛-inch across, then dice. In the large skillet over medium heat, sauté onion in butter until light brown. Meanwhile, heat stock in pot. Add sauteed onions to heated stock. Add parsley, garlic, bay leaves, and Worcestershire sauce. Bring to a boil, reduce heat, and simmer for 20 minutes. Remove parsley, bay leaves, and garlic. Place croutons in serving bowls, pour soup over, and top with a generous portion of freshly grated Parmesan cheese.

THE NASHVILLE, CHATTANOOGA & ST. LOUIS RAILWAY

CORN HOE CAKES

2 cups cornmeal
2 cups buttermilk
½ tsp. salt

½ tsp. baking soda
½ tsp. baking powder

In the saucepan, combine all ingredients well and bring just to a boil. Remove from heat and let stand 15 minutes to thicken. Drop walnut-sized spoonfuls in hot oil and fry until delicate brown. Drain on paper towel and serve hot.

BEFORE YOU BEGIN

You'll need: 2-quart saucepan, deep fryer
Preheat 4 inches frying oil to hot (380 degrees)
Preparation time: 30 minutes
Yield: 24 cakes

THE NORFOLK & WESTERN RAILROAD

FRIED CHICKEN WITH CREAM GRAVY

1 2–3 lb. frying chicken
salt and pepper
flour to coat

4 Tbsp. butter, plus more as needed
2–3 Tbsp. water

Wash and drain chicken and quarter or otherwise cut into serving pieces. Season with salt and pepper, then roll in flour. In the large skillet over low heat, melt butter and fry chicken for about 15 minutes, turning frequently to brown pieces on all sides. Cover and continue cooking over low heat for 30–45 minutes, until tender. Add 2 or 3 tablespoons of water and more butter as needed to keep moist, and turn chicken occasionally to insure even cooking. Remove chicken from pan and make gravy. To serve, place ¼ cup gravy on plate, chicken on top, and remaining gravy over.

BEFORE YOU BEGIN

You'll need: large skillet, small saucepan
Preparation time: 1¼ hours
Yield: 4 servings

GRAVY

drippings from fried chicken
3 Tbsp. flour

2 cups milk, hot
salt and white pepper to taste

Add flour to drippings remaining in skillet from frying chicken, stirring constantly to mix well. Add hot milk gradually and cook, stirring constantly until thickened. Season to taste.

THE READING LINES

CHICKEN CREOLE SOUP

BEFORE YOU BEGIN

*You'll need: 4-quart
saucepan
Preparation time:
45 minutes
Yield: 8 servings*

1 onion, diced
2 green peppers, chopped fine
2 15-oz. cans crushed tomatoes
2 qts. chicken stock
1 whole pimento, cut julienne

1 cup cooked rice
1 cup cooked chicken, diced fine
½ cup flour
salt and pepper to taste

In 4-quart saucepan, combine onion, peppers, tomatoes, and chicken stock. Bring to a boil, reduce heat, and simmer for 30 minutes. Then add pimento, rice, and chicken and heat through. Add flour, stirring constantly, to thicken. Season with salt and pepper. The finished soup should be a creamy pink color with red pimentos and green peppers floating on top.

DIAMOND CHEESE BISCUITS

BEFORE YOU BEGIN

*You'll need: large mix-
ing bowl, pastry
cutter, rolling pin,
large baking sheet,
pastry brush
Preheat oven to 350
degrees
Preparation time:
1 hour
Yield: 36 biscuits*

¼ lb. lard, softened
¼ lb. butter, softened
8 cups sifted flour
1 Tbsp. salt
2 Tbsp. sugar

2 Tbsp. baking powder
½ lb. American cheese, grated
2½ cups milk
yolk of 1 egg
1 Tbsp. light cream

In a large mixing bowl, use a pastry cutter to work lard and butter into flour until coarse. Add salt, sugar, baking powder, and grated cheese and mix all thoroughly. Slowly add milk, stirring until mixture is of biscuit-dough consistency. On a lightly floured surface, roll dough out to ¾-inch thickness. Use a sharp knife to cut dough into 2" x 3" diamond shapes. Place biscuits on ungreased baking sheet. Make an egg wash by beating the egg yolk and cream together lightly. Brush wash atop biscuits and bake until lightly browned, about 25 minutes.

THE ST. LOUIS & SAN FRANCISCO RAILWAY

FLAKED BREAST OF CHICKEN WITH SHERRY, FRISCO STYLE

1 5-lb. roasting chicken, cooked
4 Tbsp. butter
6 medium-size mushrooms, sliced thick
2 small green peppers, cut julienne
2 lbs. sweetbreads, precooked and diced
2 pimentos, cut julienne
1 Tbsp. flour

1 pt. light cream
   salt to taste
¼ tsp. cayenne
4 egg yolks, beaten
½ cup light cream, warmed
4 Tbsp. dry sherry wine

BEFORE YOU BEGIN

You'll need: 4-quart saucepan, small mixing bowl
Preparation time: 1 hour
Yield: 12 servings

Remove cooked chicken from the bone, discard skin, shred meat coarsely, and set aside. In the saucepan over medium heat, melt butter and sauté mushrooms and green peppers until tender. Add chicken, sweetbreads, and pimentos. Dust lightly with flour. Stir in the pint of cream, salt, and cayenne. Bring just to boil, reduce heat, and simmer for several minutes. Meanwhile, beat egg yolks until of lemon color, then dissolve them into the ½ cup cream. Stir egg/cream mixture into simmering ingredients to thicken. Add sherry and stir to mix. Do not return to boil after egg yolks have been added or the sauce will break. Serve hot.

RAGOUT OF TENDERLOIN TIPS STROGANOFF

2 Tbsp. butter
2 lbs. sliced tenderloin tips
1 medium onion, chopped fine
½ lb. mushrooms, sliced
1 clove garlic

1 Tbsp. butter
1 cup sour cream
1 cup dry white wine
   pinch, cayenne pepper
   salt and pepper to taste

BEFORE YOU BEGIN

You'll need: large skillet or pot, small skillet
Preparation time: 30 minutes
Yield: 8 servings

In the large skillet or pot over medium-high heat, melt the 2 tablespoons butter and sauté the sliced tenderloin tips and finely chopped onions together, turning occasionally, until tender but not too brown, about 8 minutes. Separately, in small skillet over medium heat, melt 1 tablespoon butter and sauté mushrooms until tender, about 5 minutes, adding garlic during the last minute. When completed, stir above two ingredient mixtures together. Add sour cream, white wine, cayenne pepper, salt, and pepper. Stir to mix, bring to a simmer, and let cook for 5 minutes. Serve over egg noodles cooked according to instructions.

THE ST. LOUIS SOUTHWESTERN
RAILWAY LINES

━┿━ ⊨◊⊐ ━┿━

APRICOT BAVARIAN CREAM

BEFORE YOU BEGIN

*You'll need: small
  bowl, double boiler,
  8 individual molds
Preparation time:
  2 hours
Yield: 8 servings*

1 **Tbsp. unflavored gelatin**	2 **cups whipping cream**
¼ **cup cold water**	1 **tsp. vanilla flavoring**
2 **cups apricot pulp or juice**	1 **Tbsp. lemon juice**

Soak gelatin in cold water for 5 minutes. Melt gelatin in double boiler over gently boiling water. Stir in apricots and let cool. Meanwhile, whip 1 cup cream, add vanilla flavoring and lemon juice, and fold into fruit mixture. Pour into molds and cool in refrigerator. To serve, whip remaining cup of cream. Remove fruit gelatin from molds and top with whipped cream.

━┿━ ⊨◊⊐ ━┿━

BAKED ONIONS AND RICE

BEFORE YOU BEGIN

*You'll need: 4-quart
  saucepan, 1-quart
  saucepan, grater,
  deep 2-quart baking
  dish
Preheat oven to 375
  degrees
Preparation time:
  1 hour
Yield: 6 servings*

2 **cups cooked rice**	1 **cup milk, warmed**
6 **yellow onions**	1 **tsp. salt**
2 **tsp. butter**	**pinch, cayenne pepper**
2 **Tbsp. flour**	¾ **cup grated cheddar cheese**

Cook rice (see page 153). Peel onions under water. In a 4-quart saucepan bring 3 quarts of water to a boil and parboil onions 3 minutes, until tender. Quarter the onions, separate sections, and set aside. In a 1-quart saucepan make a roux of the butter and flour. Add hot milk, salt, and cayenne pepper, and cook until smooth. Let mixture cool, then add grated cheese and bring the sauce slowly to the boil, stirring constantly, and remove from heat. In a baking dish, alternate two or three layers of rice and onions. Pour the cheese sauce over and bake until browned and bubbly, about 20 minutes. Stir to mix before serving.

BAKED SPANISH MACARONI

1 16-oz. pkg. macaroni
1 Tbsp. butter
  salt and pepper to taste
1 cup light cream
1 large white onion, chopped fine

2 stalks celery, chopped fine
2 green peppers, chopped fine
1 14½-oz. can peeled whole
    tomatoes, drained and diced
8 oz. cream cheese

Cook macaroni according to directions on package, drain, and let cool. In the 1-quart saucepan over medium-high heat, warm butter, salt, pepper, and cream. Add onion, celery, green peppers, and tomatoes. Reduce heat and simmer until tender. Meanwhile, slice cream cheese thin. Scatter half the cream cheese in a baking dish. In a large bowl, mix macaroni and sauce together and pour mixture into baking dish. Scatter remaining cream cheese on top. Bake until bubbly and browned, about 20 minutes. Serve hot.

BEFORE YOU BEGIN

You'll need: 6-quart saucepan, 1-quart saucepan, colander, 9" x 13" baking dish, large mixing bowl
Preheat oven to 350 degrees
Preparation time: 1 hour
Yield: 8 servings

OYSTERS SCALLOPED WITH RICE

3 cups cooked rice
1 pint fresh oysters
1 cup celery, chopped
2 Tbsp. butter

2 Tbsp. flour
1 cup milk, hot
½ tsp. salt
⅛ tsp. pepper

Cook rice (see page 153) and use hot. Meanwhile, drain oysters thoroughly. Place but do not pack alternate layers of rice, oysters, and celery in a baking dish. In a 1-quart saucepan over medium heat, make a roux of the butter and flour. Add hot milk, salt, and pepper and stir until smooth. Pour over the ingredients in the baking dish. Bake in oven until bubbly, about 20 minutes.

BEFORE YOU BEGIN

You'll need: 1-quart saucepan, small saucepan, deep 2-quart baking dish
Preheat oven to 375 degrees
Preparation time: 1 hour
Yield: 8 servings

PUMPKIN MERINGUE PIE

*You'll need: large mix-
 ing bowl, electric
 beater, small mix-
 ing bowl, 9-inch pie
 tin*
*Preheat oven to 375
 degrees*
*Preparation time:
 1 hour*
Yield: 1 pie

5 eggs, separated	1½ cups pumpkin pie filling
1½ cups sugar	1 heaping Tbsp. butter, melted
½ tsp. ground cinnamon	¾ cup light cream
½ tsp. ground nutmeg	1 unbaked dessert pie crust

Separate eggs, retaining three whites for meringue. Beat 5 egg yolks until of light lemon color. Continue beating, slowly adding sugar, then cinnamon, nutmeg, pumpkin, and butter. When ingredients are mixed well together, add cream and beat until smooth. Pour into unbaked pie pastry (see page 154) and bake about 45 minutes, until knife inserted in center comes out clean. Remove pie from oven and raise temperature to 400 degrees. Top pie with meringue and return to oven until browned, about 10 minutes.

MERINGUE

3 egg whites	3 tsp. sugar

Beat the whites of 3 eggs at high speed until soft peaks form. Continue beating, sprinkling sugar over beaten whites, and whip until thick but not dry.

THE SEABOARD AIR LINE RAILWAY

CREAM OF PEANUT SOUP

BEFORE YOU BEGIN

1 qt. chicken or veal stock
1 cup heavy cream

1 lb. pure peanut butter

*You'll need: small
saucepan, 1-quart
saucepan, 2-quart
saucepan, whisk
Preparation time:
1¼ hours
Yield: 8 servings*

In small saucepan over medium-low heat, warm peanut butter. Meanwhile, heat stock in the 2-quart saucepan. Add warmed peanut butter to the stock, whisk until smooth, and let simmer gently for an hour. Heat cream and add to soup, using a whisk to mix thoroughly.

FLORIDA SHRIMP CREOLE

BEFORE YOU BEGIN

4 Tbsp. butter
6 outside stalks celery, diced
3 medium onions, chopped
1 large green pepper, chopped
½ lb. fresh mushrooms, sliced
2 Tbsp. flour
2 tsp. salt
½ tsp. black pepper
2 tsp. chili powder

2 tsp. sugar
1 Tbsp. white vinegar
4 cups crushed tomatoes
¼ cup pimento, chopped
1 clove garlic, chopped fine
2 cups hot water
2 lbs. shrimp,
  cooked and cleaned
4 cups boiled rice

*You'll need: 2-quart
saucepan, 3-quart
saucepan
Preparation time:
1½ hours
Yield: 8 servings*

In the 3-quart saucepan over medium heat, melt butter and sauté celery, onions, green pepper, and mushrooms slowly, about 10 minutes. Stirring constantly, add flour to make a roux and cook 3 minutes. Add salt, pepper, chili powder, sugar, and vinegar and stir until mixed. Add tomatoes, pimento and garlic. Stirring constantly, slowly add hot water. Bring to a simmer and cook until thickened, about 1 hour. Meanwhile, cook boiled rice (see page 153). Add shrimp to creole mixture and continue to simmer until shrimp are heated through, about 5 minutes. To serve, place a ½ cup mound of boiled rice on a serving dish, and cover generously with shrimp and sauce.

THE TEXAS & PACIFIC RAILWAY

―⋅―≡◆≧―⋅―

BUTTERMILK PANCAKES

BEFORE YOU BEGIN

*You'll need: medium
mixing bowl, pan-
cake griddle or large
skillet
Preheat pancake grid-
dle to medium-high
(until a drop of
water sizzles)
Preparation time:
30 minutes
Yield: 12 6-inch pan-
cakes*

*One of the most frequently requested menu items on the Texas & Pacific, in spite of a
dinner menu that included prime-grade charcoal-broiled sirloin steak and fresh cantaloupe pie.*

2 eggs	¼ tsp. baking soda
1¼ cups buttermilk,	2 Tbsp. bacon fat, melted
(soured may be used)	2 Tbsp. sugar
½ tsp. salt	1¼ cups flour
2 tsp. baking powder	

Beat eggs thoroughly. In order, stir in buttermilk, salt, baking powder, baking
soda, fat, and sugar, and whip until well blended. Fold in the flour, stirring only
long enough to remove lumps from the mixture. Lightly grease the pancake griddle. Pour mixture into 6-inch pancakes and cook, turning once, until lightly
browned and cooked through.

―⋅―≡◆≧―⋅―

CANTALOUPE PIE

BEFORE YOU BEGIN

*You'll need: baked 9-
inch single pie crust,
strainer, ricer or
food processor,
medium saucepan,
medium mixing
bowl, electric beater
Preheat oven to 275
degrees
Preparation time:
1 hour (plus 6–12
hours to chill before
serving)
Yield: 1 pie*

*This unique desert demonstrates why Eddie Pierce of the Texas & Pacific Railroad rose
so quickly through the ranks (he became chef in only three years). Assigned to a special
train for prominent Pacific Coast fruit growers, Pierce created Cantaloupe Pie to enhance the favorable impression the trip would have on the potential shippers. One ben-
eficiary of the trip observed that in more than forty years of growing cantaloupes, he
had never tasted cantaloupe pie. If he hadn't insisted on having the recipe, we might
not have it today.*

CANTALOUPE FILLING

1 large cantaloupe, well ripened	1½ cups sugar
1 cup cold water	3 Tbsp. butter
4 Tbsp. cornstarch	⅛ tsp. nutmeg
2 Tbsp. flour	1 baked pie pastry

Dissolve cornstarch in cold water and let stand. Cut cantaloupe in half, taking
care not to lose juice. Strain juice from seeds of cantaloupe into a medium
saucepan, mashing to gain maximum juice, and discard seeds. Remove meat of
cantaloupe and put through ricer, or chop fine in food processor and put in

saucepan, conserving both meat and juice. Stir cornstarch/water mixture into saucepan and bring all to a boil over high heat. Reduce heat and continue boiling for 5 minutes. Blend flour and sugar together and add slowly to the hot mixture, stirring constantly. Add butter and nutmeg and stir until thoroughly combined. Refrigerate to cool. Meanwhile, bake a single pie pastry (see page 154) and allow to cool. Before cantaloupe mixture sets, pour into pie pastry. Top with meringue.

MERINGUE

3 egg whites, stiffly beaten	1 tsp. sugar

In mixing bowl, beat egg whites until frothy. Continue beating and slowly add sugar. Beat mixture until stiff (peaks form and hold). Cover pie with meringue. Bake in 400-degree oven until brown, about 10 minutes.

TEXAS & PACIFIC SALAD DRESSING

BEFORE YOU BEGIN

This dressing's flavor betrays its origin. It derived from early French and Spanish influences in territory covered by the Texas & Pacific, originating in a frontier town in Louisiana Purchase territory.

You'll need: medium mixing bowl, sealed 1-quart container Preparation time: 30 minutes (plus 1 hour to chill) Yield: 1 quart

½ cup chili sauce	1½ green peppers
2 cups mayonnaise	2 hard-boiled eggs, diced
¼ cup white vinegar	½ Spanish pepper,diced

In mixing bowl, mix chili sauce, mayonnaise, and vinegar well. Dice green peppers and deposit in a clean linen towel, squeezing the juice from them into dressing. Mix well, then add green pepper, hard-boiled egg, and Spanish pepper. Put into a sealed container to chill 1 hour before serving.

WABASH RAILROAD

SLOW-BRAISED SWISS STEAK, WABASH STYLE

BEFORE YOU BEGIN

You'll need: large covered skillet, large covered saucepan or skillet, tenderizing mallet
Preparation time: 1½ hours
Yield: 8 servings

2 lb. cut, top sirloin	4 Tbsp. bacon drippings
salt and pepper to taste	1 small onion, finely chopped
½ cup flour	2 cups water

Use a piece of top sirloin about 2½ inches thick by 4 inches wide. Season with salt and pepper and thoroughly pound flour into both sides until meat is ½ inch thick. In a skillet over medium-high heat, heat 2 tablespoons of bacon drippings hot enough to smoke. Sear both sides of the steak in the hot drippings until brown, about 15–30 seconds per side. Remove meat to a deep covered skillet or saucepan in which another 2 tablespoons of bacon drippings have been melted over medium heat. Add chopped onion and water. Quickly bring to a boil, cover, reduce heat, and let simmer over low heat for 1 hour.

THE RAILROADS AND THEIR CUISINES

(listed alphabetically)

Alaska Railroad
Sourdough Pancakes

Atcheson, Topeka and Santa Fe Railway System
Baked Ham with Llewellyn Sauce; Braised Duck Cumberland; Cheese Tidbit; Hungarian Beef Goulash with Potato Dumplings; Hungarian Cheese Dumplings; Lobster Americaine; Mountain Trout au Bleu; New Corn Chowder, Southern Style; St. Francis Seafood Dressing; Stuffed Zucchini Andalouse; Toasted Hot Mexican Sandwich, Santa Fe

Atlantic Coast Line Railroad
Baked Fillet of Sole with Spanish Sauce; Baked Pork Chops with Noodles Creole; Brown Betty with Fruit Sauce; Chicken Mulligatawny Soup; Cream of Lima Bean Soup; Cream Scones; Cuban Sandwich; Ybor City Style; Fricassee of Lamb with Dumplings; Orange Marmalade Pudding; Potato Salad; Seafood Cocktail Sauce

Baltimore and Ohio Railroad
Baked String Beans with Mushrooms; Corn Bread Pie; Crab Imperial à la Grady; Gourmet Sauce; Maryland Crab Cakes; Oyster Pie; Pork Chops Normandy; Shirred Sliced Turkey with Asparagus Supreme

Boston and Maine Railroad
Boston and Maine New England Clam Chowder

Canadian National Railways
Chef's Rice Salad; Chicken à la Stanley; Chicken Broth, Southern Style; Fish Chowder; Golden Pudding with Rich Orange Sauce; Graham Rolls; Meat Sauce for Spaghetti; Soufflé Rothschild; Split Pea Soup; Stuffed Calf's Liver; Tourtieres (Canadian Pork Pie)

Canadian Pacific Railway
Canadian Pacific Yellow Pea Soup; Coconut Rock; Cream Virginia Sweet Potato Soup; Fish au Gratin, Italian Style; Fried Fish, Orly Style; Lemon or Orange Meringue Pie; Parisienne Potatoes; Roast Quebec Capon, Canadian Pacific Style; Small Tenderloin, Canadian Pacific Style; Thousand Island Dressing; Venison Sauté Chasseur

Central of Georgia Railway
Honeyed Sweet Potatoes

Chesapeake and Ohio Railway
Bacon and Potato Omelet; Chesapeake Bay Fish Dinner; Cole Slaw, Mexican Style; Cream of Carrots Soup; Curried Veal; Curry of Lamb Madras; French-Style Peas; Irish Lamb Stew;

Oyster Bisque; Welsh Rarebit; Yorkshire Pudding, C&O Style

Chicago, Burlington, & Quincy Railroad
Baked Steak and Kidney Pie, Burlington Style; Baked Lima Beans; Baked Stuffed Tomato; Banana Blanc Mange; Braised Rolled Calf's Liver en Casserole, Burlington Style; Colorado Mountain Trout, *Zephyr* Style; Fried Apples; Old-Fashioned Buckwheat Cakes; Potage Alexandrina; Sherried Fruit Cocktail; Sweetbreads à la Financiere

Chicago, Indianapolis, and Louisville Railway
Hoosier Grilled Roast Beef, Monon Style; Roquefort Dressing à la Earl; Sour-Cream Salad Dressing

Chicago, Milwaukee, St. Paul & Pacific Railroad
Baked Pear Crunch with Lemon Sauce; Chicago, Milwaukee, St. Paul & Pacific Fudge; Crabmeat *Olympia* Hiawatha; Dutch Meat Loaf; Mashed Squash *Olympian;* Pork Sausage and Sweet Potatoes; Richmond Corn Cakes; Scalloped Brussels Sprouts; Scrambled Codfish Rector; Stuffed Onions; Supreme of Chicken Washington

Chicago and North Western Railway System
Chicken Mousse; Hawaiian Salad; Salamagundy Salad; Stuffed Prune Salad

Chicago, Rock Island, and Pacific Railway
Apple Fritters in Red Wine Sauce; Boneless Breast of Chicken, Hawaiian Style; Chesapeake Bay Oyster Pepper Pot; Fresh Asparagus Delmonico; Stuffed Tomato Bretonne

Delaware and Hudson Railroad
Lake Champlain Ice Fish, D&H Style

Delaware, Lackawanna, and Western Railroad
Beefsteak Pie with Mushrooms

Denver and Rio Grande Western Railroad
Boiled Black-Eyed Peas; Islander Shrimp Luau; Old-Fashioned Navy Bean Soup, Rio Grande Style; Silver Salmon Steak, Baked with Sour Cream; Spinach, German Style

Dominion Atlantic Railway
Creamed Digby Scallops on Toast

Erie Railroad
Baked Indian Pudding

Florida East Coast Railway
Florida East Coast Salad

Great Northern Railway
Anna's Hot-Stuff Sauce; Chicken Loaf; Chicken Pie, Great Northern Style; Cream of Cauliflower Soup; Gingerbread Crumb Pudding with Butterscotch Sauce; Great Northern Baked Ham; Great Northern Doughnuts; Great Northern English Beefsteak Pie; Great Northern Special Dressing; Potato Rolls; Reindeer Mulligan, Hunter Style

Gulf Mobile and Ohio Railroad
GM & O Special Sandwich; Curry of Fresh Shrimp; Blueberry Muffins

Illinois Central Railroad
Athens Parfait; Bacon and Egg Soufflé; Baked Deviled Crabmeat; Canapé Lorenzo; Clam Chowder Mid-America; Fruit Upside-Down Pudding; Curried Lobster; Illinois Central Salad Dressing; Old-Fashioned Raisin Pudding; Potatoes Romanoff; Shrimp Creole

Kansas City Southern Railway Company
Spoon Bread

Lehigh Valley Railroad
Lehigh Valley Baked Apple Dish

Louisville and Nashville Railroad
Broiled Spring Chicken on Toast, Barbecue Style; Cream of Chicken Soup with Leeks; Fresh Shrimp Gumbo, New Orleans Style; Shrimp Cocktail Sauce

Missouri-Kansas-Texas Lines (M-K-T or Katy)
Katy Kornettes; Katy Special Onion Soup

Missouri Pacific Railroad
Baked Filet of Fresh Fish; Pourtagaise; Blanc Mange (Almond–Milk Pudding); Casserole of Prime Beef; Jardiniere; Cold Sliced Breast of Turkey Isabelle; Cole Slaw; Cream of Fresh Spinach Florentine; Escallops of Veal Piquante; Fried Oysters with Remoulade Sauce; Poached Slice of Salmon Normandie; Stuffed Celery Rainbow; Sunflower Salad with Sunshine Dressing

Nashville, Chattanooga, and St. Louis Railway
Corn Hoe Cakes

New York Central System
Bisque of Crab Cardinal; Brochette of Shrimp;

Calf's Liver en Casserole Venetian; Eggs Bretagne; Lobster Newburg New York Central; Peach and Orange Sticks; Pepper Pot Louisianne; Scallopines of Pork Tenderloin with Riesling Wine Sauce; Stuffed Pork Tenderloin en Casserole; Terrine of Ragout à la Deutsch; Wheat Cakes

New York, New Haven, and Hartford Railroad
Apple, Peanut Butter, and Cheese Salad; Carrots in Mint Sauce; Chicken Cadillac; Codfish Balls; Creamed Shrimps and Oysters en Casserole; Creamed Crabmeat *Yankee Clipper;* Lobster Themidor, *Merchants Limited* Style; Rhubarb and Strawberry Pie; Savory Mushroom Dressing; Scallops à la Newburg; Washington Fruit Salad *Merchants Limited*

Norfolk and Western Railroad
Fried Chicken with Cream Gravy

Northern Pacific Railway
Baked Rabbit Pie; Boiled Halibut with Shrimp Sauce; Confetti Salad with "Our Own" French Dressing; Hawaiian Pot Roast; Herb-Buttered Beets; Honey Mayonnaise Dressing for Fruit; Northern Pacific Dark Fruit Cake; Puget Sound Clam Chowder; Rice and Ham Griddle Cakes; Special Sauce for Baked Ham; Sweet Dough Rolls

Pennsylvania Railroad
Baked Potato Pennsylvania; Corn and Green Pepper Sauté; Cream of Chicken Soup, Roquefort; Deviled Slice of Roast Beef with Mustard Sauce; Ginger Muffins; Melon Mint Cocktail; Pennepicure Pie; Potted Flank of Beef Trinidad; Salad Bowl with Pennsylvania Dressing; Stuffed Celery; Veal Cutlets in Paprika Sauce

Reading Lines
Chicken Creole Soup; Diamond Cheese Biscuits

St. Louis and San Francisco Railway (Frisco)
Flaked Breast of Chicken with Sherry, Frisco Style; Ragout of Tenderloin Tips Stroganoff

St. Louis Southwestern Railway Lines (Cotton Belt Route)
Apricot Bavarian Cream; Baked Onions and Rice; Baked Spanish Macaroni; Oysters Scalloped with Rice; Pumpkin Meringue Pie

Seaboard Air Line Railway
Cream of Peanut Soup; Florida Shrimp Creole

Southern Pacific Lines
Apple Pancakes; Avocado Cocktail; Baked Potato Surprise, Southern Pacific Style; Baked-Sugar Cured Ham Southern Pacific; California Peach and Rice Fritters; Chicken Gumbo Southern Pacific; Curried Chicken Colombo with Indian Chutney; Fillet of Sole As You Like It; Garden Salad Bowl with Southern Pacific Dressing; Spanish Beans; The Casserole

Southern Railway System
Baked Fish in Creole Sauce; Buttermilk Biscuits; Chicken Salad Sandwich; Grilled Ham Steak with Pineapple Fritters; Oysters in Cream Stew; Pecan Pie; Princesse Salad and Vinaigrette Sauce; Southern Corn Cakes with Syrup or Honey; Fresh Stewed Corn; Sweet Potatoes and Apples; Vegetable Soup

Texas and Pacific Railway
Buttermilk Pancakes; Cantaloupe Pie; Texas & Pacific Salad Dressing

Union Pacific Railroad
Apricot Pie; Barbecued Crab; Barbecued Lamb Shanks; Fricandeau of Veal; Fruit Salad Dressing; Hot Chili Roquefort Canapés; Macaroni and Cheese with Olives; Orange Tea Biscuits; Pickled Shrimp with Onion; Poached Eggs, Spanish Style with Risotto; Walnut Chicken, Hong Kong Style

Wabash Railroad
Slow-Braised Swiss Steak

Western Pacific Railroad
Arabian Peach Salad; Cocktail Sauce Ravigote; Creamed Tuna Fish with Fried Noodles au Gratin; Deviled Ham Canapé; Fresh String Beans Sauté; Grilled Sugar-Cured Ham Steak with Yorkshire Sauce; Hot Chicken Timbale with Cheese Sauce; Southern Roast-Beef Hash; Stuffed Celery; Stuffed Deviled Eggs; Western Pacific Rice Cream Pie

Fred Harvey Restaurants
Brandy Flip Pie (Chicago); Cauliflower Greens, Restelli (St. Louis); Chicken Maciel (Kansas City); Cream of Wisconsin Cheese Soup (St.

Louis); French Apple Pie with Nutmeg Sauce (Los Angeles); Hot Strawberry Sundae (Kansas City); La Fonda Pudding (Santa Fe); Plantation Beef Stew on Hot Buttermilk Biscuits (St. Louis); Poached Eggs à la Reine, Harlequin (Chicago and New Orleans); Risotto Piemontaise (Los Angeles); Roman Dressing (St. Louis)

The Pullman Company

Asparagus Vinaigrette; Chilled Salmon Steak Plate; Cinnamon Buns; Cole Slaw with Peppers; Crab Gumbo, Southern Style; Grilled Double Lamb-Chop Hot Plate; Hashed Browned Potatoes; Illinois Sandwich; Old-Fashioned Southern-Style Strawberry Shortcake; Peas in Butter; Sauté of Chicken à la Marengo

COURSE INDEX

Appetizers and Cocktail Dressings
St. Francis Seafood Dressing (Atcheson, Topeka & Santa Fe)
Seafood Cocktail Sauce (hot) (Atlantic Coast Line)
Smooth Shrimp Cocktail Sauce (Louisville & Nashville)
Melon Mint Cocktail (Pennsylvania Railroad)
Cocktail Sauce Ravigote (Western Pacific)
Avocado Cocktail (Southern Pacific)
Pickled Shrimp with Onion (Union Pacific)

Soups
New Corn Chowder, Southern Style (Atcheson, Topeka & Santa Fe)
Chicken Mulligatawny Soup (Atlantic Coast Line)
Cream of Lima Bean Soup (Atlantic Coast Line)
Clam Chowder Mid-America (Illinois Central Railroad)
Cream of Chicken Soup Roquefort (Pennsylvania Railroad)
Cream of Wisconsin Cheese Soup (Fred Harvey)
Crab Gumbo, Southern Style (Pullman Company)
Canadian Pacific Yellow Pea Soup (Canadian Pacific)
Cream of Virginia Sweet Potato Soup (Canadian Pacific)
Cream of Carrots Soup (Chesapeake & Ohio)
Oyster Bisque (Chesapeake & Ohio)
Fresh Shrimp Gumbo, New Orleans Style (Louisville & Nashville)
Puget Sound Clam Chowder (Northern Pacific)
Chicken Gumbo Southern Pacific (Southern Pacific)
Vegetable Soup (Southern Railway)
Oysters in Cream Stew (Southern Railway)
Chicken Creole Soup (Reading Lines)
New England Clam Chowder (Boston & Maine)
Fish Chowder (Canadian National)

Chicken Broth, Southern Style (Canadian National)
Split Green Pea Soup (Canadian National)
Chesapeake Bay Oyster Pepper Pot (Chicago, Rock Island & Pacific)
Old Fashioned Navy Bean Soup, Rio Grande Style (Denver & Rio Grande)
Katy Special Onion Soup (Missouri-Kansas-Texas)
Cream of Cauliflower Soup (Great Northern Railway)
Cream of Fresh Spinach Florentine (Missouri Pacific Lines)
Bisque of Crab Cardinal (New York Central)
Pepper Pot, Louisianne (New York Central)
Cream of Peanut Soup (Seaboard Air Line)
Cream of Chicken Soup with Leeks (Louisville & Nashville)
Potage Alexandrina (Chicago, Burlington & Quincy)

Salads and Salad Dressings
Great Northern Special Dressing (Great Northern Railway)
Sunflower Salad with Sunshine Dressing (Missouri Pacific Lines)
Sour Cream Salad Dressing (Chicago, Indianapolis & Louisville)
Potato Salad (Atlantic Coast Line)
Illinois Central Salad Dressing (Illinois Central Railroad)
Salad Bowl with Pennsylvania Dressing (Pennsylvania Railroad)
Roman Dressing (Fred Harvey)
Cole Slaw, Mexican Style (Chesapeake & Ohio)
Chef's Rice Salad (Canadian National)
Salamagundy Salad (Chicago & North Western)
Hawaiian Salad (Chicago & North Western)
Stuffed Prune Salad (Chicago & North Western)

Stuffed Tomato Bretonne (Chicago, Rock Island & Pacific)

Florida East Coast Salad (Florida East Coast)

Roquefort Cheese Salad Dressing (Louisville & Nashville)

Texas & Pacific Salad Dressing (Texas & Pacific)

Cape Cod Cranberry Relish (New Haven)

Sherried Fruit Cocktail (Chicago, Burlington & Quincy)

Cole Slaw (Missouri Pacific Lines)

Apple, Peanut Butter, and Cheese Salad (New Haven)

Washington Fruit Salad Merchants' Limited (New Haven)

Confetti Salad with "Our Own" French Dressing (Northern Pacific)

Honey Mayonnaise Dressing for Fruit (Northern Pacific)

Garden Salad Bowl with Southern Pacific Dressing (Southern Pacific)

Thousand Island Dressing (Canadian Pacific)

Princesse Salad and Vinaigrette Sauce (Southern Railway)

Fruit Salad Dressing (Union Pacific)

Arabian Peach Salad (Western Pacific)

Cole Slaw with Peppers (Pullman Company)

Poinsettia Salad Merchants' Limited (New Haven)

Tartar Sauce (Louisville & Nashville)

Eggs

Bacon and Egg Souffle (Illinois Central Railroad)

Poached Eggs à la Reine Harlequin (Fred Harvey)

Eggs Bretagne (New York Central)

Bacon and Potato Omelet (Chesapeake & Ohio)

Poached Eggs, Spanish Style with Risotto (Union Pacific)

Beef

Casserole of Prime Beef, Jardiniere (Missouri Pacific Lines)

Beefsteak Pie with Mushrooms (Delaware, Lackawanna & Western)

Outer Belt Bisque (Elgin, Joliet & Eastern)

Ragout of Tenderloin Tips Stroganoff (St. Louis & San Francisco)

Hungarian Beef Goulash with Potato Dumplings (Atcheson, Topeka & Santa Fe)

Stuffed Zucchini Andalouse (Atcheson, Topeka & Santa Fe)

Deviled Slice of Roast Beef with Mustard Sauce (Pennsylvania Railroad)

Potted Flank of Beef Trinidad (Pennsylvania Railroad)

Plantation Beef Stew on Hot Biscuits (Fred Harvey)

Corn Bread Pie (Baltimore & Ohio)

Stuffed Calf's Liver (Canadian National)

Hoosier Grilled Roast Beef (Chicago, Indianapolis & Louisville [Monon]

Calf's Liver en Casserole Venetian (New York Central)

Terrine of Ragout à la Deutsch (New York Central)

Slow-Braised Swiss Steak (Wabash Railroad)

Southern Roast Beef Hash (Western Pacific)

Small Tenderloin, Canadian Pacific Style (Canadian Pacific)

Roast Beef with Yorkshire Pudding C&O (Chesapeake & Ohio)

Sweetbreads à la Financiere (Chicago, Burlington & Quincy)

Baked Steak and Kidney Pie Burlington (Chicago, Burlington & Quincy)

English Beefsteak Pie (Great Northern)

Braised Rolled Calf's Liver En Casserole, Burlington Style (Chicago, Burlington & Quincy)

Meat Sauce for Spaghetti (Canadian National)

Hawaiian Pot Roast (Northern Pacific)

Dutch Meat Loaf (Chicago, Milwaukee, St Paul & Pacific)

Game

Venison Sauté Chasseur (Canadian Pacific)

Baked Rabbit Pie (Northern Pacific)

Reindeer Mulligan, Hunter Style (Great Northern)

Veal

Escallops of Veal Piquante (Missouri Pacific)

Veal Cutlets in Paprika Sauce (Pennsylvania)
Curried Veal (Chesapeake & Ohio)
Frincandeau of Veal (Union Pacific)
Stuffed Onions (Chicago, Milwaukee, St Paul & Pacific)

Fowl

Chicken Pie, Great Northern Style (Great Northern)
Chicken Loaf (Great Northern)
Cold Sliced Breast of Turkey Isabelle (Missouri Pacific Lines)
Fried Chicken with Cream Gravy (Norfolk & Western)
Chicken Mousse (Chicago & North Western)
Braised Duck Cumberland (Atcheson, Topeka & Santa Fe)
Chicken Maciel (Fred Harvey)
Shirred Sliced Turkey with Asparagus Supreme (Baltimore & Ohio)
Broiled Spring Chicken on Toast with Barbecue Sauce (Louisville & Nashville)
Flaked Breast of Chicken with Sherry (St. Louis & San Francisco)
Boneless Breast of Chicken, Hawaiian Style (Chicago, Rock Island & Pacific)
Chicken Cadillac (New Haven)
Curried Chicken Colombo with Indian Chutney (Southern Pacific)
Walnut Chicken, Hong Kong Style (Union Pacific)
Hot Chicken Timbale with Cheese Sauce (Western Pacific)
Sauté of Chicken à la Marengo (Pullman Company)
Roast Quebec Capon, Canadian Pacific Style (Canadian Pacific)
Supreme of Chicken Washington (Chicago, Milwaukee, St. Paul & Pacific)
Chicken à la Stanley (Canadian National)

Fish

Boiled Halibut with Shrimp Sauce (Northern Pacific)
Curry of Fresh Shrimp (Gulf, Mobile & Ohio)
Creamed Digby Scallops on Toast (Dominion Atlantic)

Oysters Scalloped with Rice (St. Louis Southwestern)
Lobster Americaine (Atcheson, Topeka & Santa Fe)
Baked Fillet of Sole with Spanish Sauce (Atlantic Coast Line)
Baked Fillet of Fresh Fish Pourtagaise (Missouri Pacific)
Poached Slice of Salmon Normandie (Missouri Pacific)
Fried Oysters with Remoulade Sauce (Missouri Pacific)
Baked Deviled Crabmeat (Illinois Central)
Curried Lobster (Illinois Central)
Shrimp Creole (Illinois Central)
Oyster Pie (Baltimore & Ohio)
Maryland Crab Cakes (Baltimore & Ohio)
Crab Imperial à la Grady (Baltimore & Ohio)
Lake Champlain Ice Fish (Delaware & Hudson)
Silver Salmon Steak Baked with Sour Cream (Denver & Rio Grande)
Islander Shrimp Luau (Denver & Rio Grande)
Mountain Trout au Bleu, (Atcheson, Topeka & Santa Fe)
Florida Shrimp Creole (Seaboard Air Line)
Boiled Halibut with Shrimp Sauce (Northern Pacific)
Chilled Salmon Steak Plate (Pullman Company)
Barbecued Crab (Union Pacific)
Baked Fish in Creole Sauce (Southern Railway)
Fillet of Sole As You Like It (Southern Pacific)
Lobster Thermidor, *Merchants Limited* Style (New Haven)
Creamed Crabmeat, *Yankee Clipper* (New Haven)
Scallops à la Newberg (New Haven)
Creamed Shrimps and Oysters en Casserole (New Haven)
Codfish Balls (New Haven)
Fried Fish Orly Style (Canadian Pacific)
Fish au Gratin, Italian Style (Canadian Pacific)
Chesapeake Bay Fish Dinner (Chesapeake & Ohio)
Colorado Mountain Trout, *Zephyr* Style (Chicago, Burlington & Quincy)
Brochette of Shrimp (New York Central)

Lobster Newburg on Toasted Corn Bread (New York Central)

Crabmeat Olympia Hiawatha (Chicago, Milwaukee, St.Paul & Pacific)

Scrambled Codfish Rector (Chicago, Milwaukee, St. Paul & Pacific)

Creamed Tuna Fish with Fried Noodles au Gratin (Western Pacific)

Lamb

Fricassee of Lamb with Dumplings (Atlantic Coast Line)

Irish Lamb Stew (Chesapeake & Ohio)

C&O Curry of Lamb Madras (Chesapeake & Ohio)

Barbecued Lamb Shanks (Union Pacific)

The Casserole (Southern Pacific)

Grilled Double Lamb Chop Hot Plate (Pullman Company)

Pork

Baked Ham with Llewellyn Sauce (Atcheson, Topeka & Santa Fe)

Baked Pork Chops with Noodles Creole (Atlantic Coast Line)

Pork Chops Normandy (Baltimore & Ohio)

Grilled Ham Steak with Pineapple Fritters (Southern Railway)

Baked Sugar-Cured Ham, Southern Pacific (Southern Pacific)

Baked Stuffed Tomato (Chicago, Burlington & Quincy)

Baked Ham Special Sauce (Northern Pacific)

Tourtieres Canadian Pork Pie (Canadian National)

Scallopines of Pork Tenderloin with Riesling Wine Sauce (New York Central)

Stuffed Pork Tenderloin en Casserole (New York Central)

Grilled Sugar-Cured Ham Steak with Yorkshire Sauce (Western Pacific)

Pork Sausage and Sweet Potatoes (Chicago, Milwaukee, St. Paul & Pacific)

Great Northern Baked Ham (Great Northern)

Specials

Sourdough Pancakes (Alaska)

Buttermilk Pancakes (Texas & Pacific)

Apple Pancakes (Southern Pacific)

Rice and Ham Griddle Cakes (Northern Pacific)

Wheat Cakes (New York Central)

Old-Fashioned Buckwheat Cakes (Chicago, Burlington & Quincy)

Standard French Toast (Northern Pacific)

French Toast à la Santa Fe (Atcheson, Topeka & Santa Fe)

Soo Line Special French Toast (Minneapolis, St. Paul & Sault St. Marie)

Pennsylvania Railroad Special French Toast (Pennsylvania)

French Toast, Union Pacific Style (Union Pacific)

Sandwiches

Cuban Sandwich, Ybor City Style (Atlantic Coast Line)

Toasted Hot Mexican Sandwich Santa Fe (Atcheson, Topeka & Santa Fe)

Welsh Rarebit (Chesapeake & Ohio)

Chicken Salad Sandwich (Southern Railway)

Illinois Sandwich (Pullman Company)

GM&O Special Sandwich (Gulf, Mobile & Ohio)

Vegetables

Baked String Beans with Mushrooms (Baltimore & Ohio)

Honeyed Sweet Potatoes (Central of Georgia)

Fresh Asparagus Delmonico (Chicago, Rock Island & Pacific)

Spinach, German Style (Denver & Rio Grande)

Boiled Black-Eyed Peas (Denver & Rio Grande)

Puff Potatoes (Southern Pacific)

Sweet Potato Puffs (Pennsylvania)

Buttered Beets (Union Pacific)

Potatoes Romanoff (Illinois Central)

Baked Potato Pennsylvania (Pennsylvania)

Corn and Green Pepper Sauté (Pennsylvania)

Risotto Piemontaise (Fred Harvey)

Cauliflower Greens Restelli (Fred Harvey)

Fresh Stewed Corn (Southern Railway)

Sweet Potatoes and Apples (Southern)

Macaroni and Cheese with Olives (Union Pacific)

Fresh String Beans Sauté (Western Pacific)
Asparagus Vinaigrette (Pullman Company)
Hashed Browned Potatoes (Pullman Company)
Peas in Butter (Pullman Company)
Carrots in Mint Sauce (New Haven)
Great Big Baked Potato (Northern Pacific)
Herb Buttered Beets (Northern Pacific)
Baked Potato Surprise, Southern Pacific Style (Southern Pacific)
Spanish Beans (Southern Pacific)
Parisienne Potatoes (Canadian Pacific)
French Style Peas (Chesapeake & Ohio)
Baked Lima Beans (Chicago, Burlington & Quincy)
Fried Apples (Chicago, Burlington & Quincy)
Mashed Squash *Olympian* (Chicago, Milwaukee, St. Paul & Pacific)
Scalloped Brussels Sprouts (Chicago, Milwaukee, St. Paul & Pacific)
Baked Spanish Macaroni (St. Louis Southwestern)
Baked Onions and Rice (St. Louis Southwestern)
Hungarian Cheese Dumplings (Atcheson, Topeka & Santa Fe)

Sauces

Llewellyn Sauce (Atcheson, Topeka & Santa Fe)
Cumberland Sauce (Atcheson, Topeka & Santa Fe)
Gourmet Sauce (Baltimore & Ohio)
Anna's Hot Stuff Sauce (Great Northern)
Spanish Sauce (Atlantic Coast Line; Union Pacific)
Creole Sauce (Atlantic Coast Line; Southern Railway)
Curry Sauce (Atlantic Coast Line; Denver & Rio Grande)
Italian Sauce (Canadian Pacific)
Tomato Sauce (Canadian Pacific)
Bread Sauce (Canadian Pacific)
Chasseur Sauce (Canadian Pacific)
Cream Sauce (Chesapeake & Ohio; Chicago, Rock Island & Pacific)
Financiere Sauce (Chicago, Burlington & Quincy)

Special Meat Sauce (Chicago, Milwaukee, St. Paul & Pacific)
Sauce Supreme (Baltimore & Ohio; Chicago, Milwaukee, St. Paul & Pacific)
Sweet Sauce (Great Northern)
Pourtagaise Sauce (Missouri Pacific)
Isabella Sauce (Missouri Pacific)
Sauce Normandie (Missouri Pacific)
Venetian Sauce (New York Central)
Riesling Wine Sauce (New York Central)
Shrimp Sauce (Northern Pacific)
Special Sauce for Ham (Northern Pacific; Southern Pacific)
Mustard Sauce (Pennsylvania)
Paprika Sauce (Pennsylvania)
Barbecue Sauce (Union Pacific; Louisville & Nashville)
Yorkshire Sauce (Western Pacific)
Cheese Sauce (Western Pacific)

Bread

Southern Corn Cakes with Syrup or Honey (Southern Railway)
Potato Rolls (Great Northern)
Blueberry Muffins (Gulf, Mobile & Ohio)
Corn Hoe Cakes (Nashville, Chattanooga & St. Louis)
Spoon Bread (Kansas City Southern)
Ginger Muffins (Pennsylvania)
Cream Scones (Atlantic Coast Line)
Graham Rolls (Canadian National)
Katy Kornettes (Missouri-Kansas-Texas)
Diamond Cheese Biscuits (Reading Lines)
Sweet Dough Rolls (Northern Pacific)
Buttermilk Biscuits (Southern Railway)
Orange Tea Biscuits (Union Pacific)
Fresh Cinnamon Buns (Pullman Company)
Richmond Corn Cakes (Chicago, Milwaukee, St. Paul & Pacific)
Toast Bread (Northern Pacific)
Orange Praline Toast (Illinois Central)
Cinnamon Toast (Western Pacific)

Desserts

Gingerbread Crumb Pudding with Butterscotch Sauce (Great Northern)
Great Northern Doughnuts (Great Northern)

Banana Blanc Mange (Chicago Burlington & Quincy)

Blanc Mange, Almond-Milk Pudding (Missouri Pacific Lines)

Brown Betty with Fruit Sauce (Atlantic Coast Line)

Orange Marmalade Pudding (Atlantic Coast Line)

Cranberry Pie (Alaska)

Pumpkin Meringue Pie (St. Louis Southwestern)

Apricot Bavarian Cream (St. Louis Southwestern)

Pumpkin Pie (Missouri Pacific)

Golden Pudding with Rich Orange Sauce (Canadian National)

Souffle, Rothschild (Canadian National)

Athens Parfait (Illinois Central)

Old Fashioned Raisin Pudding (Illinois Central)

Fruit Upside Down Pudding (Illinois Central)

Pecan and Orange Sticks (New York Central)

Pennepicure Pie (Pennsylvania Railroad)

Lemon or Orange Meringue Pie (Canadian Pacific)

Coconut rock (Canadian Pacific)

Baked Pear Crunch with Lemon Sauce (Chicago, Milwaukee, St. Paul & Pacific)

Fudge (Chicago, Milwaukee, St. Paul & Pacific)

French Apple Pie with Nutmeg Sauce (Fred Harvey, Los Angeles)

Hot Strawberry Sundae (Fred Harvey, Kansas City)

La Fonda Pudding (Fred Harvey, Santa Fe)

Brandy Flip Pie (Fred Harvey Chicago)

Apple Fritters in Red Wine Sauce (Chicago Rock Island & Pacific)

Baked Indian Pudding (Erie)

Lehigh Valley Baked Apple Dish (Lehigh Valley)

Cantaloupe Pie (Texas & Pacific)

NP Dark Fruit Cake (Northern Pacific)

California Peach and Rice Fritters (Southern Pacific)

Pecan Pie (Southern Railway)

Apricot Pie (Union Pacific)

Western Pacific Rice Cream Pie (Western Pacific)

Old-Fashioned Southern-Style Strawberry Shortcake (Pullman Company)

Baked Wenatchee Apple (Great Northern)

Wenatchee Apple Cake (Great Northern)

Apple Pie (Great Northern)

Apple Pan Dowdy (Great Northern)

Rhubarb and Strawberry Pie (New Haven)

Dressings

Savory Mushroom Stuffing (New Haven)

Poultry Stuffing (Chicago, Burlington & Quincy)

Hors D'oeuvres

Stuffed Celery Rainbow (Missouri Pacific)

Cheese Tidbit (Atcheson, Topeka & Santa Fe)

Canape Lorenzo (Illinois Central)

Stuffed Celery (Pennsylvania)

Stuffed Celery (Western Pacific)

Stuffed Deviled Eggs (Western Pacific)

Deviled Ham Canapé (Western Pacific)

Hot Chili Roquefort Canapés (Union Pacific)

Beverage

Horse's Neck (Pullman Company)

Hot Cocoa (St. Louis Southwestern)

For a brief general history of railroad passenger cars, the author recommends August Menchen's *The Railroad Passenger Car* (Baltimore: Johns Hopkins University Press, 1957), a book made particularly interesting by the inclusion of thirty-six first-hand accounts of early passengers' experiences riding the train, some of which are cited here. More thorough, but relying less on first-hand accounts, is John H. White, Jr.'s encyclopedic, lavishly illustrated, two-volume *The American Railroad Passenger Car* (Baltimore: Johns Hopkins University Press, 1978), which deals primarily with the evolution of passenger-car technology, but which also discusses the impact of and reactions to passenger car improvements. An excellent, detailed, readable account of one railroad's dining-car department is William A. McKenzie's *Dining Car Line to the Pacific* (St. Paul, Minn.: Minnesota Historical Society Press, 1990), an illustrated history of the Northern Pacific Railway's "famously good" food accompanied by 150 authentic recipes that Bill and his wife assembled and tested. An earlier book of generally untested or unadjusted institutional recipes, Will C. Hollister's *Dinner in the Diner* (Glendale, Calif.: Interurban Press, 1965), gives brief details on each of nineteen railroads' named trains, along with 300 recipes (NOTE: Care was taken not to duplicate here any but the most famous of these and those most clearly in need of portion reduction and testing to insure accuracy.) An account of one man's career in dining-car service is found in Paul R. McDonald's *Forty-One Years in the D. C. & H.*, 2nd edition (Waterloo, Iowa: Paul R. McDonald, 1987), which describes Jules Hansink's rise from part-time worker to superintendent on the Union Pacific. (NOTE: All footnotes for the boxed extracts appear at the end of the Notes/Bibliography section.)

1. Edwin Kachel, *A Quarter of a Century with the Traveling Public* (Seattle: Progressive Printing Co., 1937), 27.

2. H. I. Norris, (superintendent, Union Pacific Railroad Dining Car and Hotel Department), "Economic Influences on Railroad Food-Service Programs," Speech before Interstate Carrier Seminar of the U. S. Public Health Service, Kansas City, Mo. (January 21, 1955).

3. George Combe, *Notes on the United States of North America during a Phrenological Visit in 1838–39–40* (Philadelphia: 1841), quoted in Menchen, 97–100.

4. W. F. Rae, *Westward by Rail* (London: 1870), quoted in Menchen, 149–150.

5. F. Barham Zincke, *Last Winter in the United States* (London: 1868), quoted in Menchen, 144.

6. Captain Frederick Marryat, *A Diary in America* (Philadelphia: 1840), quoted in Menchen, 96.

7. J. W. Boddam-Whetham, *Western Wanderings* (London: 1874), quoted in Menchen, 159.

8. Richard Reinhardt, (ed.), *Workin' on the Railroad: Reminiscences from the Age of Steam* (Palo Alto, Calif.: American West Publishing Company, 1970), 263.

9. Arthur Bunn, *Old England and New England* (London: 1853), quoted in Menchen, 115–117.

10. Charles Mackay, *Life and Liberty in America* (New York: 1859), quoted in Menchen, 128–130.

11. Walter Thornbury, *Criss-Cross Journeys* (London: 1873), quoted in Menchen, 135.

12. Stewart H. Holbrook, *The Story of American Railroads* (New York: Crown Books, Inc., 1947), 404.

13. Major William Shepherd, *Prairie Experiences* (New York: Orange Judd Co., 1885), quoted in Reinhardt, 267.

14. J. S. Buckingham, *The Eastern and Western States of America* (London), quoted in Menchen, 101.

15. William Ferguson, *America by River and Rail* (London: 1856), quoted in Menchen, 122–128.

16. Charles George, *Forty Years on the Rail*

(Chicago: R. R. Donnelly & Sons, 1887), quoted in Reinhardt, 264–265.

17. William H. Boot, "Tales from Old Timers–No. 29," The Union Pacific Magazine (March 1926), 16.

18. Garnett Laidlaw Eskew, "The Old N. Y. Central Eating Houses," New York Central Lines Magazine (August 1924), 26–27.

19. Denice Wheeler, "Luxury Hotels Preceded Diners," The Salt–Lake Tribune (November 28, 1978), 1.

20. W. G. Marshall, Through America (London:1882), quoted in Menchen, 166–171.

21. Catherine E. Bates, A Year in the Great Republic (London: 1887), quoted in Menchen, 186.

22. Thornbury, 135.

23. The Railroad Gazette, (January 25, 1884), 73.

24. Lucius Beebe, "Dining Out," The American Heritage Cookbook and Illustrated History of American Eating and Drinking (New York: The American Heritage Publishing Company, 1964), 328.

25. Emmet R. Calhoun, "Recollections," Birmingham News (February 8, 1950), 6.

26. Joseph Husband, The Story of the Pullman Car (Chicago: A. C. McClurg & Co., 1917), 7.

27. Menchen, 12.

28. Seymour Dunbar, History of Travel in America, 4 vols. (Indianapolis, The Bobbs-Merrill Company, 1915), 1045.

29. Menchen, 17.

30. "Baltimore & Ohio Rail Road: Extension to Cumberland," Baltimore American (November 5, 1842).

31. John H. White, Jr., The American Railroad Passenger Car (Baltimore: the Johns Hopkins University Press, 1978), 314.

32. H. F. Kenney, "The Earliest Dining Cars," Railroad Gazette (December 19, 1884), 893.

33. Edward P. Mitchell, Memories of an Editor (New York: 1924).

34. Husband, 50.

35. Rae, op cit.

36. Lady Duffus Hardy, Through Cities and Prairie Lands (New York: 1881), quoted in Menchen, 176–179.

37. Benjamin Robbins Curtis, Dottings Round the Circle (Boston: 1877), quoted in Menchen, 163.

38. White, 316.

39. Charles Nordhoff, "California, How to Go There, and What to See by the Way," Harper's New Monthly Magazine (May 1872).

40. Husband, 67.

41. National Car Builder (July, 1881), 84.

42. "Vestibules, Platform Canopies, and Hoods," Railroad Gazette (March 2, 1894), 152–154.

43. Husband, 107–109.

44. "The Dining Car System," Railroad Gazette (February 24, 1882), 115.

45. White, 319–320.

46. "When Pullman Operated Dining Cars," The Union Pacific Magazine (April 1923), 18–19.

47. Adapted from portions of an unpublished manuscript provided by the Union Pacific Railroad Company Historical Archives.

48. John F. Stover, The Life and Decline of the American Railroad (New York: Oxford University Press, 1970), 197–198.

49. Beebe, 328.

50. F. M. Graves, "At a Mile a Minute Housekeeping on the Dining Car," Woman's Home Companion (March 1910), 23.

51. Kachel, 73.

52. "This is Praise," The New York Visitor (July, 1941), 19–20.

53. J. G. Pangborn, Picturesque B & O (Chicago: Knight & Leonard, 1883), 55.

54. Graves, op cit.

55. J. M. Collins, "Dining Car Forward," Erie Railroad Magazine (June, 1947), 8–9.

56. Harry I. Norris, Unpublished letter to Barbara N. Land on January 25, 1955 (Omaha: Union Pacific Railroad Company Historical Archives), 1.

57. Beebe, 329.

58. "Dining by Rail," The Railroad Gazette (June 22, 1883), 409.

59. Kachel, 41.

60. "Dining by Rail," Ibid.

61. "Chicago and North Western Railway Dining Cars Supply 'The Best of Everything'," *North Western Railway Magazine* (March 1923), 30.

62. Richard Barnitz, with Rufus Jarman, "They've Been Dining on the Railroad," *The Saturday Evening Post* (April 10, 1954), 85.

63. "Pullman Dining-Car Service on the Pennsylvania Lines West of Pittsburgh," *Railroad Gazette* (December 16, 1892), 946.

64. "Entering New York," *The New York Visitor* (April 1937), 4–6.

65. "The Operation of Dining Cars on a Trunk Line," *The Book of the Royal Blue* (November 1900), 18–20.

66. *The Extent of the Railway Dining Car Service* (Washington, D.C.: Bureau of Railway Economics, March 1924), 1–2.

67. William C. Santen, "Dinner is Now Being Served," *GM&O Historical Society News* (Issue 40–41, 1985), 13.

68. Norris, 1.

69. Barnitz, 86.

70. Beebe, 329.

71. Stover, 211–212.

72. "The Dining Car System," *Railroad Gazette* (February 24, 1882), 115.

73. "Our Dining Service," *Missouri Pacific Lines Magazine* (July 1927), 6–7.

74. Charles Frederick Carter, "The Brutal Truth About Dining Cars," *The New York Central Lines Magazine* (September, 1927), 9.

75. Ibid.

76. Kachel, 92.

77. "Railroads in the Saloon Business," *The Literary Digest* (April 27, 1912), 886–887.

78. Kachel, 46–47.

79. Kachel, 98.

80. "Katy Steward Named Railroad Man of the Year," *M-K-T Employees' Magazine* (March 1954), 2–3.

81. T. S. Robinson, "Our Professional Host–The Steward," *Illinois Central Magazine* (November 1921), 108.

82. Barnitz, 88.

83. Lawrence W. Sagle, "Meals En Route," *Trains* (January 1941), 5.

84. "Proceedings of the Nineteenth Annual Convention," *American Association of Dining-Car Superintendents* (October 19–21, 1921), 14.

85. Husband, 155.

86. Edward Hungerford, "Eating on the Train," *Harper's Weekly* (March 21, 1914), 13.

87. N. L. Patterson, "Guests Create *Panama* Menus," *Illinois Central Magazine* (January 1935), 6.

88. "This Is Praise," op cit.

89. Robinson (1921), 108–109.

90. Oh, to Be a Steward!" *Trains & Travel* (June 1952), 57.

91. William A. Wheeler, "Twenty-Seven Years on Dining Cars," *Boston and Maine Railroad Employees' Magazine* (Summer 1939), 12.

92. "This is Praise,"op cit.

93. Kachel, 17.

94. T. S. Robinson, "Behind the Scenes in a Standard Diner," *Illinois Central Magazine* (January 1922), 55.

95. Fred Rasmussen, "Rail Recipes from a B&O Chef," *The Baltimore Sun* (July 11, 1984), 2D.

96. Ibid.

97. Wheeler, 11.

98. Robinson (1922), 55.

99. L. M. Jones, "Restaurants on Wheels," *The Milwaukee Magazine* (March 1935), 4.

100. W. F. Ziervogel, "Dining Car Forces Serve 653,713 Meals in Year," *Missouri Pacific Lines Magazine*, (April 1942), 12.

101. Kachel, 92.

102. "Katy Steward Raleigh Mull Receives National Recognition," *M-K-T Employees' Magazine* (December 1953), 2.

103. *Railroad Gazette* (October 13, 1905), 355.

104. This account was compiled from a variety of sources, including: Stuart Leuthner, "James J. Heyliger, New York Central Railroad Chef," in *The Railroaders* (New York: Random House, 1983), 98–101; William A. McKenzie, *Dining Car Line to the Pacific* (St. Paul, Minn.: Minnesota Historical Society Press, 1990), 3–21; and David S. Tindall,

(Moon), *This Can't Be Me* (New York: Vantage Press, 1986), 46.

105. John F. Stover, *History of the Illinois Central Railroad* (New York: Macmillan Publishing Company, Inc., 1975), 428.

106. Lucius Beebe, "Dining on the Cars," *Holiday* (June 1953), 83–84.

107. Barnitz, 88.

108. Ibid.

109. Ibid., 33.

110. "Early Days of Pullman Cars," *Illinois Central Magazine* (March 1927), 33.

111. Waverly Lewis Root, *Eating in America: A History* (New York; Morrow, 1976), 221.

112. Daniel Boorstin, *The Americans: The National Experience* (New York: Random House, 1965) 272 .

113. Root, 221.

114. James Gray, *Business without Boundary: The Story of General Mills* (Minneapolis: University of Minnesota Press, 1954), 210–213.

115. Collins, 12.

116. H. F. Ellis, "Meals in Motion," *Atlantic Monthly* (August 1954), 93–95.

117. Freeman H. Hubbard, *Railroad Avenue* (New York: McGraw-Hill Book Company, 1945), 69–71.

118. McKenzie, 21.

119. "Why Dining Car Meals Are So Enjoyable," *Illinois Central Magazine* (November, 1922), 91.

120. John L. Ford, "Vittles on the Rails," *The Bulletin: National Railway Historical Society* 36:3, (1971) 42.

121. Don James, "Dinner in the Diner," *Railroad* (October 1965) 19.

122. Stover (1970), Ibid, 211.

123. Barnitz, Ibid, 86.

124. Kachel, Ibid, 4.

125. Barnitz, Ibid, 131.

The following notes refer to text in the boxes. Some boxed extracts are adaptions from a single source, in which case the reference is given with the text at the request of the copyright holder. Other boxed extracts are the work of the author exclusively, in which case no notes are necessary. Only those boxed extracts containing referenced material are listed here.

The Logan House:
The Station Restaurant Done Right

1. George A. Wolf, et. al. (eds.), *Blair County's First Hundred Years: 1846–1946* (Altoona, Penn.: The Mirror Press, 1945), 27;

2. Richard E. Beeler, *Altoona's Centennial Book* (Altoona, Penn: Altoona Centennial, Inc., 1949), 59–61;

3. Wolf, 134;

4. William Ferguson, *America by River and Rail* (1856), quoted in Menchen, 127;

5. Wolf, 134–135;

6. "Down Memory Lane," *Altoona Mirror* (May 6, 1977);

7. Beeler, 60;

8. Rober L. Emerson, *Allegheny Passage: An Illustrated History of Blair County* (Woodland Hills, Calif.: Windsor Publications,1984), 63.

Fred Harvey, the Harvey Houses, and Harvey Girls

Compiled from information found in the following sources:

James A. Cox, "How Good Food and Harvey 'Skirts' Won the West." *Smithsonian* (September 1987), 130–139;

James David Henderson, *Meals by Fred Harvey* (Hawthorne, Calif.: Omni Publications, 1969).

Charles W. Herbert, "The Fred Harvey Story," *Arizona Highways* (June 1968), 10 and 30–34;

Poling-Kempes, Lesley. *The Harvey Girls: Women Who Opened the West* (New York: Paragon House, 1989).

Patrice Smart, "Those Harvey Girls," *Railroad Magazine* (December 1964), 13–16;

Laura White, "Harvey Girl," *Railroad Magazine.* (February 1945), 78–100.

A fictional account of the lives led by Harvey girls may be found in: Samual Hopkins Adams, *The Harvey Girls* (New York: Random House, 1942).

A Dining Car by Definition

1. Mathias N. Forney, *The Car-Builder's Dictionary* (New York: The Railroad Gazette, 1879), 86 and 126;

2. Mathias N. Forney, *The Car-Builder's Dictionary, Revised and Enlarged Edition* (New York: The Railroad Gazette, 1888), 56, 93, and 139;

3. *The Car-Builder's Dictionary* (New York: The Railroad Gazette, 1898), 41;

4. *Car Builder's Dictionary and Encyclopedia,* 9th edition (New York: Simmons-Boardman Publishing Company, 1909), 44;

5. *1953 Car Builder's Cyclopedia of American Practice* (New York: Simmons-Boardman Publishing Corp. 1953), 24. Quotes and illustrations used by permission of Simmons-Boardman Publishing Company, Omaha, Nebraska.

One Railroad's Roster: The Southern Pacific

1. Allan Pollock "Behind the Scenes in the Dining-Car Dept.," *Southern Pacific Bulletin* (November 1927), 3.

Life on a Limited Train.

1. Paul Achard, "In American Trains," New York Central Lines Magazine (March 1930), 69.

Railroad China

1. Karl Zimmerman, "Before There Was Plastic . . ." *Americana* (February 1990), 52;

2. "The Non-Spill Coffee Cup," *The Milwaukee Magazine* (January 1946), 9;

3. "Why Dining Car Meals Are So Enjoyable," *Illinois Central Magazine* (November 1922), 92. All else: Richard W. Luckin, Dining on Rails: An Encyclopedia of Railroad China (Golden, Colo.: RK Publishing, 1990).

Song, Verse, and Silliness

1. Marie Hotson, "Dining de Luxe," *The Milwaukee Magazine* (December 1945), 15;

2. Fairfax D. Downey, "Dining Car Forward," *The Milwaukee Employees' Magazine* (February 1920), 23;

3. Arthur D. Dubin, "Some Classic Cars: Dining Cars," *Trains* (January 1960), 21;

4. Strickland W. Gillilan, "In the Dining Car," *The Book of the Royal Blue* (January 1904), 15;

5. W. H. James, "Quick Lunch Cars," *Outlook* (January 3, 1914), 11;

6. Cliff Trembly, "The Goat in the Diner," *The Great Northern Goat* (November 1930), 7;

7. "Grace-Before-Meals," *T & P Topics* (March 1955), 27;

8. T. J. Sadler, "Milwaukee Porters' and Waiters March Song," *The Milwaukee Magazine* (December 1926), 7.

Feeding the Troops

1. "The Wounded First," *The New York Visitor* (August 1944), 14;

2. Advertisement, *Pullman News* (April, 1944), inside front cover;

3. Kip S. Farrington, Jr., *Railroads at War* (New York: Coward-McCann, Inc., 1944), 156, 280, and 303;

4. E. L. Holmes, "'Keep 'Em Happy as They're Rollin' Is Escorts' Slogan," *Illinois Central Magazine* (September 1943), 35;

5. "Feeding Soldiers No Small Job," *Illinois Central Magazine* (March 1943), 11;

6. Ibid., 12;

7. Clifford Bueschel, "Sandwich Wagons Meet Trains at Three Stations," *Illinois Central Magazine* (December 1943), 3–5;

8. "Dining Car Service," document, Newberry Library file Dining Car Service 11.

George Rector and the Sixty Rector Restaurants

1. George Rector, *The Rector Cookbook* (Chicago: Rector Publishing Company, 1928);

2. Springfield Reiffel-Hamachek, "A Private Varnish Holiday Meal," *Private Varnish* (November/December 1990), 11;

3. "When Is a Tomato Not a Tomato?" *The Milwaukee Magazine* (October 1928), 9;

4. "Now Sixty Rector Restaurants in Milwaukee Dining Cars," The Milwaukee Magazine (May 1929), 10.

The Language of Dining Car Personnel
Material adapted from the following sources:
1. *The Riders Digest* (August 1945), 6;
2. *The Pullman News* (September 1922), 137;
3. Richard Barnitz with Rufus Jarman, "They've Been Dining on the Railroad," *The Saturday Evening Post* (April 10, 1954), 32;
4. David S. "Moon" *Tindall, This Can't Be Me* (New York: Vantage Press, 1986), 13;
5. Edward Hungerford, "Eating on the Train," *Harper's Weekly* (March 21, 1914), 13;
6. "At The Railroad Eating House," *Milwaukee Railway System Employees' Magazine* (January 1914), 40.

"Service Second to None"
1. David Chalmers, "First Call for Dinner: Dining Car Forward," *American Magazine* (April 1926), 56;
2. Charles Clegg, and Duncan Emrich, *The Lucius Beebe Reader* (Garden City, N.Y.: Doubleday and Company, Inc., 1967), 308.

"As Marked as that for Furnacemen"
"Proceedings of the American Association of Dining-Car Superintendents 19th Annual Convention." (October 1921), 24–26.

Creating the Menu
1. "This is Praise," (July 1941), 19-20;
2. Archibald Stowe, "Dining Car Superintendents Reveal Secrets of the Profession," *Service* (December 1937), 10;
3. T. S. Hudson, *A Scamper Through America* (New York: 1882), quoted in Menchen, 180–181;
4. *The Railroad Gazette* (February 9, 1894), 109;
5. *The Railroad Gazette* (November 23, 1894), 808;
6. *The Railroad Gazette* (February 16, 1894), 124.

The Specialty Item: The Great Big Baked Potato
Material compiled from Jay Berger, "Nostalgia: Chicken Pot Pie vs. Big Baked Potato." Mpls. St. Paul (October 1980), 109–111; William A. McKenzie, *Dining Car Line to the Pacific* (St. Paul, Minn.: Minnesota Historical Society Press, 1990), 68–69; and the author's correspondence with Edward D. Jones, Henry and Mildred Uihlein professor of plant pathology, Cornell University, dated November 17, 1987.

Promoting Shippers' Wares: Apples on the Great Northern
1. Glenn F. Wallace, "Featuring Our Own Products," *Missouri Pacific Lines Magazine* (April 1926), 5.

Feeding the Extra Crew
1. "Do You Know Your Dining Car Department?" *Cotton Belt News* (December 1945), 9;
2. Unpublished diary of S. E. Altman, provided by the Union Pacific Museum;
3. George E. Waugh, "Feeding the Extra Gang." *Milwaukee Railway System Employees' Magazine* (January 1917), 15;
4. Ibid., 16;
5. J. C. Prien, "Pioneer Days—Madison, Wis.," *Milwaukee Railway System Employees' Magazine* (November 1913), 11.

A bibliography of several hundred entries on all aspects of dining-car history and operation is available from the author, who can be contacted in care of St. Martin's Press.

SOURCES

If your interest in railroad dining extends to participation, there are a number of avenues to pursue.

To learn more about railroad history, consult any of three national organizations: the Railway & Locomotive Historical Society, Inc. (115 I Street, Sacramento, California 95814) publishes *Railroad History* semiannually and includes six regional chapters; the National Railway Historical Society (P. O. Box 58153, Philadelphia, Pennsylvania 19102) publishes *National Railway Bulletin* bimonthly and is comprised of nearly 200 local chapters. The Lexington Group in Transportation History (Department of History, St. Cloud State University, St. Cloud, Minnesota 56301) publishes *The Lexington Quarterly*. All hold annual meetings which include railroad activities ranging from facility and historical site tours to runs of steam-powered excursion trains consisting of restored older passenger equipment.

For information on the numerous historical associations devoted to specific railroads, see George H. Drury's *The Historical Guide to North American Railroads*, an excellent brief account of the more than 160 railroads abandoned or merged since 1930. Mr. Drury's equally authoritative *Guide to Tourist Railroads and Railroad Museums* directs you to more than 300 railroad attractions in North America open to the public. Of especial interest is the listing of dinner trains, many of which seek to recapture the grandeur realized on the transcontinental Limited trains. (Both books available from Kalmbach Publishing Company, 21027 Crossroads Circle, Waukesha, Wisconsin 53187)

To tap into the people who actively collect and trade railroad dining-car china, linen, and flat and hollow silverware, contact the Railroadiana Collectors Association (795 Aspen, Buffalo Grove, Illinois 60089), which publishes *Railroadiana Express* quarterly. Numerous dealers in collectibles gather at flea markets announced in *Railroadiana Express*. Several among them deal by mail order nationally and include: The Depot Attic, 377 Ashford Avenue, Dobbs Ferry, New York 10522; The Commissary, c/o Elaine C. McClellan, 1752 South Wichita, Wichita, Kansas 67213; The Private Car Limited, Third and A Streets, Belleville, Illinois 62220; and Railroad Dispatch, c/o Scott Arden, 20457 Highway 126, Noti, Oregon 97461. Authoritative reference works on dining-car collectibles include: Arthur L. Dominy and Rudolph A. Morgenfruh's *Silver at Your Service: A Collector's Guide to Railroad Dining-Car Flatware Patterns* (D & M Publishing, 197 Melville Road, Huntington, New York 11746); Richard W. Luckin's *Dining on Rails: An Encyclopedia of Railroad China* and *Teapot Treasury and Related Items* (both, RK Publishing, 621 Cascade Court, Golden, Colo. 80403–1581); Everett L. Maffett's *Silver Banquet: A Compendium on Railroad Dining-Car Silver Serving Pieces* (1870–1970), (Silver Press, P. O. Box 184, Eaton, Ohio 45320).

For those who want to sample the "lifestyles of the rich and famous," owners of private cars have formed the American Association of Private Railroad Car Owners (c/o Executive Secretary, 969 Santa Ysabel Avenue, Baywood Park, California 93402). The group's bimonthly *Private Varnish* is published by Interurban Press (1741 Gardena Avenue, P. O. Box 6128, Glendale, California 91225) and includes listings of cars available for charter, lease, or purchase.

INDEX